DICTIONARY
OF FOREIGN WORDS AND PHRASES

DICTIONARY
OF FOREIGN WORDS
AND PHRASES

*Compiled from English sources
and containing foreign words, phrases, mottos, proverbs,
place names, titles, allusions and abbreviations
from the Latin, Greek, French, Italian, Spanish,
German, Russian, Hebrew and other foreign
languages, together with English
equivalents and definitions
and a supplement in
Greek orthography*

by *Maxim Newmark* Ph.D.

Author of
*A Dictionary of Science and Technology in
English, French, German, Spanish*
Editor of
*Twentieth Century
Modern Language Teaching*

PHILOSOPHICAL LIBRARY ● NEW YORK

Copyright © 1950, renewed, Philosophical Library
Published 1950
Reprinted 1986

ISBN 0-8022-1206-9

Printed in the United States of America

M 9 8 7 6 5 4 3

INTRODUCTION

THE development of modern communications has brought about an unparalleled intermingling of peoples and languages. This has always been true in the melting-pot atmosphere of the United States; it is even more true since the United States has become the home of the United Nations and the center of international commerce and scientific research. Never before has the polyglot character of our newspapers, periodicals and creative literature been so pronounced. In almost all printed sources and in everyday speech we constantly encounter foreign words and phrases. They turn up in newspaper articles written by foreign correspondents, in novels and plays with foreign settings, in advertisements of perfumes, lingerie, or wearing-apparel, on sheets of music or program notes, in lectures and in sermons. There is no escaping them.

The absorption of these foreign words and phrases into our language is always much too rapid for assimilation, and as a result, many of them never reach the ordinary dictionaries. Yet they constantly reappear among us, from the foreign speech areas within our own country and from newly arrived immigrants, from the new political and intellectual currents in foreign countries, from the millions of soldiers and sailors who have returned from foreign service, from our diplomatic and commercial representatives returned from abroad, and from literary expatriates come home to roost. Whatever the origin of these foreign terms, they form a large part of our contemporary English vocabulary, and every literate person must at least recognize them if he wishes to be attuned to the subtler overtones of expression.

It is the purpose of this dictionary to provide English equivalents or definitions of such foreign terms. In this, it should prove of value to all those who are concerned with the English language in its esthetic, recreational, or utilitarian phases. Its particular appeal is to the editor, the journalist, the author, and the librarian, but the general reader will also find it useful in these days of war novels and travel books with their exotic backgrounds, and even more exotic vocabulary. The lecturer, the radio commentator, and the minister will no doubt look to this dictionary for many a phrase and proverb to grace their delivery. The teacher of English and of foreign languages, as well as the student of linguistics, will undoubtedly wish to consult it for their special purposes; and, I dare say, this dictionary will be conned by the writer of advertising copy, and by the restaurateur for his menus, as well as by the assiduous addict of crossword puzzles and other word games.

There is no limit to the number of foreign terms which may occur in English sources. Indeed, the very definition of what constitutes a foreign term is disputed. Neither is there any widely-accepted convention among writers of English regarding the spelling or diacritical marking of foreign terms. Least of all is there any agreement regarding the English transliteration of non-Roman alphabets. Hence, the present compilation of some 10,000 foreign terms cannot presume to be exhaustive; nor can it present itself in a normative role. It can only make the humble claim of being a faithful record of what the compiler has found in many English sources containing foreign terms. A number of unavoidable inconsistencies must therefore be expected; but these are purely formal and in no way detract from the usefulness of the equivalents and definitions.

This compilation differs from others of a superficially similar type in that it endeavors to emphasize currency of usage. A comparison between other works in this field and the present one would therefore be of no significance whatsoever as to the scope or value of either. The choice of terms has also been based on frequency of occurrence. In the absence of statistical criteria on this point, the choice has necessarily been subjective. The test of its validity must rest with time and the consultants of this dictionary.

M. N.

HOW TO USE THIS DICTIONARY

1. All entries, whether of one word or several, are in straight alphabetical order.

2. In addition to explicit cross-references, foreign terms within an article are italicized to indicate separate listing.

3. The language of the entry is indicated within square brackets, except for proper nouns and terms whose language is given in the definition.

4. A blank space within the square brackets indicates uncertainty as to the language of the entry.

5. The language within the square brackets indicates the *immediate* origin of a term; it does not indicate *ultimate* origin, or etymology.

6. The names of foreign languages not listed in the abbreviations below are given in their full form whenever they occur.

ABBREVIATIONS

abbr.	=	abbreviation	*masc.*	=	masculine
[AS]	=	Anglo-Saxon	[OE]	=	Old English
[C]	=	Chinese	[OF]	=	Old French
ca.	=	circa = approximately	[PE]	=	Pidgin English
[Du]	=	Dutch	[Pers]	=	Persian
[F]	=	French	*pl.*	=	plural
fem.	=	feminine	[Port]	=	Portuguese
[G]	=	German	[R]	=	Russian
[Gk]	=	Greek	*sing.*	=	singular
[Heb]	=	Hebrew	[Sp]	=	Spanish
[Hu]	=	Hungarian	[Swed]	=	Swedish
[It]	=	Italian	[Turk]	=	Turkish
[J]	=	Japanese	[Y]	=	Yiddish

DICTIONARY
OF FOREIGN WORDS AND PHRASES

A

a. Has [F]; the [Hu]; at; by; for; in; with [It] [Port]; by; from; of [L]; at; by; for; in; of; with [Sp]

à. At; by; for; in; to [F]

aanhangsel. Appendix [Du]

aanleidinge. Introduction [Du]

aanmerking. Note [Du]

a.a.o. See *am angeführten Ort*

aard. Earth [Du]

aardbeschrijving. Geology [Du]

aardrijkskunde. Geography [Du]

aart. Type; nature; character [Du]

a aver et tener. To have and to hold [OF]

ab. Away; off; from [G]; by; from; of [L]

A.B. See *Artium Baccalaureus*

Ab actu ad posse valet illatio. From what has happened can be inferred what will happen [L]

abaculus. Small tablet; a small tile used in mosaic pavements [L]

abacus. Tablet; calculation table; tablet placed upon the capital of a column to add to its bearing surface [L]

abaissé. Lowered; below center [F]

abajo. Down; below; downstairs [Sp]

abanico. Fan [Sp]

à bas. Down with! [F]

abatis. Knocked down; defence made of felled trees [F]

abat-jour. Day (light) deflector; light- or air-hole in a basement or cellar; skylight [F]

abat-son. Sound deflector; oblique wooden or metal sheets in steeple windows to deflect the sound of bells downwards [F]

abattoir. Slaughterhouse [F]

a battuta. In strict time; according to the beat [It]

abat-vent. Wind deflector; used in buildings to deflect wind from open casements or chimneys [F]

abat-voix. Voice deflector; canopy or other device over a pulpit or rostrum to deflect sound downwards [F]

abbandono. With abandon [It]

abbozzo. First sketch (of a painting) [It]

à beau jeu, beau retour. Tit for tat [F]

Abendbrot. Supper [G]

Abendland. The West; the occident [G]

Abendlich Glühend in Himmlischer Glut. Evening's Heavenly Light (*Meistersinger*, Act III; Wagner) [G]

Abendlied. Evening song [G]

Abendrot. Sunset glow [G]

Abendstern. Evening star [G]

a bene placito. At will; at one's pleasure [It]

ab esse. Absent [L]

Abeunt studia in mores. Studies (or pursuits) influence character [L]

ab extra. From without [L]

abgekürzt. Abridged; shortened [G]

Abhandlungen. Transactions; proceedings [G]

abhasa abhasana. Shining forth; the process of the One becoming the Many [Skr]

abheda. Indistinct [Skr]

abhinaya. Pantomime [Skr]

abies. Genus of fir trees [L]

abies balsamea. Balsam fir [L]

ab imo pectore. From the bottom of the heart [L]

ab incunabulis. From the cradle [L]

ab initio. From the beginning [L]

Ablaut. Vowel change, generally in verb forms [G]

abodah. Divine worship [Heb]

á bon chat bon rat. Tit for tat [F]

à bon marché. Cheap [F]

abonnement. Subscription [F] [Du] [Swed]

ab origine. From the beginning [L]

abortus. Fruit of an abortion [L]

ab ovo. From the egg; from the very inception [L]

ab ovo usque ad maia. From the egg even to the apples; from soup to nuts [L]

abrazo. Hug; embrace [Sp]

abrégé. Abridged [F]

Abreise. Departure [G]

abril. April [Port] [Sp]

Abriss. Outline; sketch; short treatment [G]

Abscheulicher. Monstrous one [G]

Abschied. Departure; farewell [G]

Abschiedslied. Farewell song [G]

Abschnitt. Section; sector [G]

absinthe. Wormwood; absinth; an intoxicating liquor [F]

absit invidia. No offense intended; don't take it amiss [L]

absit omen. Evil omens aside; do not infer evil from what I say [L]

absolvere. To release; set free [L]

absolvo. I acquit [L]

absque. Without [L]

absque hoc. Without this [L]

absque ulla nota. Unmarked [L]

abuelo. Grandfather (*la abuela* = grandmother) [Sp]

A buena hambre no hay pan duro. Hunger is the best sauce [Sp]

abulia. Weakening of the will [Gk]

Ab uno disce omnes. From one (instance) learn all [L]

Ab Urbe Condita. From the founding of the city (Rome); *i.e.* from the year 753 B.C. [L]

Abzug. Proof; print; discount [G]

A.C. See *Ante Christum*

acaba de publicarse. (Just) now published [Sp]

A caballo regalado no hay que mirarle el diente. Don't look a gift horse in the mouth [Sp]

acanthus. Plant of distinctly-marked foliage, used as a motif in architectural decoration; distinctive of the Corinthian capital [Gk]

A Cappella. In the church style; *i.e.* without instrumental accompaniment [It]

acatalexis. Metrically complete; carrying through the basic pattern of a line of verse [Gk]

accelerando. Accelerating; with increasing speed [It]

acciaccatura. A short grace note [It]

acciaio. Steel [It]

accolé. Stuck together; said of the juxtaposition of two heraldic shields indicating a family or national alliance [F]

accouchement. Act of giving birth to a child; delivery; lying in; period of confinement to bed during and after childbirth [F]

accoucheuse. Midwife [F]

accoudoir. Elbow-rest; ledge of a window or seat [F]

aceituna. Olive [Sp]

acequia. Ditch [Sp]

acer. Sharp; keen; genus of maple trees [L]

acera. Sidewalk [Sp]

acer saccharinum. Silver maple [L]

acer saccharum. Sugar maple [L]

ac etiam. And also [L]

acetum. Vinegar [L]

acetum italicum. Italian vinegar; mordant wit [It]

acharné. Fierce; furious; intense; tenacious; desperate [F]

acharnement. Fury; ferocity; gusto; obstinacy [F]

achat. Purchase [F]

Achtung. Respect; attention; esteem [G]

acier. Steel [F]

acierage. Steel-plating; case-hardening [F]

Aconitum. Aconite; monkshood or wolfsbane flower [L]

acortado. Abridged [Sp]

acroama. Thing heard; play; lecture (*pl.* acroamata) [Gk]

A cruce salus. Salvation (comes from) the cross [L]

ac si. As if [L]

acta. Records; registers; minutes; journals; documents [L]

acta eruditorum. Contributions [L]

Action Française. Pro-monarchist party in France [F]

actus. Act [L]

actus curiae. Act of the court [L]

actus Dei. Act of God [L]

acus. Needle [L]

ad. At; by; for; in; with [It]; by; for; to; at; near; on account of; until; upon [L]

A.D. See *Anno Domini*

adagietto. A tempo slower than adagio; a short composition in *adagio* tempo [It]

adagio. A slow tempo, slower than *andante*, but not so slow as *largo*; a dance in which the woman leaps to her partner or is lifted from the floor as they whirl [It]

ad alium diem. At another day [L]

adam. Man [Heb]

ad arbitrium. At pleasure; at will [L]

Ad astra per ardua. To the stars through difficulties [L]

Ad astra per aspera. To the stars through difficulties (motto of Kansas) [L]

a datu. From the date [L]

ad calendas Graecas. At the Greek calends (*i.e.* never) [L]

ad captandum vulgus. To capture (the fancy of) the mob [L]

addendum. Something to be added; a supplement; additional comment (*pl.* addenda) [L]

addio. Farewell [It]

Addio Alla Madre. Farewell, Dear Mother (*Cavalleria Rusticana*; Mascagni) [It]

adelantado. Head; superior; governor; presiding official [Sp]

aden. Acorn; gland [Gk]

adeps. Fat [L]

ad esse. Present [L]

Adeste Fideles. O Come, All Ye Faithful [L]

ad eundem. To the same degree; of equivalent value or rank [L]

à deux. For two; between two [F]

ad fidem. In allegiance [L]

ad finem. To the end [L]

ad hoc. For this purpose; a dubious assumption or argument arbitrarily introduced as explanation after the fact [L]

Adhyatman. The Absolute; the Oversoul [Skr]

adiantum. Unwetted; species of fern; black maiden-hair fern [Gk]

adiaphora. Indifferent things, *i.e.* neither good nor bad [Gk]

ad idem. To the same point [L]

adieu. Farewell [F]

adin. One [R]

ad infinitum. To infinity; for ever; on and on [L]

ad interim. In the meantime [L]

adiós. Goodby [Sp]

ad lib(itum). At pleasure; to any extent; freely [L]

ad litteram. To the letter; exact [L]

Ad majorem Dei gloriam. To the greater glory of God [L]

ad manum. At hand [L]

ad nauseam. To (the point of) disgust; to a disgusting extent [L]

adnyaton. Impossible thing; a form of *hyperbole* [Gk]

adobe. Sun-dried brick [Sp]

Adonai. God; the Supreme Being [Heb]

Adonis. Handsome youth loved by Venus; beau; dandy

Adonis aestivalis. Summer Adonis; a flower [L]

adonius versus. A poetic line consisting of a dactyl followed by a spondee or trochee [L]

adoxographi. Ignoble writings [Gk]

ad quem. To whom; the terminus or end-point to which something tends [L]

ad quod. To which; the terminus or end-point to which something tends [L]

ad rem. To the purpose; to the point [L]

adresboek. Directory [Du]

adresnaya kniga. Directory [R]

adscriptus glebae. Bound to the soil (said of a serf in medieval times) [L]

ad sum. I am here [L]

ad summam. To the (full) sum; on the whole; in short [L]

aduana. Custom-house [Sp]

adulter. Corrupter; seducer; counterfeiter [L]

adultera. Adulteress [L]

ad unguem. To the (finger-) nail; with great precision or nicety [L]

ad unguem factus. Highly finished [L]

ad valorem. To the (extent of the) value; in proportion to the value [L]

advena. Alien [L]

ad verbum. Word for word [L]

adversa. Things noted; things at hand [L]

adversaria. Memoranda; commonplace books; things written on the opposite page; commentaries [L]

Adversa virtute repello. By courage I repel adversity [L]

adversus bonos mores. Against good morals [L]

Advienne que pourra. Happen what may [F]

ad vitam. For life [L]

ad vitam aut culpam. For life or until fault; *i.e.* during good behavior [L]

advocare. Call to one's aid; defend; vouch for [L]

advocatus diaboli. Devil's advocate [L]

adytum. Forbidden place; sanctum [Gk]

aedificare. To build a house [L]

aedificatum. That which is built (*pl.* aedificia) [L]

aeger. Sick; ill; note testifying to a student's illness [L]

aegis. See *aigis*

Aeneid. Roman epic based on Homer's *Odyssey* (Vergil) [L]

Aeolus. God of the winds [Gk]

aeon. See *aion*

aequilibrium indifferentiae. State of exact balance between two actions, the motives being of equal strength [L]

aequitas. Equity [L]

aequus. Equal; even [L]

aere perennius. More enduring than bronze [L]

Aeroflot. Russian airline network [R]

aeronavtika. Aeronautics [R]

aerostación. Aeronautics [Sp]

aes. Brass; money; coin [L]

aes alienum. Borrowed money; debt [L]

Aesculapius. Roman god of medicine; a physician [L]

aesculus. Buckeye tree [L]

aesthetikos. Perceptive [Gk]

aestimatio capitis. Estimation of the head; *i.e.* price or value of a man [L]

aet. See *aetate*

aetas. Age [L]

aetate. In (the) age; of (the) age [L]

aetheling. Nobleman [AS]

aevum. Eternity [L]

afbeelding. Illustration [Du]

afdeeling. Division; section [Du]

affaire de coeur. Affair of the heart; love affair [F]

affaires. Business [F]

affectus. Disposition; intention; impulse or affection of the mind [L]

affettivo. Affecting; sad; pathetic [It]

affettuoso. Tenderly expressive [It]

affinitas. Relationship; affinity; relationship by marriage [L]

afflatus. Breathed upon; inspiration; wind [L]

afflitto. Sorrowfully; mournfully [It]

affrettando. Quickening the tempo [It]

afgekort. Abridged [Du]

afhandling. Dissertation; thesis [Swed]

aficionado. Fan; amateur [Sp]

à fond. Fundamentally; at bottom; thoroughly [F]

a fortiori. With stronger (reason); all the more; more certainly [L]

Afrikaans. Dutch dialect spoken in the Union of South Africa [Du]

Afrikaner. Native of South Africa, of European origin [Du]

afskrift. Facsimile [Swed]

aga. Commander; ruler; officer [Turk]

agathobiothik. The good life [Gk]

Agenbite of Inwit. See *Ayenbite*, *etc.*

agenda. Things to be done; items of business at a meeting [L]

agenesia. Sexual impotence [Gk]

agenfrida. Owner; master [AS]

agens. Agent [L]

agent provocateur. Provoking or instigating agent; one who tempts others into incriminatory action; a spy hired for this purpose [F]

ager. Field [L]

agere. To act [L]

agevole. Lightly; easily [It]

aggadah. Tale; narrative [Heb]

agilita. Agility; lightness [It]

agio. Ease; currency conversion fee; differential between two currencies [It]

agitato. Agitated; restless; fast [It]

agitka. Propaganda poem [R]

aglio. Garlic [It]

agnates. Male descendants [L]

agnello. Lamb [It]

agnomen. Nickname; title [L]
agnostos. Unknowing [Gk]
Agnus Dei. Lamb of God; section of the Mass beginning with these words (compositions by Bizet, Mozart, *etc.*) [L]
agon. Contest; conflict [Gk]
agora. Market [Gk]
agosto. August [It] [Sp]
agotado. Out of print [Sp]
agréation. Preliminary assurance that a prospective diplomat will be acceptable to a foreign country [F]
agréé. Commercial lawyer [F]
agrégation. Admission to a fellowship after an examination [F]
agrégé. Certified as a professor after an examination [F]
agrément. A receiving country's approval of a sending country's diplomat [F]
agréments. Musical embellishments [F]
agricola. Farmer [L]
aguador. Water-carrier [Sp]
agua fresca. Cool water [Sp]
aguardiente. Hard liquor, generally of inferior quality [Sp]
agudeza. Point; acuity; conceit [Sp]
aguinaldo. Present [Sp]
agurtsof. Cucumbers [R]
Aham brahma asmi. I am *brahman* [Skr]
ahamkara. "I-maker"; the principle generating the consciousness of one's ego or personal identity [Skr]
ahanta. "I-ness"; selfhood [Skr]
Ah! Fuyez, Douce Image. Flee, Fair Vision (*Manon*, Act III; Massenet) [F]
ahí. There [Sp]
ahimsa. Non-injury; the ethical principle of the Hindu religion [Skr]
Ahnung. Presentiment; suspicion; notion [G]

ahora. Now [Sp]
à huis clos. With closed doors; in private [F]
ai. Love [C]
aide de camp. Field aide; officer acting as messenger and *liaison* man for a general [F]
Aide toi, le ciel t'aidera. Heaven helps those who help themselves [F]
aigis. Shield of Zeus or Athene; symbol of rule or authority; impregnable defence [Gk]
aigrette. Egret; tuft of feathers; crest of feathers or hair; a spray of precious gems [F]
aiguille. Needle; sharp peak [F]
aiguillette. Point; tag; shoulder-knot; aiglet [F]
aile. Wing [F]
aileron. Wing-piece; inverted consoles at the sides of a dormer window [F]
aîné. Elder (son) [F]
aînesse. Right of the eldest born; primogeniture [F]
ainsi de suite. And so forth [F]
Ainsi soit-il. So be it [F]
aion. Aeon; long period of time [Gk]
Air De La Fleur. Flower Song (*Carmen*, Act II; Bizet) [F]
Air des Bijoux. Jewel Song (*Faust*, Act III; Gounod) [F]
Ais. A-sharp [G]
aisthanomai. Perceive [Gk]
aisthesis. Feeling; perception [Gk]
aitia. Cause [Gk]
aitiologeo. To inquire into [Gk]
ajedrez. Chess [Sp]
ajuar. Dowry in household goods [Sp]
akasa. Ether; space [Skr]
akhates. Chalcedony; ruby [Gk]
akolouthos. Follower; acolyte [Gk]
akrasia. Incontinence [Gk]
aksara. Syllable; imperishable [Skr]

Akten. Documents; filed papers [G]

al. The [Arab]

ala. Wing [L]

à la. In the manner (style) of; according to [F]

A la bonne heure! Very good; that's right [F]

à la bourgeoise. In family style; in middle-class style [F]

à la carte. According to the bill (of fare); as specified in the bill (of fare); as distinguished from *table d'hôte* [F]

à la grecque. In Grecian style; an architectural design resembling twisted ribbon, used on moulding [F]

A la guerra, con la guerra. Fight fire with fire [Sp]

à la marengo. Stewed with oil, mushrooms and truffles [F]

alameda. Grove of poplars; walk or drive lined with poplars [Sp]

álamo. Poplar [Sp]

à la mode. In the fashion; term applied to ways of serving various dishes [F]

à l'ancienne. Old-fashioned; old-style [F]

A la Recherche du Temps Perdu. Remembrance of Things Past (Novel cycle; Proust) [F]

à la rigueur. Strictly (speaking) [F]

alazon. Braggart [Gk]

alba. Dawn [L]; parting song at dawn; *aubade* [Provençal]

Albaicín. Suburb of Granada; dwelling-place of gypsies [Sp]

albergo. Hotel [It]

Albigenses. Men of Albi (Albiga), a sect of reformers of the 13th century in southern France persecuted for criticism of clerical corruption

alborada. Dawn; morning song [Sp]

Al buen entendedor, media palabra le basta. A word to the wise is sufficient [Sp]

Al buen pagador, no le duelen prendas. An honest debtor makes sacrifices to pay his debts [Sp]

Albumblatt. Album page or leaf; a short musical composition of an occasional quality [G]

albumen. Whiteness; white (of an egg) [L]

albus. White [L]

albus liber. White book [L]

alcalde. Mayor; justice of the peace [Sp]

alcázar. Fortified palace of the Moorish kings; name applied to modern structures of pseudo-Arabian design [Arab]

al contado. In cash [Sp]

alcornoque. Cork tree [Sp]

alcuna. Some; a little [It]

alegría. Joy; a *flamenco* dance [Sp]

alemán. German [Sp]

Alençon. Town in N.W. France; type of lace with floral motifs [F]

alexandrin. French heroic verse of 12 syllables [F]

Al fine, e poi la coda. To (the point marked) *fine*, and then (play) the *coda* [It]

alfombra. Carpet; measles [Sp]

alforjas. Saddle-bags [Sp]

al fresco. In the fresh (air); in the open; in the *fresco* style (of painting) [It]

algodón. Cotton [Sp]

algos. Pain [Gk]

alguacil. Warrant officer; constable; bailiff [Sp]

alguien. Someone [Sp]

Alhambra. Palace of the Moorish kings in Granada, Spain [Sp]

Al hierro caliente, batir de repente. Strike while the iron is hot [Sp]

Al hombre osado, la fortuna le da la mano. Fortune favors the bold [Sp]

Alianza Democrática. Democratic Alliance; a Chilean coalition party [Sp]

Alianza Popular Revolucionaria Americana. American People's Revolutionary Alliance (a political party in Peru) [Sp]. See also *Apra*

alias. Otherwise; at another time; in another manner; abbr. of *alias dictus* [L]

alias (dictus). Otherwise (called) [L]

alibi. Elsewhere; plea of being elsewhere when an alleged act took place; an excuse accounting for whereabouts during a crime [L]

alienus. Another's; belonging to another [L]

alimenta. Means of support; *i.e.* food, clothing and shelter [L]

Aliquando bonus dormitat Homerus. Even good Homer sometimes nods; even the best authors are sometimes dull [L]

aliquot. Some number of; said of a part contained by a whole an integral number of times [L]

Alis volat propriis. She flies with her own wings (motto of Oregon) [L]

Aljamiado. Spanish written in Arabic script [Sp]

Alkoran. See *Koran*

alla breve. 2-2 rhythm [It]

Allah. Mohammedan name of God [Arab]

alla milanese. Milan style [It]

alla prima. At the first (touch); said of a painting done at once without retouching [It]

allargando. Growing broad; louder and slower [It]

alla Tedesca. In the German style [It]

alla vostra salute. To your health [It]

allegretto. Light; cheerful; not as fast as *allegro* [It]

allegro. Quick; lively; rapid and cheerful [It]

alleluia. See **hallelujah**

allemand. German [F]

Allerseelen. All Souls' Day [G]

Allez! Indeed! I assure you [F]

allgemein. General; universal [G]

allgemeingültig. Universally valid [G]

allí. There [Sp]

alliage. Alloy [F]

Allí fué Troya. There was a terrific row [Sp]

Allium. Species of bulbous plants which includes onions, leeks, chives and garlic [L]

Allmacht. Omnipotence; Almighty [G]

allmählich. Gradually [G]

allo—. See *allos*

Al loco y al toro darles corro. Make way for a madman and a bull [Sp]

alloeostropha. Irregular stanzas; poem consisting of these [Gk]

allons. Let's go; come [F]

Allons donc! Nonsense! [F]

allos. Other [Gk]

allouette. See *alouette*

alluvio maris. Washing up of the sea; formation of land from the sea [L]

alma. Soul [Sp]

almacén. Magazine [Sp]

alma mater. Fostering mother; school or college from which one graduates [L]

al mana. The measure [Arab]

Al mentiroso le conviene ser memorioso. A liar should have a good memory [Sp]

almuerzo. Lunch [Sp]

Al necio y al aire, darle calle. Never contradict a fool [Sp]

Al Nostri Monti. Home To Our Mountains (*Il Trovatore*, Act IV; Verdi) [It]

alnus. Alder [L]

aloe. Plant with spike-shaped flowers; purgative derived from juice of this plant [Gk]

A l'oeuvre on connait l'artisan. A craftsman is known by his work (La Fontaine) [F]

Aloha Oe. Farewell to Thee [Hawaian]

alors. Well then; so; at that time [F]

alouette. Lark; a French children's song [F]

alpaca. Small, domesticated goat of Peru; fiber or hair from this goat, used in weaving fabrics [Sp]

alpargata. Rope-soled sandal [Sp]

Alpenstock. Alpine stick; iron-tipped staff used in climbing [G]

Alpenverein. Alpine mountaineer club [G]

alpha. First letter of the Greek alphabet (Aα); beginning [Gk]

alpha-omega. First and last; beginning and end; whole [Gk]

alporgata. Sandal [Sp]

Als Adam grub und Eva spann. When Adam delved and Eve span [G]

al segno. To the sign [It]

als ob. As if; the philosophy that knowledge rests on a series of fictions which are not verifiable but pragmatically justifiable [G]

Also Sprach Zarathustra. Thus spake Zarathustra (Nietzsche-Richard Strauss) [G]

alt. High [It]; Old [G]

alter. Other [L]

altercatio. Forensic argumentation; cross-questioning [L]

alter ego. Other I; one's other self; a close friend [L]

Alter ipse amicus. A friend is a second self [L]

Alternat. Alternation; sequence in which countries sign a treaty [G]

Altertum. (Classical) antiquity [G]

Altertumskunde. Archaeology [G]

Altertumswissenschaft. Archaeology [G]

alterum non laedere. Not to injure others [L]

altesse. Highness [F]

Althaea officinalis. Marsh Mallow; a flower [L]

Althaea rosea. Hollyhock [L]

Altiora peto. I seek higher things [L]

altiplano. High plateau [Sp]

altissimo. Highest [It]

alto. High; a low female voice; viola [It]

alto relievo. High-relief; said of sculptured figures or designs which project considerably from the block out of which they are cut [It]

al ud. A type of lute [Arab]

alumna. Foster-daughter; graduate of an institution (*pl.* alumnae) [L]

alumnus. Foster-son; graduate of an institution (*pl.* alumni) [L]

aluta. Leather [L]

alveolus. Little hollow; trough; bucket [L]

Al villano dale el pie y se tomará la mano. Give him an inch and he'll take a yard [Sp]

Alyssum maritimum. Sweet Alyssum; a flower [L]

A.M. See *Anno Mundi*; *Ante Meridiem*; *Artium Magister*

amabile. Amiable; gentle [It]

A mal tiempo, buena cara. Face your troubles cheerfully; smile at your troubles [Sp]

am angeführten Ort. At the place mentioned; *loco citato* [G]

amant. Lover [F]

amanuensis. Hand servant; clerk; stenographer; private secretary who takes dictation [L]

amapola. Poppy [Sp]

amarillo. Yellow [Sp]

Amarna. See *Tel-el-Amarna*

Amaterasu. Sun-goddess of the *Shinto* religion [J]

Amazon. Name of a race of female warriors in Scythia; a masculine woman [Gk]

ambi-. On both sides [L]

ambitus. Going around; path between adjacent houses; unlawful buying of public office; unit of thought; period [L]

amblysia. Blunting; speech intended to soften the effect of dire tidings [Gk]

ambrosia. (Food of) the nonmortal, *i.e.* the gods; anything tasty or fragrant [Gk]

A.M.G.D. See *Ad majorem Dei gloriam*

âme. Soul [F]

âme damnée. Damned soul; one condemned to destruction or an evil end; a fanatical follower; a tool [F]

amen. Certainty; a devout wish or expression of agreement [Heb]

amende honorable. Honorable amends; public apology and reparation [F]

a mensa et toro. From board and bed [L]

amentia. Total lack of mental capacity [L]

a merveille. Remarkably well; wonderfully [F]

Amici probantur rebus adversis. Friends are tested by adversity [L]

amictus. Garment; amice; square of white linen on shoulders of a celebrant priest [L]

amicus. Friend [L]

amicus curiae. Friend of the court; disinterested and impartial adviser [L]

Amicus humani generis. A friend of the human race [L]

amigo. Friend [Sp]

amir. Title of Mohammedan ruler [Arab]

amir al. Commander of the sea [Arab]

amo. Master [Sp]

amoeba. Change; microscopic organism which changes shape [Gk]

amog. Amuck; in a frenzied state [Malay]

Amontillado. A Spanish wine [Sp]

amoraim. Speakers; commentators; authorities of the *Gemara* [Heb]

Amor con amor se paga. One good turn deserves another [Sp]

amore. Love [It]

amoretti. Tiny cupids represented in paintings and designs [It]

amorini. Cupids; love-gods; tiny figures often represented in art [It]

amoroso. Amorously; tenderly [It]

amortissement. Amortization; liquidation; termination (of a building), *i.e.* a pyramidal ornament at the top of a structure [F]

amour. Love; love affair; intrigue [F]

amour propre. Self-love; self-esteem [F]

amphi-. Both; same; around [Gk]

amphibole. Ambiguity resulting from uncertain construction of a sentence [Gk]

amphibrachus. One long syllable flanked by two short ones; a metrical pattern in verse [Gk]

amphora. A two-handled Grecian vase, often awarded as a prize; a Roman unit of capacity [Gk]

amplificatio. (Arguments) against the accused [L]

ampulla. Flask of globular form [L]

Am Stillen Herd. By the Silent Hearth (*Meistersinger*, Act I; Wagner) [G]

Amt. Office [G]

Amtorg. Trading company representing the Russian government in trade relations with the United States [R]

A mucho hablar, mucho errar. Much talking, much erring [Sp]

amuck. See **amog**

an. Year [F]

ana-. Back; up; anew; again [Gk]

-ana. Pertaining to; connected with [L]

anabasis. Going up; military advance; work by Xenophon [Gk]

anaclasis. Metrical variation to improve scansion [Gk]

anacoenosis. Referring a question to the reader or audience [Gk]

anaconda. Boa; python [Sp]

anacrusis. Extra syllable at the beginning of a line of poetry [Gk]

anadi. Having no beginning [Skr]

Anadyomene. She who rose from the sea; a name for the goddess *Aphrodite* [Gk]

Anagallis arvensis. Common Pimpernel or Poor Man's Weatherglass flower [L]

anaglyph. Bas-relief (sculpture) [Gk]

anagnorisis. Transition from ignorance to knowledge; dramatic discovery or realization [Gk]

anagoge. Mystical interpretation [Gk]

anakephaliosis. Recapitulation at the end of an argument [Gk]

anakoluthon. That which does not follow; a phrase or sentence lacking grammatical sequence; an inconsistency [Gk]

Anakreon. Greek lyric poet; poetry written in the style and meter ascribed to him; convivial and amatory poetry in a light, superficial vein [Gk]

analekta. Gleanings; pickings; literary selections [Gk]

anamnesis. Recollection [Gk]

ananas. Pineapple [F]

ananda. Joy; happiness; bliss; beatitude [Skr]

Ananke. Fate; necessity [Gk]

anapale. Pantomime dance representing combat [Gk]

anapest. Metrical foot consisting of two short syllables followed by a long one [Gk]

anaphrodisia. Frigidity; incapacity for sexual intercourse [Gk]

anastrophe. Withholding of expected words for suspense or stress [Gk]

anathema. Accursed thing; solemn curse [Gk]

anchois. Anchovy [F]

Anchusa. Genus name of Forget-me-not [L]

ancien régime. Old regime; period before the French Revolution [F]

ancilla. Handmaiden [L]

ancora. Again; yet [It]

andante. Slow, even tempo; a movement in this tempo [It]

andantino. A little less slow than *andante* [It]

Andenken. Commemoration [G]

An Die Ferne Geliebte. To the Distant Beloved (Song Cycle; Beethoven) [G]

An die Freude. Ode to Joy (Schiller; Beethoven) [G]

andra handen. Second hand [Swed]

androgynus. Hermaphrodite [Gk]

âne. Ass; donkey [F]

Anemone quinquefolia. American Wood Anemone or Windflower [L]

anemos. Wind [Gk]

Anfang. Beginning; inception [G]

angaria. Forced public service [L]

Angelus. Angel (prayer beginning: *Angelus Domini nuntiavit Mariae*, The angel of the Lord announced to Mary; title of a painting by Millet) [L]

Angelus Domini. Herald or Angel of the Lord; observance of the Incarnation; Roman Catholic prayer beginning with these words [L]. See also *Angelus*

angewandt. Applied [G]

angina. Choked condition; quinsy [L]

angina pectoris. Choked condition of the chest; spasm of chest as result of heart ailment [L]

anglais. English(man) [F]

Angleterre. England [F]

Angostura. Narrowness; straits or narrows; distress; name of a South American bark, or a tonic brewed from it [Sp]

Angriff. Attack [G]

Angst. Anxiety; fear; dread [G]

Anhang. Appendix (to a book or composition); *coda* (music) [G]

anima. Soul [L]

anima mundi. Soul of the World; the Holy Ghost [L]

animato. Animated; with spirit [It]

animis opibusque parati. Ready in soul and resource (part of the motto of South Carolina) [L]

animo. With intention, disposition, design, or will [L]

Animo et fide. By courage and faith [L]

Animum fortuna sequitur. Fortune follows courage [L]

animus. Mind; intention; disposition; design; will; enmity; hostile or bitter feeling [L]

Anmerkung. Note [G]

anna. East Indian coin=one-sixteenth of a *rupee* [Hindu]

Annahme. Acceptance; assumption [G]

Annam. See *Viet Nam*

année. Year [F]

anni. See *annus*

anni nubiles. Marriageable years [L]

anno aetatis suae. In the ——year of his age [L]

Anno Domini. In the year of (our) Lord [L]

Anno Mundi. In the year of the world (used in ancient chronology) [L]

anno regni. In the year of the reign [L]

Anno Urbis Conditae. In the year of the founding of the city (Rome); *i.e.* 753 B.C. [L]

annulus et baculus. Ring and staff; symbols of a bishop's investiture [L]

annus. Year (*pl.* anni) [L]

annus et dies. A year and a day [L]

annus luctus. Year of mourning [L]

Annus Mirabilis. The Wonderful Year (a poem by Dryden relating the events of the year 1666) [L]

año. Year [Sp]

anoche. Last night [Sp]

Año Nuevo. New Years [Sp]

An Poblacht Abu. Up the Republic [Gaelic]

Anschauung. View; direct perception or intuition [G]

Anschluss. Union; annexation; the union of Austria and Germany [G]

an sich. In itself [G]

Ansicht. View; opinion [G]

Ansichtslosigkeit. "Point of viewlessness"; objectivity; the state of having no preconceptions [G]

antar-atman. Inner self [Skr]

ante. Before [L]

ante bellum. Before the war; (in the U.S., before the Civil War) [L]

ante Christum. Before Christ [L]

ante meridiem. Before midday [L]

ante omnia. Before all things; first of all [L]

ante res. Before things [L]

Antes que te cases mira lo que haces. Look before you leap [Sp]

anthos. Flower [Gk]

anthropopathia. Imputation of human feelings to animals or lifeless things [Gk]

anthropos. Man [Gk]

anthypophora. Asking, then giving the answer [Gk]

antibacchius. Metrical foot of two long syllables and a short [Gk]

Antike. The (classical) antique; classical antiquity; Greco-Roman civilization and culture [G]

antinomia. Contradiction or inconsistency in the laws; inconsistency or conflict between two propositions or authorities [L]

antipasto. Appetizer [It]

antiphon. Statement and response (*pl.* antiphona) [L]

antiphrasis. Use of a word to mean its opposite [Gk]

antiporta figurata (ornata). Frontispiece [It]

antiquaille. Antique rubbish; antiques of little value or interest [F]

Antiquar. Second-hand bookseller; antiquarian [G]

Antirrhinum. Snapdragon [L]

antistrophon. Response to a first strophe in the Greek dramatic chorus; antistrophe; argument turned against an adversary [Gk]

antisyzygy. Union of opposites [Gk]

antitheton. Opposition of ideas; antithesis; *oxymoron* [Gk]

antonomasia. Substitution of an epithet for a proper name [Gk]

antrum. Cave; cavity (*pl.* antra) [L]

an und für sich. In and for itself; referring to a system of internal relations independent of external relations [G]

A otro perro con ese hueso. Tell it to the marines [Sp]

à outrance. To the extreme; to an excessive degree; to the death [F]

apache. Dance which enacts a fight between a Paris gangster and his *gamine* [F]

apaideutas zeteseis. Undisciplined dialectic [Gk]

apanage. Allowance of lands or money for maintenance of the King's sons [F]

aparithmesis. A formal list, as in recapitulation [Gk]

a parte ante. From the part before; referring to duration previous to a given event [L]

a parte post. From the part after; referring to duration subsequent to a given event [L]

apathia. No feeling; in Stoic philosophy, freedom from emotion [Gk]

apectrum hyemale. Putty root; an orchid variety; sticky substance used as an adhesive [L]

aperçu. Perceived; (keen) perception or insight; summary exposition of a subject; an insight not in itself analytical; apperception [F]

apéritif. Appetizer; aperient [F]

apertum factum. Overt act [L]

à peu près. Nearly [F]

Apfelkuchen. Apple cake [G]

aphasia. Loss of power of articulate speech [Gk]

aphelia. Simplicity [Gk]

aphonia. Loss of speech due to injury or disease of the vocal organs [Gk]

Aphrodite. Goddess of love in Greek mythology [Gk]

a piacere. At pleasure; at will; as desired [It]

apices litigandi. Fine points or subtleties of litigation [L]

apnoea. Difficulty in breathing [Gk]

apo. By; from [Gk]

apocope. Seeming to deny what is really affirmed [Gk]

apocrypha. Of unknown authorship [Gk]

apodioxis. Indignant rejection of an argument as absurd [Gk]

Apollo. God of light, knowledge, music and purity [Gk]

apologia. A speech or essay in defense [Gk]

Apologia Pro Vita Sua. A Defence of His Life (Cardinal Newman's autobiography) [L]

apomnemoneumata. Memoirs [Gk]

apophthegm. Pointed saying [Gk]

aporemata. Questions; puzzles [Gk]

aporia. A theoretical difficulty or puzzle; the expression or implication of doubt [Gk]

aposiopesis. Break in the midst of a sentence [Gk]

a posteriori. Following after; said of inductive reasoning, beginning with observed facts and inferring general conclusions from these [L]

apostrophe. Invocation; entreaty; rhetorical device to divert attention from matter under consideration [Gk]

apotheosis. Deification; the raising of a mortal to the gods [Gk]

appassionato. Passionately [It]

Applicatio est vita regulae. Application is the life of a rule [L]

appliqué. Applied; said of ornaments applied or fixed to the surface of an object [F]

appoggiatura. A long grace note [It]

appui. Support; prop; fulcrum [F]

Apra. Political party in Peru; antiforeign and pro-Indian social movement; Alianza Popular Revolucionaria Americana [Sp]

après. After [F]

après-midi. Afternoon [F]

Après-Midi D'Un Faune. Afternoon of a Faun (Mallarmé; Debussy) [F]

Après moi le déluge! After me, the deluge! (attributed to Louis XV and to Mme. de Pompadour [F]

a prima vista. At first sight [It]

a priori. Ascertained by reason alone rather than by sense impressions; non-empirical; presumptive; deductive [L]

Aprismo. The *Apra* movement or doctrines [Sp]

à-propos. Something said, done, or happening aptly or opportunely; with reference to [F]

aprovechamiento. Approvement; improvement and enjoyment of public lands [Sp]

apud. By; in; with; among [L]

aqua dulcis. Sweet or fresh water [L]

aquae manalis. Hand-washing vessel, used in church for washing the hands by the celebrant of the liturgy [L]

aqua fortis. Nitric acid [L]

aqua marina. Green water; a precious stone used by gemengravers in ancient times [L]

aqua regia. Nitric acid [L]

aquarius. Water-bearer [L]

aqua vitae. Water of life; distilled spirits; brandy; whiskey [L]

aquí. Here [Sp]

A quien madruga, Dios le ayuda. The early bird catches the worm [Sp]

Aquí hay gato encerrado. Something's up; there's some mystery here [Sp]

aquila. Eagle [L]

Aquilegia. Columbine [L]

a quo. From which; the starting point from which something proceeds [L]

A quoi bon? What's the use? [F]

arabesque. Having a design of delicate tracery; a musical composition with tonal embroidery [F]

arabilis. Arable land [L]

arancia. Orange [It]

arator. Plowman [L]

Aratra Pentelici. Plowshares of Pentelicus (Ruskin's lectures on sculpture, 1870) [L]

Araucano. Peruvian Indian [Sp]

Arbeiter. Worker(s) [G]

Arbeit macht das Leben süss. Work adds zest to life [G]

Arbeitsdienst. Labor Service [G]

Arbeitsunterricht. Work instruction; activity program in teaching [G]

arbiter bibendi. Toastmaster; judge of the drinking; master of the feast [L]

arbiter elegantiarum. Director of amusements at the imperial court in ancient Rome; one whose opinion or taste is authoritative; a judge of style or taste [L]

arbitrios. Merchandise tax [Sp]

arbor. Tree; plant; mast [L]

arbor consanguinitatis. Family tree [L]

arbor vitae. Tree of life; name of an evergreen shrub [L]

arbre fourchu. Forked tree; a design in the decorative and graphic arts [F]

arca. Bow [L]

Arcades ambo. Rascals both (*i.e.* both Arcadians) [L]

arcana. An ark for covering or containing sacred objects; a sheltered and secluded area; occultism (*arcanum*) [Gk]

arcana caelestia. Celestial mysteries [L]

arcana imperii. State secrets [L]

arcanum. See *arcana*

arc boutant. Flying buttress [F]

Arc de Triomphe. Arch of Triumph; erected in Paris by Napoleon, to mark the victories of the Grand Army of the Republic [F]

arc-en-ciel. Rainbow [F]

arche. The first in a series; origin; principle; first cause [Gk]

arco. A bow [It]

are. Are=square dekameter= 100 square meters=1076.441 square feet [F]

A Rebours. Against the Grain (novel; Huysmans; 1884) [F]

arena. Sand [Sp]

arenales. Sandy beaches [Sp]

areopagite. Lawyer or chief judge in Athens; court of the *Areopagus* or "hill" in Athens [Gk]

Areopagus. Hill of Mars; meeting place of the highest tribunal in Athens [Gk]

arestovannyi. Suppressed [R]

aretai ethikai. Moral virtues [Gk]

arête. Sharp mountain ridge [F]

Arete. Virtue; the activity of reason [Gk]

A rey muerto, rey puesto. The king is dead; long live the king! [Sp]

argent. Money; silver [F]

argentarius. Money-lender [L]

argentum. Silver; money [L]

argentum album. Virgin silver; uncoined silver bullion [L]

argentum Dei. God's money; money given as a bond or guarantee of good faith [L]

argot. Thieves' slang; jargon [F]

argumenta. See *argumentum*

argumenta contra. Arguments against; subdivision of some treatise in scholastic philosophy [L]

argumentum. Argument; exposition; table of contents (*pl.* argumenta) [L]

argumentum ad baculum. An argument based on an appeal to fear or a threat [L]

argumentum ad crumenam. Argument based on appeal to material interests [L]

argumentum ad hominem. An irrelevant or malicious appeal to personal circumstances; the diversion of an argument from facts to the personality of the opponent [L]

argumentum ad ignorantiam. A misleading argument used in reliance on people's ignorance [L]

argumentum ad judicium. A reasoning based on the common sense of mankind and the judgment of the people [L]

argumentum ad misericordiam. An argument based on an appeal to pity and related emotions [L]

argumentum ad populum. An argument aimed to sway popular feeling or win popular support by appealing to sentimental weaknesses rather than facts and reasons [L]

argumentum ad rem. An argument to the point, as distinguished from an evasive argument such as *argumentum ad hominem* [L]

argumentum ad verecundiam. An argument using venerable authority, great men, ancient customs, *etc.*, to produce an illusion of proof; argument so phrased that its answer risks a breach of propriety [L]

argumentum a fortiori. An argument from analogy which shows that the proposition advanced is more admissible than one previously conceded by an opponent [L]

argumentum ex concesso. An inference founded on a proposition which an opponent has already admitted [L]

argumentum ex silentio. Conclusion based on absence of data [L]

Ar Hyd Y Nos. All Through the Night [Welsh]

aria. A vocal solo passage in an opera [It]

aria cantabile. A song of marked smoothness [It]

aria da capo. A vocal form with trio which has a repeat of its first section [It]

aria di bravura. A brilliant *aria* aimed to display vocal technique [It]

aria di mezzo carattere. *Aria* of moderate character [It]

aria di portamento. A song making frequent use of vocal *portamento*, which involves a sweep of the voice toward the next note before the time of the preceding note is finished [It]

aria parlante. A song in spoken style, less abrupt than *recitativo* [It]

Aries. Ram [L]

arioso. A short composition, less regular in form than an *aria* [It]

arista. Ear of corn [L]

aristos. Best [Gk]

arlecchino. Harlequin; clown [It]

arma. Arms; weapons; armor; heraldic arms [L]

arma dare. To dub a knight [L]

armata vis. Armed force [L]

Arma tuentur pacem. Arms maintain peace [L]

Arma virumque cano. Arms and the man I sing (first words of Virgil's *Aeneid*; title of a play by G. B. Shaw) [L]

arme blanche. Sword; lance [F]

armes parlantes. Speaking (coats of) arms; arms and crests suggested by the name of the family that bears them [F]

Armut. Poverty [G]

arpeggio. Harp-like; the notes of a chord played in swift succession [It]

arpent. Ancient French measure of land; in Louisiana it equals the square of 192 feet [F]

arraché. Torn away; erased [F]

arrack. Juice; fermented cocopalm liquor [Arab]

arras. Marriage gift from husband to wife [Sp]

Arras. Arras (cloth); a woven fabric used in France in the 14th century as tapestry; name of a French city [F]

arrastre. Dragging; haulage; ramp [Sp]

arrendamiento. Contract of letting or hiring an estate or land [Sp]

arriba. Above; up; upstairs [Sp]

arriere pensee. Ulterior motive; mental reservation [F]

Arrivederci. Goodby [It]

arriviste. Upstart; pusher; unscrupulous person [F]

arrondi. Curved; rounded [F]

arrondissement. Administrative unit of the national government in France; subdivision of a *département* [F]

arroz con pollo. Rice with chicken [Sp]

ars. Art [L]

ars amandi. Art of loving [L]

ars amatoria. Art of lovers (Ovid) [L]

ars combinatoria. Art of combining simple concepts to derive complex ones [L]

Ars est celare artem. The art consists in concealing the art [L]

ars gratia artis. Art for art's sake [L]

arsis. Stressed syllable of a metrical foot [Gk]

Ars longa, vita brevis. Art (is) long, life (is) short; art is long and time is fleeting [L]

ars magna. The great art [L]

ars moriendi. Art of dying (well) [L]

Ars Poetica. Art of Poetics (title of poetics by various authors, especially that by Horace) [L]

artel. Agricultural unit of a semi-collectivized farm [R]

Artemis. The moon-goddess; patroness of hunters [Gk]

Artes, Scientia, Veritas. Arts, Science, Truth (motto of University of Michigan) [L]

artha. Object; goal [Skr]

artichaut. Artichoke [F]

articulo mortis. See *in articulo mortis*

Artium Baccalaureus. Bachelor of Arts [L]

Artium Magister. Master of Arts [L]

arud. Science of prosody [Arab]

as. Unity [L]; ace [F]

As. A-flat [G]

asana. Sitting; posture; an aid to mental discipline used in *Yoga* [Skr]

Aschermittwoch. Ash Wednesday [G]

Asclepia. Milkweed; silkweed [L]

Ashkenazim. Polish - German Jews, as distinguished from Spanish-Portuguese Jews, or *Sephardim* [Heb]

asi. So; thus [Sp]

Asilo Infantile. Kindergarten [It]

asinus. Ass [L]

askesis. Exercise (of ritual) [Gk]

aski. Term applied to blocked marks in Nazi Germany; *Ausländersonderkonten für Inlandbezahlungen*, special foreign accounts for domestic payments [G]

asor. A stringed musical instrument mentioned by David in the Bible [Heb]

aspectant. Facing; face to face; said of figures in heraldic devices [F]

asperge. Asparagus [F]

assai. Very; extremely; much [It]

assiette. Plate [F]

assisa. Assize; court [L]

assumpsit. He undertook; he promised [L]

asteismus. Ingenious mockery [Gk]

astika. Orthodox [Skr]

Astraea Redux. Astraea Returned (poem by Dryden about the goddess of Justice) [L]

Astrakhan. City in S.E. Russia; Lamb skin from this city, sometimes called *karakul*

astratto. Abstract [It]

astron. Star [Gk]

Asunción. Assumption [Sp]

asyndeton. Omission of conjunctions as a rhetorical device [Gk]

atavus. A fourth grandfather back [L]

ataxia. Disorder of animal functions; unsteadiness of limbs [Gk]

Ate. Doom [Gk]

atelier. Workroom; studio [F]

a tempo giusto. In equal time [It]

ateneo. *Athenaeum* [Sp]

athanasia. Immortality; painless death [Gk]

athenaeum. Temple of Athene, Goddess of Wisdom; meeting place of ancient philosophers, poets and orators; lecture hall; title of various periodicals [Gk]

Athene. Goddess of wisdom, gentleness and art [Gk]

athlon. Prize [Gk]

athroeismus. Enumeration [Gk]

atman. Self; soul; ego [Skr]

à tort et à travers. At random; blindly; hit or miss [F]

à tout prix. At any price [F]

atrium. Central court in ancient Roman buildings; in Byzantine architecture, a courtyard outside a building [L]

atropos. An ancient string instrument [Gk]

attacca. Musical direction to attack or start a passage incisively [It]

attaché. Official of a nondiplomatic government department attached to a diplomatic post; person attached to an ambassador's suite or to a foreign legation; court attendant [F]

attentat. He attempts; anything wrongfully attempted; an attempted assassination [L]

atti. See *atto*

atto. Act; document; protocol; proceeding; transaction (*pl.* atti) [It]

aubade. A song at dawn; morning song [F]

au besoin. In (case of) need [F]

au bleu. Blue-style; said of fish boiled in white wine and flavored [F]

A.U.C. See *Ab Urbe Condita*

Au Clair de la Lune. In the Light of the Moon (French song with music attributed to Lulli) [F]

au contraire. On the contrary [F]

au courant. Well-posted; informed [F]

auctoritas. Authority [L]

Audaces fortuna juvat. Fortune favors the bold [L]

Audentes fortuna juvat. Fortune aids the daring [L]

au détail. Retail [F]

Audi alteram partem. Hear the other side [L]

audition colorée. Association of sounds with colors [F]

auditor. Hearer [L]

au fait. At home; informed [F]

Aufbau. Construction; structure; reconstruction [G]

Aufenthalt. Abode (Schubert) [G]

Auffassung. Comprehension; apprehension; nature; composition [G]

Auf Flügeln des Gesanges. On Wings of Song (Mendelssohn) [G]

Aufforderung zum Tanz. Invitation to the Dance (Weber) [G]

Aufgabe. Task; assignment; problem; exercise; homework [G]

Aufgeschoben ist nicht aufgehoben. Postponed is not abandoned [G]

Aufklärung. Enlightenment; solution of a problem or puzzle; reconnaissance [G]

Auflage. Printing; edition [G]

Auflösung. Dissolution (Schubert) [G]

au fond. At bottom; basically [F]

Aufsatz. Essay; composition [G]

Augenarzt. Oculist; ophthalmologist [G]

Augenblick. Instant; moment [G]

au grand sérieux. Quite seriously [F]

au gras. With fat; dressed with meat gravy [F]

au gratin. Baked with a topping of grated cheese or crumbs [F]

Augustana Confessio. The Augsberg Confession [L]

au jus. In the natural gravy or juice [F]

aula. Hall; court [L]

aulos. An ancient flute [Gk]

au miroir. Fried (eggs) sunny side up [F]

a.u.n. See *absque ulla nota*

au naturel. In the natural state; in the nude; plain or unaffected; referring to plain cookery [F]

au pied de la lettre. Literally; to the letter [F]

aura. Breeze; emanation; enveloping atmosphere [Gk]

aura popularis. The popular breeze; popular favor or acclaim [L]

aurea aetes. Golden Age [L]

aurea mediocritas. The golden mean [L]

au revoir. Goodby (till we meet again) [F]

auripigmentum. Rich-colored pigment used by the ancients [L]

auris. Ear [L]

Aurora. Dawn; goddess of the morning [L]

aurora borealis. The northern aurora; *i.e.* the northern lights [L]

Au royaume des aveugles les borgnes sont rois. In the kingdom of the blind the one-eyed are kings [F]

Aus dem Regen in die Traufe. Out of the frying-pan into the fire [G]

Aus den Augen, aus dem Sinn. Out of sight, out of mind [G]

Aus der Tiefe Rufe Ich. Out of the Deep I Call to Thee (Bach) [G]

Ausdruck. Expression [G]

ausführlich. Thorough; complete; exhaustive [G]

Ausgabe. Edition; issue [G]

Ausgewanderte. Expatriates; *émigrés* [G]

Ausgleich. Equalization; equitable agreement [G]

Aushängebogen. Proofs; advance sheets [G]

Auslandsdeutscher. German national or person of German origin living outside of Germany [G]

Auslegung. Interpretation; explanation; commentary [G]

Auslese. Selection; assortment; *élite*; the pick; the flower; the choicest (wine) [G]

Aus Meinen Tränen Spriessen. Out of my Tears Spring Forth (Heine-Schumann) [G]

Auspex. The Diviner; *i.e.* Observer of the Birds (a poem by Lowell) [L]

auspicium. Bird-watching; *i.e.* divining of omens [L]

Aussage. Statement; declaration; utterance [G]

Ausschuss. Committee [G]

Aussitôt dit, aussitôt fait. No sooner said than done [F]

Austausch. Exchange; barter [G]

Auszug. Extract [G]

Autarchie. Self-sufficiency [G]

Aut Caesar aut nullus. Either Caesar or nobody (motto of Caesar Borgia); all in all or not at all [L]

Autobahn. Auto highway [G]

autoclesis. Self-inviter; introduction of an idea by refusing before being requested [Gk]

auto da fé. Act of faith; sentence of the Inquisition; burning at the stake [Port]

autos. Self [Gk]

autostrade. Auto highway [It]

autour. About [F]

autre. Other [F]

autrefois. Formerly; before; at another time [F]

Autre temps, autre moeurs. Other times, other customs [F]

autunno. Autumn [It]

Aut vincere aut mori. Either to conquer or to die; victory or death [L]

auxesis. Peak; climax; amplification [Gk]

auxilium ab alto. Aid from on high [L]

Avanguardia. Italian fascist youth organization [It]

avant. Before [F]

avantail. Front visor of a helmet covering the whole face [F]

avant-garde. Vanguard [F]

avant propos. Preface; foreword [F]

avarie. Loss and damage in sea transportation [F]

Ave atque Vale. Hail and Farewell [L]

avec. With [F]

Ave Caesar, morituri te salutant. Hail Caesar, those who are about to die salute thee (greeting of the gladiators before combat) [L]

Ave Maria. Hail Mary (Luke 1-28; various anthems; Schubert, Gounod, *etc.*; prayer or song of Annunciation) [L]

avenir. Future [F]

Aventine. Famous hill in Rome [It]

aventurine. A delicate type of glass manufactured with copper filings as an ingredient; a greenish-yellowish color [F]

A verbis ad verbera. From words to blows [L]

Avete capito? Do you understand? [It]

aveu. Avowal; admission; confession [F]

aveugle. Blind (man) [F]

avidya. Ignorance; nescience; the state of mind unaware of true reality [Skr]

a vinculo matrimonii. From the bond of matrimony [L]

avion. Airplane [F]

avis. Bird [L]

Avnos. Council of Liberation; a Yugoslav partisan group [ ]

avocat. Advocate; lawyer [F]

avoirdupois. System of weights in the U.S. and Britain; weight; mass [OF]

a vostro beneplacito. At your pleasure [It]

à votre santé. To your health [F]

avoué. Barrister; attorney [F]

avtor. Author [R]

avtorizovamyi. Authorized [R]

a vuestra salud. To your health [Sp]

avunculus. Uncle [L]

avus. Grandfather [L]

avushchi. Vegetables [R]

Axios! He is worthy! [Gk]

axis. Axle (*pl.* axes) [L]

ayer. Yesterday [Sp]

Ayenbite of Inwyt. Remorse of Conscience (title of a religious work in Kentish dialect by Dan Michel, 1340) [OE]

ayuntamiento. Congress; municipal council [Sp]

aza. Gum [Pers]

azad. Free [Hindu]

azafrán. Saffron [Sp]

azucarillo. Meringue crushed in cold water [Sp]

azul. Blue [Sp]

azulejo. Bluish (tile); a glazed Mauro-Spanish tile used in the 15th century [Sp]

azzurro. Blue [It]

B

baba. Sweet yeast cake; very light plum cake [F]

babbo. Dad [It]

baboo. Gentleman; Mr.; half-anglicized Hindu [Hindu]

babov. Beans [R]

babushka. Triangular scarf or shawl worn over the head and tied under the chin [R]

baccarat. A card game [F]

bacchanale. Pertaining to *Bacchus*; riotous [F]

bacchanalia. Festival of *Bacchus*; drunken revelry [Gk]

Bacchantes. Worshippers of *Bacchus* [Gk]

bacchius. Metrical foot of one short syllable followed by two long ones [Gk]

Bacchus. The wine-god; a stout, convivial person; also called *Dionysus* [Gk]

Bach. Brook [G]

Bächlein. Brooklet [G]

bacillus. Little staff; rod-shaped microscopic organism (*pl.* bacilli) [L]

bacio. Kiss [It]

Bacio di bocca spesso cuor non tocca. The heart is often missed where the mouth is kissed [It]

baculus. Rod; staff; wand [L]

Bad. Bath; in place names, indicates a locality noted for its mineral springs, present or past [G]

badaya. Javanese court dancer [ ]

badinage. Banter [F]

badinerie. Pleasant foolery; a light, jocular musical composition [F]

Baedeker. A famous guide-book for European travelers [G]

bagatelle. Trifle; short musical composition [F]

bagel. Doughnut-shaped roll of hard dough [Y]

bagnio. Brothel; bath house [It]

bagno. Bath(room) [It]

bague. Ring; annular moulding [F]

baguette. Moulding with a semi-circular profile [F]

Baha'i. Asiatic religious faith emphasizing the unity of all religions [Pers]

baignoire. Theatre box [F]

bailarina. Female dancer [Sp]

baile. Dance [Sp]

baile flamenco. Gypsy dance [Sp]

bailie. Magistrate; bailiff [Scotch]

bain. Bath [F]

bain-marie. Double boiler used in heating sauces [F]

baird. Poet; minstrel; bard [Gaelic]

baiser. Kiss [F]

bajadere. Indian temple dancer [Port]

bakhshish. Tip; gratuity [Pers]

baklava. Oriental pastry made of dough, honey, nuts and butter [R]

balalaika. A three-stringed musical instrument with a triangular sound-box [R]

balata. Chicle [Sp]

baldachino. Canopy [It]

baldio. Waste land; public domain [Sp]

Balilla. Italian fascist youth organization; name of a national boy hero of the 18th century [It]

ballare. To dance [It]

ballerina. *Ballet* dancer [It]

ballet. A pantomime performance of a story to musical accompaniment; a musical composition written for such purposes [F]

Ballet Russe. Russian Ballet [F]

Ballo in Maschera. Masked Ball (Verdi) [It]

ballon d'essai. Trial balloon; feeler [F]

balloné. Ballet step involving a bend and kick [F]

ballotage. Second ballot between two highest-ranking candidates [F]

balmoral. Heavy shoe with a separate tongue [Scotch]

balompié. Football [Sp]

balshoya. See *bolshoya*

balteus. Baldric; a sword or dagger holder of the ancient Romans [L]

bambino. Baby (*pl.* bambini) [It]

ban. Governor [Hungarian]

banat. Province [Hungarian]

banausos. Vulgar; illiberal [Gk]

banco. Seat; bench; bank [It]

Band. Volume [G]

bandeau. Narrow band or ribbon [F]

banderilla. Small dart with a streamer, used for baiting bulls [Sp]

banderillero. Dart-man; bull-fighter who sticks the *banderillas*, or darts, into the back of the bull's neck [Sp]

bandurria. An extra large Spanish guitar [Sp]

banlieue. Suburbs; outskirts [F]

banni nuptiarum. Banns of matrimony [L]

banqueroute. Bankrupt [F]

banquette. Small bench; narrow window seat [F]

banyan. Merchant; shop-keeper; commercial agent [Hindu]

baragaria. Concubine [Sp]

baranini. Lamb [R]

barato. Cheap [Sp]

barba. Beard [L]

barbacoa. Barbecued meat [Sp]

barba rossa. Red beard [It]

Barbera. An Italian wine [It]

Barbiere di Siviglia. Barber of Seville (Rossini) [It]

barbitos. An ancient harp [Gk]

barcarolle. Boatsong [It]

barde. Strip of bacon [F]

barditus. Sword dance; battle-cry of early Germanic tribes [L]

Bar-le-duc. Type of currant jelly [F]

bar-mitzva. Confirmation [Heb)

baroque. Over-ornamental; obscured by over-elaborate design; a style that sacrifices harmony and proportion to dynamism; eccentric; obscure; flamboyant [F]

barouche. Four-wheeled carriage with collapsible half-head [F]

barraca. Low, thatched cabin [Sp]

barrera. Barrier; barricade; fence [Sp]

barroso. Muddy; pimpled; reddish [Sp]

barrucco. Rough pearl [Sp]

barshchina. Labor rent; rent for farms paid off in labor on an owner's estate [R]

Baruch. Blessed; first word of many Hebrew prayers; a proper name [Heb]

bas. Low; inferior; subordinate; stocking [F]

bas bleu. Bluestocking; female intellectual [F]

bashi-bazouk. Mercenary of Turkish irregulars [Turk]

basileus. King [Gk]

basilica. A public building among the ancient Greeks and Romans; a church or cathedral built on the plan of the ancient basilica; ancient compilation of law [Gk]

basis. Step; a metrical verse of two feet, as recited to the choric dance [Gk]

Basis virtutum constantia. Constancy is the basis of the virtues [L]

bas-relief. A sculpture or design done on a flat surface and projecting from it [F]

basse taille. A process of enameling on precious metals [F]

basso cantante. Singing bass; type of voice classified just above the *basso profundo* [It]

basso continuo. The figured bass [It]

basso profundo. Deep bass; the lowest type of voice [It]

bastante. Enough [Sp]

Bastille. Old state prison captured and destroyed by the people of Paris on July 14, 1789; any prison-fortress [F]

bastinado. Beating on the soles of the feet; cudgel [Sp]

batavus. Dutch [L]

bateau. Boat [F]

bathos. Height; depth; a fall from the lofty to the ludicrous [Gk]

batik. Hand-died fabric of the Dutch East Indies [ ]

batinki. Shoes [R]

batiste. A lightweight wool cloth; a type of cambric [F]

Batrachomyomachia. Battle of the Frogs and Mice [Gk]

batrakhos. Frog [Gk]

battement. Beating; ballet step involving beating movement of the free leg, the supporting leg remaining stationary [F]

batterie de cuisine. Complete set of cooking utensils [F]

Batti, Batti, O Bel Masetto. Scold me, O Dear Masetto (*Don Giovanni*, Act I; Mozart) [It]

battue. Beaten; driving of game; wholesale slaughter [F]

battuta. Beat or measure [It]

Baukunst. Architecture [G]

bavarder. To gossip [F]

Bavaroise. Tea sweetened with syrup and orange juice [F]

bayadere. See *bajadere*

bayou. Creek; stream; outlet from a swamp, pond, or lagoon to a river or the sea [Choctaw]

Bd. See *Band*

Beata Beatrix. Blessed Beatrice (Rossetti) [L]

Beati possidentes. Blessed (are) they that possess; possession is nine points of the law [L]

beau. Handsome; fine; nice; beautiful [F]

beau geste. Magnanimous gesture [F]

beau idéal. Highest ideal [F]

beau monde. Fashionable society [F]

Beaune. A red Burgundy [F]

beaux arts. Fine arts [F]

beaux esprits. See *bel esprit*

beaux yeux. Pretty eyes [F]

Bebung. Trembling; *tremolo* [G]

Béchamel. Rich, white sauce [F]

bêche-de-mer. Sea-slug; jargon English (South Pacific) [F]

Becken. Basin; cymbals [G]

Beckmesser. A musical hack; name of a character in Wagner's *Meistersinger* [G]

bedeutend. Significant [G]

Bedeutung. Meaning [G]

bednyak. Poor peasant [R]

bega. Land measure equal to one-third of an acre [Bengalese]

Begriff. Concept; notion [G]

Begriffsbildung. Formation of concepts [G]

begum. Lady; princess; woman of high rank [Hindu]

Behörde. Authority; commission [G]

beige. Natural; undyed; unbleached [F]

beignet. Fritter [F]

Beiheft. Supplement [G]

Beilage. Supplement [G]

Bei Nacht sind alle Katzen grau. In the dark all cats are gray [G]

Beira Mar. Famous bay-side avenue in Rio de Janeiro [Port]

Beitrag. Contribution (*pl.* Beiträge) [G]

bekendmaking. Publication [Du]

bel canto. Pure *legato* singing or playing [It]

bel esprit. Cultivation of literature; witty person; affected person; fop (*pl.* beaux esprits) [F]

belladonna. Beautiful lady; poisonous nightshade plant; drug for dilating the pupils of the eyes [It]

belle âme. Beautiful soul; sensitive person [F]

Bella Figlia Dell' Amore. Fairest Daughter of the Graces (*Rigoletto*, Act IV; Verdi) [It]

belles-lettres. The humanities; grammar; eloquence; poetry; literature and criticism; esthetics of literature [F]

belleza. Beauty [Sp]

Bellis. English Daisy [L]

bellum. War [L]

Bel Paese. Beautiful country; reference to Italy; an Italian cheese [It]

Belshazzar. The last Babylonian king, at whose feast handwriting appeared on the wall, forecasting the fall of Babylonia. See *Mene, Mene Tekel, etc.*

belyi. White [R]

bema. Orator's tribune; proscenium; pulpit; sanctuary [Gk]

Bemerkungen. Observations; remarks; comments [G]

bémol. Any flat (music) [F]

ben. Son [Heb]

bene. Well; in proper form; legally; sufficiently [L]

Benedicite. Bless ye; praise ye; first word of a canticle of the Anglican Church [L]

Benedictine. Pertaining to St. Benedict and his order; a *liqueur* [F]

Benedict(us). Blessed; St. Benedict (b. A.D. 480), founder of the Benedictine order of monks; first word of a section of the Mass [L]

beneplacito. By your leave [It]

bengaline. A poplin-like fabric [F]

ben trovato. Well-invented; well-conceived; plausible [It]

berceuse. Lullaby [F]

beret. Round, visorless cap with a short tassel [F]

bergamot. A perfume; a coarse tapestry; a variety of pear [F]

Bergbau. Mining [G]

berger. Shepherd (*fem.* bergère) [F]

bergère. See *berger*

Berggeist. Mountain spirit [G]

Bergschrund. Crevice [G]

Bergsteiger. Mountain climber [G]

Bericht. Report [G]

Bernstein. Amber [G]

bersaglieri. Sharpshooters [It]

Bertillon. System of anthropometry used chiefly for identification of criminals [F]

bésame. Kiss me [Sp]

besant. A heraldic figure in the shape of a disc; a round architectural ornament on a flat surface [F]

Besatzung. Garrison; crew; occupation (of a town, *etc.*) [G]

beseelt. Imbued with soul; inspired; full of spirituality [G]

besoin. Need [F]

Bestellung. Order [G]

bestiarium. Collection of animals; animal fables; allegorical poems of the 12th and 13th centuries representing human virtues and vices in the form of animals [L]

beta. 2nd letter of the Greek alphabet (B β)

betal. See *betel*

betel. Leaf used for chewing by East Indians and Siamese [Malayan]

bête noire. Pet abomination [F]

Beth. House; second letter of the Hebrew alphabet [Heb]

bêtise. Nonsense; foolishness; stupidity [F]

béton. Concrete; cement and pebble mixture [F]

béton armé. Reinforced concrete [F]

betreffend. Concerning [G]

betula. Genus name of birch trees [L]

beurre. Butter [F]

beurre noir. Black butter sauce [F]

bevollmächtigt. Authorized[G]

Bewährung. Verification; proof [G]

bewegt. Agitated; full of motion or movement [G]

Beweis. Proof [G]

bewerker. Editor [Du]

bewusst. Conscious; aware [G]

Bewusstsein. Consciousness [G]

Bewusstsein überhaupt. Consciousness in general [G]

bey. Master; governor; official [Turk]

bezgl. See *bezüglich*

bez goda. No date [R]

Beziehung. Relation(ship); connection; reference [G]

beziehungsweise. Respectively; as the case may be [G]

bezüglich. Regarding; in reference to [G]

bezw. See *beziehungsweise*

Bhagavad Gita. Song of the Blessed One (title of a famous Indian philosophic epic) [Skr]

bhakti. Division; share [Skr]

bhang. Indian hemp (a narcotic) [Hindu]

bhasya. Speaking; commentary [Skr]

bheda. Different; distinct [Skr]

bhedabheda. Different (yet) not different [Skr]

bhugia. A vegetable dish popular in India [ ]

bhuta. Become; that which has become [Skr]

biacca. White lead [It]

biadetto. A blue, cuprous pigment [It]

bianco. White [It]

bianco secco. Dry white; a white pigment used in *fresco* painting [It]

bianon. Violent retort to an argument [ ]

Bibamus, moriendum est. Let us drink, for we must die (Seneca) [L]

bibelot. Trinket; knick-knack; miniature edition; tiny book[F]

bibite fresche. Cool drinks [It]

biblia pauperum. Books of the poor; medieval books [L]

biblioteca. Library [It] [Sp]

bibliotheca. Library; book collection; bibliography or catalogue [L]

Bibliothek. Library [G]

bibliothèque. Library [F]

bicchiere. Glass [It]

biche. Hind; girl; darling; light woman [F]

bicorne. Two-horned, crescent-shaped hat, such as worn by admirals [F]

bidet. Sitzbath [F]

Biedermeier. A style of furniture in the 19th century; middle-class domesticity; literary period in Germany, 1815-1848; preoccupation with minor things of only personal interest

Biegsamkeit. Flexibility [G]

bien aimée. Dearly beloved [F]

bien conservado. In good condition [Sp]

Biene. Bee [G]

bien entendu. Of course [F]

bienes. Goods; property [Sp]

bienes comunes. Common property [Sp]

bienséance. Decorum; consistency with manners and morals of a particular time [F]

Bierstube. Tavern [G]

biffato. Canceled [It]

biffé. Canceled [F]

bijdragen. Contributions [Du]

bijou. Jewel (*pl.* bijoux) [F]

bijouterie. Jewelry [F]

bildende Künste. Formative arts, *i.e.* architecture, sculpture, painting [G]

Bildung. Formation; cultivation; education [G]

billa vera. True bill [L]

billet. Bill; note; ticket; billet (for quartering soldiers); oblong figure on a shield [F]

billet doux. Love note; mash note [F]

billig. Cheap [G]

biltong. Strip(s) of sun-dried meat [Du]

Biographia Literaria. Literary Biography (title of a critical work by Coleridge, 1817) [L]

biremis. A double-banked galley [Gk]

birra. Beer [It]

bis. Twice; once more; continued; to be repeated [L]; Until [G]

Bis dat qui cito dat. He gives twice who gives soon [L]

bise. North wind in Switzerland [F]

Bis pueri senes. Old men are children twice [L]

bisque. Thick soup usually made from shell-fish; ice cream containing finely chopped nuts [F]

bistecca. Steak [It]

bistre. A brown color with a yellowish tint; an artist's sketch done in this color [F]

bistro. Wine merchant; restaurant keeper [F]

Bis vincit qui se vincit in victoria. Twice conquers he who conquers himself in the victory [L]

bitka. Croquettes [R]

bitochki. Meat croquettes [R]

Bitterling. Bitter mineral spring; small species of carp; yellowwort [G]

bizcocho. Biscuit; hardtack; *bisque*; plaster [Sp]

blad. Leaf; sheet [Du] [Swed]

bladwijzer. Index; table of contents [Du]

blague. Pretentious talk or conduct [F]

blanchir. To bleach; whiten [F]

blanc mange. Pudding made of milk, sugar, vanilla, and other ingredients according to style; *e.g.* cornstarch, coconut, chocolate, *etc.* [F]

blanquette. White meat in thick cream sauce [F]

blasé. Jaded; wearied by dissipation [F]

blaue Blume. Blue flower; symbol of romantic longing [G]

blessé. Wounded [F]

blinchiki. Pancake served with sour cream, jam, or sugar, sometimes stuffed with cottage cheese [R]

blini. Buckwheat-flower pancakes [R]

blintzes. Cottage-cheese or meat wrapped in thin dough [Y]

Blitzkrieg. Lightning war [G]

blonde de veau. Stock of veal broth [F]

blucher. Type of shoe in which the tongue is a continuation of the vamp or front part of the shoe [G]. See also *Blücher*

Blücher. German general who introduced the open-throat laced shoe as an army shoe in 1910. See also *blucher*

Blut und Boden. Blood and soil; a *Nazi* theory that emphasizes the identification of character with geographic locality [G]

Blut und Eisen. Blood and iron [G]

bnai. Sons [Heb]

B'nai B'rith. Sons of the Covenant; a Jewish fraternal organization [Heb]

boca. Mouth [Sp]

bocage. Copse; grove [F]

bocce. Lawn bowling; bowling balls [It]

boccia. Bowling ball (*pl.* bocce) [It]

Boche. German (contemptuous) [F]

Bockbier. Dark beer of the early spring brew [G]

bodega. Wine cellar [Sp]

bœuf. Ox; steer; beef [F]

boeuf à la mode. Beef, larded and pot-roasted [F]

boek. Book [Du]

boekenbeschrijving. Bibliography [Du]

Boer. Peasant; South African of Dutch origin [Du]

Bogen. Bow; arc; curve; slur or tie (music); sheet of paper [G]

Bohême. Bohemia; home of the gypsies; dwelling place of artists and others who flout middle-class conventions [F]. See also *Vie de Bohême*

böhmisch. Bohemian [G]

boina. Basque beret [Sp]

bois. Wood(s) [F]

boisson. Beverage [F]

boîte. Box; chest; case; shack [F]

boiteux. Lame [F]

boksamling. Library [Swed]

bolas. Leather thongs with balls at the ends, used by the *gaucho* to capture animals [Sp]

bolero. A dance of moderate pace, in 3-4 rhythm, accompanied by castanets; a short jacket [Sp]

bolivar. Unit of currency in Venezuela [Simon Bolivar, national hero]

Bolsheviki. Majority party; that founded by Lenin, now the Communist Party of the Soviet Union [R]

bolshinstvo. Majority [R]

bolshoya. Large [R]

bombardon. The bass tuba [F]

bombe. Bomb; shell; dessert consisting of frozen mixture in a mold [F]

bombe glacée. Mold of ice cream or ices [F]

bombilla. Sipper [Sp]

bombos. An ancient wind instrument, somewhat like the modern bass clarinet [Gk]

bombyx. An ancient wood-wind instrument resembling the modern clarinet [Gk]

bomolochos. One who hangs about altars; beggar; clown [Gk]

bomphiologia. Words full of wind; pompous speech; bombast [Gk]

bon. Good; fine; all right [F]

bona. Good(s); property; possession(s) [L]

bonae fidei. In good faith [L]

bonae fidei emptor. Purchaser in good faith [L]

bona fide. In good faith [L]

bona fides. Good faith [L]

bona gratia. By mutual consent [L]

bon ami. Good friend [F]

bonanza. Fair weather; prosperity; run of luck; large output (of a mine); prosperous [Sp]

bonbon. Candy [F]
bon gré, mal gré. Willing or unwilling [F]
bonheur. Happiness [F]
bonhommie. Geniality [F]
bonito. Pretty [Sp]
Bon jour. Hello; Good day [F]
bon marché. Cheap [F]
bon mot. Witty saying [F]
bonne. Nursemaid; servant; good [F]
bonne bouche. Sweet (dessert); tidbit [F]
bon sens. Good sense [F]
bon ton. Good breeding; of the fashionable world [F]
bonum per se. Good in itself [L]
bon vivant. Gourmand [F]
bon voyage. Happy trip [F]
boreas. North wind [Gk]
bordarii. Tenants renting a "bord" or cottage [L]
Borgen macht Sorgen. Borrowing makes for sorrowing [G]
borné. Limited; narrow-minded [F]
Borotbist. Member of a Ukrainian nationalist party which was suppressed in 1918 [R]
borracho. Drunkard [Sp]
borrachita. Intoxicator; drunkard [Sp]
borrado. Canceled [Sp]
borschok. Strong *consommé* [R]
borscht. Russian soup made of beets [R]
borzoi. Wolfhound [R]
bös. Evil; wicked; naughty; angry [G]
bosco. Wood; forest [It]
bossage. Embossment; relief or projection [F]
Botschaft. Message (Brahms) [G]
botte. Cask; butt; bundle; thrust, lunge [F]
bottega. Shop; studio; art shop [It]
bouche. Mouth [F]

bouchée. Mouthful; small pastry shell or pepper case filled with creamed meat or fish [F]
bouclé. Fabric woven from twisted yarn so as to produce small loops on its surface [F]
boudin. Black pudding of forcemeat and blood [F]
boudoir. Lady's private sitting-room; small, intimate reception room, part of or outside of a lady's bedroom [F]
bouffant. Puffed (said of a style of full sleeve or skirt) [F]
bougran. Buckram [F]
bouillabaisse. Mixed seafood soup [F]
bouilli. Boiled; boiled beef [F]
bouillon. Clear soup, particularly of beef [F]
boulanger. Baker [F]
Boulangisme. Political party led by General Boulanger, French minister of war (*ca.* 1888), accused of treason [F]
boule de neige. Snowball; a species of tulip [F]
boulevardier. Pleasure-seeker; man or style in the France of the Second Empire; irreverent young man; frequenter of cafés and theaters [F]
bouquet d'herbes. Bunch of vegetables; parsley, thyme, and scallions [F]
Bourbon. A French dynasty, 16th to 18th centuries; an extreme conservative; a whiskey [F]
bourdon. A drone bass accompaniment; the organ pipes which produce this tone; a pilgrim's staff [F]
bourgeois(e). Middle class (person); conventional [F]
Bourgeois Gentilhomme. Middle-class Gentleman (play by Molière) [F]
bourgeoisie. The middle class [F]
Bourgogne. Burgundy [F]

Bourguignote. Ragout of truffles [F]

bourrée. Peasant dance in 4-4 time; originated in Auvergne and executed with a skipping step somewhat like the polka [F]

bourse. Purse; stock-exchange [F]

boustrophedon. Ox-turning; written alternately from right to left and left to right, as in some ancient inscriptions [Gk]

bouteille. Bottle [F]

Boutez en Avant. Strike out; push ahead [F]

boutique. Shop; booth; stall [F]

boutonnière. Button - maker; button-hole, button-hole flower or ornament [F]

bouts-rimés. Rhymed ends (of lines of poetry); detached rhyme-pairs (as in a rhyming dictionary) [F]

bouwerye. Farm [Du]

bouwkunde. Architecture [Du]

bouwmeester. Farmer [Du]

bozero. Advocate; attorney [Sp]

Brabançonne. National Air of Belgium [F]

brachys. Short [Gk]

Brahma. The impersonal, pantheistic world-soul; the Absolute; the Creator or creative principle of the universe in the Hindu religion [Skr]

Brahman. The real [Skr]

braisé. Braised [F]

braisière. Saucepan with ledges on the lid for holding charcoal [F]

branle. A category of costumed pantomime dances [F]

Branntwein. Brandy [G]

brasero. Charcoal burner; braizier [Sp]

brassard. Armpiece; part of a suit of armor that protects the arm; ornament or insignia on a sleeve [F]

Bratsche. Viola [G]

Brauhaus. Brewery [G]

Braut. Bride [G]

bravura. Requiring or displaying great dexterity; spirit; skill [It]

brebis. Sheep [F]

breve. Writ (*pl.* brevia) [L]

breveté. Patented [F]

breviarium. Compilation of laws [L]

Brevi manu. Off-hand; summarily [L]

bride. Bridle; string; loop; connecting tie in lace [F]

Brie. A French town; a soft, white cream cheese [F]

Brief. Letter; epistle [G]

Briefmarke. Postage stamp [G]

Briefmarkenkunde. Philately [G]

brio. Vivacity; dash; spirit [It]

brioche. Bun; cake; blunder [F]

brisé. Broken; ballet step somewhat like the *entrechat* except that only one foot does the beating [F]

brise-bise. Curtain to prevent draft [F]

brocatelle. An imitation brocade; a fabric with ornamental, raised designs [F]

broccoli. A variety of cauliflower that is green instead of white [It]

broché. Fabric with a raised woven design; sewed (said of books) [F]

brochette, Skewer [F]

brochure. Pamphlet [F]

broderskap. Guild [Swed]

bronteon. Brazen vessels filled with stones; thunder machine used in ancient drama [Gk]

brouillé. Mixed; confused; fallen out with; run foul of [F]

bruit. Noise [F]

brujo. Wizard; sorcerer; magician [Sp]

Brumaire. Second month of the calendar used during the French Revolution [F]

Brunhilde. The bravest of Wotan's war-like daughters; any strong, large-proportioned female [G]

brut. Rough; raw; unadulterated (wine) [F]

brutum fulmen. Empty noise or threat [L]

Bücherbesprechung. Book review [G]

Bücherei. Library; printing office [G]

Bücherkunde. Bibliography [G]

Buchhandel. Book trade [G]

bucolicum. Pastoral poem; bucolic [L]

Buddha. "The Enlightened One;" name of the founder of Buddhism; small image of Buddha [Skr]

Buenas tardes. Good afternoon [Sp]

Buenos días. Good morning [Sp]

bueyes. Oxen [Sp]

buffo. A singer who plays comic roles; the comedian in an opera [It]

buffon. Clown [F]

Bühne. Stage [G]

bulla. Seal; amulet; charm [L]

bumaga. Paper [R]

Bummelzug. Local train [G]

Buna. A synthetic rubber [G]

Bund. League; union [G]

Bundesrat. Federal Council (upper house of the parliament of the West German Republic, 1949); upper house of the *Reichstag*, 1871-1918; Swiss federal executive council [G]

Bundesrepublik. Federal Republic (of Western Germany) [G]

Bundestag. Federal Assembly (lower house of the parliament of the West German Republic 1949) [G]

Bunker. Fortified underground shelter [G]

bunraku. Puppet play [J]

buñuelos. Fritters [Sp]

Buona notte. Good night [It].

Buona sera. Good evening [It]

Buon giórno. Good morning [It]

Burg. Citadel; fortress [G]

bürgerlich. Bourgeois; civil [G]

Bürgermeister. Mayor [G]

Burgtheater. State-supported theater in Vienna [G]

burin. Graver; engraving tool [F]

burladero. Sheltering wall or fence in a bull ring [Sp]

burletta. Musical farce; burlesque [It]

burnoose. A hooded cloak [Arab]

burro. Butter [It]; Donkey; burro [Sp]

bursa. Purse [L]

buryi. Brown [R]

busca. Search; quest [Sp]

Burschenschaft. Student corps; fraternity [G]

bushido. Way of the warrior; ethical code of the *samurai* or feudal warrior class [J]

Butterbrot. Sandwich [G]

butyrum. Butter [Gk]

Butzenscheibenlyrik. Stained-glass poetry; artificial poetry idealizing medievalism [G]

buxus. Beech; boxwood, used for engraving [L]

byggningskonst. Architecture [Swed]

bylina. Narrative folksong [R]

C

c-. See also *k-*

ca. See *circa*

cabaletta. A musical composition with an accompaniment that suggests a galloping horse [It]

caballero. Knight; cavalier; gentleman [Sp]

caballo. Horse [Sp]

cabaña. Hut; cabin; cottage[Sp]

cabaret. Tavern; restaurant [F]

cabbala. Tradition; Jewish oral tradition; occult lore [Heb]

cabeza. Head [Sp]

caboché. Full-faced; on heraldry said of the head of an animal that faces the spectator [F]

cabochon. A polished but uncut precious stone in a gold setting [F]

cabotage. Right to engage in coastwise shipping [F]

cabriole. Ballet step executed with both feet in the air and both legs beating together but not crossing [F]

cacciatore. Huntsman (style); parts of chicken potted in tomato and paprika sauce [It]

cacemphaton. Lewd allusion; foul play on meaning or sound; *double entendre*; ill-sounding expression; use of a common word having another and obscene reference [Gk]

cache. Hiding place; hidden storage [F]

cachet. Seal; stamp; mark (of genius, *etc.*) [F]. See also *lettre de cachet*

cachucha. A rapid Andalusian dance in triple rhythm [Sp]

Caciocavallo. A hard, Italian cheese, white in color and shaped like a gourd [It]

cacique. American Indian chief [Sp]

cacoethes loquendi. Itch for speaking; irresistible desire to speak [L]

cacoethes scribendi. Itch for writing; scribbler's itch [L]

cacozelon. Affected diction or style [Gk]

cada. Each [Sp]

Cada cerdo tiene su San Martín. Every dog has his day[Sp]

Cada día gallina, amarga la cocina. Constant repetition wearies [Sp]

Cada oveja con su pareja. Birds of a feather flock together [Sp]

Cada uno habla como quien es. We speak according to our lights [Sp]

cadenza. An elaborate solo passage coming near the end of an instrumental composition or song [It]

cadere. To fall [It]

cadet. Younger son; student at a military or naval academy [F]

Cadet Rousselle. A French folksong, author unknown [F]

44

Cadit quaestio. The question falls; there is no room for further argument [L]

cadran. Dial; clock face; instrument dial; dial plate [F]

cadre. Frame; skeleton; outline; design; nucleus of an organization [F]

caduceus. Serpent - entwined staff with winged top, carried by Mercury; herald's wand; symbol of peace; insigne of the Medical Corps [L]

Caeca invidia est. Envy is blind [L]

caelatura. Said of raised work on metal; chased [L]

Caelitus mihi vires. My strength is from heaven [L]

caeruleus. Blue [L]

caesura. A cutting (of a verse of poetry); a stop or break in a line of poetry [L]

Caetera desunt. The rest is missing [L]

caeteris paribus. Other things being equal [L]

caeterus. Other; another; the rest [L]

café. Coffee; restaurant [F]

café au lait. Coffee with milk [F]

café chantant. Cabaret [F]

café cantante. Restaurant having singing and dancing [Sp]

café noir. Black coffee [F]

café-terrasse. Outdoor café [F]

caffè espresso. Special coffee, Italian style [It]

caftan. Long tunic [Turk]

Cagoulards. Hooded men; the name of a semi-fascist French political organization before and during World War II [F]

cahier. Notebook; register; journal [F]

caique. Rowboat [Turk]

Ça ira! It will succeed! (French revolutionary song, 1789) [F]

caisse. Chest; box; drum; cashier's cage; cashier; treasury; treasurer [F]

caisson. Coffer; case; chest; sunken panel in a ceiling; ammunition box [F]

calabaza. Gourd; pumpkin [Sp]

calabozo. Jail; cell [Sp]

calamus. Reed [L]

calando. Growing softer and slower [It]

calceus. Shoe; boot [L]

calculus. Little stone; pebble (used in counting); branch of higher mathematics [L]

calèche. Open carriage; *barouche* [F]

calendae. Calends; first day of the month in the ancient Roman calendar [L]

Calendula officinalis. Pot Marigold [L]

caliente. Hot [Sp]

caliga. Soldier's nail-shod shoe [L]

caliph. Spiritual head of the Mohammedans; successor to Mohammed [Arab]

calix. A drinking-cup having two small handles and set on a stem ending in a base [Gk]

calle. Street [Sp]

callejon. Narrow passage or lane [Sp]

Callistephus chinensis. China Aster [L]

calmato. Calm; tranquil; quiet [It]

caló. Language of the Spanish gypsies [Sp]

caloroso. Warm; animated [It]

calot. Skull cap [F]

calunnia. Slander [It]

Calvados. *Département* of France; apple brandy made there [F]

calx. Stone [L]

calzolaio. Shoemaker [It]

camaieu. A painting in imitation of a cameo [F]

camaraderie. Comradeship; good fellowship [F]

camarón. Shrimp [Sp]

cambiale. Order [It]

cambio. Change; exchange [Sp]

Camelots du Roi. Royalist faction in France, disbanded in 1936 [F]

Camembert. A French cheese

camera. Chamber [L]

camera lucida. Bright chamber; device using a prism to project the image of an object upon a sheet of drawing paper [L]

camera obscura. Dark chamber; device used to project a reduced and inverted image upon a surface in a dark chamber; predecessor of the box camera [L]

camera stellata. Star chamber [L]

cameriere. Servant [It]

Camicie Rosse. Red Shirts; army of 1,000, organized by Garibaldi for the liberation of Sicily [It]

camilla. Table with aproned sides [Sp]

camino. Road; highway [Sp]

camino de Santiago. The Milky Way [Sp]

camino real. Royal highway [Sp]

camion. Wagon; truck [F]

Camisards. French Protestants who revolted against the Edict of Nantes, 1685 [F]

Camorra. Secret society [It]

campane. Bells [It]

campanes. Small bells, woven or carved, used as a *motif* in ornamentation [F]

campanile. A bell tower [It]

Campanula rotundifolia. Bluebells of Scotland; Harebell [L]

campeador. Warrior; champion [Sp]. See also *El Cid Campeador*

campione. Sample [It]

campo. Field [It] [Sp]

campo santo. Sacred field; cemetery [It] [Sp]

campus. Field [L]

cana. Measure of length equal to 5 to 7 feet [Sp]

canaille. The rabble; common herd [F]

canapé. Slice of bread or toast, or a cracker, spread with highly flavored food and served as an appetizer [F]

canard. Duck; hoax [F]

canasta. Basket; a South American card game [Sp]

canasto. Pannier; basket [Sp]

can-can. Dance involving high kicking and display of *lingerie* [F]

cancer. Crab; malignant tumor [L]

cancionero. Collection of songs and lyrical poetry of a particular epoch [Sp]

cancrine. Crab-like; verse that reads the same backward as forward; *palindrome* [L]

Candida pax. White-robed peace [L]

Candide. Character in a book of that name by Voltaire; an optimist [F]

canephorus. Basket-bearer [Gk]

caneton. Duckling [F]

cannelon. Meat stuffed, rolled up, and roasted or braised [F]

canon. Rule; law; "round" song; select list of Greek writers [L]

cañón. Deep, narrow valley; gorge; canyon [Sp]

Canossa. See *Nach Canossa, etc.*

canotier. Canoer; large-brimmed sailor hat [F]

cansado. Tired [Sp]

canson. Lyric of from 5 to 7 stanzas [OF]

cantabile. In a smooth, singing style [It]

cantar. To sing; epic poem; lay [Sp]

Cantar de mío Cid. Lay of the Cid; Spanish epic (*ca.* 1140)

cántaro. Jar [Sp]

cantata. A short composition for one or more voices, in *oratorio* form [It]

Cantate. O sing [L]

cantharus. A two-handled vase or cup, sacred to Bacchus [Gk]

canticula. Short song [L]

canticum. Part of a play to be sung or chanted [L]

cantilena. A melody; a melodious passage [It]

Cantique des Cantiques. Song of Songs [F]

canton. Political subdivision of Switzerland [F]

Cantuar. (abbrev. for *cantuariensis*) Of Canterbury [L]

cantus firmus. Fixed song; the chief melody in troubadour music, sung by a tenor [L]

canus. Gray [L]

canzone. Song [It]

capa. Cape [Sp]

cap à pie(d). Head to foot; said of a knight armed head to foot [F]

capa y espada. See *comedia, etc.*

capeador. Bullfighter who teases the bull with the cape [Sp]

capeline. A large hat with a soft brim; a small skull cap worn under a helmet [F]

capias. Take thou; writ of arrest [L]

capilotade. Poultry hash [F]

capinera. Wren [Sp]

capitis diminutio. Loss of status [L]

capo. The beginning; the head or top [It]

capriccio. Musical composition in free form having a capricious or bizarre style [It]

capriccioso. Capriciously; fancifully [It]

capricornus. Goat-horned; goat [L]

caput. Head [L]

caput mortuum. Dead head; residue; worthless person [L]

Caput Mundi. Head of the world; reference to Rome [L]

cara. Dear [L]; Face [Sp]

carabinieri. Military police [It]

caracul. See *karakul*

carafe. Water bottle [F]

carátula. Title page [Sp]

carbonados. Black diamonds used for industrial purposes [Port]

Carbonari. Charcoal burners; members of Italian republican secret society [It]

carbón de leña. Charcoal [Sp]

carbón de piedra. Hard coal [Sp]

carbone bianco. White coal; water power [It]

carcan. Iron collar [F]

carcanet. Necklace of pearls or precious stones [F]

carcer. Prison [L]

carceres. Stalls for horses in the ancient Roman circus [L]

carciofi. Artichokes [It]

caricare. To overload; to exaggerate [It]

carior. Dearer [L]

carissima. Dearest [It]

carita. Feeling; tenderness [It]

caritas. Charity [L]

Carmagnole. French revolutionary song (1789); a round dance to the *Carmagnole*; a patriotic costume of the French Revolution [F]

carmen. Song; poem; lyric; canto [L]

carmen figuratum. Shaped verse; verse printed in the shape of an object [L]

carmen solutum. Prose poem [L]

Carmen Triumphale. Song of Triumph (poem by Southey) [L]

carnaliter cognovit. He knew carnally; *i.e.* had intercourse with; raped [L]

carne. Meat [It]

47

carnivora. Carnivorous or flesh-eating order of mammals [L]

caro. Dear [It]; Flesh [L]

Caro Mio Ben. My Dear One (Giordani) [It]

Caro Nome. Dearest Name (*Rigoletto*, Act II; Verdi) [It]

carpa. Itinerant tent show in Mexico [Sp]

carpe diem. Seize the day; enjoy the present [L]

Carpe diem, quam minimum credula postero. Enjoy the day, trusting the morrow as little as possible (Horace; *Odes*; 1-11-8) [L]

carpentum. Covered carriage used by Roman ladies in ancient times [L]

Carrara. City in Italy famous for its marble quarries [It]

carré. Square(d) [F]

Carro di Tespi. Thespian chariots; traveling theaters [It]

carrus. Cart [Gk]

carta. Chart(er); letter; deed[L]

carte blanche. White or blank card; unlimited authorization; free hand [L]

cartel. Group of corporations organized for the purpose of controlling the market; French inter-party coalition; agreement for exchange of prisoners [F]

Cartel des Gauches. Coalition of leftist parties [F]

cartera. Portfolio [Sp]

cartero. Mailman [Sp]

Carthago delenda est. Carthage must be destroyed (Cato's repeated exhortation to the Roman Senate) [L]

cartouche. Cartridge; an ornament with an empty space for an inscription; any oval design [F]

carus. Dear; costly; precious; loved [L]

caryatides. Figures of women which serve as columns in classical architecture [Gk]

caryatis. A dance, in the nude, in honor of Diana, and symbolising innocence [Gk]

casa. House [Sp]

casa de huéspedes. Boarding-house [Sp]

Casa de dos puertas, mala de guardar. A house with two doors is hard to guard [Sp]

cascara sagrada. A laxative [Sp]

cassava. A form of tapioca [F]

casse-noisette. Nut-cracker [F]

casserole. Coarse clay saucepan used both for cooking and serving; case or mold of potato, rice, or bread, in which meat or vegetables are cooked [F]

cassia. Any plant of the genus *cassia*; a medicine or laxative [L]

Casta Diva. Queen of Heaven (*Norma*, Act I; Bellini) [It]

castanea. Chestnut tree [L]

castañeta. Castanet; snapping of the fingers [Sp]

castanopsis. Chinquapin tree [L]

castañuelas. Castanets [Sp]

castellano. Castillian (Spanish) [Sp]

castello. Castle [Sp]

castra. Camp [L]

castrati. Castrated ones; male with a female voice [It]

castrum. Camp [L]

casus. Case; event; chance; accident [L]

casus belli. Occurrence giving rise to war; war-like incident [L]

casus foederis. Provision of a treaty requiring one of the parties to act [L]

cata-. Down; against; through; concerning [Gk]

catabasis. Descending or post-climatic action of a play [Gk]

catachresis. Improper use of a

term; unsuccessful figure of speech [Gk]

catalán. Catalan (language); native dialect of north-eastern Spain [Sp]

catalecta. Detached literary pieces; collection of poems attributed to Vergil [Gk]

catalla. Chattels; dead goods [L]

catalogue raisonné. Commentated catalogue, discussing subject, history and style of works of art [F]

catastasis. Narrative part of the introduction of a speech [Gk]

cathedra. Armchair; papal throne; bishop's throne [L]. See also *ex cathedra*

catorce. Fourteen [Sp]

cattleya. Variety of orchid, often worn as a *corsage* [L]

cattura. Caption [It]

caucho. Rubber [Sp]

caudillo. Chief; title used by Franco [Sp]

causa. Cause; reason; occasion; motive; inducement [L]

Causa causae est causa causati. The cause of a cause is the cause of the thing caused [L]

causa causans. Immediate cause [L]

causa efficiens. Efficient or effective cause [L]

causa formalis. Formal cause [L]

causa materialis. Material cause [L]

causa mortis. In view of (approaching) death [L]

causa proxima. Immediate cause [L]

causa sine qua non. Necessary or inevitable cause; cause without which the effect in question could not have happened [L]

causa sui. Cause of itself [L]

cause célèbre. Celebrated case; an unusual or remarkable case or trial; sensational trial [F]

causerie. Chat; informal talk; one of a series of periodical essays on literary themes [F]

Causeries du Lundi. Monday Talks (criticism; St. Beuve, 1856-69) [F]

cautela. Care; caution; vigilance [L]

cautio. Security; bail; bond [L]

Ça va. All right; fine [F]

cavaedium. Open part of an ancient Roman house; open quadrangle [L]

cavaliere servente. Man devoted to a married woman, as in the medieval system of courtly love [It]

Cavalleria Rusticana. Rustic Chivalry; title of an opera by Mascagni [It]

Ça va sans dire. That goes without saying [F]

cavatina. Short song; melodious air; smooth, aria-section of a *scena* [It]

caveat. Let him beware [L]

Caveat actor. Let the doer beware [L]

Caveat emptor. Let the buyer beware [L]

Caveat venditor. Let the seller beware [L]

Caveat viator. Let the traveler beware [L]

Cave canem! Beware of the dog! [L]

caviar. Salted roe of sturgeon; anything rare and exclusive [Turk]

Cedant arma togae. Let arms give way to the toga (Cicero) [L]

Cela m'est égal. It's all the same to me [F]

Cela ne fait rien. That makes no difference [F]

Cela va sans dire. That goes without saying [F]

celeste. Celestial; heavenly; a musical instrument like a miniature piano, having a bell-like tone [It]

Celeste Aïda. Heavenly Aïda (*Aïda*, Act I; Verdi) [It]

cella. Cell; store-room; separate chamber in a bath; sanctuary in ancient temples [L]

celtis. Chisel [L]

cembalo. Harpsichord [It]

cena. Supper [It]

cénacle. Guest chamber (scene of the Last Supper); intimate circle of disciples; literary group or *coterie* [F]

cenaculo. Guest chamber (scene of the Last Supper) [It]

C'En Est Fait! It is Done! (*Hérodiade*, Act III; Massenet) [F]

Ce n'est que le premier pas qui coûte. It is only the first step that costs (dearly) [F]

censo. Annuity; ground rent [Sp]

centaur. Fabulous creature, half man, half horse [Gk]

Centaurea cyanus. Cornflower; Bachelor's Button; French Pink [Gk]

centavo. One-hundredth of a *peso*, in various South American countries [Sp]

centesima. One-hundredth [L]

centiare. Centare = 1 square meter = 1.19 square yards [F]

centigramme. Centigram = 0.01 gram [F]

centime. One-hundredth of a *franc* [F]

centimètre. Centimeter = 0.01 meter [F]

cento. Hundred [It]

centon. Patched cloth; a literary patchwork of the classics [L]

centum. Hundred; name given to a classification of languages based on resemblance of sound in their words for 100; distinguished from the *satem* languages [L]

cèpe. An edible plant [F]

cera. Wax; seal [L]

Cerberus. Three-headed watch-dog at the entrance to Hades [Gk]

cerca. Near [Sp]

cerebrum. Brain [L]

cerf. Stag [F]

cerise. Cherry [F]

certiorari. To be made more certain; writ to procure records of a lower court [L]

Certum est quia impossibile est. It is true because it is impossible (Tertullian) [L]

certus. Certain; sure [L]

Ces. C-sharp [G]; These [F]

cesellato. Tooled [It]

Cessante causa, cessat effectus. The cause ceasing, the effect ceases [L]

cessé de paraître. Discontinued [F]

cesta. Long, spoon-shaped basket tied to the wrist and used in *jai-alai* [Sp]

c'est à dire. That is to say [F]

C'est dommage. It's a pity [F]

cestino. Basket; hamper; lunch basket [It]

C'est la vie. That's life [F]

cestrum. Etching needle; stylus [L]

cestus. Boxing-glove; brass knuckles [L]

ceteris paribus. Other things being equal [L]

cf. See *confer*

C.G.I.L. See *Confederazione, etc.*

C.G.T. See *Confédération Générale, etc.*

ch-. See also under *h-*

Chablis. Small town in the Yonne *Département* of France; famous white Burgundy wine [F]

chaconne. Slow, dignified dance in triple rhythm [F]

chacta. A Peruvian liquor distilled from sugar cane [Sp]

Chacun à son goût. Every one to his taste [F]

Chacun pour soi. Every one for himself [F]

chai. Tea [R]

chainik. Tea kettle [R]

chaise longue. Long sofa or *boudoir* reclining chair [F]

châlet. Rustic house; Swiss cottage [F]

challis. A light dress-fabric [Hindu]

chalumeau. Shepherd's pipe; a reed [F]

chalupa. Corn pancake [Sp]

chamade. Signal announcing willingness to parley or surrender [F]

Chambre de Députés. Chamber of Deputies; one of the two branches of the French parliament, elected on the basis of one deputy for each 70,000 inhabitants [F]

chameau. Camel; low woman [F]

Chamorro. Native of Guam having the status of an American national [Sp]

Champagne. Ancient province of France; sparkling wine made from grapes grown in the Champagne region; any sparkling wine similar to it [F]

champignon. Mushroom [F]

champ-levé. Raised field; a process of engraving similar to *cloisonné* [F]

Champs Elysées. Elysian Fields (famous avenue in Paris) [F]

ch'ang. Invariable laws or principles; constant virtues [C]

chanson. Song; an ancient troubadour verse-form [F]

Chanson Indoue. Song of India (Rimsky-Korsakoff) [F]

chansonnier. Collection of troubadour poetry [F]

chantage. Blackmail [F]

chanteuse. (Female) singer [F]

Chantilly. French town near Paris; delicate lace with floral motifs [F]

chaperon. Hood or bonnet worn by knights; escutcheon on forehead of a horse [F]

char à bancs. Small wagon [F]

characteristica universalis. Universal characters or ideographs, conceived by Leibniz for the formulation of knowledge [L]

charcuterie. Pork - butcher's shop [F]

chargé(e). Loaded; charged; burdened; entrusted; overaccentuated; over-emphasized; in heraldry, said of a shield carrying a figure [F]

chargé d'affaires. Subordinate class of diplomat in charge of an embassy or legation, either temporarily (*ad interim*), or permanently (*ad hoc*) [F]

charivari. Raucous music; uproar [F]

charogne. Carrion; corpse; blackguard [F]

Charon. Ferryman of departed souls across the river Styx, in Greek mythology [Gk]

charta. Charter; deed [L]

Charta de Foresta. Laws of the Forest; collection of English laws during the reign of Henry III [L]

chartae libertatum. Charters (grants) of liberties; *i.e. Magna Charta* and *Charta de Foresta* [L]

Chartreuse. A greenish *liqueur*; a dish of mixed vegetables; a greenish hue or shade [F]

charue. Plow [F]

chashku kofya. Cup of coffee [R]

chasse. Chase; hunt; chaser (*i.e. liqueur* after coffee) [F]

chassé. Chased; hunted; ballet step involving movement of one foot from its place by means of a touch from the other; gliding dance step [F]

chassé croisé. Double *chassé*; idle maneuvering [F]

chasseur. Hunter; light-cavalry trooper; pursuit plane [F]

chassis. Frame [F]

chast. Part [R]

chastnoe izdanie. Privately printed [R]

chat. Cat (*fem.* chatte) [F]

château. Palace; castle; name of various French wine companies [F]

châtelaine. Key chain; lady of a manor [F]

chaud-froid. A jellied sauce [F]

chauffe-pied. Foot-warmer [F]

chaussée. Highway; causeway; raised embankment [F]

chauve-souris. Bat; flittermouse; a masked costume [F]

Chauvin. Name of an admirer and follower of Napoleon; used as the basis of the word "chauvinism", or exaggerated patriotism; jingo; violet patriot [F]

chaye. Being; creature [Heb]

chayote. Pear-shaped fruit with a large stone [Sp]

che. Stringed instrument [C]

cheetah. Leopard [Hindu]

chéchia. A brimless, conical hat somewhat like a *fez* [ ]

chechita. See *chéchia*

Che cosa hai? What's the matter with you? [It]

chedar. School [Heb]

chef. Chief; boss; head cook [F]

chef de cabinet. Chief departmental assistant to a French cabinet minister [F]

chef d'œuvre. Masterpiece [F]

Che Gelida Manina. Your tiny hand is frozen (*La Bohème*, Act I; Puccini) [It]

Cheiranthus. Wallflower; a perennial [Gk]

Cheka. Communist secret police organization for suppression of anti-revolutionary activities, 1917-22; later reorganized as the *OGPU* [R]

chemin. Road [F]

chemin de fer. Railroad [F]

chemisier. Shirtmaker [F]

cheng. Organ-like musical instrument [C]

ch'eng. Honesty, sincerity; reverence; seriousness; fulfilment of the self [C]

chenille. Caterpillar; grub; soft-pile cotton or rayon yarn; fabric made from such yarn [F] .

chen jen. The true man [C]

cheniscus. Goose's head; ornament affixed to stern or prow of ancient vessels [Gk]

cheniskos. See *cheniscus*

Che ora è? What time is it? [It]

cher. Dear; expensive (*fem.* chère) [F]

Cherchez la femme! Look for the woman (as the cause or instigator) [F]

chérie. Sweetheart [F]

cherven. Red [R]

chernyi. Black [R]

Che sarà sarà. What is to be will be [It]

Chetnik. Member of Yugoslav resistance forces after the country was invaded by the Nazis in 1941; led by General Mikhailovich [ ]

chetverg. Thursday [R]

chetvertnoi. Quarterly [R]

chetvertyi. Fourth [R]

chetyre. Four [R]

chetyrnadtsat. Fourteen [R]

cheval. Horse (*pl.* chevaux) [F]

chevalier. Knight; first and lowest grade of the *Légion d'Honneur* [F]

chevalier d'industrie. Adventurer; swindler [F]

chevaux. See *cheval*

chevaux-de-frise. Barrier consisting of spikes set in timber [F]

chevelure. Hair; tresses [F]

chevet. Head (of a pillow); pillow; bedside; apse (of a church) [F]

cheveux. Hair [F]

cheville. An expression used

solely to round off a sentence or a verse [F]

chevreuil. Roe; deer; venison [F]

chevron. Rafter; joist; V-shaped object or design; V-shaped strip on the sleeve of a uniform; continuous V-shaped decoration [F]

chez. Near; at the home (house) of [F]

chi. 22nd letter of the Greek alphabet $(X\chi)$; moving power; force; spirit [C]

chianti. Red Italian wine [It]

chiao. Doctrine(s); religion [C]

chiarezza. Clearness; purity; neatness [It]

chiaroscuro. Bright (and) dark; the art of distributing light and shade in a picture; writing in which contrasts are mingled [It]

chiasmus. Cross; a balanced passage in which the second part reverses the order of the first, using forms of the same word [Gk]

chibouk. Long tobacco pipe [Turk]

chic. Style; elegance; skilful execution or touch (in art) [F]

chicane. Shrewd cunning; swindling; use of tricks and artifice [F]

chicha (morada). Fermented corn or fruit drink of Peru [Sp]

chi-chi. Trim; bow [F]

chico. Small boy; youngster [Sp]

chien. Dog [F]

chienne. Bitch [F]

chiesa. Church [It]

chifa. Peruvian name for a Chinese restaurant [ ]

chiffon. Rag; cloth; lightweight silk *crêpe*; whipped or frothy ingredients in pies and desserts [F]

chignon. Hair arranged over a pad at the nape of the neck [F]

chih. Memory; purpose; will; wisdom [C]

chile con carne. A Mexican dish of red peppers minced and mixed with meat [Sp]

chilli. Dried capsicum seed [Sp]

chimaera. Fabulous monster; hideous dream; impossible conception [Gk]

Chi Mi Frena. What Restrains Me? (*Lucia di Lammermoor*, Act II; Donizetti) [It]

chinchilla. A squirrel-like rodent; its fur [Sp]

ching. Essence; purity; spirit; tranquillity; villain in a play [C]

Chi niente sa, di niente dubita. Who knows nothing, doubts nothing [It]

chinois. Chinese [F]

chirographum. Hand-written document; voucher of debt [L]

chirurgie. Surgery [F]

Chi tace acconsente. Silence implies consent [It]

chitarrone. Type of large guitar [It]

chiton. Ancient garment worn next to the skin [Gk]

chlamys. Loose dress worn by the ancients and fastened by a brooch at the shoulder [Gk]

chlyeb. Bread [R]

choisi(e). Chosen; selected [F]

choliambus. An irregular iambic line [Gk]

cholodno. Cold [R]

chopine. Venetian clog-shoe with high sole [It]

choragium. Property room in the ancient theater [Gk]

choriambus. A metrical foot consisting of a long syllable, two shorts, and a long [Gk]

chorodidascalus. Teacher or trainer of the chorus [Gk]

chose. Thing; matter [F]

chose jugée. Settled matter; thing already decided [F]

chou. Cabbage; a term of endearment [F]; comedian [C]

Chouannerie. Collective term for various royalist uprisings during the French Revolution [F]

chou-fleur. Cauliflower [F]

chrestomathie. Selection of reading material for language instruction or study of rhetoric [F]

chroma. Color [Gk]

chronicon. List of historical events; a chronology [Gk]

chronique scandaleuse. Collection of scandalous gossip [F]

Chronos. God; time [Gk]

Chrysanthemum frutescens. Marguerite; Paris Daisy [L]

chrysos. Gold [Gk]

chtiri. Four [R]

chton. Earth [Gk]

chü. Verse; lyric; song [C]

chufa. An edible tuber of the sedge family; flavoring prepared from it; sherbet so flavored [Sp]

chung yung. Golden mean [C]

chupe de camarones. Shrimp soup [Sp]

chü ping. Criticism of opera [C]

Churriguerismo. Term denoting decadent architectural style of the 13th century [Sp]

churros. Fritters [Sp]

chute. Fall; slide [F]

chutzpa. Gall; nerve [Y]

ciborium. Food chalice; sacred vessel in which the host was kept; tabernacle with ornate canopy used for this purpose in early churches [Gk]

cicerone. Guide; connoisseur [It]

cicoria. Dandelion [It]

Cid. Chieftain [Arab] [Sp]. See also *Cantar de mio Cid*; *El Cid Campeador*

ci-devant. Former; late [F]

Cielito Lindo. Beautiful Heaven (Fernandez) [Sp]

Cielo E Mar! Heaven and Ocean! (*La Gioconda*, Act II; Ponchielli) [It]

ciencia. Science [Sp]

ciento. Hundred [Sp]

cierra. Inclosure; corral (for bulls) [Sp]

ci gît. Here lies [F]

cimetière. Cemetery [F]

cinco. Five [Sp]

cincuenta. Fifty [Sp]

cinquain. Unit of five; verse-form of five lines [F]

cinquanta. Fifty [It]

cinque. Five [It]

cinquecento. Five hundred; in art history, used as an abbreviation for *mille cinquecento*, fifteen hundred, and applied to Italian art of the 16th century [It]

cinquefoil. Perennial flower of the rose family, popularly known as five-fingers; heraldic device [L]

cinzolino. Violet-reddish color; zinzolin [Sp]

ciociara. Neapolitan costume dance based on the theme of the fickle lover [It]

cipolino. Small onion; a kind of marble with white and green wavy lines forming a grain that resembles the cross-section of an onion [It]

cipolla. Onion (*pl.* cipolle) [It]

cippus. Column or pedestal bearing a memorial inscription [L]

cir. See *circa*

circ. See *circa*

circa. About; approximately [L]

circuitus verborum. Circumlocution [L]

circulus in definiendo. (Vicious) circle in definition; a logical fallacy [L]

circulus in probando. (Vicious) circle in proving; a logical error involving premisses which assume the conclusion to be established [L]

circulus vitiosus. Vicious circle, a logical fallacy [L]

circumambages. Methods or devices of *periphrasis* [L]

circus. Circle; large stadium;

itinerant tent-show featuring abrobats, clowns, and animals [Gk]

cire. Wax [F]

ciré. Waxed; glazed; glossy patent-leather finish [F]

cirrus. Curly lock of hair; fleecy cloud [L]

Cis. C-sharp [G]

cis-. On this side of [L]

ciselé. Chiseled; tooled [F]

Cistok. Bulletin [R]

cit. Awareness [Skr]

citatio. Summons; citation [L]

citi. Spirit; highest intelligence [Skr]

citole. Musical instrument [F]

Cito maturum, cito putridum. Soon ripe, soon rotten [L]

citoyen. Citizen [F]

citrioli. Cucumbers [It]

Citroen. A French auto

città. City [It]

ciudad. City [Sp]

Civilitas successit barbarum. Civilization succeeds barbarism (motto of Minnesota) [L]

civiliter. Civilly; in a civil character or position; in civil, as distinguished from criminal, proceedings [L]

civis. Citizen [L]

Civis Romanus sum. I am a Roman citizen [L]

civitas. Body of people living under the same laws; city; state [L]

Civitas Dei. City of God (St. Augustine, 354-430) [L]

civitas diaboli. City of the devil [L]

Clair de Lune. Moonlight (Debussy) [F]

claque. Hired applauders [F]

claret. Any red wine; a reddish color [F]

clarino. Clarinet [It]

clarté. Clarity; lucidity [F]

classiarius. Seaman [L]

clausula. Clause; sentence [L]

clavele. Carnation [Sp]

clavelito. See *clavele*

claves curiae. Keys of the court; officers of the court [L]

clef. Key; wrench [F]. See also *roman à clef*

clerc. Clerk; clerical; intellectual [F]

clericus. Clerk; priest [L]

cliché. Stereotype; photographic negative; hackneyed phrase [F]

clientèle. Customers; patrons [F]

clipeus. An ancient shield [Gk]

clique. Set; party; exclusive group; *coterie* [F]

cloaca. Sewer [L]

cloche. Bell; gardener's bell glass; helmet-shaped hat [F]

cloisonné. Type of enamel work in which the hollows for depositing the enamel are formed by welding strips of wire to a metal surface; an object or objects ornamented in this fashion [F]

cloky. See *cloqué*

cloqué. Blistered; reference to fabrics finished with a blistered effect [F]

clôture. Parliamentary procedure whereby debate is closed [F]

clou. Nail; peg; situation upon which a story hangs [F]

Cluny. A simple, coarse bobbin lace; a museum in Paris [F]

cnawan. To know [AS]

cobarde. Cowardly; fainthearted [Sp]

cobla. Stanza [OF]

coca. A South American shrub, the leaves of which are chewed by the natives; its liquor is used as the basis for "cola" drinks [Sp]

cochon. Pig; swine [F]

cocido. Boiled meat and vegetables [Sp]

cocinera. (Female) cook [Sp]

cocotte. Loose woman [F]

coda. Concluding passage (music) [It]

Code Civil. The civil code or

55

body of civil law; the *Code Napoléon* [F]

Code Napoléon. Code embodying the civil law of France, promulgated in 1804 [F]

code noir. The black code; laws once regulating slavery in the French colonies [F]

codetta. Short *coda* or extra concluding passage (music) [It]

codex. Collection of laws; book; manuscript written on parchment (*pl.* codices) [L]

Codex Justinianeus. Justinian Code; body of laws compiled on the order of Emperor Justinian, in A.D. 528 [L]

codex rescriptus. Manuscript with superimposed writing; palimpsest [L]

codices. See *codex*

Coelitus mihi vires. My strength is from heaven [L]

coeur. Heart [F]

cofradía. Religious society [Sp]

Cogitationis poenam nemo patitur. No one is punished for his thoughts [L]

Cogito, ergo sum. I think, therefore I am (*i.e.* exist) (Descartes) [L]

cognac. Cognac brandy [F]

cognatus. Relation by the mother's side; cognate; relation or kinsman generally (*pl.* cognati) [L]

cognitio. Cognition; acknowledgment (*pl.* cognitiones) [L]

cognomen. Family name; surname [L]

cognoscendum. Object of a cognition [L]

cognoscente. Connoisseur; expert (*pl.* cognoscenti) [It]

cognoscere. To know [L]

coif. Close-fitting, hood-like cap [F]

coiffeur. Hair-dresser; barber [F]

coiffure. Hair-dress; hair-style [F]

coin. Corner [F]

Cointreau. A *liqueur* [F]

coitus. Sexual intercourse [L]

colazione. Lunch [It]

Colchicum. Autumn Crocus; Meadow Saffron [L]

Coliseum. Amphitheater in ancient Rome; name given to large sports structures [L]

collage. Pasting; an art technique of pasting pictures and materials on to a canvas [F]

collectanea. Collection [L]

collegium. Assembly; society; company; corporation; army; class of men; body of bishops; college or assemblage (*pl.* collegia) [L]

colligatus. Bound [L]

colline. Hill [F]

Cologne. See *eau de Cologne*

colon. Limb; member [Gk]

colón. Monetary unit of San Salvador [Sp]

colonus. Tenant; husbandman [L]

colophon. Summit; finishing touch; statement on last page of a book concerning publisher, author, *etc.*; publisher's trade mark or emblem; name of a periodical [Gk]

coloratura. Embellishments or ornamental passages in vocal music; a soprano who sings such music [It]

Colossus. Gigantic statue of Apollo in ancient Rome; any enormous thing or person [Gk]

colportage. Book trade; peddling; retailing [F]

colporteur. Pedlar; spreader of news; book salesman [F]

colorado. Red [Sp]

coltello. Knife [It]

colum. Wine strainer [L]

columbaria. Dove-cotes; recesses for depositing urns in ancient tombs; in architecture, holes in a wall for the insertion of timbers [Gk]

Columna Bellica. Column of war in ancient Rome [L]

comare. Godmother; gossip; friend; confidante; female symbol of death [It]

Combien? How much? [F]

come. As; like; the same as [It]

comedia de capa y espada. Cloak and sword comedy; pertaining to the Spanish classical drama [Sp]

comédie. Play of manners and customs [F]

comédie de moeurs. Comedy of manners [F]

Comédie Française. State theater of France, situated in Paris [F]

comédie humaine. Human comedy; comedy of manners, less exalted than a tragedy; title of a work by Balzac [F]

comédie larmoyante. Sentimental middle-class drama of the 18th century [F]

comes. Follower; attendant; count; earl [L]

Come si chiama Lei? What is your name? [It]

Come si dice? How do you say? [It]

Cominform. Communist Information Bureau (replaced *Comintern*, 1945) [R]

Comintern. The Third International [R]

comitadji. Balkan irregulars [Serbian]

comitas. Comity; courtesy [L]

comitas inter communitates. Comity of nations [L]

Comitas inter gentes. Courtesy between nations [L]

Comité des Forges. Organization of French iron, steel, and munitions industries [F]

comma. Chip [Gk]

commande. Order [F]

commandeur. Commander; 3rd grade of the *Légion d'Honneur* [F]

commandité. Limited partnership [F]

comme ci, comme ça. So, so [F]

comme il faut. Proper; in accordance with etiquette [F]

commedia dell' arte. Comedy of the guild (of professional players); 16th century Italian actors famous for improvisation [It]

commis. Clerk [F]

commiseratio. Plea for the accused [L]

commissar. Russian administrative official [R]

commissariat. Government department or ministry [R]

commoratio. Dwelling lengthily upon a valid point [L]

Commune. Self-governing town or village; name of the committee of the people in the French Revolution (1793); group desiring absolute self-government in Paris (1871); administrative subdivision headed by a *Maire* [F]

communes loci. Commonplaces; commonly accepted ideas [L]

communicare. To share [L]

communiqué. Communication; official statement; dispatch [F]

comodo. Easily; conveniently; quietly [It]

comos. Group of revellers (in an ancient festival in honor of *Dionysus*) [Gk]

Compiègne. Yeast cake sweetened with fruit; forest where the armistice of World War I was signed [F]

compluvium. Rain collector; open space in the roof of ancient Roman houses [L]

compos mentis. Sound of mind [L]

compos sui. Having the use of one's limbs [L]

compote. Stew; fruits stewed in syrup [F]

compra. Purchase [It] [Sp]

compra y venta. Purchase and sale [Sp]

compris. Understood; taken together; included [F]

compromis. Agreement to submit a dispute to arbitration [F]

compte. Account [F]

compte rendu. Report; critical review [F]

Comsomol. See *Komsomol*

comte. Count [F]

con. With [It] [Sp]

con amore. With love; in an eager, enthusiastic manner [It]

conatus. Drive; force; urge [L]

con buena fe. With (in) good faith [L]

conca. Hollow; valley; vessel [It]

concerto. Musical composition of several movements for one or more solo instruments with orchestral accompaniment [It]

concetto. Conceit (*pl.* concetti) [It]

concha. Shell [Sp]

concièrge. Janitor [F]

concordat. Compact; agreement between the Pope and a ruler or state [L]

concursus. Meeting [L]

concursus Dei. Concurrent activity of God [L]

Condiciones rompen leyes. Circumstances alter cases [Sp]

conditiones sine quibus non. Conditions for which there are no substitutes [L]

Confédération des Présidents. Steering committee in the French Chamber of Deputies [F]

Confédération Générale du Travail. General Confederation of Labor; the chief French confederation of labor unions [F]

Confederazione Generale Italiana del Lavoro. General Confederation of Italian Labor [It]

confer. Compare [L]

confitures. Jam [F]

confrère. Fellow member; colleague; partner; associate [F]

Confessio Amantis. Confession of a Lover (poem by John Gower) [L]

confessio fidei. Confession of faith; statement of creed [L]

con fuoco. With fire; with passion [It]

congé. Dismissal; leave; permission; clearance; passport[F]

congé d'élire. Leave to elect; royal permission to a chapter to elect a bishop [F]

congou. Black tea [C]

Congregatio de Propaganda Fide. Committee of cardinals in charge of foreign missions[L]

conjugium. Marriage [L]

conjunctis viribus. With united forces [L]

con moto. With motion; with movement; fast [It]

connaissance. Cognition; awareness; acquaintance [F]

connaisseur. Knower; connoisseur, expert (especially in one of the fine arts) [F]

Connais-Tu Le Pays? Knowest Thou the Land? (*Mignon*, Act I, Thomas) [F]

con mucho gusto. Gladly [Sp]

conocimiento. Knowledge [Sp]

connoissement. Bill of lading [F]

connubium. Marriage [L]

conquistadores. Conquerors; Spanish explorers in America [Sp]

conscientia. Knowledge [L]

conseil. Council [F]

conseil de famille. Family council [F]

consejo. Council [Sp]

consensus gentium. Agreement of people [L]

Consilio et animis. By wisdom and courage [L]

consistoire. Consistory of cardinals convoked by the Pope [F]

consistorium. State council of the Roman emperors; assembly of cardinals convoked by the Pope [L]

consolatio. Consolation; a poetic *genre* for the assuaging of grief [L]

console. Console table; table with ledges supported by brackets [F]

consommé. Concentrated meat soup [F]

consortium. International financial control agency; union of fortunes; marriage [L]

consuetudo. Custom; usage; established practice [L]

Consuetudo est altera lex. Custom is another law [L]

contadino. Peasant [It]

conte. Tale; short story [F]

conte de noël. Christmas tale [F]

conte-dévot. Pious tale (in verse) [F]

contenido. Contents [Sp]

conteur. Story-teller; narrator [F]

contra. Against; confronting; opposite to; on the contrary; on the other hand [L]

contra naturam. Contrary to nature [L]

contrabasso. Double-bass viol [It]

contra bonos mores. Against good morals [L]

contradictio in adjecto. Logical inconsistency between a noun and its modifying adjective; *e.g.* "round square" [L]

contra jus commune. Against common law (justice) [L]

Contra negantem principia non est disputandum. There is no disputing against one who denies first principles [L]

contra pacem. Against the peace [L]

contrat social. Social contract; theory that man left the state of nature to enter into a social compact with his fellow men; (title of a work by Rousseau) [F]

contre. Against; counter [F]

contre basse. Double-bass viol [F]

contredanse. Quadrille dance or air [F]

contretemps. Adverse occurrence; an unexpected dilemma; sudden accident or confusion [F]

controversiae. Fictitious civil or criminal cases; controversies [L]

Convallaria majalis. Lily-of-the-Valley [L]

convenances. The conventional proprieties [F]

conventus. Congress; convention; meeting [L]

Convolvulus japonicus. California Rose [L]

Copacabana. Crescent-shaped beach in Rio de Janeiro [Port]

copeck. Small Russian coin [R]

copertina. Cover; wrapper [It]

copla. Couplet; ballad; stanza; phrase of a song or dance [Sp]

copula. Connective; the verb "to be" as a connective between subject and predicate [L]

coq-à-l'âne. "Cock to ass"; dramatic monologue used for comic effect [F]

coq au vin. Chicken braised with wine [F]

Coq d'or. The Golden Cock (composition by Rimsky-Korsakoff) [F]

Coquelin. Most famous actor of France (1841-1909)

coquerelles. Winter cherries; a heraldic design [F]

coquetterie. Coquetry; flirtatiousness; affectation; in art, graceful figures painted in a bright and fresh tone [F]

coquille. Shell [F]

coquin. Rascal; rogue [F]

cor. Horn; trumpet [F]

coram. Before; in the presence of [L]

coram judice. Before a judge [L]

coram populo. In public; in sight of all [L]

cor anglais. English horn [F]

corazón. Heart [Sp]

corbeau. Crow; raven; corbel; grappling-iron [F]

corbie. Steps in the roof of a gabled house [Scotch]

corcho. Cork [Sp]

Corcovado. Hunchback; great cliff outside of Rio de Janeiro [Port]

corda. String; cessation of the soft pedal (piano playing) [It]

cordax. Burlesque dance by the comic chorus in early Greek drama [Gk]

cordillera. Mountain range [Sp]

cordoba. Monetary unit of Nicaragua [Sp]

cordon. Strand; string; rope; cord; ribbon; edging; girdle [F]

cordonnet. Twist; braid; milled edge of coins; thick thread which outlines the pattern of lace [F]

cordon sanitaire. Quarantine belt; a political line designed to prevent the spread of an undesired ideology [F]

Cordova. City in Spain; ornamented leather [Sp]

corium. Type of armor made of leather [L]

cornemuse. Bagpipe [F]

corneus. Horny [L]

corno. Horn; trumpet [It]

corno inglese. English horn [It]

cornu. Horn [L]

cornu copiae. Full horn; horn of plenty; symbol of peace and prosperity [L]

cornus. Genus of the dogwood tree [L]

corolla. Little crown (of a flower) [L]

corona. Crown; projecting edge of a cornice; any crown-shaped representation or ornament [L]

coronach. Highland dirge [Gaelic]

coronati. Crowned [It]

coronado. Crowned; awarded a prize [Sp]

coroplastae. Shapers of dolls; name given by the Greeks to artists who fashioned small images of clay or *terra-cotta* [Gk]

corps de ballet. Ballet troupe or group [F]

corpus. Body; collection of men, laws, or articles; physical substance; principal sum or capital [L]

Corpus Christi. Feast of the Body of Christ on Thursday after Trinity Sunday [L]

corpus delicti. Body of a crime; corpse of a murdered man; charred remains of a burned house; substantial fact that a crime has been committed [L]

corpus juris. Body of law; book containing collection of laws [L]

corpus juris canonici. Body of the canon (ecclesiastical) law [L]

corpus juris civilis. Body of the civil law; Justinian Code [L]

corregido. Corrected; revised [Sp]

corrida (de toros). Bullfight [Sp]

corrigenda. See *corrigendum*

corrigendum. Thing(s) to be corrected (*pl.* corrigenda) [L]

corsage. Bodice; bust; chest; flowers worn on the bodice of a dress [F]

corsi. Courses; fluxes [It]

cortège. Procession [F]

Cortes. Legislative assembly; parliament or congress of Spain or Portugal [Sp]

Cortesía de boca vale mucho y poco cuesta. Courteous speech is worth much and costs little [Sp]

corvée. Feudal obligation to contribute free labor to the state; forced labor; labor service [F]

coryphaeus. Leader of the ancient Greek dramatic chorus. [Gk]

coryphée. Minor female dancer in a *corps de ballet* [F]

cosa. Thing; matter [Sp]

cosaque. Sweet cooky [F]

cosecha. Harvest [Sp]

Cos'è questo? What's this? [It]

cosí-cosí. So-so [It]

Cosí fan tutte. That is the way of all women; that is the way of the world (opera by Mozart) [It]

costumbrismo. Realism in prose fiction on manners and customs; character writing [Sp]

côte. Hillside vineyard; coast [F]

côté. Corner; side; direction [F]

Côte d' Ivoire. Ivory Coast [F]

Côte d'Or. Gold Coast; *département* in southern France famous for its Burgundy wine [F]

Côte d'Azur. Azure Coast (the French Mediterranean coast) [F]

coterie. Group; set; circle [F]

cothurnatus. Wearing the *cothurnus*; elevated emotion and dignity proper to tragic roles [L]

cothurnus. High boot worn by the ancient Greeks and Romans, particularly by actors [L]

cotización. Quotation [Sp]

couchant. Lying down; reclining [F]

cou-de-pied. See *coup de pied*

coulisse. Slideway; groove on stage floor for shifting scenes; the side scenes or flats; wing (of a stage) [F]

coup de dés. Cast of the dice [F]

coup de glotte. Glottal catch, as before accented vowels [F]

coup de grâce. Finishing stroke [F]

coup de main. Bold stroke; help; sudden attack [F]

coup de maître. Master stroke [F]

coup de pied. Kick [F]

coup de plume. Literary attack [F]

coup de soleil. Sunstroke [F]

coup d'essai. First trial [F]

coup d'état. Sudden forcible seizure of government; sudden stroke of policy [F]

coup de tête. Rash act [F]

coup de théâtre. Successful dramatic device: sensational surprise; dramatic moment or action; a hit [F]

coup d'oeil. Overall view; glance [F]

coupé. Cut; shorn off; type of ballet step in which one foot is displaced by a kick from the other; small car [F]

cour. Court [F]

courante. A dance during the time of Louis XIV [F]

coureur de bois. Forest runner; a French hunter or trapper during the days of the French colonial empire in North America and Canada [F]

courier. Official messenger carrying diplomatic correspondence [F]

couronne. Crown [F]

couteau. Knife [F]

coûte que coûte. At all costs [F]

couture. Dressmaking [F]

couturier. Dressmaker [F]

couvert. Cover; envelope [F]

crambe repetita. Cabbage dished-up again; annoying repetition [L]

crambo. Rhyme(s); a game in which rhymes must be made with a given word [ ]

crampon. Grappling iron; iron spike used in mountain climbing [F]

crastino. On the morrow; the day after [L]

creacionismo. A post-modernist esthetic movement; creationism [Sp]

créancier. Creditor [F]

crèche. Crib; public nursery [F]

creda. Wednesday [R]

Credat Judaeus. Tell that to the Jews; expression of incredulity (Horace, *Satires*) [L]

credentia. See *credenza*

credenza. Table or bench for vessels used in church services; small table used for pre-tasting food (to guard against poisoning); small cupboard for gold and silver plate [It]

Crédit Mobilier. Company formed for banking, for construction of public works, or operation of major enterprises [F]

credo. I believe; belief, creed [L]

Credo In Un Dio Crudel. I Believe in a Cruel God (*Otello*, Act II; Verdi) [It]

Credo quia absurdum est. I believe because it is absurd; an expression of trust in absolute faith [L]

Credo ut intelligam. I believe in order that I may understand [L]

creencia. Belief; faith [Sp]

crème. Cream [F]

crème de la crème. Pick of the crop; the *élite* [F]

crème de menthe. Peppermint *liqueur* [F]

créole. Native of the West Indies; referring to a style of cookery [F]

crêpe. Type of silk, rayon, or wool fabric; veil made of this fabric; crape; a silk *chiffon*; a pancake [F]

crêpe de Chine. Chinese crape; a silk fabric made of tightly twisted yarns [F]

crêpe maroquin. Morocco crape; a heavy silk fabric [F]

crêpes suzette. Thin pancakes [F]

crepis. Boot [Gk]

crépuscule. Twilight [F]

Crescat scientia, vita excolatur. Let knowledge increase, let life be perfected (motto of the University of Chicago) [L]

crescendo. Gradual increase in power and volume [It]

Crescit eundo. It increases by going; it grows as it goes (Lucretius; 6-341) (motto of New Mexico) [L]

Crescite et multiplicamini. Increase and multiply (motto of Maryland) [L]

crevasse. An irregular crack [F]

criado. Servant (*fem.* criada) [Sp]

crime d'état. Treason [F]

crimen innominatum. Nameless crime; crime against nature; crime of perversion [L]

crime passionel. Crime of passion; sex murder [F]

crinein. To judge; decide [Gk]

criollismo. Literary movement in Venezuela emphasizing native, "creole" scenes and types [Sp]

criophorus. One who carries a ram; name given to *Hermes* [Gk]

crise. Crisis [F]

Cristo de los Andes. Giant statue erected in 1904 at the summit of the Andes on the boundary between Argentina and Chile [Sp]

critique. Criticism; book or drama review; critical evaluation after military maneuvers [F]

crochet. Hook; knitting needle; a type of handmade lace; a personal trait or idiosyncrasy [F]

croissant. Crescent; crescent-shaped breakfast rolls [F]

Croix de Feu. Fiery cross; French fascist organization in the 1930's [F]

Croix de Guerre. War Cross; decoration awarded by the French Government [F]

cromlech. Prehistoric stone monument [Welsh]

crónica. Chronicle [Sp]

croquette. Rissole; fried ball or cake of meat or fish covered with bread crumbs [F]

croquis. Sketch; pattern [F]

crotala. Wooden castanets used by the ancients [Gk]

croupier. Man who rakes in the money at a gambling table; presiding chairman [F]

croustade. Bread or rice case for creamed meat or fish [F]

croutons. Small cubes of toasted bread served with soup [F]

cruce signati. Marked with a cross; crusaders [L]

Crudel! Perchè Finora. Cruel One! Why Have You? (*Marriage of Figaro*, Act III; Mozart) [It]

crux. Cross; difficult or cardinal point [L]

crux criticorum. Puzzle of critics [L]

Crux spes unica. The cross (is) the only hope (motto of Notre Dame University) [L]

cruz. Cross [Sp]

cruzeiro. Unit of currency in Brazil [Port]

cuadrilla. Group of various classes of bull-fighters; troupe of bull-fighters; the matador's *entourage* [Sp]

Cuando te dieren el anillo, pon el dedillo. Don't let opportunities slip by [Sp]

Cuánto? How much? [Sp]

cuarenta. Forty [Sp]

cuarto. Room [Sp]

cuatro. Four [Sp]

cubierta. Cover; wrapper [Sp]

cucaracha. Cockroach [Sp]

cucchiaio. Spoon [It]

cuchillas. Plains of Uruguay [Sp]

cucina. Kitchen [It]

cuenta. Bill [Sp]

cuento. Tale; narrative [Sp]

cuero. Leather [Sp]

cui. For whom [L]

Cui bono? To what purpose? For whose benefit? [L]

cuidado. Care [Sp]

cuir. Leather [F]

cuisine. Kitchen; cookery [F]

cuisinier. Cook; *chef* [F]

cuivre. Copper [F]

Cujusvis hominis est errare. It is (natural) for any man to make a mistake (Cicero) [L]

cul-de-sac. Blind alley; dead end [F]

culotte. See *sans culottes*

culpa. Fault; blame; negligence [L]

Culpae poena par esto. Let the punishment fit the crime [L]

Culpam poena premit comes. Punishment follows on the heels of crime [L]

culte du moi. Cult of Self [F]

culteranismo. Cultism; affected elegance of style [Sp]

cum grano salis. With a grain of salt; with allowance for exaggeration [L]

cum laude. With praise; with honor in a college class [L]

cum notis variorum. With *variorum* notes [L]

cum onere. With the burden; subject to an existing charge [L]

cumpleaños. Birthday [Sp]

cum privilegio. By privilege; referring to a monopoly granted by a king [L]

Cum tacent, clamant. While they are silent, they speak out; their silence is in itself an admission (Cicero) [L]

cunades. Affinity; alliance; relation by marriage [Sp]

cuoio. Leather [It]

cura. Care; charge; guardianship [L]

curator. Caretaker; guardian[L]

curé. Parish priest [F]

curia. Court; manor; Roman senate (chamber); any court of justice [L]

Curia advisari vult. The court will advise [L]

curia domini. Lord's court [L]

curia regis. King's court [L]

curriculum. Year; course of a year; set of studies for a particular grade or period; course of study [L]

curriculum vitae. Course of (one's) life; outline of one's career [L]

cursus. Metrical pattern of Latin prose [L]

custodes. See *custos*

custos. Custodian; guard; keeper; warden; conserver; inspector; observer (*pl.* custodes) [L]

custos morum. Guardian of manners [L]

cuvée. Vat; blend of wines from different vintages or vineyards [F]

cyathus. Drinking cup with one handle [Gk]

cygne. Swan [F]

cyma. Wave; curved molding [Gk]

cyma recta. Curved molding with convex part nearest the wall [Gk]

cyma reversa. Curved molding with concave part nearest the wall [Gk]

cymatium. Architectural molding [L]

cynghanedd. Symphony; Welsh verse-form

Cyrano de Bergerac. Celebrated French writer and duellist (1620-55); title of a play by Rostand; type of romantic hero with a long nose

cywydd. Welsh verse-form

czar. Title of the Russian sovereign from 1547 to 1918; title of the King of Bulgaria from 1908 to 1945; man appointed to regulate an industry; anyone having absolute authority [R]

czardas. A Hungarian dance

czarina. Title of the Empress of Russia [R]

czarowitz. Title of the eldest son of the *czar* and *czarina* [R]

D

d. See *denarius*

d'. Of; from; some; any [F]

da. There; then; since; because [G]; By; from; in; with; as; at [It]; Yes [R]

d'abord. At first [F]

da capo. From the beginning[It]

da capo al segno. From the beginning to the sign [It]

d'accord. In agreement; agreed [F]

Dachshund. Short-legged dog; badger hound [G]

dactyl. Metrical foot consisting of one long syllable followed by two short ones [Gk]

Dadaism. School of art and literature (1917-24) ignoring logical relationships between thought and expression [ ]

dado. Stone cube forming the chief part of a pedestal [It]

daedala. Primitive sculpture in ancient Greece [Gk]

dahabeeyah. Nile sailing boat [Arab]

Dail. Parliament [Gaelic]

Dail Eireann. Lower house of the Irish legislature [Gaelic]

daimio. Feudal vassal [J]

daimon. Spirit [Gk]

daina. Form of Latvian folk poetry [ ]

dak. Relay transport or post [Hindu]

Dalai Lama. Grand or Chief Lama of Thibet [Thibetan]

daldans. Pantomime dance [Swed]

Da liegt der Hund begraben! There's the rub! [G]

dal segno. From the sign [It]

dame. Lady [F]

Dämmerung. Twilight [G]

Damnunt quod non intelligunt. They condemn what they do not understand (Cicero) [L]

Dandin. Character in a play of that name by Moliere; a husband dominated by his wife [F]

dan direach. Classical mode of old Gaelic poetry [Gaelic]

danse du ventre. Oriental dance involving sinuous movement of the lower torso; belly dance [F]

Danse Macabre. Dance of Death (Saint-Saëns) [F]

Danse rituelle du feu. Ritual Fire Dance (De Falla) [F]

dar. Gift [R]

Dariole. Sweet *pâté* baked in a mold [F]

D'Artagnan. Hero of Dumas' novel, *The Three Musketeers*

das. The (in phrases, see also under the next following word) [G]

Das Beste ist gut genug. The best is good enough (Goethe) [G]

Dasein. Presence; existence [G]

Das Ewig-Weibliche. The eternal feminine (Goethe) [G]

65

das heisst. That is; *id est* [G]

Das Kapital. Capital (Marx) [G]

Das Leben ist die Liebe. Life is love (Goethe) [G]

Das Universum ist ein Gedanke Gottes. The universe is a thought of God (Schiller) [G]

Dasvidanya. Goodby [R]

data. See *datum*

Dat, dicat, dedicat. He gives, devotes and dedicates [L]

Dat, donat, dicat. He gives, presents, dedicates [L]

datum. Thing given; first principle; date (*pl.* data) [L]

daube. Meat or fowl baked in sauce [F]

Dauphin. Old French title of nobility; title of the eldest son or heir presumptive of French kings [F]

davai. Faster; move on [R]

Da y ten y harás bien. Be generous but prudent [Sp]

D.C. See *da capo*

D.D. See *Divinitatis Doctor*

D.D.D. See *Dono, Dedit, Dedicavit; Dat, Donat, Dicat*

de. The [Du]; By; from; in; of; some; with; any [F]; About; from; of [L]; By; for; from; in; of; to; with [Sp]

de aequitate. In equity [L]

de ambitu. Concerning bribery [L]

débâcle. Collapse (title of a novel by Zola) [F]

Debajo de la mala capa hay un buen bebedor. Appearances are often deceptive [Sp]

débat. Debate; contest in verse [F]

débauché. One led astray; dissolute person [F]

De Beata Vita. On the Good Life (St. Augustine) [L]

de bene esse. Conditionally; provisionally; in anticipation of future need [L]

de bone memorie. Of good memory; of sound mind [L]

de bono et malo. For good and ill [L]

de bono gestu. For good behavior [L]

débris. Remains; waste; rubbish; wreck [F]

début. First appearance; beginning [F]

deca-. Ten [Gk]

de caetero. Henceforth [L]

décagramme. 10 grams [F]

décamètre. Dekameter = 10 meters = 32 feet, 8 inches [F]

Decembrists. Revolutionary members of the Russian nobility whose unsuccessful revolt was suppressed in December 1825 [R]

decemvir. One of a group of ten men; member of a board appointed in 410 B.C. to revise and codify Roman law (*pl.* decemviri) [L]

decanus. Dean; officer having supervision over ten [L]

deceptio visus. Optical illusion [L]

dechado. Sample [Sp]

décigramme. Decigram = 0.1 gram [F]

décima. Stanza of ten lines [Sp]

decimae. Tenths; tithes [L]

decime. Tenth of a *franc* [F]

décimètre. Decimeter = 0.1 meter [F]

decimo. Tenth [It]

decimus. Tenth [L]

Decipi quam fallere est tutius. It is safer to be deceived than to deceive [L]

deciso. Decidedly; boldly [It]

De Civitate Dei. On the City of God (philosophical work on the state; St. Augustine) [L]

Deckel. Cover [G]

de claro die. By daylight [L]

déclassé. Reduced or fallen in the social scale [F]

décolletage. Low-necked effect; informal effect [F]

décolleté. Low-necked (said of dresses) [F]

décor. Room setting; stage setting; set [F]

décor simultané. Stage - set having several locales at once; multiple set [F]

decrementum. Decrease; addition of lesser things or ideas; descending action of a play [L]

decrescendo. Gradually diminishing in power and volume [It]

decreta. See *decretum*

decretum. Decree (*pl.* decreta) [L]

de die in diem. From day to day [L]

dedo. Finger; toe [Sp]

de facto. In fact; in deed; actually [L]

de fide. As a matter of faith [L]

défraîchi. Soiled [F]

D.G. See *Dei Gratia*

dégagé. Disengaged; unconstrained [F]

degollada. Low-necked; *décolleté* [Sp]

dégoût. Distaste; disgust; aversion [F]

de gratia. Of grace or favor; by favor [L]

De gustibus non est disputandum. About tastes there is no disputing; there is no accounting for tastes [L]

de haut en bas. Patronizingly; condescendingly [F]

Deh Vieni Alla Finestra. Open Thy Window (*Don Giovanni*, Act II; Mozart) [It]

Dei Gratia. By the grace of God [L]

de integro. From the beginning [L]

Dei plena sunt omnia. All things are full of God [L]

Dei Sponsa. The Bride of God (poem by Patmore) [L]

Dei sub numine viget. It flourishes under the will of God (motto of Princeton University) [L]

déjeuner. Lunch [F]

de jure. Of right; legitimately; by law; lawful; by right [L]

dekabr. December [R]

Del dicho al hecho hay gran trecho. It's a long way from saying to doing [Sp]

dele. Erase; delete [L]

deleatur. Let it be destroyed or erased [L]

Delenda est Carthago. Carthage must be destroyed; the fight must be carried to a finish (Cato) [L]

deletus. Canceled [L]

Delft. Dutch town noted for its earthenware; earthenware produced in . this town, or in imitation of it.

delicato. Delicate; smooth [It]

del(ineavit). (He) has drawn (it); an abbreviation following the name of the original artist of a drawing which has been reproduced [L]

delirium tremens. Trembling delirium; brain disease of alcoholics [L]

Del plato a la boca se pierde la sopa. There's many a slip twixt the cup and the lip [Sp]

delta. 4th letter of the Greek alphabet ($\Delta\delta$)

de luxe. Luxurious; extra-fancy; of the highest elegance [F]

de mal en pis. From bad to worse [F]

démarche. Step; measure; action; diplomatic step or decisive diplomatic move [F]

démenti. Official denial of rumor or allegation [F]

dementia. Form of insanity resulting from brain disorder [L]

dementia praecox. *Dementia* of adolescence [L]

67

Demeter. Goddess of agriculture [Gk]

demi-. Half [F]

demie-tasse. Half a cup; small cup of black coffee [F]

demi-monde. Class of women of questionable repute; fringe of society (title of a novel by Dumas *fils*) [F]

demiourgos. Artisan; craftsman; term used by Plato to designate the intermediary maker of the world [Gk]

demireliure. Half-bound [F]

demi-teinte. Half-tone [F]

demi vol. Single-wing design on a shield [F]

De mortuis nil nisi bonum. About the dead nothing (should be said) except good [L]

De nada. You are welcome; not at all; don't mention it [Sp]

denarius. Chief silver coin of the ancient Romans (*pl.* denarii); penny [L]

De Natura Rerum. Of the Nature of Things (title of a philosophical treatise by Lucretius) [L]

Den Gelehrten ist gut predigen. A word to the wise is enough [G]

denier. Penny; farthing; a weight used as a measure for synthetic yarn, equal to the number of .05-gram weights in a standard 450-meter skein [F]

Denkschrift. Memorial volume [G]

Denn alle Schuld rächt sich auf Erden. For all guilt is avenged upon earth (Goethe) [G]

De noche, todos los gatos son pardos. At night all cats are gray [Sp]

dénouement. Unknotting; unraveling (of the complications of a plot) [F]

de nouveau. Anew; afresh [F]

de novo. Anew; afresh; a second time [L]

dens-canis. Dogtooth; type of violet: *Erythronium dens-canis* [L]

dentelle. Lace [F]

Deo duce. God is my leader [L]

Deo favente. With God's favor [L]

Deo Optimo Maximo. To God the best and greatest [L]

Deo, patriae, amicis. For God, country and friends [L]

Deo volente. God willing [L]

département. Largest national administrative subdivision of France; one of 92 such units, three of which are in Algeria [F]

De pilo pendet. It hangs by a hair [L]

Déposons Les Armes. Let us Lay Down Our Arms (*Faust*, Act IV; Gounod) [F]

dépôt. Deposit; railroad station; military supply dump; assembly station [F]

De Profundis. Out of the Depths (Psalms 130-1; title of poems by Mrs. Browning, Oscar Wilde, and others) [L]

depuis. Since [F]

Depuis le Jour. Since the Day (*Louise*, Act III; Charpentier) [F]

der. The (in phrases, see also below succeeding word) [G]

déraciné(e)(s). Uprooted [F]

de rebus. Of things [L]

derecho. Right; law; impost; tax [Sp]

de règle. Proper; customary [F]

De Rerum Natura. Concerning the Nature of Things (Lucretius) [L]

Der ewige Jude. The eternal Jew; the wandering Jew [G]

dergleichen. And the like [G]

Der Historiker ist ein rückwärts gekehrter Prophet. The historian is a retrospective prophet (F. von Schlegel) [G]

De rien. Not at all [F]

de rigueur. Indispensable; absolutely necessary; as required by strict etiquette [F]

derma. Skin [Gk]

dernier. Last [F]

dernier cri. The last word; the latest style [F]

Der Mensch denkt, Gott lenkt. Man proposes, God disposes [G]

Der Schein trügt. Appearances are deceptive [G]

Der Tod, Das Ist Die Kühle Nacht. Death is Like the Cool of Night (Heine-Brahms) [G]

Des. D-flat [G]; From (of) the; some [F]

dés. Dice [F]

desayuno. Breakfast [Sp]

De Senectute. Concerning Old Age (Cicero) [L]

desesperado. Desperate [Sp]

déshabillé. In a state of informal undress; negligently dressed.

deshevoc. Cheap [R]

desiat. Ten [R]

desiatyi. Tenth [R]

desiderata. See *desideratum*

desideratum. That which is desired (*pl.* desiderata) [L]

Desideria. Longings (poem by Wordsworth) [L]

designatum. That which is designated [L]

Des Knaben Wunderhorn. The Child's Magic Horn (of Plenty) (collection of folk tales by the Grimm Brothers) [G]

dessus-dessous. In front and behind [F]

destra. Right hand; right [It]

Desunt caetera. The rest is missing; *i.e.* the quotation is incomplete [L]

détaché. Detached; staccato (in violin music) [F]

de tempore in tempus. From time to time [L]

détente. Release of tension; end of strained relations [F]

detritus. Wearing away; erosion [L]

de trop. Superfluous; unwanted [F]

deuil. Mourning; grief [F]

deus. God [L]

Deus est qui regit omnia. There is a God who rules all things [L]

deus ex machina. God from the machine; introduction of a god in a play in order to untangle the plot; outside intervention to resolve a crisis [L]

Deus lux mea. God (is) my light (motto of the Catholic University of America) [L]

Deus miseratur. God be merciful [L]

Deus nobis fiducia. God (is) our trust (motto of George Washington University) [L]

Deus tecum. God (be) with thee [L]

Deus vobiscum. God (be) with you [L]

Deutsche Reichsbahn. German Railroad(s) [G]

Deutsches Nachrichtenbüro. German News Office or agency; the official *Nazi* news agency [G]

Deutschland über alles. Germany Above All; patriotic anthem by von Fallersleben; the melody is the same as that of the former Austrian anthem, by Joseph Haydn [G]

Deutlichkeit. Distinctness [G]

Deutschordensdichtung. Literature produced by the Knights of the Teutonic Order (14th cent.) [G]

devant. Before [F]

de verbo in verbum. Word for word [L]

de verborum significatione. Of the signification of words [L]

devianosto. Ninety [R]

devianostyi. Ninetieth [R]

deviat. Nine [R]
deviatnadtsat. Nineteen [R]
deviatnadtsatyi. Nineteenth [R]
deviatyi. Ninth [R]
de vive voix. Out loud; *viva voce* [F]
devoir. Duty; task [F]
De Vulgari Eloquentia. On the Eloquence of the Vernacular (Dante, 1307) [It]
dexter. Right-handed; on the right; skilful [L]
dextrochère. Heraldic device showing a right arm [F]
dgl. See *dergleichen*
d.h. See *das heisst*
dharma. Right; virtue; duty [Skr]
dhyana. Meditation [Skr]
di. By; from; of; to; with [It]
día. Day [Sp]
diable. Devil [F]
diaconicum. Side vault in the ancient Christian *basilica* [L]
Día de Año Nuevo. New Year's Day [Sp]
Día de la Raza. Day of the Race; Hispanic Day; coincides with Oct. 12th, Columbus Day [Sp]
Día de los Reyes. Religious holiday on Jan. 6th; Day of the Magi [Sp]
diadumenos. Statue of a youth binding a wreath or diadem about his head [Gk]
diaeresis. Coincidence of the end of a metrical foot and of a word; break or pause at that point [Gk]
dialego. Discourse; debate [Gk]
diallage. Concentration of various arguments upon a single point [F]
dialogue intérieur. Internal dialogue; soliloquy; stream of consciousness dialogue [F]
dianoia. Intellectual virtues; the faculty or exercise of thinking [Gk]
Dianthus barbatus. Sweet William [L]

Dianthus caryophyllis. Carnation [L]
Dianthus plumarius. Garden Pink [L]
diario. Daily; journal; newspaper [Sp]
diaspora. Dispersion, scattering; the countries through which the Jews were dispersed; Jews living in these countries [Gk]
diatim. Daily; every day; from day to day [L]
dibbuk. See *dybbuk*
dibrach. Metrical foot of two short syllables [Gk]
dicaiologia. Giving one's reasons; statement containing the reason therefor; admitting but condoning a fact [Gk]
dichalogia. See *dicaiologia*
dicho y hecho. No sooner said than done [Sp]
Dichter. Poet; creative writer [G]
Dichterliebe. Poet's Love (Song Cycle; Heine-Schumann) [G]
Dich, Teure Halle. Oh Hall of Song (*Tannhäuser*, Act II; Wagner) [G]
Dichtkunst. Art of poetry; poetics [G]
Dichtung. Poetry; creative writing or composition [G]
diciannove. Nineteen [It]
diciassette. Seventeen [It]
diciotto. Eighteen [It]
dicta. See *dictum*
dictamen. Art of writing prose, especially letter writing [L]
dictum. Saying; pronouncement; remark; observation (*pl.* dicta) [L]
dictum de dicto. Report upon hearsay [L]
dictum de omni et nullo. Maxim of all and nothing; the maxim that whatever may be predicated of a whole may also be predicated of any of its parts [L]

Dictum sapienti sat est. A word to the wise is sufficient [L]

Dichtung und Wahrheit. Poetry and Truth (title of Goethe's autobiography; 1811 *ff.*) [G]

didaktikos. Taught [Gk]

didascaliae. List of plays presented at Athens (title of a work by Aristotle) [Gk]

die. The (in phrases, see also below succeeding word) [G]

Die Baukunst ist eine erstarrte Musik. Architecture is frozen music (Goethe) [G]

dieci. Ten [It]

diecinueve. Nineteen [Sp]

dieciocho. Eighteen [Sp]

dieciséis. Sixteen [Sp]

diecisiete. Seventeen [Sp]

Die Forelle. The Trout (Schubert) [G]

Die Leiden des jungen Werthers. The Sorrows of Young Werther (Goethe) [G]

Die Lotosblume. The Lotus Flower (Heine-Schumann) [G]

Diem perdidi. I have lost a day [L]

Die Natur weiss allein, was sie will. Nature alone knows what her purpose is (Goethe) [G]

dierkunde. Zoology [Du]

dies. Day; date.—*Dominica*, Sunday;—*lunae*, Monday;—*Martis*, Tuesday;—*Mercurii*, Wednesday; *Jovis*, Thursday;—*Veneris*, Friday;—*Saturni*, Saturday [L]

dies a quo. Day from which [L]

Die Schöne Müllerin. The Maid of the Mill (song cycle; Schubert) [G]

dies datus. A given day [L]

dies dominicus. The Lord's day, *i.e.* Sunday [L]

dièse. Sharp (music) [F]

Diesel. Referring to compression ignition type of internal-combustion engine, invented by Rudolf Diesel [G]

Dies Irae. Day of Wrath (Judgment); Latin hymn of the 13th century, set to music by Mozart, Gounod, Verdi, and others; part of the Requiem Mass [L]

dies non. Day that does not count [L]

Dieu. God [F]

Dieu et Mon Droit. God and My Right (motto of the royal arms of England, first assumed by Richard I) [F]

Die Wacht am Rhein. The Watch on the Rhine; former German national anthem (verses by Schneckenburger; music by Karl Wilhelm) [G]

Die Weisheit ist nur in der Wahrheit. Wisdom lies only in truth (Goethe) [G]

Die Weltgeschichte ist das Weltgericht. History is Judgment (Schiller) [G]

Die Winterreise. Winter Journey (song cycle; Schubert) [G]

diez. Ten [Sp]

Die Zauberflöte. The Magic Flute (Mozart) [G]

differentia. Factors which distinguish a thing from its general class or *genus* [L]

difunto. Dead; defunct; dead person [Sp]

digitalis. Foxglove; dried foxglove leaves used as a heart tonic [L]

digitus. Finger [L]

dii penates. Household gods [L]

Diktat. Dictation; dictatorial order [G]

Diktatur. Dictatorship [G]

diluendo. Dying away into silence [It]

Dime con quien andas y te diré quién eres. We judge people by their friends [Sp]

diminuendo. Gradually diminishing in power or volume [It]

dindon. Turkey [F]

dindonneaux. Young turkey [F]

dinero. Money [Sp]

Ding an sich. Thing in itself; Kantian term referring to what lies beyond human experience or knowledge [G]

dionysia. Dances in honor of *Bacchus*; festival of *Dionysus* [Gk]

Dionysus. God of vintage, also called *Bacchus* [Gk]

Dios da el frío conforme a la ropa. God tempers winds to the shorn lamb [Sp]

Dios se lo pague. May God reward you [Sp]

diota. Ancient two-handled vase [Gk]

diopter. Vision slit; sighting device; unit of refracting power of a lens with focal length=1 m. [Gk]

diplois. Part of the ancient Greek costume drawn up over a girdle at the waist [Gk]

diplos. Double [Gk]

dipsa. Thirst [Gk]

Directoire. Directory (style); the period of the French Directory, 1795-99 [F]

Dirigo. I direct (motto of Maine) [L]

diritta. See *dritta*

Dirndl. Young girl or miss; peasant-girl style of clothes [G]

Dis. D-sharp [G]

discere docendo. To learn through teaching [L]

Disciplina praesidium civitatis. Instruction (is) the safeguard of the state (motto of the University of Texas) [L]

discobolus. Discus thrower; quoit player [Gk]

diseur. Monologist [F]

diseuse. Female monologist [F]

disjecta membra. Scattered parts [L]

dispiacere. Displeasure [It]

distich. Couplet [Gk]

distinctio rationis. Mental distinction [L]

dithyramb. Greek lyric form [Gk]

distingué. Distinguished; having an air of high social position [F]

distrait. Distraught; distracted; absent-minded; inattentive [F]

dit. Says; said; called [F]

Ditat Deus. God enriches (motto of Arizona) [L]

diurnus. Daily [L]

diva. Goddess; female opera star [It]

diverbium. Dialogue or spoken verse in Latin drama, as distinguished from *canticum*, verse to be sung [L]

divertissement. Diversion; a brief and lively piece (ballet or sketch) given between two acts [F]

dives. Rich [L]

Divide et impera. Divide and rule [L]

Divina Commedia. Divine Comedy (Dante; 1302 *ff.*) [It]

Divinitatis Doctor. Doctor of Divinity [L]

divisa. Badge; emblem; device [Sp]

divisi. Divided; separated [It]

divozione. Primitive form of religious drama [It]

dlia. For [R]

D.N.B. See *Deutsches Nachrichtenbüro*

dobavlenie. Appendix; supplement [R]

Dobir den! Hello! [R]

Do'brii ve'tcher! Good evening! [R]

Dobroe utro! Good morning! [R]

doce. Twelve [Sp]

Docendo discitur. One learns by teaching [L]

Docendo discimus. We learn by teaching [L]

docere. To teach [L]

dochimiacus. Metrical foot of three long and two short syllables [Gk]

docta ignorantia. Learned ignorance [L]
dodeca. See *dodeka*
dodecagon. Plane-figure having twelve sides [Gk]
dodecahedron. Solid figure having twelve surfaces [Gk]
dodeka. Twelve [Gk]
dodicesimo. Twelfth [It]
dodici. Twelve [It]
dogma. Opinion; a public decree [Gk]
d'ogni mese. Monthly [It]
d'ogni settimana. Weekly [It]
doklady. Papers [R]
dokus. See *tuches*
dolabra. An ancient axe [L]
dolce. Sweet(ly) [It]
dolce far niente. Sweet idleness [It]
dolce stil nuovo. Sweet new style; descriptive of Dantean poetry [It]
dolente. Sad; mournful [It]
dolium. Spherical earthenware vessel [L]
Dolmetscher. Interpreter; translator [G]
doloroso. Sadly; sorrowfully [It]
Dom. Cathedral [G]
dom. House [R]
D.O.M. See *domino optimo maximo*
domani. Tomorrow [It]
Domei. Official Japanese news agency.
domenica. Sunday [It]
Domine, dirige nos. Lord, direct us (motto of the City of London) [L]
domingo. Sunday [Sp]
dominica palmarum. Palm Sunday [L]
dominium eminens. Eminent domain [L]
domus Dei. House of God [L]
Domino optimo maximo. To the Lord, supreme and mighty (motto of the Benedictine Order; *abbr.* D.O.M.) [L]
dominus. Lord; sir; owner; master; husband [L]

Dominus illuminatio mea. The Lord is my light (motto of Oxford University) [L]
Dominus Mea Illuminatio. The Lord My Light (Blackmore) [L]
Dominus vobiscum. The Lord be with you [L]
Domus Procerum. House of Lords [L]
don. Gift [F]
donatio. Gift [L]
Dónde? Where? [Sp]
Donde hay gana, hay maña. Where there's a will there's a way [Sp]
Donde las dan, las toman. As ye sow, so shall ye reap [Sp]
donna. Lady; woman [It]
donné(e). Given; given data [F]
Donner. Thunder [G]
Donnerwetter. Thunderstorm; confound it! [G]
Dono, Dedit, Dedicavit. (The author) has given and dedicated for a gift [L]
Don Quixote. Idealistic, impractical, self-sacrificing person; chief character and title of Cervantes' novel, 1605-15 [Sp]
donum. Gift [L]
dopo. After [It]
dopo la guerra. After the war [It]
Dopolavoro. After work; Italian fascist organization for leisure time activities [It]
Doppelgänger. Phantom double [G]
doppio. Double [It]
dorado. Gilt [Sp]
doré. Gilt; gilded [F]
Dorf. Village [G]
Dorfgeschichte. Village tale [G]
dormant. Asleep; sleeping [F]
dormer. To sleep; the upper story in the roof of a house [F]
d'orsay. Sandal or pump with low-cut sides [F]. See also *Quai D'Orsay*
dorsum. Back [L]

dorure. Beaten egg-yolks [F]

dos. Two [Sp]

Dos de Mayo. May 2nd; patriotic holiday celebrating the Spanish uprising against French rule in 1808 [Sp]

Dos moi pou sto, kai tan gan kinaso. Give me a place to stand and I will move the earth (attributed to Archimedes)[Gk]

dossier. File; systematic notes [F]

Dosvidanio! Goodby! [R]

dottore. Doctor; professor; pedant [It]

douane. Customs office [F]

douanier. Customs officer [F]

double entendre. See *double entente*

double entente. Expression with two meanings, one usually indelicate [F]

douce. Sweet; gentle; quiet-mannered [F]

doucement. Sweetly; softly; gently [F]

douceur. Bribe; tip [F]

douloureux. Sad; painful [F]

doux. Sweet; gentle; soft [F]

Dove Sono I Bel Momenti? Where Are the Lovely Moments? (*Marriage of Figaro*, Act III; Mozart) [It]

doxa. Opinion [Gk]

Dozent. Instructor [G]

Drachen. Dragon; kite [G]

drachma. Unit of Greek currency [Gk]

dragée. Sugar-almond; sugar-plum; small shot [F]

Dramatis Personae. The persons of the drama [L]

drame avec soi. Dialogue with himself; soliloquy [F]

drame bourgeois. Middle-class tragedy [F]

Drang nach Osten. Drive to the east; trend of expansion towards the east [G]

drap d'or. Cloth of gold [F]

dravya. Substance [Skr]

Dresden. City in Germany; porcelain ware originating in that city or in imitation of it [G]

dritta. Right (hand); straight (road) [It]

droit. Law; right; justice; equity [F]

droit d'auteur. Copyright [F]

droit du seigneur. Lord's right (to have the bride before his vassal) [F]. See also *jus primae noctis*

droshky. Carriage; cab [R]

Druck. Pressure [G]

Druckerei. Printing office [G]

Druckfehler. Misprint; *errata* [G]

Druze. Religious sect in southern Syria [ ]

D.S. See *dal segno*

duan. A poem or canto thereof [Gaelic]

Du Bist Wie Eine Blume. Thou Art Like a Flower (Heine-Schumann) [G]

duce. Leader [It]. See also *Il Duce*

duces tecum. Bring with you; writ or subpoena requiring party summoned to bring with him some document or piece of evidence to be inspected by the court [L]

Ducit amor patriae. The love of country leads me [L]

ductus. Stylistic pattern of a speech [L]

ductus figuratus. Figurative or indirect style [L]

ductus simplex. Straightforward style or intention [L]

ductus subtilis. Stylistic device of intending the opposite of what is said [L]

Dudelsackpfeife. Bagpipe [G]

due. Two [It]

dueña. Chaperone [Sp]

Duft. Fragrance; aroma [G]

Dulag. See *Durchgangslager*

Dulce est desipere in loco. It is delightful to relax upon occasion [L]

Dulce et decorum est pro patria mori. Sweet and fitting is it to die for one's country (Horace, *Odes*; 3-2-13) [L]

Dulce quod utile. What is useful is sweet [L]

Dulcinea. Country wench, idealized by Don Quixote as a "Queen of Love and Beauty" [Sp]

dum. While; as long as; until; upon condition that [L]

Duma. Russian parliament from 1905 to 1917; council [R]

Dum docent, discunt. (Men) while they teach, learn (Seneca) [L]

Dum spiro spero. While I breathe I hope (Vergil, *Aeneid*; 2-799) [L]

Dum tacet, clamat. While it is silent, it speaks out; silence is in itself an admission (motto of the Woodmen of the World) [L]

Dum vita est, spes est. While there is life, there is hope [L]

Dum vivimus, vivamus. While we live, let us live [L]

dunque. Now [It]

Dunque Io Son. Then I am the one *(Barber of Seville,* Act II; Rossini) [It]

duodecimo. See *in duodecimo*

duolo. Grief; sorrow [It]

duomo. Cathedral [It]

dur. Hard [F]

Dur. Major key [G]

durak. Fool; imbecile [R]

dura mater. Outer membrane of the brain [L]

durbar. East Indian court; audience; *levée* [Persian]

Durchgangslager. (P.W.) Transit camp [G]

durchgestrichen. Canceled [G]

durchkomponiert. Said of an art-song or *Kunstlied* in which music is set for an entire poem rather than having the same music repeated for each stanza [G]

durée. Duration [F]

duvet. Eiderdown quilt; pubic hair [F]

Dux femina facti. A woman the leader of the deed; *Cherchez la femme* [L]

D.V. See *Deo Volente*

dva. Two [R]

dvadtsat. Twenty [R]

dvadtsatyi. Twentieth [R]

dvienadtsat. Twelve [R]

dvienadtsatyi. Twelfth [R]

dvugodovalyi. Biennial [R]

dvukhmesiachnyi. Bimonthly [R]

dvukhnedelnyi. Biweekly [R]

dybbuk. Bewitched person; person in a trance [Y]

dyesit. Ten [R]

dyevit. Nine [R]

dynamis. Power; a source of change; the capacity of passing to a different state; potentiality [Gk]

dys. Hard; bad [Gk]

dyspareunia. Incapacity of a woman for sexual intercourse except with difficulty and pain [Gk]

E

e. And [It]; From; of [L] (For Greek words beginning with *e*, see also under *he-*)

E.A.M. See *Ethnikon Apeleutherotikon Metopon*

eau. Water [F]

eau de cologne. Cologne (water); perfumed toilet water [F]

eau de vie. Aqua vitae; spirits; brandy [F]

eau forte. Aqua fortis; nitric acid; etching or print produced by chemical process [F]

eau sucrée. Water sweetened with sugar [F]

ébauche. First sketch (of a painting) [F]

ebda. See *ebenda*

ebenda. In the same place; *ibidem* [G]

ec-. See also *ek-*

écarté. Card game for two [F]

E cattivo vento che non è buono per qualcuno. It's an ill wind that blows no one any good [It]

ecbasis. Digression [Gk]

Ecce Ancilla Domini. Behold the Handmaid of the Lord (Luke 1-38; the *Annunciation*, by Rossetti) [L]

Ecce Homo. Behold the Man (presentation of Christ to the multitude by Pilate; John 19-5) [L]

Ecce quam bonum. Behold how good (Psalms, 133-1)

(motto of the University of the South) [L]

Ecce, Quomodo Moritur. Behold! The Way of Death [L]

Ecce signum. Behold the sign (*i.e.* the proof) [L]

ecclesia. Assembly; church [L]

échafaud. Scaffold [F]

echando flores. Paying compliments [Sp]

échappé. Escaped; type of ballet step [F]

échelle. Scale; ladder [F]

echinus. Convex projection under the *abacus* of the Doric capital [Gk]

echt. Real; genuine [G]

éclair. Pastry or cake shell filled with whipped cream or custard [F]

éclaircissement. Clarification; explanation [F]

éclat. Brilliant success; prestige [F]

ecloga. Eclogue; pastoral dialogue in verse [L]

école maternelle. French equivalent of the *Kindergarten* for children 2 to 6 [F]

école normale. Normal school; teacher-training school [F]

école primaire. Primary school; tuition-free public school for pupils 6 to 13 [F]

e contra. From the opposite; on the contrary [L]

écorché. Flayed, skinned; stripped (of bark); anatomical figure used to study muscles and veins [F]

écossais. Scottish; in Scottish style [F]

ecphonema. Outcry; exclamation [Gk]

ecplexis. Enthralment [Gk]

Ecrasez l'infâme! Crush the infamy; down with the infamous system (slogan of Diderot and Voltaire before the French Revolution) [F]

écrevisse. Crayfish; crab; lobster [F]

écriture. Writing; style [F]

écrivain. Writer; clerk [F]

ed. And [It]

edad. Age [Sp]

Edda. Either of two collections of Old Norse literature (ca. 1200)

Edelweiss. White-flowered Alpine plant [G]

E.D.E.S. See *Ellinikos, etc.*

edición de bolsillo. Pocket edition [Sp]

édition de luxe. Handsome edition [F]

édition de poche. Pocket edition [F]

editio princeps. First or original edition [L]

editus. Put forth; promulgated; brought forth; born [L]

edizione portatile. Pocket edition [It]

efendi. Master; title of officials and members of the learned professions; general title of respect [Turk]

Effectus sequitur causam. Effect follows the cause [L]

effendi. See *efendi*

effrayé. Frightened; design of rearing horse in heraldry [F]

effusio sanguinis. Shedding of blood [L]

e.g. See *exempli gratia*

égalité. Equality [F]

égaré(e). Strayed; lost; in a maze; confused [F]

égarement. Confusion [F]

église. Church [F]

ego. I; self; myself [L]

Eheu! fugaces labuntur anni! Alas! the fleeting years glide away (Horace) [L]

Ehret die Frauen! Honor women! (Schiller) [G]

Ehrlich währt am längsten. Honesty is the best policy [G]

eicon. Image; presentation of physical resemblance by portrait or imagery [Gk]

eidola. Images; insubstantial forms; phantoms [Gk]

eidos. Form [Gk]

eidyllion. Short, descriptive poem [Gk]

Eifersucht. Jealousy [G]

Eigenart. Character(istic) [G]

Eigenlob stinkt. Self-praise is no recommendation [G]

Ei incumbit probatio qui dicit non qui negat. The proof lies upon him who affirms, not upon him who denies [L]

eikon. Image [Gk]

Eile mit Weile. Make haste slowly [G]

Eili, Eili. My Lord, My Lord [Heb]. See also *Eli, etc.*

Einband. Binding [G]

Einbildung. Imagination [G]

Eine Hand wäscht die andere. One good turn deserves another [G]

Eine Kleine Nachtmusik. Little Nocturne (Mozart) [G]

einfach. Simple; plain; simply [G]

Ein' Feste Burg ist Unser Gott. A Mighty Fortress is Our God (Luther) [G]

Einfluss. Influence [G]

Einfühlung. "In-feeling"; empathy; projection of subjective feeling into an object [G]

Einführung. Introduction [G]

eingebunden. Bound [G]

eingegangen. Discontinued [G]

Einheitspartei. United Party. See *Sozialistische Einheitspartei*

Einleitung. Introduction [G]

Einsamkeit. Loneliness [G]

Einsam Wachend in der Nacht. Lonely Watch I Here Tonight (*Tristan und Isolde*, Act II; Wagner) [G]

einschliesslich. Including; inclusively [G]

Einstellung. Attitude; focus; adjustment; setting of a dial or instrument [G]

Eisen und Blut. Iron and blood (a phrase used by Bismarck) [G]

eisteddfod. Musical, literary, and dramatic contest (*pl.* eisteddfodau) [Welsh]

ejemplar. Copy [Sp]

ejido. Common; public land; communal land system in Mexico [Sp]

ejusdem generis. Of the same class [L]

ek. From; of [Gk]. See also under *ec-*

ekkyklema. Primitive revolving stage [Gk]

eklegein. To select [Gk]

ekpaideusis. Education [Gk]

ekphonesis. Outcry; exclamation Gk][

ekstasis. Displacement; trance [Gk]

ekzempliyar. Copy [R]

el. The (in phrases, see also below [Sp]

El Amor Brujo. Love, th Magician (De Falla) [Sp]

élan. Vivacity [F]

élan vital. Vital urge or force; term used by Bergson to denote the source of causation and evolution in nature [F]

E.L.A.S. See *Ellinikos Laikos, etc.*

elatton horos. Minor term (of a syllogism) [Gk]

El Caudillo. See *Caudillo*

El Cid Campeador. Warrior Chieftain; Spanish hero

El dinero es mal amo, pero buen criado. Money is a good servant but a bad master [Sp]

El Dorado. The gilded (land); fictitious country rich in gold, once believed to be in South America [Sp]

eleemosynae. Possessions of the church [L]

elegantia. Elegance; careful choice of diction [L]

elegit. He has chosen [L]

elektrichestvo. Electricity [R]

elektrum. Amber; an alloy of gold and silver used by the ancient Greeks and Romans for making coins [Gk]

elenco degl' indirizzi. Directory [It]

El Escorial. Palace near Madrid; burial place of Spanish kings [Sp]

élève. Pupil [F]

Eli, Eli, lama sabachthani? My God, My God, why hast thou forsaken me? (Matt. 27–46) [Heb]

elisir. Elixir; potion [It]

élite. Elect; select few; upper class [F]

elixir vitae. Quintessence of life; a potion that prolongs life [L]

El Libertador. The Liberator; name of revolutionary hero of South America, especially Simón Bolívar or José de San Martín [Sp]

Ellinikos Dimokratikos Ethnikos Stratos. Greek National Democratic Army; right-wing political organization, 1944-5

Ellinikos Laikos Apeleutheratikos Stratos. Hellenic Peoples' Army of Liberation; the fighting forces of the *E.A.M.*

elocutio. Clarity and propriety of speech; proper composition and pronunciation [L]

éloge. Eulogy [F]

Elohim. God; the Supreme Being [Heb]

éloigner. Remove to a distance [F]

El pan, pan, y el vino, vino. Plain facts in plain words; to call a spade a spade [Sp]

El que calla, otorga. Silence gives consent [Sp]

élu(e). Elect(ed) [F]

E Lucevan Le Stelle. The Stars were Shining (*La Tosca*, Act III; Puccini) [It]

Elzevir. Name of a Belgium book-printing house in the 16th century; book issued by this firm

embarras de choix. More choices than one knows how to deal with [F]

embarras de richesse. More wealth than one knows how to deal with [F]

embatai. Soft shoe worn by Greek women and effeminates [Gk]

embolimon. Choral interlude in tragedy [Gk]

embolus. Blood-clot [L]

embonpoint. Plumpness [F]

embouchure. Mouth of a river; outlet of a valley; mouthpiece of an instrument; art of using a mouthpiece [F]

emendatio. Emendation; improvement; correction [L]

emeritus. To have earned one's pay completely; having earned discharge (referring to a retired professor) [L]

emeth. Truth [Heb

émeute. Popular uprising [F]

emigrado. Exile; *émigré* [Sp]

émigré. Emigrated; emigrant; exile(d); specifically, one who leaves a country as a result of revolution or persecution [F]

emmeleia. Ancient religious dances [Gk]

Emollit mores nec sinit esse feros. Makes gentle the character and does not allow it to be unrefined (Ovid; motto of the University of South Carolina) [L]

Empfindung. Sensation; sensitiveness; feeling; emotion [G]

empressement. Display of cordiality [F]

Empta dolore docet experientia. Experience teaches (when) bought with pain [L]

emptio. Purchase [L]

emptor. Buyer; purchaser [L]

Emunot ve-Deot. Doctrines and Religious Beliefs (title of a work by Saadia, a Hebrew philosopher of the 10th century [Heb]

en. And [Du]; at; by; for; in; with [F]; at; by; in [Gk]; for; in; on [Sp]; a; an; one [Swed]

en arrière. In the rear; behind [F]

en avant. Forward; in front; onward [F]

en bloc. In a bloc; as a unit [F]

En boca cerrada no entran moscas. A wise head keeps a closed mouth [Sp]

en brochette. Impaled on a skewer [F]

encargo. Commission [Sp]

encarpa. Decoration consisting of fruit or flowers [Gk]

en casserole. See *casserole*

enceinte. Circumference; surrounding wall of city or fort; pregnant; with child [F]

enchainements. Sequences; step-combinations [F]

encheiridion. Handbook; manual [Gk]

encierro. Enclosure; corral [Sp]

enclavé. Keyed in; a joint formed by one square, projecting piece fitting into another; a geographical feature having this shape; territory enclosed by that of a foreign power [F]

encoignure. Corner table, triangular in shape [F]

encomboma. Garment fastened around the waist by a large bow [Gk]

encomium. Laudatory speech or poem [L]

en coquilles. In the shell [F]

encore. Again; repeat [F]

encuadernación. Binding [Sp]

en cueros vivos. Naked [Sp]

encyclios paideia. Program of cultural studies [Gk]

encyclopédistes. Collaborators on Diderot's rationalistic *Encyclopédie*, 1751-76 [F]

endecha. Dirge; elegy [Sp]

Ende gut, alles gut. All's well that ends well [G]

en déshabillé. In undress [F]

endormi(e). Asleep; sleeping [F]

endosser. To endorse [F]

endoxa. Prevailing beliefs [Gk]

endromis. Heavy, warm robe worn by ancient Greek athletes [Gk]

endyadis. One by two; figure of speech in which an idea is expressed by two nouns and a conjunction; *e.g.* "We drink from cups and gold" [Gk]

endymatia. Costumed dances as a form of entertainment [Gk]

energeia. Vividness [Gk]

energico. Energetic [It]

enero. January [Sp]

en fait. In fact; in deed; actually [F]

enfant prodigue. Prodigal son [F]

enfants perdus. Lost children; forlorn hope [F]

enfant terrible. Bad boy; overweening, precocious youngster; young "terror" [F]

enfant trouvé. Foundling [F]

enfer. Hell; purgatory [F]

en fête. In a festive state [F]

enfin. Finally; at last [F]

en garçon. As a bachelor [F]

englouti. Engulfed; inundated [F]

engobage. Glaze; glazing [F]

engobe. Glaze; white paste applied to the surface of pottery [F]

en grande tenue. In full dress [F

en gros. In gross; total [F]

en haut. Above; on high [F]

enjambement. Carrying the sense of a poetic line over to the next line [F]

enkyklios paideia. (Complete) circle of education [Gk]

en masse. In a mass; all together; wholesale [F]

ennui. Boredom [F]

ennuyé. Bored [F]

en papillote. Said of fried food wrapped in oiled or buttered paper [F]

en passant. In passing; incidentally; by the way [F]

en pension. In a boarding-house [F]

en plein jour. In broad daylight; in the open [F]

en rapport. In agreement; in harmony [F]

en règle. In due form [F]

en route. On the way [F]

ens. Being; existence; thing [L]

ens a se. Being in itself; thing as such [L]

ensayo. Essay [Sp]

en seguida. At once; immediately [Sp]

enseignement. Instruction; teaching [F]

ensemble. Together; group; aggregate or totality; whole; set or collection which works, fits, or belongs together; musical or theatrical group; dress outfit [F]

enseñanza. Instruction; teaching [Sp]

Ense petit placidam sub libertate quietem. With the sword she seeks peaceful rest under liberty (motto of Massachusetts) [L]

ens legis. Creature of the law; artificial entity; legal fiction [L]

ens rationis. Being or existence as conceived by the intellect or mind; creature of reason [L]

ens realissimum. Purest or most real being [L]

entablature. Horizontal architectural unit surmounting columns; top moulding of a piece of furniture [F]

Entartung. Degeneration [G]

entasis. Swelling in the middle of a column [Gk]

Entbehren sollst du! Thou shalt renounce! (Goethe) [G]

entelecheia. Completed realization; purposeful spiritual activity [Gk]

entendu. Understood; settled [F]

entente. International agreement of friendship or alliance; group of states bound by this agreement [F]

Entente Cordiale. Anglo-French agreement of 1904, settling differences regarding Africa [F]

Entführung. Seduction [G]

Entführung Aus Dem Serail. Abduction from the Seraglio (Mozart) [G]

Enthüllung. Disclosure; revelation [G]

Entia non sunt multiplicanda praeter necessitatem. Entities are not to be multiplied unless necessary; a statement of the logical rule of economy known as "Occam's Razor" [L]

entourage. Surrounding company; body of courtiers and retainers; group of admirers and followers [F]

en-tout-cas. Umbrella used as a parasol [F]

entr'acte. Interval between acts; brief entertainment between acts; music played during intermission [F]

entre. Among; between; in; with [F]

entrechat. Ballet step involving a jump and repeated crossing of the feet (an *entrechat-quatre* indicates two crossings of the feet, an *entrechat-six*, three crossings, *etc.*) [F]

entrecoupe. Vacant space between two architectural vaults [F]

entredeux. Narrow strip of lace or embroidery used between joined pieces of a dress; piece of furniture between two doors or posts [F]

entrée. Entrance; dish served between heavy courses at a formal dinner [F]

entremés. Interlude; short play [Sp]

entremet. Side-dish served between courses; interlude [F]

entre nous. Between you and me [F]

entrepôt. Trans-shipment port; bonded warehouse; commercial center [F]

entrepreneur. Enterpriser; one who undertakes to finance or manage an enterprise [F]

entresol. Suite of low-pitched rooms between two floors of a house, generally between the ground floor and first floor [F]

entretien. Conversation; talk; upkeep; care; preservation [F]

Entweder-Oder. Either-or; alternative [G]

Entwicklung. Development [G]

enumeratio. Recapitulation [L]

environs. Environment; surroundings; neighborhood [F]

envoi. Postscript to a poem [F]

En voiture! All aboard! [F]

eo die. On that (the same) day [L]

eon. See *aion*

eo nomine. Under (by) that name [L]

epagoge. Process of establishing a general proposition by induction; seeing the universal in the particular [Gk]

epanodos. Return to main theme (after a digression) [Gk]

epanorthosis. Correction of a statement (while making it) [Gk]

épater le bourgeois. Stamp on the middle class; indicates scorn of the bohemian artist for the conventional citizen; to confound the Philistines [F]

épaulette. Shoulder piece; shoulder knot; epaulet [F]

epauxesis. Sudden climax [Gk]

épergne. Table ornament [F]

eperotesis. Short, emphatic question [Gk]

ephemerides. See *ephemeris*

ephemeris. Almanac; calendar (*pl.* ephemerides) [Gk]

epi-. Upon; beside; over [Gk]

épi. Ear of corn; any shape or design resembling it; ornament surmounting a pointed roof [F]

épice. Spice [F]

epicerie. Grocery [F]

épicier. Grocer [F]

Epigaea repens. Trailing Arbutus; Mayflower [L]

epigone. Successors and imitators; born afterwards [Gk]

epigoneion. Ancient string-instrument, somewhat like a harp [Gk]

Epigonendichtung. Literature imitative of a previous era [G]

epimythium. Final moral of a fable [Gk]

epinicium. Song or ode commemorative of a victory [Gk]

epiparados. Second entrance (of the tragic chorus) [Gk]

epiphonema. Striking figure or emphatic remark at the end of a passage or speech [Gk]

epiplexis. Argument by censure or shame [Gk]

episcopus. See *episkopos*

episkenion. Upper story or roof behind the Greek stage [Gk]

episkopos. Overseer; inspector; bishop [Gk]

episodium. That which comes between the choral odes, *i.e.* an act, in Greek tragedy [Gk]

episteme. Science; knowledge [Gk]

epistola. Letter; charter (*pl.* epistolae) [L]

epistyle. Horizontal beam on capitals of columns [Gk]

episyntheton. Use of various kinds of foot in a meter [Gk]

epitasis. Intensification of conflict toward the climax of a drama [Gk]

epithalamion. Marriage song; hymeneal [Gk]

epithalamium. See *epithalamion*

épîtres. Epistles; letters [F]

epitrite. Metrical foot of one short and three long syllables [Gk]

epizeuxis. Redoubling; immediate repetition [Gk]

E Pluribus Unum. From many, one (motto of the United States) [L]

éponge. Sponge; spongy fabric with a curly surface [F]

épopée. Epic [F]

epos. Word tale; song; heroic poem or poetry [Gk]

époux. Husband; spouse [F]

Eppur si muove. Nevertheless, it does move (imputed to Galileo, shortly after being forced to renounce his ideas about the motion of the earth) [It]

épreuve. Proof; print [F]

epsilon. 5th letter of the Greek alphabet (Eε)

épuisé. Exhausted; out of print [F]

équerre. Square [F]

eques. Knight [L]

era. Threshing floor [Sp]

erabilis. Maple tree [L]

Erbarme Dich. Have Mercy [G]

Erblichkeit. Heredity [G]

eretz. Earth; land; country [Heb]

Erfahrung. Experience [G]

Erfüllung. Fulfilment [G]

Ergänzung. Completion; supplement [G]

ergo. Therefore; hence; because [L]

ergon. Work [Gk]

erhaben. Lofty; elevated; sublime [G]

Erin go bragh. Ireland forever [Gaelic]

Erinnerung. Remembrance [G]

Eripuit caelo fulmen, mox sceptra tyrannis. He wrested the lightning from the sky, then the scepters from tyrants (inscription by Turgot on Houdon's bust of Franklin) [L]

Eri Tu? Was it Thou? (*The Masked Ball*, Act III; Verdi) [It]

Erkenntnis. Cognition; realization; insight; intuition; recognition [G]

Erkenntnislehre. Theory of knowledge; epistemology [G]

Erkenntnistheorie. Theory of knowledge; epistemology [G]

Erlebnis. Experience [G]

Erlkönig. Erl-king (king of the elves in Goethe's dramatic ballad [G]

Ernährung. Nutrition [G]

Ernst. Earnestness; seriousness[G]

eroica. Heroic [It]

Eros. God of love; Cupid; love [Gk]

erotema. Question with an obvious answer [Gk]

erotesis. Rhetorical question [Gk]

Erotik. Eroticism; a love song; composition on a love-theme[G]

erotomania. Form of *nymphomania* or *satyriasis*; morbid propensity for falling in love; love-sickness [Gk]

Errare humanum est. To err is human [L]

erratum. Error (*pl.* errata) [L]

Ersatz. Replacement; substitute; synthetic (substance); shoddy; cheap; artificial [G]

Erscheinung. Appearance; phenomenon; apparition; specter [G]

Erstlingsdrucke. Incunabula [G]

Erst wäg's, dann wag's. Look before you leap [G]

Eruditio et Religio. Learning and Religion (motto of Duke University) [L]

Erwartung. Expectation [G]

erworben. Acquired [G]

Erythronium americanum. Trout-Lily or Adder's-Tongue [L]

Erythronium dens-canis. Dogtooth Violet [L]

Erythronium grandiflorum. Glacier-Lily [L]

erythros. Red [Gk]

Erzählung. Narrative; recountal [G]

Erziehung. Raising; rearing; bringing up; education [G]

Erziehungslehre. Theory of education; pedagogy [G]

Erziehungswesen. Education [G]

Es. It; E-flat [G]

esaurito. Out of print [It]

escalier. Stairway [F]

escamotage. Juggling; sleight of hand; pilfering [F]

escargots. Snails [F]

escarpe. Inclined rear section of a trench [F]

Eschscholtzia californica. California Poppy [L]

escribano. Notary [Sp]

escritoire. Writing desk [F]

escritor. Writer [Sp]

escritura. Writing; written document [Sp]

escudo. Unit of currency in Portugal [Port]

escuela. School [Sp]

Eselsbrücke. Asses' bridge; *pons asinorum* [G]

es decir. That is to say [Sp]

E sempre l'ora. It is always time [It]

Es irrt der Mensch so lang' er strebt. Man errs as long as he strives (Goethe) [G]

Es ist vollbracht. It is fulfilled (*St. John Passion*, No. 58; Bach) [G]

E Sogno? O Realtà? Am I Awake? Or Do I Dream? (*Falstaff*, Act II; Verdi) [It]

espada. Sword; nickname for a *matador* [Sp]

espadrille. Spanish rope-soled sandal with canvas uppers [Sp]

España. Spain [Sp]

español. Spanish [Sp]

Esperanto. Hopeful; an auxiliary language devised in 1887 by Zamenhof

esparto. Type of grass used for paper-making [Sp]

esperanza. Hope [Sp]

espiègle. Roguish [F]

espoir. Hope [F]

esponjado. Mixture of egg-whites and sugar, baked crisp [Sp]

espressivo. With expression [It]

esprit. Spirit; intelligence; wit [F]

esprit fort. Freethinker [F]

esprit d'escalier. Stairway wit; the witty comment that occurs to one after leaving an argument [F]

Esprit des Lois. Spirit of the Laws (Montesquieu) [F]

esprit gaulois. Gallic wit [F]

espumante. Foam; liquid sugar used to give a foamy head to mixed drinks [Sp]

esquisse. Sketch; outline [F]

esse. To be; existence; the reality of something [L]

Esse est percipi. To be is to be perceived; the doctrine that the world exists only for the mind, expressed by Bishop Berkeley [L]

essenhamen. Poem on manners intended for training in etiquette [OF]

Esse quam videri. To be rather than to seem (motto of North Carolina) [L]

esse quid. To be or being thus; the quiddity [L]

Está bien! Right! [Sp]

Estados Unidos. United States [Sp]

estación. Station; season [Sp]

estado. State; condition [Sp]

estaminet. Wine or coffee shop [F]

estampie. Medieval song with dancing; accentual rhythm to tapping feet [F]

estancia. Large plantation or ranch [Sp]

estate. Summer [It]

Est autem vis legem simulans. Violence may also put on the mask of law [L]

Est Est Est. An Italian wine [It]

estestvoispytatel. Naturalist [R]

estilo. Style [Sp]

estilo plateresco. Ornate style [Sp]

Est modus in rebus. There is a medium in all things (Horace) [L]

Esto Perpetua. Let her be eternal (motto of Idaho) [L]

Est quaedam fiere voluptas. There is a certain pleasure in weeping [L]

estrade. Platform; stand; stage [F]

Estrellita. Little Star (Ponce) [Sp]

estribillo. Little stirrup; introductory lines of a song [Sp]

estufat. Sirloin of beef pickled in red wine [R]

Es tut nichts, der Jude wird verbrannt! It doesn't matter;

the Jew will be burned! (from Lessing's *Nathan der Weise*) [G]

et. And [F] [L]

eta. 7th letter of the Greek alphabet (Hη)

età. Age [It]

et al. See *et alii (aliae)*; *et alibi*; *et alius*

et alibi. And elsewhere [L]

et alii (aliae). And others [L]

et alius. And another (*pl.* et alii) [L]

étape. Stage; step [F]

état. State [F]

étatisme. Statism; theory of extreme government control[F]

Etats Généraux. Estates General; assembly of representatives of the three estates or orders of France, 1392-1789 [F]

Etats Unis. United States [F]

etc. See *et cetera*

et caetera. And others; and other things; and so on [L]

et cetera. And other things; and so forth [L]

Et discere et rerum exquirere causas. Both to learn and to investigate the causes (of things) (motto of the University of Georgia) [L]

été. Summer; been [F]

Et ego in Arcadia. And I have been in Arcadia; *i.e.* I, too, have been an idealist [L]

E Tenebris. Out of the Darkness (Oscar Wilde) [L]

Ethica. Ethics; title of many philosophical works on this subject [L]

ethos. Custom; character [Gk]

Ethnikon Apeleutherotikon Metopon. National Liberation Front; leftist political organization in Greece, 1944-5 [Gk]

étoile. Star [F]

Eto otchen chorosho. This is very good [R]

et passim. And everywhere; and scattered here and there (in a work) [L]

être. To be; being [F]

Etruscan. Referring to Etruria; referring to vases made in this place in imitation of Greek pottery [Gk]

et seq. (et sq.). See *et sequens*.

et seqq. (et sqq.). See *et sequentes*

et sequens. And the following; and what follows (*pl.* et sequentes; et sequentia) [L]

et sequentes. See *et sequens*

et sequentia. And what follows [L]

et sic de ceteris. And so of the rest [L]

et sic de similibus. And so of the like [L]

et sic fecit. And he did so [L]

et sic ulterius. And so further; and so on (forth) [L]

Et tu Brute? Thou, too, Brutus? (spoken by Caesar to Brutus as he saw him among his assassins; Shakespeare: "Julius Caesar"; Act III, Sc. I); a reference to any friend turned enemy [L]

étude. Study; short musical composition [F]

étudiant. Student [F]

étui. Small box or case; sheath [F]

étuvée. Stew(ing) [F]

et ux. See *et uxor*

et uxor. And wife [L]

etwas. Somewhat; some; something [G]

etymon. Basic component or meaning; root (word) [Gk]

eucalyptus globulus. Black gum tree [L]

eudaimonia. Happiness; wellbeing; harmonious satisfaction of all rational powers [Gk]

Euphorbia pulcherrima. Poinsettia; Mexican Flame-Leaf[L]

Euphrosyne. The Joyous One (one of the Three Graces) [Gk]

Eureka! I have found it! (attributed to Archimedes; motto of California) [Gk]

eurythmia. Beauty of proportion; grace of composition; harmonious balancing of lines in a figure or groups in a large painting [Gk]

eutopia. The good place [Gk]

eutrapelia. Hair-splitting [Gk]

Evangelium. Good Tidings; the New Testament [Gk]

évolution créatrice. Creative evolution; a principle of Bergson's philosophy (title of a treatise by Bergson) [F]

ewig. Always; eternal; forever [G]

Ewigkeit. Eternity [G]

ewig Weibliche. Eternal feminine [G]

examen. Trial; test; investigation [L]

exarch. Bishop of the Eastern Orthodox Church [Gk]

exargasia. Literary embellishments [Gk]

excambium. Exchange [L]

ex capite. From memory [L]

ex cathedra. From the chair; authoritative; having the weight of authority; pontifical [L]

Excelsior. Higher (motto of the State of New York) [L]

Exceptio probat regulam. The exception proves the rule [L]

exceptis excipiendis. The proper exceptions having been made [L]

ex concessis. From the premises already granted [L]

excudit. Published; issued [L]

ex curia. Out of court [L]

excursus. Detailed discussion; digression [L]

exeat. Let him go out; leave of absence [L]

exedra. Semicircular bench [Gk]

exegesis. Explanation; explanatory digression; clarification of a passage in the Bible [Gk]

exegetes. Roman officials who interpreted sacred law, dreams, omens and oracles [L]

Exegi monumentum aere perennius. I have raised a monument more enduring than brass (Horace) [L]

exemplaire. Copy [F]

exempli gratia. For the purpose of example; for example; for instance [L]

exemplum. Copy; pattern; example; illustrative story in a sermon (*pl.* exempla) [L]

exergue. Space on a coin or medal outside the main design [F]

exequatur. Formal permission by a state to a consular officer of another state to perform the functions of his office [L]

exercitus. Army; armed force [L]

exeunt. They go out [L]

Exeunt omnes. All retire [L]

ex. From; out of; by; on account of; according to [L]

ex facie. From the face; apparently; evidently [L]

ex facto. From a fact or action; actually [L]

Ex fide fortis. Strong through faith [L]

existere. To emerge [L]

Exitus acta probat. The outcome justifies the deeds (Ovid) (Washington's motto) [L]

ex libris. From the library of; book plate [L]

ex more. According to custom [L]

ex natura rei. From the nature of things [L]

ex nihilo. Out of nothing [L]

Ex nihilo nihil fit. Nothing comes of nothing (Lucretius) [L]

exodium. Farce or light piece played after a tragedy [L]

exodos. End of a play [Gk]

ex officio. By virtue of office [L]

exomis. Short, sleeveless tunic [Gk]

86

exordium. Laying of the warp (for weaving); initial stage; introduction to a discourse; any beginning [L]

Ex Ore Infantium. Out of the Mouth of Babes (Psalms, 8-2; poem by Francis Thompson) [L]

exostra. Projecting balcony (permitting an actor to enter the stage from above) [Gk]

ex parte. On one side only; by or for one party; unilateral [L]

ex pede Herculem. From the foot of Hercules; *i.e.* from the part one can measure or judge the whole [L]

Experientia docet stultos. Experience teaches even fools [L]

Experto crede. Believe one who speaks from experience [L]

exposé. Statement; account; recital; explanation [F]

expositio. Explanation; interpretation; exposition [L]

ex post facto. After the fact [L]

ex quocunque capite. From whatever source [L]

ex tempore. In consequence of time; by lapse of time; without preparation or previous thought [L]

exterus. Foreigner; alien [L]

extra. Beyond; except; without; out of; outside [L]

extrados. Upper convex surface of a vault or arch [L]

extraneus. Foreigner [L]

Extra pecuniam non est vita. Without money (property) there is no life [L]

extremis. See *in extremis*

exuere patriam. To renounce one's country; expatriate oneself [L]

Ex uno disce omnes. From one you may learn all [L]

ex vi termini. From the force of the term; from the very meaning of the expression [L]

ex voluntate. Voluntarily [L]

ex voto. As a vow; marble tablet or inscription expressing the accomplishment of a vow [L]

ezardar. Hindustan farmer [ ]

ezhednevnyi. Daily [R]

ezhegodnik. Year book [R]

ezhegodnyi. Annual [R]

ezhenedelnyi. Weekly [R]

F

fabliau. Short tale in verse (France; 12th and 13th centuries) [OF]

fabula. Comedy; farce [L]

fabula Atellana. Atellan farce; ancient south Italian farce originated in the town of Atella [L]

fabula crepidata. Roman tragedy based upon Greek models [L]

fabulae amatoriae. Love stories [L]

fabula palliata. Cloak comedy; Roman comedy, especially of Plautus and Terence [L]

façade. Outside surface of a building, especially the front [F]

facchino. Porter [It]

faccia. Page [It]

facere. To do [L]

facere sacramentum. To take an oath [L]

facere totum. Do-all [L]

fâché. Annoyed; angry [F]

facies. Face; countenance; external appearance or view [L]

facile princeps. Easily first [L]

Facinus quos inquinat aequat. Guilt makes equal those whom it stains [L]

facio. I do (make) [L]

façon de parler. Manner of speaking [F]

facta. See *factum*

facta armorum. Feats of arms [L]

facta, non verba. Deeds, not words [L]

Facta sunt potentiora verbis. Deeds are more powerful than words [L]

factotum. A do-all; jack of all trades; handyman [L]. See also *facere totum*

factum. Deed; act; fact; circumstance (*pl.* facta) [L]

Factum est. It is done [L]

Factum infectum fieri nequit. A thing done cannot be undone [L]

factum probandum. Fact to be proved [L]

factum probans. Fact tending to prove (another fact) [L]

factura. Invoice [Sp]

facture. Invoice [F]

facultas. Power; faculty; ability [L]

faex populi. Dregs of the people [L]

fagioli. Beans [It]

fagot. Bunch of parsley, thyme, *etc.*, tied up with a bay leaf [F]

fagotto. Bassoon [It]

fagus. Beech [L]

faible. Weak (point) [F]

faïence. Glazed pottery [F]

faille. Originally a Flemish fabric with a coarse grain; *grosgrain* silk or rayon [F]

faillite. Bankruptcy; failure [F]

fainéant. Do-nothing; idler [F]

faire. To do; to make; to cause [F]

faire le salon. To write a review of an art exhibit [F]

faire mon devoir. Do my duty [F]

faisan. Pheasant [F]

fait. Done; thing done or accomplished; deed; act; fact [F]

fait accompli. Accomplished fact; thing already done [F]

faja. Sash [Sp]

fakir. Religious beggar; poor man; mendicant [Hindu]

Falange Española. Spanish fascist organization started in 1933 by General Primo de Rivera and later merged with the *Falange Española Tradicionalista* [Sp]

Falange Española Tradicionalista. Spanish fascist party started in 1937 and headed by the *Caudillo*, General Francisco Franco [Sp]

falsa demonstratio. False designation; erroneous description [L]

falsetto. Imitation of a female voice by a male singer; very high head tones in the male voice [It]

Falsus in uno, falsus in omnibus. False in one thing, false in everything [L]

Faltboot. Folding boat; light, portable canoe or boat [G]

fama. Fame; reputation; character; report (of common opinion) [L]

Fama nihil est celerius. Nothing is swifter than rumor [L]

familiares regis. Persons of the king's household [L]

famosus libellus. Libelous or slanderous writing [L]

fandango. Spanish dance, accompanied by castanets [Sp]

fanfaronade. Fanfare; boast [F]

fanfreluche. Excessive ornamentation; bauble; gewgaw; tinsel [F]

fang hsin. Lost heart, *i.e.* one who has strayed from righteousness [C]

fang shu. Divination; magic [C]

fan tan. A card game [C]

fantoccini. Puppet show [It]

fantoche. Marionette; puppet [F]

farandole. Lively, rapid dance in 4-4 or 6-8 rhythm [F]

Farbe. Color; dye [G]

Farbenindustrie. Dye industry; German chemical trust [G]

farce. Forcemeat [F]

farceur. Clown; comedian; joker; mystifier [F]

farci. Stuffed [F]

fare, fac. Speak, do [L]

farinha. Flour made from tubers of the *manioc* plant; staple food of Brazil [Port]

farol. Lantern [Sp]

far niente. Doing nothing [It]

farrago. Mixed cattle feed; medley [L]

farrago libelli. Miscellaneous contents of a book [L]

farruca. A *Flamenco* dance [Sp]

fas. Right; justice; divine law[L]

fasces. Bundle of twigs surrounding an axe, the symbol of the Roman magistrate's authority [L]

fascismo. Roman symbol of authority; bundle of rods around an axe; fascism [It]

fasti. Lawful (days); calendar of festivals and anniversaries; chronicle or register of events; annals; almanach [L]

Fastnachtspiel. Shrovetide or Carnival play [G]

Fata obstant. The fates oppose; *i.e.* it is impossible [L]

Fata viam invenient. The fates will discover a way [L]

fatrasie. Medieval comedy depending on confusion and absurdity for comic effect [F]

fatua mulier. Whore [L]

fatum. Fate [L]

fatuus. Idiot; fool [L]

faubourg. Suburb [F]

Faulheit. Laziness [G]

faute de mieux. For want of (anything) better [F]

fauteuil. Armchair; box seat [F]

fauve. Fawn-colored; tawny [F]

fauvette. Warbler [F]

faux. False; counterfeit [F]

fauxbourdon. Medieval system of musical notation [F]

faux pas. False step; error in tact or etiquette; blunder [F]

fazzoletto. Handkerchief [It]

fe. Faith [Sp]

febbraio. February [It]

fec. See *fecit*

feciales. Ambassadors [L]

fecit. He made (it); term appearing on works of art, the artist's name preceding [L]

Fedora. Name of the hero in one of Sardou's plays; soft felt hat with the crown creased lengthwise [F]

Fehmgericht. Secret tribunal usurping functions of a regular court [G]

Feis. A traditional Irish festival [Gaelic]

Feld. Field [G]

Feldherr. General [G]

Felicia amelloides. Blue Daisy; Blue Marguerite [L]

felix. Happy; fortunate [L]

Felix qui potuit rerum cognoscere causas. Happy is the man who has been able to learn the causes of things [L]

fellah. Egyptian peasant (*pl.* fellaheen) [Arab]

felo de se. Suicide [L]

Fels(en). Rock; cliff [G]

felucca. Mediterranean sailing vessel [It]

feminalia. Short breeches worn by the ancient Romans after the *toga* had gone out of fashion [L]

femme. Woman; wife [F]

femme de chambre. Chambermaid [F]

femme de charge. Housekeeper [F]

femme fatale. Woman of fate; seductive enchantress [F]

femme incomprise. Misunderstood wife or woman [F]

fer. Iron [F]

ferae naturae. Of wild nature; untamed; wild [L]

feria. Vacation; holiday; weekday (*pl.* feriae) [L]

feria. Market; fair; bazaar; holiday; repose [Sp]

fermé(e). Closed [F]

fermenta cognitionis. Seeds of knowledge [L]

Ferntrauung. Long-distance wedding (instituted by the Nazis for morale purposes between troops on distant fronts and their sweethearts at home) [G]

ferre. To bear [L]

ferrovia. Railroad [It]

ferrum. Iron; horseshoe [L]

fesse. Buttock; rump; bottom [F]

Festa del Grillo. Annual festival in the city of Florence [It]

Festa del Lavoro. Labor Day, April 21st [It]

Festa del Redentore. Annual festival in the city of Venice [It]

Festa dello Statuto. Constitution Day (first Sunday in June; commemorating granting of constitution by King Carlo Alberto to the people of Piedmont in 1848) [It]

Fester Wille führt zum Ziel. Where there's a will, there's a way [G]

Festina lente. Make haste slowly [L]

Festschrift. Volume of learned papers in honor of a scholar; commemorative essays; memorial volume [G]

Festspiel. Festival play [G]

Festspielhaus. Festival Play-House (theater built in Bayreuth, Germany, 1876, for the performance of Wagner's operas) [G]

festum stultorum. Feast of fools [L]

Festung. Fortress [G]

Festung Europa. Fortress of Europe; term for German-occupied Europe in World War II [G]

fête. Festival; entertainment; birthday or saints' day [F]

fête-champêtre. Outdoor festival or entertainment [F]

feu. Fire [F]

feu de joie. Firing of guns as a token of rejoicing; bonfire [F]

feudum. Feudal right; fief; fee [L]

feuille. Leaf; journal; newspaper [F]

feuilletage. Puff paste [F]

feuilleton. Literary or critical article published regularly in a newspaper; section of a novel published serially in a newspaper; newspaper literature; paper; review [F]

feurig. Fiery; ardent [G]

feux d'artifice. Fireworks [F]

fez. Felt or cloth hat, usually red, cylindrical in shape, and with a tassel (worn by men as the national headdress in Turkey before World War II) [Turk]

fiacre. Cab; hack [F]

fiammiferi. Matches [It]

fiancée. Betrothed [F]

fiasco. Bottle [It]

fiat. Let it be done; an order for an act to be done; authority for such act [L]

Fiat. Name of an Italian automobile [It]

Fiat justitia. Let justice be done [L]

Fiat justitia, ruat coelum. Let justice be done, though the heavens should fall [L]

Fiat lux. Let there be light (Genesis, 1-3) (motto of Clark University) [L]

ficelles. Tricks (of the artist's trade); dodges; subterfuges [F]

fichu. Pitiful; done for; neckerchief; triangular scarf tied around the shoulders [F]

fictile. Pottery; vases; tools of the potter's art [L]

Fictio cedit veritati. Fiction yields to truth [L]

Fide et fiducia. By faith and confidence [L]

fidelitas. Fidelity; fealty [L]

fideliter. Faithfully [L]

Fidei defensor. Defender of the Faith [L]

fides. Faith; honesty; trust; veracity; honor [L]

Fides servanda est. Faith must be kept [L]

fidicula. Stringed instrument [L]

Fi donc! For shame! [F]

fiducia. Pledge; mortgage [L]

fidus Achates. Faithful follower (Achates, a disciple of Aeneas) [L]

Fiera del Levante. Fair of the East; annual fair of East European countries held in Bari, Italy [It]

fieri. To be made; to be done [L]

fiesta. Festival [Sp]

Figaro. Character in a play by Beaumarchais, *Le Barbier de Séville*, and in a opera based on it by Rossini; a clever and wily valet; a Paris newspaper [F]

figlia. Daughter [It]

Figli della Lupa. Sons of the wolf; fascist youth organization comprising boys 6-8 years old [It]

figlio. Son [It]

figura causae. Stylistic pattern of a speech [L]

filar la voce. To prolong a tone with the voice; to let the tone diminish gradually [It]

filet. Long thin strips of boneless meat or fish [F]

filet mignon. Tenderloin of beef; choice steak [F]

fileuse. Spinner [F]
filigrane. Watermark [F]
filidh. Learned poet or minstrel [Gaelic]
filius. Son; child (*pl.* filii) [L]
Filius est pars patris. A son is part of the father [L]
filius nullius. Son of nobody, *i.e.* a bastard [L]
fille. Girl; daughter [F]
Fille Aux Cheveux De Lin. Maiden with the Flaxen Hair (Debussy) [F]
fille de joie. Woman of pleasure; courtesan [F]
fille d'honneur. Maid of honor [F]
filoselle. Floss silk [It]
fils. Son [F]
fils naturel. Natural son (title of a play by Diderot) [F]
filum. Thread; line; file [L]
fin. End [F]
finado. Dead; deceased [Sp]
financière. Flavored ragout [F]
Finch' Han Dal Vino. For a Carousal (*Don Giovanni*, Act I; Mozart) [It]
fin de siècle. End of the century; decadence [F]
fine. End [It]
fine champagne. Liqueur brandy [F]
fines herbes. Minced parsley, chives, *etc.* [F]
finis. End; limit; boundary [L]
Finis opus coronat. The end crowns the work [L]
finnan haddie. Smoked haddock [Scottish]
finocchio. Fennel [It]
finster. Dark; gloomy [G]
fioriture. Embellishments in singing [It]
Firenze. Florence [It]
firman. Passport; grant of privileges [Turk]
Fis. F-sharp [G]
fiscus. Treasury [L]
flabellum. Fan [L]
flaccus. Limp [L]

flagellum. Whip; scourge [L]
flagrans. Burning; raging; in actual perpetration; going on now [L]
flagrante delicto. In the very act of committing the crime [L]
Flak. Anti-aircraft gun or fire [G]
Flamenco. Dancing or music of Spanish-Gypsy origin [Sp]
Flammenwerfer. Flame-thrower [G]
flan. Custard [F]
flâneur. Idle saunterer; an esthetic dilettante; an idler [F]
flauto. Flute [It]
flatus vocis. Breath of the voice; vocal utterance [L]
flavus. Yellow [L]
flèche. Arrow; slender spire [F]
Fledermaus. Bat (Johann Strauss) [G]
fleur. Flower [F]
fleur de lis. Lily; insignia of France; design used as a general symbol of purity, nobility and sovereignty [F]
fleuron. Small flower design used as an ornament in classical architecture [F]
Fleurs du Mal. Flowers of Evil (collection of poems by Baudelaire, 1857) [F]
fleuve. River [F]
Floréal. Eighth month of the calendar used during the French Revolution [F]
Floreat et crescat. May it flourish and increase [L]
florida. Flowery [Sp]
florilegium. Gathering or collection of flowers; anthology [L]
floruit. He flourished; period when a person lived [L]
Flöte. Flute [G]
Flügel. Wing; grand piano [G]
Flugschrift. Pamphlet [G]
fluvius. River; flood [L]
fluxus. Flow [L]
foedus. League; treaty; compact [L]

foetus. Unborn child; embryo [L]

foglio bianco. Blank page; fly-leaf [It]

Föhn. Hot south wind in the Alps [G]

foi. Faith [F]

foies gras. Goose livers [F]

foja. Leaf [Sp]

Folge. Consequence; series [G]

folie. Madness [F]

folie de grandeur. Megalomania [F]

folio. See *in folio*

folium. Leaf [L]

folleto. Pamphlet [Sp]

fonda. Hotel [Sp]

fondant. Candy made from melted sugar or honey; melting; melted sugar [F]

fondé(e). Founded [F]

fonds. Fund [F]

fondue. Melted; melted cheese [F]

Fonopostal. Argentine postal service for transmission of recorded messages

fons et origo. Source and origin [L]

fons malorum. Source of evils [L]

Fons Vitae. Fountain of Light [L]

Fontainebleau. Chateau near Paris; scene of the abdication of Napoleon I, 1814, and other historic events [F]

fonte. Cast iron [F]

force majeure. Superior or irresistible force [F]

Forderung des Tages. Demand of the hour [G]

Forelle. Trout [G]

forensis. Belonging to or connected with a court [L]

förlagsrätt. Copyright [Swed]

forlana. Pantomime dance executed by a trio [It]

forma. Form [L]

Forma dat esse. Form gives being [L]

formaggio. Cheese [It]

format. Size of a book; the external make-up of a book, size, binding, style, paper, *etc.* [L]

Formenlehre. Accidence [G]

Formtrieb. Instinct for form; formal instinct [G]

fornkunskap. Archeology [Swed]

Foro d'Italia. Italian forum; stadium in Rome, formerly named *Foro Mussolini* [It]

Forsan et haec olim meminisse juvabit. Perchance it will be a joy hereafter to remember even these things [L]

Fors Clavigera. Fortune with the Nail; reference to an Etruscan design showing Atropos driving a nail into a beam (Ruskin; Horace, *Odes*, 1-35) [L]

Forscher. Investigator; scientist; researcher [G]

Forschung. Investigation; science; research [G]

Forstwesen. Forestry [G]

fort. Strong; fort [F]

forte. Strong; loud [It]

fortior. Stronger [L]

fortiori. See *a fortiori*

fortis. Strong [L]

fortissimo. Very loud; very strong [It]

Fortiter in re. With firmness in action [L]

Fortiter in re, sed suaviter in modo. Unflinching in principle, but gracious in method [L]

Fortuna caeca est. Fortune is blind (Cicero, *De Senectute*, 15-54) [L]

Fortuna fortes juvat. Fortune aids the brave [L]

forum. Paved court in Rome; court of justice; place of jurisdiction or litigation [L]

forza. Force; power [It]

Forza Del Destino. Force of Destiny (Verdi) [It]

forzats. End-paper; flyleaf [R]

forzando. Forced; accented; emphasized [It]

fossa. Ditch; trench; pit [L]

fosse. Ditch; trench [F]

fou. Fool; crazy [F]

fouetté. Whipped; a ballet step involving a swing of one leg with a snap at the finish [F]

foujdar. Police magistrate [Hindu]

foulard. Light twill-weave silk fabric; handkerchief or tie made of this fabric [F]

four. Oven [F]

fourberie. Cheating; knavery; imposture; deceit [F]

fourchette. Fork [F]

Fourier. French pre-Marxist socialist.

foyer. Promenade in a theater [F]

fra. Among; in; friar [It]

frais. Expense; charges; costs [F]

fraise. Strawberry [F]

framboise. Raspberry [F]

franc. French (Belgian and Swiss) unit of currency, equal to 100 *centimes* [F]

franc-tireur. Member of irregular troops [F]

frango. Break [L]

frangipane. Perfume of red jasmine; kind of pastry [F]

fra poco. In a little while [It]

frappé. Struck; beaten; whipped; iced or semi-frozen [F]

Frascati. An Italian wine [It]

frater. Brother (*pl.* fratres) [L]

fratres. See *frater.*

Frau. Mrs.; woman; wife [G]

Frauenliebe und Leben. A Woman's Love and Life (song cycle, Schumann) [G]

Frauenlob. Praise of women [G]

Fräulein. Miss; young lady; governess [G]

fraus pia. Pious fraud; deception intended for a good purpose [L]

fraxinus. Ash [L]

frei. Free [G]

Freie Bühne. Free Theater (founded by Otto Brahm in Berlin, 1889) [G]

Freiheit. Freedom [G]

Freiheit ist nur in dem Reich der Träume. Freedom exists only in the realm of dreams (Schiller) [G]

Freiheitsdichtung. Patriotic literature during wars of liberation against Napoleon [G]

frein. Brake; restraint [F]

Freischütz. Yeoman hunter; marksman; opera by Weber [G]

fremd. Strange; foreign [G]

freneticus. Frenzied person; madman [L]

frère. Brother [F]

fresco. Mural painting done on a fresh surface of lime and gypsum, making retouching impossible [It]

frescura. Insult; impudence [Sp]

frère. Brother [F]

Freude. Joy [G]

freudig. Joyfully [G]

Freut euch des Lebens. Rejoice in Life (first words of a folk-song) [G]

Freya. Wife of *Wotan* [G]

fricandeau. Dish made of boned veal; slice of fried or stewed veal [F]

fricassé. Fricassee; diced meat in thick sauce [F]

frigorifico. Meat-packing plant [Sp]

frijoles. Kidney beans [Sp]

Frimaire. Third month of the calendar used during the French Revolution [F]

frisch. Fresh; lively [G]

Frisch gewagt ist halb gewonnen. A good beginning is half the battle [G]

friseur. Hair-dresser (*fem.* friseuse) [F]

frisson. Shiver; shudder; thrill [F]

frit. Fried [F]

Fritillaria biflora. Black Lily [L]

fritos. Fried potatoes or fish [Sp]

Frl. See *Fräulein*

fromage. Cheese [F]

frontis grabado. Frontispiece [Sp]

frontón. Three-walled court for playing *jai-alai* or *pelota* [Sp]

Front Populaire. Popular Front; coalition of French liberal parties under the leadership of Léon Blum (1936-9) [F]

Frosch. Frog [G]

frottola. Musical ballad [It]

frou-frou. Rustling of a dress; swishing [F]

Fructidor. Twelfth month of the calender used during the French Revolution [F]

fructus. Fruit(s); produce; profit; compensation [L]

früh. Early [G]

Frühlingslied. Spring Song (Mendelssohn) [G]

Fruimur pro iucunditate. We enjoy (things) for pleasure [L]

frumenta. Grain [L]

frustra. In vain; to no purpose [L]

frustum. Piece; part of a solid body [L]

frutta. Fruit [It]

fuego. Fire [Sp]

fuente. Fountain [Sp]

fuga. Flight [L]

Fugaces labuntur anni. The years glide fleeting on [L]

fugato. Having the characteristics of a *fugue* [It]

Fuggiam Gli Ardori. Flee from these burning skies (*Aïda*, Act III; Verdi) [It]

fughetta. A very short *fugue* [It]

Fugit hora. Time flies [L]

fugue. Form of musical composition in which different voices or instruments take up the themes successively [It]

Führer. Leader; guide [G]

Führerprinzip. Leader-principle; doctrine that the leader embodies the will of the people and can make decisions for them [G]

fu kuei. Ragged beggar [C]

fulcrum. Bedpost; support; point of support [L]

fumoir. Smoking room [F]

functus officio. Having fulfilled the function; discharged the office; referring to an officer whose term has expired [L]

fundamentum divisionis. Principle according to which a *genus* is divided into *species* [L]

fundición de hierro. Cast iron [Sp]

fungus. Spongy plant; mushroom; spongy growth [L]

funiculare. Cable railroad in mountains [It]

funkelnagelneu. Brand-new; as new as a shining pin [G]

fuoco. Fire; passion [It]

fuori vendita. Not for sale [It]

fur. Thief [L]

furioso. Furious; vehement [It]

furiosus. Madman [L]

furlana. Rapid Venetian dance in 6-8 rhythm [It]

furor. Insanity [L]

furor poeticus. Frenzied inspiration [L]

Fürst. Prince [G]

furtum. Theft [L]

fuscus. Brown [L]

fusil. Rifle; gun [F]

G

Gabe. Gift [G]

gabella. Tax; rent; excise; custom [L]

gabelle. Salt tax [F]

gabinetto. Cabinet; closet; toilet [It]

gaffe. Gross blunder [F]

gage d'amour. Pledge of love [F]

gaillard. Lively dance; a jolly fellow [F]

gai saber. Gay science; troubadour poetry [OF]

gaita. Native bag-pipe used in Galicia, Spain [Sp

gaku. Picture stretched in a frame [J]

Galanthus nivalis. Common Snowdrop [L]

galea. Helmet [L]

galeón. Ship [Sp]

galette. Light, salted cake [F]

gallego. Portuguese dialect spoken in Galicia, Spain [Sp].

gallo. Cock-fight [Sp]

galop. Gallop; a rapid dance in 2-4 rhythm [F]

gamay. A hardy grape vine [F]

gamin. Urchin; tomboy [F]

gamine. Hoyden; hussy [F]

gamma. 3rd letter of the Greek alphabet (Γγ)

gammelong. Musical bells [Javanese]

gamos. Marriage [Gk]

ganancias. Gains; profits [Sp]

ganapane. Porter [Sp]

ganiff. See *ganov*

ganov. Thief [Y]

gant. Glove [F]

Ganymede. Cup-bearer to *Zeus* [Gk]

garbanzos. Chick-peas [Sp]

garbha. Seed; germ [Skr]

garçon. Boy; waiter; minor dancer in a *corps de ballet* [F]

garde du corps. Bodyguard [F]

gare. Railroad station [F]

Gargantua. Novel by Rabelais; symbol of a man with sensual appetites [F]

garicho. Hot [R]

garni. Garnished; furnished [F]

garrotin. A *Flamenco* dance [Sp]

Gasse. Lane; street [G]

Gasthaus. Inn; hotel [G]

gâteau. Cake (*pl.* gâteaux) [F]

gate sauce. "Spoil sauce"; nickname for a cook's assistant [F]

Gato escaldado del agua fría huye. A burnt child dreads the fire [Sp]

Gattin. Spouse [G]

Gattung. Species; type; *genre* [G]

Gau. District; administrative unit in the *Nazi* party [G]

gauche. Left; awkward; tactless [F]

gaucherie. Awkwardness; tactlessness [F]

gaucho. Cowboy of the *pampas* [Sp]

Gaudeamus igitur. Let us be joyful [L]

gaudium. Joy; delight (*pl.* gaudia) [L]

96

gaufre. Wafer [F]

Gaul. Horse; nag [G]

Gauleiter. District leader of the *Nazi* party [G]

Gaullist. Follower of General Charles de Gaulle, leader of the French resistance in World War II

gavotte. Dance with a suggestion of syncopation [F]

gavyadini. Beef [R]

gazetta. Coin; gazette [It]

gazpacho. Stewed tomatoes, bread and olive oil [Sp]

Gazza Ladra. Thieving Magpie (Rossini) [It]

Gebet. Prayer [G]

Gebrannte Kinder scheuen das Feuer. A burnt child dreads the fire; once bit, twice shy [G]

Geburt. Birth [G]

Geck. Fop; fool [G]

Gedanke. Thought [G]

Gedicht. Poem [G]

Gefehlt ist gefehlt. A miss is as good as a mile [G]

gefilte fish. Filled or stuffed fish [Y]

geflügelte Worte. Winged words; title of a collection of sayings [G]

Gefühl. Feeling; sentiment; expression in utterance, singing, or performing [G]

Gegenreformation. Counter-Reformation [G]

Gegenstand. Object; thing; item, article; subject (of a sentence) [G]

Gegenwart. Present (time) [G]

Gehalt. Content; salary [G]

geheftet. Sewed [G]

Geheime Staatspolizei. Secret state police [G]

Geheimnis. Secret [G]

gehend. Going; progressing; the same as *andante* (music) [G]

Geige. Fiddle [G]

geisha. Professional entertainer [J]

Geist. Spirit; intellect; sensibility [G]

Geistesgeschichte. History of thought [G]

Geisteswissenschaften. Intellectual sciences as distinguished from *Naturwissenschaften*, natural sciences; cultural or socio-historical sciences [G]

gekliben. Gathered; chosen; selected [Y]

Gelände. Terrain; cross-country [G]

Geländeläufer. Cross-country runner [G]

gelato. Ices; sherbet [It]

gelb. Yellow [G]

Geld. Money [G]

gelée. Jelly; jelled [F]

gelehrt. Learned [G]

Gelehrter. Learned man; savant; pedant [G]

Gemälde. Painting [G]

Gemara. Completion; the latter part of the *Talmud* [Heb]

gemeenteraad. Corporation [Du]

Gemeinschaft. Community [G]

gemelles. Twins [F]

Gemini. Twins; Constellation of Castor and Pollux; a sign of the zodiac [L]

gemma. Gem; precious stone [L]

Gemse. Chamois; Alpine goat [G]

Gemshorn. Name of an organ stop having a thin and delicate tone [G]

Gemüt. Mind [G]

gemütlich. Congenial; easy-going; cosy [G]

Gemütlichkeit. Congeniality; coziness [G]

gendarme. Policeman [F]

gendarmerie. Force of *gendarmes* [F]

gêne. See *sans gêne*

geneeskunde. Medicine [Du]

genera. See *genus*

Generalife. Summer palace of the Moorish kings in Granada, Spain

generator. Begetter; producer [L]. See also *genetrix*

genesis. Coming into being; the Biblical account of creation in the Book of Genesis [Gk]

genetrix. One who brings forth or bears; mother [L]

Genie. Genius; term applied to writers of the *Sturm und Drang* [G]

génie civil. Civil engineering [F]

Genio e Follia. Genius and Insanity (Lombroso; 1864) [It]

genitor. Begetter; father [L]

genius loci. Guardian angel of a place [L]

genouillères. (Leather or metal) knee-pieces (in armor) [F]

gennaio. January [It]

genre. Type; style; kind; sort; referring to painting or sculpture, the subjects of which are taken from real (everyday) life, as contrasted with grand historical or religious subjects [F]

gens. Tribe; clan [L]

gentes. People [L]

gentile. Graceful; elegant [It]

gentiles. Members of a *gens* [L]

gentilhomme. Gentleman [F]

genus. General class or division comprising several *species*; a man's lineage; first of a series of universal ideas (*pl.* genera) [L]

genus homo. The *genus* man; classification of man among the vertebrates [L]

Genuss. Pleasure [G]

Geopolitik. Geopolitics; pseudo-science based on the premise that the destinies and relationships of nations depend on geographical factors [G]

Georgius Rex. King George [L]

Gerbera. African Daisy [L]

Gerechtigkeit. Justice [G]

Germania. Germany; feminine figure symbolic of Germany; title of a work by Tacitus [L]

Germinal. Seventh month of the calendar used during the French Revolution; title of a novel by Zola [F]

Ges. G-flat (music) [G]

gesammelt. Collected; gathered [G]

gesamt. Complete; whole [G]

Gesamtausgabe. Complete edition [G]

Gesamtkunstwerk. Total or organic work of art [G]

Geschlecht. Race; sex; gender [G]

Geschütz. Gun; cannon [G]

Gesellschaft. Society; company [G]

Gesellschaft mit beschränkter Haftung. Limited liability company [G]

gesta. See *gestum*

Gestalt. Form; figure; configuration; structural pattern [G]

Gestapo. See *Geheime Staatspolizei*

Gesta Romanorum. Deeds of the Romans (collection of tales relating to the times of the Roman emperors) [L]

gestio. Behavior; conduct [L]

gestum. Deed; act; thing done (*pl.* gesta) [L]

Gesundheit. Health [G]

Gesundheitslehre. Hygiene [G]

get. Divorce [Y]

geta. Raised wooden shoe [J]

Gewehr. Gun; rifle [G]

ghazel. Lyric form in Persian poetry; spinning [Arab]

ghazi. Conqueror; title of Mustapha Kemal, first president of the Turkish Republic; fanatical Mohammedan fighter [Arab]

ghee. Buffalo-milk butter [Hindu]

ghisa. Cast iron; pig iron [It]

ghurra. Earthenware vessel [Hindu]

giallo. Yellow [It]

giallolino. Naples yellow, a pigment used by artists [It]

giaour. Infidel [Pers]

gibier. Game [F]

gigantomachia. War of the giants (against the gods) [Gk]

gigot. Leg of mutton [F]

gigue. Small, high-pitched viol used by old French *jongleurs* or minstrels [F]

Gilgamesh. Sumerian epic, *ca.* 2000 B.C.; a mythical Babylonian king

gillie. A shoe or slipper with laces that tie around the ankle [Scottish]

Ginnasio. Academic high school [It]

Gioconda. See *La Gioconda*

giocoso. Merry; humorous [It]

giorno. Day [It]

Giovani Fascisti. Young fascisti; youth organization for boys over 18 [It]

giovedì. Thursday [It]

Giralda. Moorish tower in Seville, Spain

girandole. Candelabrum; diamond ornament; fireworks [F]

girofle. Clove [F]

giroflée. Gilliflower [F]

giroflet. See *giroflée*

girante. Drawer of a bill [It]

Gironde. River formed by the confluence of the Garonne and the Dordogne, flowing towards the Bay of Biscay; famous wine-growing region [F]

Girondins. Political party led by the deputies of Gironde, suppressed in 1793 [F]

girouette. Weathercock; vane; whirligig [F]

Gis. G-sharp (music) [G]

gittern. Type of guitar [F]

giudizio. Judgment; verdict [It]

giugno. June [It]

giuoco di mano. Practical jokes [It]

giustizia. Justice [It]

giusto. Exact; in exact time; moderate; not excessive [It]

gitanita. Little gypsy [It]

gitano. Gypsy [Sp]

gl'. See *gli*

glacé. Smoothly polished; glazed; iced; sugared [F]

glacis. Defensive slope of a fortress [F]

gladius. Sword [L]

Glaube. Belief; faith [G]

glaucoma. Dimness or defect of vision from opacity of the vitreous humor [Gk]

glaukos. Blue-green; light gray [Gk]

gleditsia. Species of locust tree [L]

Gleichschaltung. Co-ordination; bringing into line [G]

Gleich und gleich gesellt sich gern. Birds of a feather flock together [G]

Gletscher. Glacier [G]

gli. The (*pl.*) (in phrases, see also below succeeding word) [It]

Gli affari vanno bene. Business is good [It]

glissade. Glide [F]

glissando. Gliding; sliding toward a tone instead of attacking it (violin playing); a scale played by dragging a finger along the keys (piano playing) [It]

Gli Stati Uniti. The United States [It]

Gli Uccelli. The Birds (Respighi) [It]

Glocke. Bell [G]

Glockenspiel. Carillon; an instrument of flat-steel plates giving off bell-like tones when struck by a mallet [G]

Gloria. Section of the mass, in church music [L]

Gloria in excelsis (Deo). Glory to God in the highest (Luke, 2-14) [L]

Gloria Patri. Glory be to the Father [L]

Gloria tibi. Glory be to thee [L]

Gloriosa superba. Spider Lily or Climbing Lily [L]

glossa. Gloss; explanation; interpretation; commentary; annotation (*pl.* glossae) [L]

Glück. Fortune; happiness; good luck [G]

glücklich. Happy; fortunate [G]

Glückliche Reise! Have a nice trip; *bon voyage* [G]

Glück und Glas, wie bald bricht das! Fortune is fickle [G]

gluten. Glue; nutritious part of white flour [L]

glutinare. To paste [L]

glyph. Slit; groove; notch; in architecture, channels or flutings; as a root in English words, referring to designs in precious stones, either incised or in relief [Gk]

glypt-. Pertaining to cut, etched, or engraved figures in metal or stone; pertaining to sculpture or the plastic arts in general [Gk]

Glyptothek. Museum of sculpture in Munich [Gk]

glyptotheka. Sculpture gallery; sculpture collection [Gk]

G.M.B.H. See *Gesellschaft mit, etc.*

Gnade. Grace; mercy [G]

Gnädige Frau. Madame (a form of address in Germany and Austria) [G]

Gnädiges Fräulein. Miss [G]. See also *Gnädige Frau*

Gneiss. Laminated rock of quartz, feldspar and mica [G]

gnocchi. Dumpling made from maize or *semolino*; dish made with flower, eggs, and grated cheese, served with a sauce [It]

gnom-. Mark; token; maxim [Gk]

gnosis. Knowledge [Gk]

Gnothi seauton. Know thyself .[Gk]

Gobelins. Parisian tapestry factory established during the reign of Louis XIV; tapestry manufactured there [F]

gobemouche. Credulous gossiper; one who swallows flies [F]

gobierno. Administration; government [Sp]

god. Year [R]

godet. Cup; bowl; calyx; triangular section set in to give fullness to the bottom of a skirt [F]

godichnyi. Annual [R]

god izdaniya. Date of publication [R]

godnyi. Available [R]

goedkoop. Cheap [Du]

Golem. Graven image (brought to life and used for evil purposes) [Heb]

goliardus. Jester; buffoon; juggler [L]

gollandskii. Dutch [R]

golondrina. Swallow [Sp]

golos. Voice [R]

gonfalon. Battle-flag; banner of honor [F]

gongorismo. Complexity of verbal devices; strangeness of diction and construction; over-elaborate and eccentric style (early 17th century) [Sp]

goniff. Thief [Y]

gopak. A lively dance [R]

Gorgonzola. Cylindrically-shaped cheese streaked with green mold [It]

gorn. Forge [R]

gornoe delo. Mining [R]

gorod. Town [R]

gorovoi. Annual [R]

Gosplan. Russian State Planning Commission [R]

gosudarstvennyi. Political [R]

gosudarstvo. State [R]

Götterdämmerung. Twilight of the gods (great conflagration signalizing the destruction of the world); title of an opera by Wagner [G]

Gott erhalte Franz den Kaiser.
God Preserve Our Emperor
Franz (former Austrian anthem;
music by Joseph Haydn) [G]

Gott mit uns! God with us
(motto of the Kings of Prussia)
[G]

Gott sei Dank! Thank Heavens!
[G]

gouache. Method of water-color
painting using opaque colors
diluted in a mixture of water,
gum, and honey [F]

goulash. Beef stew [Hu]

goulu. Glutton [F]

gourmand. Glutton [F]

gourmandise. Gluttony [F]

gourmet. Judge of good foods
and wines; epicure [F]

goût. Taste; style; inclination [F]

goutte. Drop; gout [F]

goy. Gentile; Christian [Y]

G.P.U. Branch of the Soviet
Government for combatting the
counter-revolution (*abbr.* of
Gossudarstvennoye Politiches-
koye Upravleniye [R]

grabado. Engraving; plate [Sp]

Grad. Degree [G]; City [R]

gradatim. Step by step; gradually [L]

gradine. Toothed chisel used by
sculptors [F]

gradior. Step [L]

gradus. Step; degree; grade [L]

gradus (ad Parnassum). Dictionary used in writing Latin
verse; "step to Parnassus" [L]

Graf. Count; title of nobility
(*Gräfin*=countess) [G]

graffiti. Black drawings on a
white ground, transferred to
stone or plaster; decorations in
stone or plaster made by this
method [It]

Gräfin. See *Graf*

gramma. Letter (*pl.* grammata)
[Gk]

grammatici. Grammarians [L]

grammaticus. Grammarian;
teacher of grammar [L]

grammatikos. Pertaining to
letters or literature [Gk]

gramme. Gram; weight of a
cubic centimeter of water at
4° C. =11 grains troy [F]

grana. Nickname for Parmesan
cheese [It]

gran cassa. Bass drum [It]

Gran Chaco. Disputed area between Bolivia and Paraguay
[Sp]

grand. Big; large; great [F]

grand croix. Grand cross; 5th
and highest grade of the *Légion
d'Honneur* [F]

grande dame. Lady of society;
dignified or haughty lady; a
lady of breeding and reserve; a
gracious hostess [F]

Grand Guignol. Paris theatre
founded 1897; type of blood-
curdling play [F]

grande parure. Full dress [F]

grande tenue. Full dress [F]

grande toilette. Elaborate dress
[F]

grand officier. Grand officer;
4th grade of the *Légion d'Honneur* [F]

grand prix. Grand prize; first
prize [F]

grands battements. See *battement*

grand sujet. Role below *première
danseuse* in a *corps de ballet* [F]

grand veneur. Huntsman sauce;
a rich sauce generally for venison [F]

granita. Ice-pudding [It]

graphein. To write [Gk]

gras. Fat [F]

gratiae. Graces [L]

Gratia et Veritas. Grace and
Truth (motto of Goucher College) [L]

gratin. Said of dishes prepared
with cheese, bread-crumbs, *etc.*
[F]

gratinée. Sprinkled with grated
cheese or crumbs [F]

gratis. Freely; without pay [L]

gratis dictum. An unfounded assertion; voluntary statement [L]

grau. Gray [G]

Grau, teurer Freund, ist alle Theorie. Gray, dear friend, is all theory (Goethe) [G]

gravamen. Thing complained of [L]

Graves. Vineyards on the left bank of the Garonne; district of fine wines [F]

gravicembalo. Primitive precursor of the piano [It]

gravis. Heavy [L]

gravure. Engraving; plate [F]

grazia. Grace; elegance [It]

Graziano. Pedant doctor; stock figure in *commedia dell' arte* [It]

Grazie. Thank you [It]

grecheskii. Greek [R]

grège. Raw (silk); undyed and unfinished fabric; any fabric "in the gray"; gray goods [F]

gremio. Guild; trade union [Sp]

grenadine. Liqueur of pomegranates; silk dress fabric; larded fillets of veal; type of carnation [F]

grenouille. Frog [F]

Grenzen. Limits; boundaries [G]

grès cérame. Stoneware [F]

Gretsiya. Greece [R]

grève. Strike [F]

griadushchee. Future [R]

Griechenland. Greece [G]

griffe. Decorative leaf connecting the base of a column with the pedestal [F]

Grille. Mood; caprice [G]

gringo. American from the U.S. [Sp]

grisaille. Painting in imitation of a bas-relief, having only white, gray and black tones; gray monochrome painting [F]

gris(e). Gray [F]

grisette. Working-class girl [F]

grob. Coarse; boorish; vulgar [G]

Grobian(us). Coarse fellow; boor [L] [G]

Groschen. Small coin of Austria [G]

grosgrain. Coarse grain; rayon warp, cotton-filled fabric with crosswise ridges, generally woven in ribbon widths [F]

grosse caisse. Bass drum [F]

Grossraumwirtschaft. Large area economy; Nazi doctrine justifying extension of Germany's boundaries [G]

grosso. Full; grand; great [It]

grottesco. Grotesque [It]

Grundbegriff. Basic concept [G]

Grundfragen. Fundamental problems [G]

Grundlage. Basis; foundation [G]

Grundlinien. Basic outline; fundamentals [G]

Grundriss. Outline; ground plan [G]

Grundsatz. General law or proposition; basic principle [G]

Grundzüge. Basic features; fundamentals [G]

Gruss. Greeting; salute [G]

Gruyère. A type of Swiss cheese

guanaco. Species of the llama family; fur or wool from this animal [Sp]

guanaquito. See *guanaco*

guaracha. A Spanish dance [Sp]

guardia. Policeman [It]

gubernator. Pilot; helmsman [L]

gudki. Whistles [R]

gueule. Mouth; jaw; muzzle [F]

Guerre à mort. War to the death [F]

gueridon. Decorative flower or lamp stand [F]

guerrilla. Little war; warfare by irregulars [Sp]

gueules. Gules; a heraldic term for red, shown on a shield by parallel, vertical lines [F

guía. Guide; handbook; guidebook; right of way [Sp]

güícharo. See *güiro*

guichet. Ticket window; post-office window, *etc.* [F]

Guignol. Character in French puppet show. See also *Grand Guignol*

guilder. Unit of currency in Holland [Du]

guilloche. Design consisting of undulating and crossed lines [F]

guillotine. Beheading machine used during the French Revolution and named after its inventor, J. I. Guillotin [F]

guimpe. Sleeveless frock; jumper [F]

guipure. Type of fine lace [F]

güiro. Puerto Rican instrument; a gourd in which ridges are cut across which wires are scraped [Sp]

guisarme. Scythe-like weapon [F]

guitarra. Guitar [Sp]

gule. Rose [Arab]

Gurkha. One of ruling Hindus in Nepal; East-Indian British soldier [Skr]

guru. Hindu spiritual teacher [Skr]

gusto. Taste; pleasure [It] [Sp]

Guter Mut macht gutes Blut. A contented mind is a continual feast [G]

Güterwagen. Freight car [G]

gwerz. Narrative ballad [Breton]

Gymnasium. Secondary school leading to the university; building(s) in which the ancient Greeks engaged in sports and games [Gk]

gymnopoedia. Religious dances in worship of Apollo [Gk]

gyne. Wife [Gk]

gyo retsu. Traditional parade [J]

Gypsophila paniculata. Common Baby's Breath; a flower [L]

H

h-. See also under *ch-*

H. For Greek words beginning with *h*, see also under the succeeding vowel; *e.g. Hellenikos.* See under *Ellenikos*

habañera. Cuban dance in moderate tempo and usually in triple rhythm [Sp]

habeas corpus. You have the body; writ to bring a party before a court or judge [L]

Habeas corpus ad subjiciendum. Writ to produce the detained person to submit to whatsoever the judge or court shall consider on his behalf [L]

habendum et tenendum. To have and to hold [L]

habentes homines. Men of substance; rich men [L]

habet. He has it; he is hit [L]

habilis. Fit; suitable; useful; proved; authentic; stable [L]

Habima. Platform; stage; name of a troupe of Hebrew actors [Heb]

Habló el buey y dijo mú. When fools speak, they utter nonsense [Sp]

hace calor. It is warm [Sp]

hacer. Make; do [Sp]

hachures. Hatchings; parallel or crossed lines to suggest contours, used in engravings and maps [F]

hacienda. Farm and plantation; manor house [Sp]

Hackbrett. Chopping-board; a name sometimes given to the dulcimer because this instrument was played by striking the strings with a hammer [G]

Hadassah. A name of Esther; women's Zionist organization [Heb]

Hadji. Mohammedan pilgrim to Mecca [Arab]

haecceitas. "Thisness"; particular nature or being; individual quality or essence [L]

Haec est conventio. This is an agreement [L]

Haec meminisse juvabit. See *Haec olim meminisse, etc.*

Haec olim meminisse juvabit. To remember these things hereafter will be a pleasure (Virgil) [L]

haereditas damnosa. Burdensome or debt-ridden inheritance [L]

haeres. Heir (*pl.* haeredes) [L]

Haeres est alter ipse. An heir is another self [L]

hafiz. Mohammedan who knows the Koran by heart [Pers]

Hágame el favor. Please [Sp]

Haganah. Defense; Palestinian fighting forces [Heb]

Haggadah. Instruction; teaching; summary of talmudic lore and biblical themes [Heb]

Hahn. Rooster; cock [G]

haik. Cloak [Arab]

haiku. Short poem of 17 syllables [J]

haima. Blood [Gk]

Hakenkreuz. Swastika; crooked or hooked cross; symbol of Nazism [G]

halaeha. Law [Heb]

halb. Half [G]

haleine. Breath; wind [F]

Hallelujah! Praise the Lord! [Heb]

halling. Boisterous dance for men, featuring high kicks and jumps [Norwegian]

halutz. Pioneer (*pl.* halutzim) [Heb]

halva. Oriental dessert consisting of a paste made of nuts, honey, and sweet cream [R]

hamamelis virginiana. Witch-hazel tree [L]

hamartia. Error; sin [Gk]

Hammerklavier. Pianoforte[G]

hanap. Type of metal drinking cup in the Middle Ages [OF]

Handbuch. Handbook; manual [G]

Handel. Trade; commerce [G]

Handel ist Handel. A bargain is a bargain [G]

Handlung. Action; plot [G]

Handschrift. Manuscript [G]

Hanse. Hanseatic (League); alliance of German maritime cities for protection and furtherance of commercial interests [G]

Hanswurst. Buffoon; clown [G]

Hanukkah. Feast of Lights [Heb]

hapax legomenon. Once said; word of which only one use is recorded [Gk]

harasho. Good [R]

hareng. Herring [F]

haricot. Bean; a thick stew dressed with vegetables [F]

haricot de mouton. Irish stew [F]

haricots verts. Green string-beans [F]

Harpagon. Character in Molière's play *L'Avare*; symbol of a miser [F]

hartebeest. Kind of antelope [Du]

Hasenpfeffer. Jugged hare [G]

hasid. Pious or devout person (*pl.* hasidim) [Heb]

Hasidim. Jewish religious sect founded 1750 in the Ukraine by Israel ben Eliezer [Heb]

hasta. Until [Sp]

Hasta luego. Goodby; so long [Sp]

Hat der Bauer Geld, hat's die ganze Welt. A fool and his money are soon parted [G]

hatti. Turkish edict [Pers]

haupia. Coconut pudding [Hawaian]

Hausfrau. Housewife [G]

Hausmärchen. Household Tales (J. and W. Grimm; 1812) [G]

hausse. Rise (in price) [F]

hautbois. Oboe [F]

haut(e). High [F]

Haute Couture. Group of famous French designers and dressmakers [F]

hauteur. Haughtiness [F]

havildar. Sepoy sergeant [Pers]

Hay que bailar al son que se toca. Adapt yourself to circumstances [Sp]

hay sol. The sun is shining [Sp]

Haz bien y no mires a quién. Do good to all [Sp]

h.e. See *hoc est*

hebdomadaire. Weekly [F]

Hecha la ley, hecha la trampa. Make a law and it is evaded [Sp]

hectare. Hectare=square hectometer=10,000 square meters= 2.47 acres [F]

hectogramme. 100 grams [F]

hectomètre. 100 meters=110 yards approx. [F]

hedone. Pleasure [Gk]

Heft. Number (of a book or edition); instalment or section of a publication; signature (binding); fascicle; notebook or copybook; handle; hilt; fastener; pin; clip [G]

heftig. Violent; vehement [G]

hegumenos. Head of the monks in the Greek Church [Gk]

Heil! Hail! [G]

Heiland. Savior; Redeemer [G]

Heil Hitler! "Hail Hitler!" (the official words of greeting under the Nazi regime, known as "der deutsche Gruss", the German greeting or salutation [G]

heilig. Holy [G]

Heimat. Home(land) [G]

Heimatkunst. Local color; regionalism [G]

heimatlos. Homeless; referring to persons who have no nationality [G]

Heimweh. Homesickness; nostalgia [G]

Heimwehr. The Austrian clerical-fascist political militia founded in 1927 and suppressed by the Germans; Home guard, the German regular army [G]

hekaton. Hundred [Gk]

helados. Ices [Sp]

Heldenleben. Hero's Life (Richard Strauss) [G]

Heldentenor. Heroic tenor [G]

Heldentod. Heroic death; death of a hero [G]

Helianthus. Sunflower [Gk]

helios. Sun [Gk]

Hellas. Greece [L]

Helleborus. Hellebore; member of the Buttercup family of flowers [L]

Helvetia. Switzerland [L]

Hemerocallis. Day Lily [L]

hemi-. Half [Gk]

hemiplegia. Paralysis of one side of the body [Gk]

hemistich. Half a line of verse; short line in a stanza [Gk]

hennin. High, cone-shaped headdress worn by women in the 15th century, generally with a long veil [Arab]

Henomenai Politeiai. United States [Gk]

Hepatica. Liverleaf Plant; member of the Buttercup family [L]

hephaestion. Metrical critic; grammarian [Gk]

Hephaestos. Son of Zeus, deformed at birth; god of fire and of arts of the smith [Gk]

hepta-. Seven [Gk]

heptagon. Seven-sided plane figure [Gk]

Hera. Consort of Zeus; queen of the heavens and of fertility [Gk]

Heraa Suomi! Awake, Finland! [Finnish]

Heracles. Son of Zeus; personification of strength [Gk]

Herausgeber. Editor; publisher [G]

Herbst. Autumn [G]

Heregeld. Tax levied for maintenance of an army [AS]

hermano. Brother [Sp]

hermeneutics. System or science of construction and interpretation [Gk]

Hermes. Son of Zeus and Maia; messenger of the gods [Gk]

hermoso. Beautiful [Sp]

hermosura. Beauty [Sp]

Herouth. Freedom (name of a political party in Israel) [Heb]

Herr. Mr.; lord; sir; master; gentleman [G]

Herrenmoral. Moral(s) of the master(s); aristocratic morality [G]

Herrnhüter. Moravian pietistic sect [G]

Herr Ober! Waiter! [G]

Hersteller. Manufacturer [G]

herus. Master [L]

Herz. Heart [G]

Herzog. Duke [G]

hetaera. See *hetaira*

hetaeria. Company; society; college [L]

hetaira. Courtesan [Gk]

heteros. Other; different [Gk]

hetman. Polish commander [Polish]

Heuchera americana. Alum Root [L]

heure. Hour [F]

heuriskein. To discover [Gk]

hexa-. Six [Gk]

hexaemera. Ancient and medieval versions of the creation epic as inspired by the book of *Genesis* [Gk]

hexagon. Six-sided plane figure [Gk]

hexahedron. Six-sided solid figure; cube [Gk]

hiatus. Split; gap; cleft; break in a line of poetry [L]

Hibiscus moscheutos. Swamp Rose-Mallow [L]

Hibiscus syriacus. Rose of Sharon or Shrub-Althea [L]

Hic et ubique. Here, there, and everywhere [L]

Hic jacet. Here lies; an epitaph [L]

Hic Jacet (Sepultus). Here lies (buried) [L]

hicoria. Genus of hickory trees [L]

hidalgo. Nobleman; man of property; gentleman [Sp]

hiems. Winter [L]

Hiera Anagraphe. Holy Writ [Gk]

hierba mate. Paraguayan tea [Sp]

hieros. Sacred [Gk]

hierro. Iron [Sp]

hijo. Son [Sp]

hilandera. Spinner [Sp]

himation. Garment consisting of a square mantle, worn by the ancient Greeks [Gk]

Hindustani. Popular speech of North India, used as an auxiliary language by 230 million people

Hin ist hin. What's gone is gone [G]

hirtlich. Pastoral; rustic [G]

Hispania. Spain [L]

Histadruth. Organization; workers' federation in Palestine [Heb]

his testibus. These are witnesses [L]

histor. Learned [Gk]

historié(e). Illuminated (letters in a medieval manuscript) [F]

Historismus. Academic history-writing [G]

histrio. Actor (*pl.* histriones) [L]

Hitlerjugend. Hitler youth; *Nazi* youth organization [G]

hiuen. Musical whistle used in China [C]

hiver. Winter [F]

H.J. See *Hic Jacet*

hlaford. Lord [AS]

Hobot ha-Lebabot. Duties of the Heart [Heb]

hoc. This [L]

hoc anno. In this year [L]

hoc est. This is (used in explanations, like *i.e.*) [L]

Hoch! Hail! [G]

Hochdeutsch. High German (as distinguished from Low German; the standard language of educated Germans as distinguished from local dialects) [G]

Hochmut. Pride; arrogance [G]

Hochzeit. Wedding [G]

hoc loco. In this place [L]

hoc nomine. In this name [L]

hoc tempore. At this time [L]

hoc titulo. This title; under this title [L]

hoc verbo. This word; under this word [L]

hoc volo. This I wish [L]

hoi polloi. Common people; rabble [Gk]

hojas. Leaves; sheets [Sp]

hokku. See *haiku*

Hollandaise. Sauce made of egg yolks, melted butter, and lemon juice [F]

holo-. Whole [Gk]

homagium reddere. To renounce homage [L]

homard. Lobster [F]

hombre. Man [Sp]
homilos. Crowd [Gk]
homines. Men [L]
Hominum causa jus constitutum est. Law is established for the benefit of man [L]
homme. Man [F]
homme d'affaires. Business man [F]
homme d'esprit. Man of intellect; wit [F]
homo. Man; human being (*pl.* homines) [L]
homo additus naturae. Man added to Nature (Bacon) [L]
homoeoteleuton. Occurrence of similar endings of words or lines [Gk]
homo faber. Man the maker; technical expert [L]
homo sapiens. Discerning man; man as a thinking animal; the *genus* man [L]
Homo sum; humani nihil a me alienum puto. I am a man; I consider nothing human to be strange to me (Terence) [L]
Homunculi quanti sunt. What an insignificant creature is man (Plautus) [L]
honeste vivere. To live honestly or virtuously [L]
Hon(n)i soit qui mal y pense. Evil to him who evil thinks (motto of Great Britain) [F]
honorarium. Free gift; gratuitous payment [L]
honorarium donum. Gift (made on appointment) to a post of honor; fee for services rendered [L]
Honores mutant mores. Honors change manners [L]
Honos alit artes. Honor nourishes the arts [L]
honte. Shame [F]
hookah. Water pipe with long tube [Arab]
hoppo. Collector; supervisor [C]
hora. Hour [L] [Sp]

hora fugit. The hour flies [L]
Hora Novissima. New Hour (title of an early Latin poem) [L]
Horas non numero nisi serenas. I number none but shining hours (inscription for a sun-dial) [L]
horca. Gallows; hanging [Sp]
horchata. Soft drink of crushed almonds or *chufa* root [Sp]
horme. Impulse [Gk]
hormos. An ancient Greek dance, performed in the nude [Gk]
horribile dictu. Horrible to be told [L]
hors d'affaire. Out of danger [F]
hors de combat. Disabled [F]
hors de concours. Beyond competition [F]
hors de propos. Aside from the purpose [L]
hors de saison. Out of season [F]
hors d'oeuvres. Side dishes; relishes, served at the beginning of a meal [F]
Horst Wessel Lied. *Nazi* song written by Horst Wessel, a storm troop leader who was shot in 1930 [G]
hortus. Garden [L]
hortus conclusus. Enclosed garden; private sanctuary [L]
hortus siccus. Dry garden; herbarium; collection of dried plants [L]
hospes. Guest [L]
hospitium. Inn; household (*pl.* hospitia) [L]
hospodar. Governor [Turk]
hossonah. Wedding [Y]
hostes humani generis. Enemies of the human race [L]
hostia. Host-bread; consecrated wafer in the eucharist [L]
Hostis honori invidia. An enemy's hatred is an honor [L]
Hôtel des Invalides. Hospital for invalid soldiers; famous building in Paris [F]

hôtel de ville. City or town hall [F]

Hôtel Dieu. Lord's Hospital (famous Paris building) [F]

houppelande. Dress or coat with fitted waist, long sleeves and skirt, worn in the 18th century [F]

houri. Nymph of the Moslem paradise; beautiful woman [Arab]

howdah. Litter; seat on elephant's back [Arab]

hsiang. Phenomenon; form or image (C)

hsiao. Filial piety; love of parents [C]

hsi-chü. Play; comedy [C]

hsin. Heart; mind; good faith; belief; trust [C]

hsu. Emptiness; non-existence [C]

hsuan. Mysterious; abstruse; profound [C]

hsu wu. Absence of desire [C]

hua. Change [C]; Fruit segments [Hawaian]

h.t. See *hoc titulo*

huapango. Mexican song and dance festival [Sp]

huarache. Mexican laced leather sandal [Sp]

hubris. See *hybris*

huerta. Garden; reference to the fertile land of Valencia, Spain [Sp]

Hügel. Hill [G]

Huir del fuego y dar en las brazas. Out of the frying-pan into the fire [Sp]

huis. Door [F]

huitain. Group of 8 lines of verse [F]

huître. Oyster [F]

huîtres en coquille. Scalloped oysters [F]

hula-hula. Hawaian dance involving graceful movements of the arms and hips [Hawaian]

Humani nihil a me alienum puto. I consider nothing human to be strange to me (Terence) [L]

Humanum est errare. To err is human [L]

humerus. Shoulder; bone of upper arm [L]

humus. Ground; vegetable mould [L]

Hunc tu caveto. Beware of him [L]

hun mang. Golden Age [C]

Hüttenkunde. Metallurgy [G]

h.v. See *hoc verbo*

Hyacinthus orientalis. Dutch Hyacinth [L]

hybris. Insolence; transgression of divine command or moral law [Gk]

Hydra. Fabulous animal represented as a dragon with seven heads, slain by Hercules [Gk]

hyle. Materials; matter [Gk]

hymeneia. Wedding dances[Gk]

hymnarium. Hymnal [L]

Hymne Au Soleil. Hymn to the Sun (*Coq d'Or*, Act II; Rimsky-Korsakoff) [F]

hymnos. Song in praise of gods or heroes [Gk]

hypaethrum. Latticed window over the entrance to a Greek temple [Gk]

hyper-. Over; above [Gk]

hyperbaton. Transgressor; transposition of words [Gk]

hyperbole. Exaggeration [Gk]

hyphaeresis. Contraction; omission of letters [Gk]

hypnos. Sleep [Gk]

hypo. By; from [Gk]

hypocaustum. Underground furnace with flues in the ancient Roman baths and houses [L]

hypochondriasis. Exaggerated fear concerning health; state of suffering from an imaginary disease [Gk]

hypophora. Objection raised against an argument [Gk]

hyporchema. Choral lyric sung during pyrrhic dances in honor of Apollo [Gk]

hypostasis. Foundation; basis [Gk]

hypotheca. Pledge; mortgage [L]

hypotyposis. Representation of something as though present [Gk]

hypozeugma. Use of several subjects with one verb [Gk]

hypsos. Elevated [Gk]

hysteron proteron. Making the consequent an antecedent; putting the cart before the horse; the logical error of explaining a thing in terms of something which presupposes it [Gk]

I

i. The [It]; (for Latin words beginning with *i*, see also under *j*)

Iacta alea est. The die is cast (Julius Caesar) [L]

iambic. A dance in honor of Mars [Gk]

iambus. Foot [Gk]

ib. See *ibidem*

ibericus. Spanish [L]

Iberis. Candytuft; a garden flower [L]

ibid. See *ibidem*

ibidem. In the same place; in the same work [L]

ibex. Species of goat [L]

ich. I; ego; self [G]

Ich bin der Geist, der stets verneint. I am the spirit that always denies (Mephistopheles in Goethe's *Faust*) [G]

Ich Denke Dein. I Think of Thee (Kerner-Schumann) [G]

Ich dien'. I serve (motto of the Prince of Wales) [G]

Ich Grolle Nicht. I Bear Thee No Grudge (Schumann) [G]

Ich habe gelebt und geliebet. I have lived and loved (Schiller) [G]

ici. Here [F]

Ici on parle français. French is spoken here [F]

icosahedron. Solid figure with 20 equal plane sides [Gk]

icthys. Fish [Gk]

ictus. Push; blow; rhythmic accent [L]

id. See *idem*

idanta. "This-ness"; the state of being a "this", *i.e.* an object of knowledge [Skr]

idée fixe. Fixed idea; prejudice [F]

idée mère. Mother idea; basic idea; original conception [F]

Ideenlehre. Theory of ideas [G]

idem. The same (author) [L]

idem quod. The same as [L]

ideo. Therefore [L]

Ides. 15th (13th) of the month in the Roman calendar [L]

id est. That is [L]

id genus omne. All that class; all of that ilk [L]

idion. Property; attribute [Gk]

Ido. Offspring; a system of reformed *Esperanto*, devised 1907 by Couturat and De Beaufront

idoneus. Sufficient; competent; responsible; fit or proper [L]

i.e. See *id est*

ieri. Yesterday [It]

Iesous Hemeteros Soter. Jesus, our Savior [Gk]

Iesus Hominum Salvator. Jesus, Savior of Men [L]

Iesus Nazarenus Rex Iudaeorum. Jesus of Nazareth, King of the Jews (inscription on the cross of Christ) [L]

I frutti proibiti sono i piu dolci. Forbidden fruits are the sweetest [It]

I.G. See *Interessengemeinschaft*

I.G. Farben. See *Farbenindustrie*

ignis. Fire [L]

ignis fatuus. Foolish fire; phosphorescent glow; delusive goal; will-o'-the-wisp [L]

ignis judicium. Trial by fire [L]

ignoramus. We do not know; an ignorant person [L]

Ignorantia juris non excusat. Ignorance of the law is no excuse [L]

Ignorantia legis neminem excusat. Ignorance of the law excuses no one [L]

ignoratio elenchi. Ignorance of the refutation; arguing outside the case; fallacy of irrelevance [L]

ignotum per ignotius. Unknown by more unknown; explanation clear as mud (*i.e.* more obscure than what is explained) [L]

I.H.S. See *In Hoc Signo*; *Iesus Hominum Salvator*

ikkarim. Dogmas [Heb]

il. He [F]; The [It]

Il Bacio. The Kiss (Arditi) [It]

Il Carnevale. Period of merry-making, dances and masquerades between Epiphany and Ash Wednesday [It]

Il Duce. The Leader; title of Benito Mussolini [It]

ilex opaca. American holly tree [L]

il faut. It is necessary [F]

illud. That [L]

illuminati. Enlightened ones; scholars; religious or political radicals [L]

Il Mio Tesoro. To My Beloved (*Don Giovanni*, Act II; Mozart) [It]

Il n'y a pas de quoi. Don't mention it [F]

Il n'y a que le premier pas qui coûte. It is only the first step that costs (*i.e.* that is difficult) [F]

Il Penseroso. The pensive man; a dreamer (title of a poem by Milton) [It]

Il Piacere. Pleasure (title of a novel by D'Annunzio; 1889) [It]

il primo maggio. The first of May [It]

Ils ne passeront pas. They shall not pass (French slogan at Verdun in 1916) [F]

il y a. There is (are) [F]

imagines. Images [It]

imago. Likeness; image [L]

Imam. See *Iman*

Iman. Mohammedan priest; prince having spiritual power [Arab]

imbroglio. Confusion; complication [It]

imennoi. Cumulative [R]

I Mille. The Thousand (army organized by Garibaldi for the liberation of Sicily) [It]

immer schlimmer. Worse and worse; from bad to worse [G]

Imp. See *Imperator*

impasto. Application of very thick oil-color to the surface of a canvas [It]

Impatiens. Genus of Snapweed or Touch-Me-Not [L]

impedimenta. Baggage; army supplies; anything impeding progress [L]

impensis. Publisher [L]

imperator. Emperor; commander [L]

imperium. Absolute power; right to command [L]

imperium in imperio. A government within a government; supreme authority delegated by another [L]

impluvium. Cistern to catch rain-water [L]

impos animi. Weak of mind [L]

impotentia coeundi. Frigidity; incapacity for sexual intercourse [L]

impotentia generandi. Sexual impotence [L]

imprenta. Printing office [Sp]

impresor. Printer [Sp]

imprimatur. Let it be printed; license to print (usually referring to that granted by the Church); sanction [L]

imprimerie. Printing office [F]

imprimeur. Printer [F]

imprimis. In the first place [L]

in absentia. In absence [L]

in actu. In the very act; in reality [L]

in aeternum. Forever [L]

in ambiguo. In doubt [L]

inamorato. See *innamorato*

In arduis virtus. Virtue in difficulties [L]

in articulo mortis. At the point of death [L]

In bello parvis momentis magni casus intercedunt. In war, important events are the results of trivial causes (Caesar) [L]

Inbrunst. Fervor; passion [G]

in camera. In chambers; in private [L]

incipitur. It is begun [L]

incisura. Lines used to deepen tones of a painting, generally in *fresco* painting [L]

In coelo quies. Rest in heaven [L]

in commendam. In trust [L]

inconnu(e). Unknown [F]

in corpore. In body or substance; in a material thing or object [L]

incunabula. "Cradle books"; volumes printed before the beginning of the 16th century, shortly after the invention of printing [L]

inde. Thence; thereupon; for that cause [L]

in delicto. In fault [L]

In Deo speramus. In God we hope (motto of Brown University) [L]

index. Pointer; indicator (*pl.* indices) [L]

Index Expurgatorius. Term applied to books marked with an asterisk in the *Index Librorum Prohibitorum*, indicating those which may not be read until corrected [L]

Index Librorum Prohibitorum. Index of Prohibited Books; list of books condemned by the authorities of the Catholic Church [L]

indiano. Spaniard who returns to Spain after residing in South America [Sp]

Indigo tinctoria. Indigo-plant from which the dye is produced [L]

in dorso. On the back [L]

in dubio. In (case of) doubt [L]

In Dulci Jubilo. In Sweet Rejoicing [L]

in duodecimo. In 12 (leaves); book consisting of sheets folded 4 times to give 12 leaves [L]

in esse. In being; in a state of existence [L]

Inest sua gratia parvis. Little things have their peculiar charm [L]

in exitu. In issue [L]

in extenso. In extended form; in full [L]

in extremis. In (the last) extremity; in the last illness; at the point of death [L]

inf. See *infra*

in facto. In the state of completion; completed [L]

In Fernem Land. In a Distant Land (*Lohengrin*, Act III; Wagner) [G]

inferno. Hell (title of the first part of Dante's *Divina Commedia*) [It]

in fieri. In being made; in process of formation or development; incomplete [L]

in fine. In the end; in short [L]

in flagrante (delicto.) Taken in the act of committing the offence; red-handed [L]

in folio. In the page; reference to once-folded sheet of printing paper giving two leaves or four pages [L]

in foro conscientiae. In the tribunal of conscience; morally rather than legally [L]

in forma pauperis. In the condition of a pauper; not liable to costs in an action [L]

infra. Below; underneath; within [L]

infra aetatem. Under age [L]

infra dig(nitatem). Beneath one's dignity [L]

infra regnum. Within the realm [L]

infulae. Small pendant bands hanging from a mitre in ecclesiastical costume [L]

in genere. In kind; in the same *genus* [L]

ingle. Boy [Y]

ingenue. Innocent; naive girl; theatrical role of such a character [F]

Inghilterra. England [It]

In Hac (Cruce) Salus. In this (cross) safety [L]

Inhalt. Content(s) [G]

Inhaltsverzeichnis. Index; table of contents [G]

in hoc. In this; in respect to this [L]

In Hoc Signo. In this sign (*i.e.* the crucifix) [L]

In hoc signo spes mea. In this sign is my hope [L]

In hoc signo vinces. In this sign (*i.e.* the cross) thou shalt conquer (motto of the Emperor Constantine) [L]

in intellectu. In the intelligence; in conception [L]

iniquum est. It is inequitable or unjust [L]

initio. At the beginning [L]

in jure. In law; according to law [L]

Injuria non excusat injuriam. One wrong does not justify another [L]

in limine. On the threshold; at the outset [L]

in loc. See *in loco*

in loco. In place; instead [L]

in loco parentis. In the place of a parent; instead of a parent [L]

in loco citato. In the place cited [L]

In lumine tuo videbimus lumen. In thy light shall we see light (Psalms, 36-9; motto of Columbia University) [L]

in medias res. Into the midst of things; into the heart of the subject; without preface or introduction [L]

in mediis rebus. In the midst of things [L]

In medio tutissimus ibis. You will go safest in the middle; a middle course is safest (Ovid) [L]

in malam partem. In a bad sense [L]

In Memoriam. In Memory (seen on epitaphs, and also the title of many elegies; Tennyson; Mary Lamb; Edwin Arnold; *etc.*) [L]

In maxima potentia minima licentia. In the greatest power there is the least freedom [L]

innamorati. Young lovers [It]

innamorato. Lover (*fem.* innamorata) [It]

innig. Inwardly; sincere, earnest; profound; subjective [G]

in nomine Dei. In the name of God [L]

in nomine Domini. In the name of the Lord [L]

inorodtsi. Aliens [R]

in nubibus. In the clouds; non-existent; vague [L]

in nuce. In a nutshell [L]

innuendo. Meaning; that is [L]

in octavo. In eight (leaves); book consisting of sheets folded twice to give 8 leaves [L]

in omnia paratus. Prepared for all things [L]

in omnibus. In all things; on all points [L]

in omnibus caritas. In all things, charity [L]

in perpetuo. In perpetuity; forever [L]

in pace. In peace [L]

in pari causa. In an equal cause [L]

in pari delicto. In equal fault [L]

in pari materia. Upon the same matter or subject [L]

in partibus infidelium. In infidel countries (*i.e.* not Roman Catholic) [L]

in perpetuum. Forever; in perpetuity [L]

in petitio principii. See *petitio principii*

in pleno. In full [L]

in posse. In possibility; potentially [L]

in primis. Among the first [L]

in principio. At the beginning [L]

in promptu. In readiness; at hand [L]

In propria causa nemo judex. No one can be judge in his own cause [L]

in propriae personae. In (one's own) person [L]

in puris naturalibus. In a state of nudity; stark naked [L]

in quarto. In four (leaves); book consisting of sheets folded twice to give 4 leaves [L]

inquisitio post mortem. Inquest after death [L]

in re. In (a) thing, *i.e.* in something existing outside the mind; in the matter of [L]

in rebus. In things [L]

in rem. Proceedings or actions against the thing rather than against a person [L]

in rerum natura. In the nature of things; in the realm of actuality [L]

I.N.R.I. See *Jesus* (or *Iesus*) *Nazarenus, etc.*

in saecula saeculorum. For ages of ages; for ever and ever [L]

insalata. Salad [It]

inscribiente. Clerk; professional letter writer [Sp]

in se. In itself [L]

in secula seculorum. For ages of ages; for ever and ever [L]

insigne. Mark (*pl.* insignia) [L]

insignia. See *insigne*

in situ. In position; at rest [L]

in solido. For the whole; as a whole [L]

insouciance. Carelessness; indifference [F]

insouciant. Careless; indifferent [F]

in specie. Specific(ally); in kind; in the same or like form [L]

instantané. Snapsnot; sketch[F]

instanter. Urgently; immediately [L]

in statu quo. In the condition in which it was [L]

in statu quo (ante). In the same situation as before [L]

Institut de France. Official name of a group of learned societies [F]

institutiones. Institutes; works containing the elements of a science; collection of laws [L]

insula. Island [L]

intaglio. Decoration cut lower than the surface of a precious stone; a stone cut in this style; a style, the reverse of the cameo; a method of printing [It]

in tantum. In so much; so far; so greatly [L]

In te, Domini, speravi. In Thee, O Lord, have I trusted [L]

integer. Whole; untouched; whole number [L]

Integer vitae scelerisque purus. Upright in life and pure of guilt (Horace) [L]

Integralista. Member of Brazilian pro-Nazi organization which was suppressed in 1938 [Port]

intellectus agens. Active intellect [L]

intellectus possibilis. Passive intellect [L]

intelligentsia. Intellectuals; the educated and cultured class [R]

in tenebris. In darkness [L]

inter. Among; between [L]

inter alia. Among other things [L]

inter alios. Between other persons [L]

Interessengemeinschaft. Community of interests; cartel; trust [G]

interim. Meanwhile; an intervening time [L]

Interlingua. See *Latino sine flexione*

intermezzo. Music played during intermission in the theater or at the opera [It]

Internationale. Song of the revolutionary working - class movement; first sung in 1871; music by Degeyter; words by Pottier [F]

inter nos. Between us [L]

internuncio. Papal minister of a class below that of *nuncio* [It]

inter pares. Between peers or equals [L]

interpellation. Formal question on policy by a member of the French Chamber of Deputies [F]

in terrorem. As a warning [L]

inter vivos. Among the living; between the living; referring to gifts given while the donor is still alive [L]

intime. Intimate [F]

in toto. On the whole; entirely [L]

intra. In; near; within [L]

intrados. Concave surface of the stones of an arch [Sp]

intra muros. Within the walls [L]

in transitu. In transit; on the way [L]

intra parietes. Between walls; among friends; out of court [L]

intrecciare. To weave or braid [It]

Introit. Entrance; introduction (of a musical composition, *etc.*); beginning of a talk; beginning of the Mass [L]

in vacuo. In a vacuum; unrelated to reality; without object; isolated [L]

Invalides. Palace designed by Mansard at the order of Louis XIV; tomb of Napoleon [F]

inverno. Winter [It]

invicem. In turn [L]

invictus. Unconquered [L]

invierno. Winter [Sp]

in vino veritas. In wine (there is) truth [L]

inzhenernoe iskusstvo. Engineering [R]

Io mi chiamo. My name is [It]

iota. 9th letter of the Greek alphabet (Iι); smallest Greek letter; minutest quantity possible; jot [Gk]

Ipomaea. Genus of the Morning-Glory [L]

Ipsa scientia potestas est. Knowledge is power (Bacon) [L]

ipse. He himself; the same [L]

Ipse dixit. He himself said (it); the master himself has spoken; a dogmatic assertion [L]

ipsissima verba. The very words; an exact quotation [L]

ipsissimis verbis. In the very words [L]

ipso facto. By the very fact; in the very nature of the deed [L]

ipso jure. By the law itself [L]

i.q. See *idem quod*

irae et lacrimae. Resentment and tears [L]

Irgun Zvai Leumi. National Military Organization; extremist Zionist group in Palestine [Heb]

Ir por lana y salir trasquilado. The deceiver is often deceived [Sp]

irredenta. See *Italia irredenta*

Iskra. Spark; revolutionary newspaper edited by Lenin [R]

iskusstvo. Art [R]

Islam. True faith; Mohammedanism [Arab]

isos. Equal [Gk]

ispolu. Half-and-half system; payment of half the harvest as rent for a farm [R]

issledovanie. Research [R]

Ita est. It is so; so it stands [L]

Ita lex scripta est. Such is the law [L]

Italia irredenta. Italy unredeemed; name applied to former Italian territory held by other powers after World War I [It]

Ita te deus adjuvet. So help you God [L]

item. Likewise [L]

Ite, missa est. Go, the service is finished; *i.e.* the Mass has been celebrated [L]

iter. Path [L]

iteratio. Repetition [L]

iterum. Again [L]

iuft. Russian leather [R]

ivre. Drunk; intoxicated [F]

Ivrit. Modern Hebrew [Heb]

iz. For; from; of [R]

izdanie. Edition; issue; publication [R]

izdatel. Publisher [R]

izquierdo. Left [Sp]

izuchenie. Study [R]

izvestyia. News; report [R]. See also *Izvestia*

Izvestia. Official newspaper of the Soviet Union, published in Moscow

izvlechenie. Extract [R]

J

j. See also under *i*

ja. Yes [G]

jabot. Frill at the neckline of a shirt or waist [F]

jacere. To throw [L]

Jacobins. Members of the French revolutionary group led by Marat, and meeting in a former Jacobin convent [F]

Jacta est alea. The die is cast [L]

jacquard. Jacquard loom (invented by Joseph-Marie Jacquard); fabric with large figured motifs woven on the loom of that name [F]

Jacquerie. Peasant mob or revolt in France, 1358 [F]

Jacques Bonhomme. Symbolic character for France, as John Bull for England [F]

Jagannatha. Juggernaut [Skr]

Jäger. Hunter [G]

Jahrbuch. Yearbook; annual [G]

Jahresbericht. Annual report [G]

jai-alai. Type of handball game played with special rackets on a three-walled court [Basque]

jaleo. Dance with accompaniment of finger-snapping, hand-clapping, and shouted or chanted phrases [Sp]

jamás. Never; ever [Sp]

jamais. Never [F]

jambe. Leg; shank; stem [F]

jambon. Ham [F]

jamón. Ham [Sp]

jam satis. Already enough [L]

Janus. Two-faced Roman god whose temple was opened in time of war and closed in time of peace [L]

japonaiseries. Japanese objects of art [F]

Jarabe Tapatío. Mexican Hat Dance [Sp]

jardin. Garden [F]

Jardin des Plantes. Botanical Gardens (in Paris) [F]

jardinière. Mixed vegetables in their own sauce; richly decorated flower vase [F]

jaune. Yellow [F]

Jawohl! Yes indeed; yes, sir! [G]

Je Crois Entendre Encore. I Hear as in a Dream (*Pearl Fishers*, Act I; Bizet) [F]

jehad. War against unbelievers; holy war or crusade; Mohammedan Holy War [Arab]

Je me fie en Dieu. I trust in God [F]

jen. Man; true manhood; virtue; the golden rule; love of all men and things [C]

Je ne sais quoi. I know not what; an indescribable something [F]

Je réserve la suite. I reserve (decision pending) what follows; I am not responsible for the consequences [F]

Jérez. Sherry (town in southwestern Spain, noted for its sherry wine) [Sp]

Jesus, hominum Salvator. Jesus, Savior of mankind [L]

Jesus Nazarenus Rex Judaeorum. Jesus of Nazareth, King of the Jews (inscription on the cross of Christ) [L]

jeté. Thrown; ballet step with both feet off the floor simultaneously and receipt of the descending weight on one foot [F]

jeton. Gambling chip [F]

jeu. Play (*pl.* jeux) [F]

jeu d'esprit. Intelligence game; play of wits; general term for charades, puzzles, tongue-twisters, quizzes, *etc.* [F]

jeune premier. Juvenile lead [F]

jeunesse. Youth [F]

jeunesse dorée. Gilded youth; young elegants [F]

jeu parti. Debate poem [F]

jeu(x). Game(s) [F]

jeux de bourse. Speculation on the stock exchange [F]

jícara. Small cup [Sp]

jihad. See *jehad*

jinnee. Reincarnated spirit in human or animal form (*fem.* jinneeyeh; *pl.* jinn) [Arab]

jinrickisha. Man-drawn two-wheeled carriage [J]

jipi-japa. "Panama" hat (manufactured in Ecuador and Colombia [Sp]

jiva. Life; the individual soul [Skr]

jodhpur. Short riding boot; name of a state in India

Johannisberger. A Rhine wine [G]

Johannistag. Midsummer day [G]

joie de vivre. Joy in living [F]

joli(e). Pretty; beautiful [F]

jongleur. Minstrel; juggler [F]

jornada. Day's journey [Sp]

jota. Regional dance of Aragon, Spain [Sp]

jour. Day [F]

jour de fête. Festival; birthday [F]

journal intime. Intimate diary; confessional [F]

joven. Youth; young (man) [Sp]

jube. Loft or gallery of a church [F]

Jubilate. O be joyful [L]

Juchtenleder. Russian leather [G]

Judaeus. Jew [L]

Jude. Jew [G]

Judenhetze. Organized persecution of the Jews [G]

judex. Judge (*pl.* judices) [L]

jueves. Thursday [Sp]

Jueves Santo. Holy Thursday [Sp]

Jugend. Youth [G]

juglans. Butternut tree [L]

juglans nigra. Black walnut [L]

jugum. Yoke [L]

Juif. Jew [F]

Juive. Jewess [F]

julienne. Referring to clear vegetable soup with vegetables cut in strips; fried potatoes cut in thin, match-like strips [F]

Juncta juvant. Alta petit. Union is strength. It seeks the heights (motto of Cincinnati University) [L]

Jungfrau. Virgin; maiden [G]

Jüngling. Youth; youngster [G]

Junimea. Youth Party [Rumanian]

Junker. East Prussian nobleman; member of the landed gentry [G]

Junkers. Type of heavy bomber or transport plane [G]

Juno. Consort of Jupiter; Latin equivalent of *Hera* [L]

junta. Administrative or legislative council [It] [Sp]; Secret political council; faction [L]; Committee; convention; union [Sp]

Junta Política. Political coalition of 50 party-leaders who founded the *Falange Española Tradicionalista* [Sp]

junto. Group banded together for a political plot [Sp]

jupe. Skirt; petticoat [F]

Jupiter. Ruler of the gods; Latin equivalent of *Zeus* [L]

Jupiter pluvius. Jupiter of the rain; reference to rainy weather [L]

jupon. Petticoat [F]

jura. Rights; laws (*pl.* of *jus*) [L]

Jura naturae sunt immutabilia. The laws of nature are unchangeable [L]

jura regalia. Royal rights [L]

jure. By right; by the law [L]

jure belli. By the law of war [L]

jure divino. By divine right [L]

jure gentium. By the law of nations [L]

jurer. To swear [F]

juris. Of right; of law [L]

Juris praecepta sunt haec: honeste vivere; alterum non laedere; suum cuique tribuere. The precepts of the law are these: to live honorably; to hurt nobody; to render to everyone his due [L]

jus. Right; justice; law [L]

jus belli. Law of war [L]

jus canonicum. Canon law [L]

jus civile. Civil law [L]

jus civitatus. Right of citizenship [L]

jus et norma loquendi. The law and rule of speaking; common usage [L]

Jus ex injuria non oritur. Right does not rise out of wrong [L]

jus gentium. Law of nations [L]

jus in re. A right in a thing [L]

jusjurandum. Oath [L]

jus non scriptum. Unwritten law [L]

jus primae noctis. The right of the first night; the right of a lord to spend the first night with the bride of his vassal [L]

jusqu'à. Up to; until [F]

jus soli. Law of the soil; rule of a child's nationality being determined by place of birth [L]

jus sanguinis. Law of the blood; rule of a child's nationality being determined by parentage [L]

juste milieu. Golden mean [F]

justitia. Justice; jurisdiction; office of a judge [L]

justitia omnibus. Justice for all (motto of the District of Columbia) [L]

juvenis. Youth [L]

juxta. Near; following; according to [L]

K

k. See also under *c*

kabuki. Operetta [J]

kaddish. Prayer for the dead [Heb]

kadi. Mohammedan judge [Arab]

kadoches. Fever [Heb]

kadrilj. A Swedish folk-dance [Swed]

Kaffeeklatsch. Gab-fest [G]

Kagda? When? [R]

Kahk pajivayiti? How are you? [R]

Kahn. Boat [G]

kai. And [Gk]

Kaiser. Emperor [G]

kakemono. Hanging picture (having a rod at the lower end so that it can be rolled up) [J]

kala. Creatorship; authorship; time [Skr]

Kalb. Calf [G]

Kalevala. Finnish epic

kalmia latifolia. Mountain laurel [L]

kalpana. Imagination [Skr]

Kalte Hände, warmes Herz. A cold hand, a warm heart [G]

kama. Desire [Skr]

kamarinskaia. A lively dance for men [R]

Kamerad. Comrade (interjection of German soldier wishing to surrender) [G]

kami. Holiness; spirit; divinity; anything that inspires and overawes with a sense of holiness [J]

kamikaze. Divine wind; suicide dive-bomber pilot; tactics of suicide bombing [J]

Kammer. Chamber [G]

Kampf. Battle; struggle; conflict [G]

Kampf ums Dasein. Struggle for existence [G]

kanklys. A peasant harp [Lettish]

Kann er was? Can he do anything? Does he know anything? [G]

kanon. Rule [Gk]

kaolin(e). Clay used for making fine porcelain; porcelain ware made of this clay [C]

Kapellmeister. Band or orchestra leader; director of music in a chorus or orchestra [G]

kappa. 10th letter of the Greek alphabet (Kϰ)

Kapelle. Chapel; orchestra; band [G]

Kapp Putsch. Reactionary attempt to overthrow the German Republic in March 1920, led by Wolfgang Kapp [G]

kapusti. Cabbage [R]

kaputt. Done; lost; spoiled; broken [G]

karakul. A short, curly-haired fur; Persian lamb [Place]

karana. Cause [Skr]

karandash. Pencil [R]

kardia. Heart [Gk]

karma. Action, movement; deed; cause; in Indian philosophy, the law of retribution determining the nature and circumstances of incarnation [Skr]

karpos. Fruit [Gk]

Kartenlegerin. Fortune teller [G]

Kartoffelklösse. Potato dumplings [G]

kartoshki. Potatoes [R]

kasha. Steamed buckwheat groats [R]

kasher. Right (with respect to dietary laws) [Heb]

Kasten. Box; chest; coffer; crate [G]

kata-. Down; against; through; concerning [Gk]. See also under *cata-*

kategorikos. Affirmative; predicative [Gk]

kat' exochen. Pre-eminently; *par excellence* [Gk]

katharsis. Purification; purgation; the purging of the emotions of pity and fear effected by tragedy, according to Aristotle's theory [Gk]

katholikos. Universal [Gk]

katok. Calendar [R]

Katori chas? What time is it? [R]

Katzenjammer. Hangover [G]

Kauderwelsch. Jargon; gibberish [G]

Kauf. Purchase [G]

Kauf ist Kauf. A bargain is a bargain [G]

kavass. Policeman; servant [Turk]

kavya. Poetic composition [Skr]

Kdyz mne stará matka. Songs My Mother Taught Me (Dvorak) [Czech]

keddah. Elephant hunt [Hindu]

Keine Antwort ist auch eine Antwort. Silence gives consent [G]

Kellner. Waiter [G]

Kennst du das Land, wo die Zitronen blühn? Knowst thou the land where the lemon trees bloom? (opening lines of Mignon's song in Goethe's *Wilhelm Meister*) [G]

kephale. Head [Gk]

képi. Straight-peaked cap [F]

Keren Hayesod. National Foundation Fund (for Palestine) [Heb]

Kerl. Fellow [G]

kermis. Fair [Du]

Kern. Kernel; nucleus [G]

Kessel. Boiler; cauldron; pot; pocket of terrain [G]

kevala. Alone [Skr]

kh-. See also *ch-*

khan. Ruler or official in Central Asia [Turk]

khasi. Method of mural decoration in India and Persia; a type of mosaic work [Skr]

khavyar. See *caviar*

Khedive. Viceroy of Egypt [Turk]

khidmutgar. Table servant [Hindu]

khmer. Architectural monuments of ancient Cambodia [Pers]

kholst. Linen [R]

khutor. Tract of land [R]

khvostism. Following from behind [R]

kibbutz. Co-operative settlement [Heb]

kibitzer. Heckler; card-game watcher; one who offers unsolicited advice [Y]

Kieselguhr. A fine earth used for industrial purposes [G]

kilki. Anchovies [R]

kilogramme. Kilogram=1,000 grams=2.2 lbs. [F]

kilomètre. 1,000 meters=1,093 yards [F]

Kimpai. Imperial Japanese secret military police [J]

kin. A string instrument [C]

Kindergarten. Children's garden; class for pre-grade school children [G]

Kinder, Küche, Kirche. Children, kitchen, church (province of women in German nationalistic doctrine) [G]

Kindermärchen. (Children's) fairy tale(s) [G]

Kinderspiel. Child's play [G]

Kinderstück. Children's Piece; musical composition for children [G]

kinesis. Motion; change [Gk]

kinnor. Lyre or harp [Heb]

kiosque. Small circular or polygonal structure surmounted by a dome [Turk]

Kirche. Church [G]

Kirchhof. Churchyard [G]

Kirsche. Cherry [G]

Kirschwasser. Cherry water; cherry brandy or liqueur [G]

kishkes. Intestines [Y]

kismet. Fate; destiny [Turk]

kithara. An ancient string-instrument [Gk]

Kladderadatsch. Slap-Bang! (name of a comic paper) [G]

Klage. Complaint; plaint; lament [G]

Klang. Sound [C]

Klarheit. Clarity [G]

Klavier. Piano [G]

Kleider machen Leute. Fine feathers make fine birds; clothes make the man [G]

klein. Little; small [G]

Kleinbürger. Member of lower middle class; *petit bourgeois* [G]

Kleinbürgertum. Lower middle class; *petite bourgeoisie* [G]

kleptomania. Pathological urge to steal [Gk]

Kletterschuhe. Climbing shoes; mountaineer's boots [G]

klino. Bend [Gk]

Knesset. Parliament [Heb]

kniga. Book [R]

Knittelvers. Short verse-form in rhymed couplets with 4 stresses and 8 or 9 syllables [G]

knout. Whip [R]

Kobold. Brownie; elf; spirit (living in mines) [G]

kodashim. Holy things [Heb]

kohl. Antimony powder used to darken eyelids [Arab]

Kohlrabi. A variety of cabbage [G]

koinai ennoiai. Common notions; *i.e.* good, evil, existence of God, *etc.* [Gk]

koiné. Branch of a language common to an area [Gk]

koinos. Common [Gk]

koinos bios. Common life [Gk]

koinos topos. Common or general topic; commonplace; commonly accepted point of view [Gk]

Kokuikai. State Strength Society; unofficial planning group for economic policy [J]

kolia. A type of *danse du ventre* [Gk]

Köln. (City of) Cologne [G]

Kol Nidre(i). All vows [Heb]

Kölnisch(es) Wasser. See *eau de Cologne*

kolo. A peasant dance [Serbian]

Kommandatura. Inter-allied governing authority of Berlin after World War II; military occupation headquarters [R]

Komm', Süsser Tod. Come, Sweet Death (Bach) [G]

Komsomol. Communist youth organization [R]

König. King [G]

Konditorei, Pastry shop [G]

konsequent. Consistent [G]

konsequenter Naturalismus. Consistent or absolute naturalism [G]

Kontrabass. Double-bass viol or "bull fiddle" [G]

Konzentrationslager. Concentration camp [G]

Konzertmeister. Chief violinist of an orchestra [G]

Konzertstück. Concerto; concert-piece [G]

kooperativnyi. Co-operative [R]

kopek. One-hundredth of a *ruble* [R]

kopje. Small hill [Du]

kopros. Dung [Gk]

Koran. Book; the sacred book of the Mohammedans [Arab]

koros. Satiety [Gk]

kosher. Adhering to Jewish dietary laws; legitimate; approved; correct [Y]. See also *kasher*

kosmos. World [Gk]

kothornos. See *cothurnus*

kotleti. Hamburgers [R]

koulebiaka. Meat or cabbage pie [R]

kourbash. Whip [Turk]

ko wu. Investigation of things [C]

kozatski. Cossack dance [R]

Kraft. Force; power; strength [G]

Kraft durch Freude. Strength through Joy (Nazi morale organization) [G]

kräftig. Powerful; strong; forceful; energetic [G]

Krähe. Crow; raven [G]

krakowiak. A dance in 2-4 rhythm [Polish]

Krasnaya Svezda. Red Star; publication of the Russian army [R]

krasnyi. Red [R]

krateros. Strong [Gk]

kratkii obzor. Abstract [R]

Kraut. Herb; abbr. of *Sauerkraut*; derisive term for German (soldier) [G]

Kredit-Anstalt. Credit institution; Vienna banking institution which failed in June 1931 [G]

Kreis. Circle; group; clique; region; county [G]

Kremlin. Citadel of Moscow; center of Soviet administration; synonym for Soviet government [R]

kreutzer. Austrian copper coin [G]

Kreuz. Cross [G]

Kreuz und Krone. Cross and Crown; Pain and Sorrow (Bach) [G]

Kreuzzug. Crusade [G]

Krieg. War [G]

Kriegsgefangener. Prisoner of war [G]

Kriegspiel. War game; maneuvers [G]

Krishna. Deity of India; one of the embodiments of *Vishnu* [Skr]

Kritik der reinen Vernunft. Critique of Pure Reason (title of a philosophical work by Kant) [G]

Kritik der Urteilskraft. Critique of Judgment (Kant) [G]

kritikon. Sensory discrimination [Gk]

krona. Unit of currency in Sweden

krone. Unit of currency in Denmark and Norway

krotala. Clappers, used to accompany dancers [Gk]

kuan hua. Speech of officials; Mandarin Chinese [C]

Kuchen. Cake [G]

kudos. Glory [Gk]

Kugellager. Ball-bearing [G]

kukri. Gurkha curved knife [Hindu]

kulak. Middle-class farm owner employing hired labor at a profit [R]

Kultur. Culture (as a spiritual concept; often distinguished from civilization, a more material concept) [G]

Kulturbund. Cultural league or union [G]

Kulturgeschichte. History of culture or civilization [G]

Kulturkammer. Chamber of culture (Nazi government agency in control of cultural activities) [G]

Kulturkampf. Cultural struggle; Prussian struggle in 1870's and 1880's to bring the Catholic Church under State domination [G]

kumbaloi. Cymbals, used by the ancient Greeks [Gk]

Kümmel. Caroway seed or *liqueur* [G]

kung. Respect; courtesy; politeness [C]

Kunst. Art [G]

Kunstgeschichte. History of art [G]

Kunstlehre. Theory of art; esthetics [G]

Künstler. Artist [G]

Kunstlied. Art-song; a lyrical form of vocal music in which music is set for an entire poem rather than having the same music repeated for each stanza [G]

Kunstmärchen. Literary tale [G]

Kunstwerk. Work of art [G]

Kuomintang. National People's Party; National Party Government [C]

Kupferstich. Copper-plate engraving [G]

kuritsi. Chicken [R]

Kursaal. Building or hall for those visiting a health resort[G]

Kürze ist der Rede Würze. Brevity is the soul of wit [G]

kuznitsa. Blacksmith shop; smithy [R]

kyanous. Blue [Gk]

kylin. Design of a dragon; symbol of good omen [C]

Kyrie Eleison. Lord, have mercy (section of the Mass) [Gk]

kyrielle. Verse-form in couplets [F]

L

l'. The (in phrases, see also below succeeding word) [F] [It]

L. Fifty [L]. See also *libra*

la. The (in phrases, see also below succeeding word) [F] [It] [Sp]

laager. Encampment; wagons in defensive circle [Du]

labarum. A standard, carried in war before Roman emperors [L]

labia. Lip [L]

La Bohème. Bohemia; opera by Puccini, 1898, depicting life among the bohemian artists of the *Quartier Latin* in Paris [F]. See also *La Vie de Bohème*

Laborare est orare. To labor is to pray (motto of the Benedictine monks) [L]

Labor est etiam ipsa voluptas. Labor is pleasure itself [L]

Labor omnia vincit. Labor conquers all (motto of the Universities of Illinois and Oklahoma) [L]

L'Aborrita Rivale A Me Sfuggia. My detested rival has escaped me (*Aida*, Act IV, Verdi) [It]

Lac des Cygnes. Swan Lake; a ballet by Tchaikowsky [F]

La Calunnia. Slander (*Barber of Seville*, Act I, Rossini) [It]

lacerna. Loose garment worn by the Romans over the *toga* [L]

lâche. Loose; slack; sluggish; coward(ly) [F]

Là Ci Darem La Mano. Give Me Your Hand (*Don Giovanni*, Act I, Mozart) [It]

La caridad bien ordenada empieza por uno mismo. Charity begins at home [Sp]

La Cathédrale Engloutie. The Sunken Cathedral (Debussy) [F]

laconicum. Hot-room in ancient baths [Gk]

La costumbre es otra naturaleza. Habit is second nature [Sp]

Lacrima Christi. Tear of Christ; name of an Italian wine [L]

lacuna. Ditch; furrow; gap (*pl.* lacunae) [L]

Laden. Shop; store [G]

Ladino. Jew descended from Spanish refugees of 1492; dialect spoken in Switzerland [Sp]

ladno. All right [R]

La Donna E Mobile. Woman is Fickle (*Rigoletto*, Act IV; Verdi) [It]

ladrón. Thief; cutpurse [Sp]

laelia. Variety of orchid [L]

laesa majestas. Lese-majesty; injured majesty; high treason [L]

laesio. Injury [L]

La fame non vuol leggi. Hunger knows no law [It]

La Fille Aux Cheveux De Lin. The Maiden with the Flaxen Hair (Debussy) [F]

lag. Law [Swed]
lagarto. Lizard [Sp]
Lager. Camp; store; storage; bearing or pillow block; light beer [G]
La Gioconda. Mona Lisa (wife of Francesco del Giocondo, painted by Da Vinci) [It]
La Giovine Italia. Young Italy; secret society led by Mazzini, working for Italian liberation [It]
lai. Romantic tale; love poem [OF]
laicus. Layman [L]
laid(e). Ugly [F]
laine. Wool [F]
laissez aller. Lack of constraint; freedom of manners or conduct [F]
Laissez donc! Nonsense! [F]
laissez faire. Let things go (as they may); let one do (as he will); classical economic theory that economic matters will take care of themselves without regulation by the state [F]
lait. Milk [F]
laitue. Lettuce [F]
La Juive. The Jewess (title of an opera by Halévy) [F]
lakh. 100,000 *rupees* [Skr]
La letra con sangre entra. Spare the rod and spoil the child [Sp]
L'Allegro. Cheerfulness; liveliness (title of a poem by Milton) [It]
lama. Buddhist priest [Thibetan]
lambda. 11th letter of the Greek alphabet (Λλ)
lamé. Trimmed with gold or silver leaf; a fabric using metal threads [F]
lamentoso. Lamenting, sorrowful, mournful [It]
L'amour est un oiseau. Love is like a bird (*Carmen*, Act I; Bizet) [F]
L'Amour Sorcier. See *El Amor Brujo*
Länder. States; provinces [G]

Ländler. Country dance [G]
Landser. Doughboy (World War I) [G]
Landsturm. Home Guard; Reserves [G]
Landwehr. Home Guard; Reserves [G]
Landwirtschaft. Agriculture [G]
La necesidad carece de ley. Necessity knows no law [Sp]
langouste. Lobster; crayfish [F]
langsam. Slow(ly) [G]
langue. Tongue; language [F]
langue de chat. Cat's tongue (a confectionery) [F]
langue d'oc. Historical name for the language of southern France [F]
langue d'oïl. Historical name for the language of northern France [F]
languendo. Languishing [It]
lanku. Primitive African instrument resembling a guitar [L]
La nuit, tous les chats sont gris. All cats are grey in the dark [F]
lanza. Lance [Sp]
Laocoon. Priest who warned the Trojans not to accept the Greeks' gift of the wooden horse; represented as being devoured by serpents together with his two sons [Gk]
lapin. Rabbit [F]
lapis. Stone [L]
lapis-lazuli. An opaque blue stone veined with white [ ]
La Plus Que Lente-Valse. As Slowly as Possible-Waltz (Debussy) [F]
La pobreza no es vileza. Poverty is no crime [Sp]
L'appétit vient en mangeant. The more you eat, the more you want [F]
L'Apprenti Sorcier. See *Zauberlehrling*
La Prensa. Press; newspaper in Argentina; Spanish daily in New York City [Sp]

lapsus calami. Slip of the pen; clerical error [L]

lapsus linguae. Slip of the tongue [L]

lapsus memoriae. Lapse of memory [L]

lapsus pennae. Slip of the pen [L]

la race, le milieu, et le moment. Race, environment, time; three aspects by which Taine explained the quality of a culture [F]

lararium. Shrine in which the Romans placed images of the *lares et penates*, household gods [L]

lardon. Strip of bacon [F]

la reata. Quirt; riding-whip [Sp]

La Reine de Saba. The Queen of Sheba (Gounod) [F]

lares et penates. Household gods; spirits of deceased persons supposed to protect every Roman house; guardian angels [L]

largamente. Broadly; with fullness [It]

l'argent. Money [F]

larghetto. A tempo somewhat faster than *largo* [It]

largo. A broad, slow tempo [It]

Largo Al Factotum. Room for the Factotum (*Barber of Seville*, Act I; Rossini) [It]

larix. Larch tree [L]

larix laricina. Tamarack [L]

larmoyant(e). Tearful; sentimental [F]

l'art pour l'art. Art for art's sake [F]

larva. Ghost (*pl.* larvae) [L]

lasagne. Strips of macaroni [It]

Lascia Ch'Io Pianga. Leave Me to Languish (Handel) [It]

Lasciate ogni speranza, voi ch'entrate. All hope abandon, ye who enter here (Dante, *Inferno*, 3-9) [It]

Lasciate Mi Morire. Let Me Die [It]

lashkar. Camp; body of armed tribesmen [Hindu]

lassus. Weary [L]

lata culpa. Gross negligence [L]

latere. To be hidden [L]

lathyrus adoratus. Sweet Pea [L]

latine. In Latin [L]

Latino sine flexione. Latin without inflections; auxiliary language devised by Peano in 1903

lator. Bearer; messenger; maker of laws [L]

latro. Robber; thief [L]

latte. Milk [It]

lauda. Medieval Italian song to the Lord (*pl.* laudi) [It]

laudare. To name, cite, or quote; to show one's title or authority [L]

laudatio. Praise; laudatory poem [L]

laudator temporis acti. Praiser of the past; one who lauds the good old times (Horace; *Ars Poetica*; 1-173) [L]

laudo. Praise [L]

lau lau. Beef, pork, and fish mixture [Hawaian]

laurier. Laurel [F]

Lausbub(e). Rascal [G]

laus Deo. Praise be to God [L]

Laut. Sound [G]

lavabo. Lavatory; washroom [L]

Lavandula. Lavender [L]

L'Avare. The Miser (play by Molière) [F]

lavandera. Laundress [Sp]

l'avenir. Future [F]

la vie. Life [F]

La Vie de Bohème. Bohemian Life; dramatization of Murger's novel, *Scènes de la Vie de Bohème*, 1849; source of the libretto for Puccini's *La Bohème* [F]

lazo. Bond; tie [Sp]

Lazurstein. Ultramarine [G]

lazzarone. Neapolitan loafer and beggar [It]

lazzo. Improvised trick (*pl.* lazzi) [It]

lb. See *libra*

l.c. See *loco citato*

le. The (in phrases, see also below succeeding word) [F]

Le Barbier de Séville. The Barber of Seville (title of a play by Beaumarchais; an opera based on it by Rossini) [F]

Le Bateau Ivre. The Drunken Ship (title of a poem by Rimbaud) [F]

Leben. Life [G]

Leben Sie wohl! Farewell! [G]

Lebensraum. Living space [G]

Leberwurst. Liverwurst [G]

lebhaft. Lively; animated [G]

l'échafaud. The scaffold [F]

lecteur. Reader [F]

lectio difficilior. The harder reading; principle of choice between two variant readings in manuscripts [L]

lecture. Reading [F]

lecythus. Greek vase ornamented with figures [Gk]

Leder. Leather [G]

leer. Empty; vacant [G]

lega. Alloy [It]

legatissimo. Extremely smooth and fluent [It]

legato. Bound; smooth; with no pause between notes [It]

legatura. Binding [It]

legein. Discourse [Gk]

leges. See *lex* [L]

legge. Law [It]

leggiero. Light; easy; delicate [It]

Légion d'Honneur. Military and civil order established by Napoleon; granted also to foreign citizens for service to France [F]

lego. Say [Gk]

Legum Baccalaureus. Bachelor of Laws [L]

Legum Doctor. Doctor of Laws [L]

legumi. Vegetables [It]

Lehrbuch. Textbook [G]

Lehre. Theory; doctrine; lesson [G]

Lehrgedicht. Didactic poem [G]

Lehrling. Apprentice [G]

Lehrtheater. Didactic theatre [G]

Leiche. Corpse; body [G]

Leid. Sorrow; suffering; injury [G]

Leiden des jungen Werthers. Sorrows of Young Werther (title of a novel by Goethe; 1774) [G]

Leidenschaft. Passion; suffering [G]

leidenschaftlich. Passionate(ly) [G]

Leinwand. Linen; canvas; cloth [G]

Leise Flehen Meine Lieder. Softly My Songs Implore (Schubert's *Serenade*) [G]

Leitfaden. Guide; manual [G]

Leitmotiv. Guiding theme or motive, characteristic of Wagnerian music; any recurrent theme in a poem or narrative [G]

lejos. Far [Sp]

Le Juif Errant. The Wandering Jew; an ancient French song [F]

lekidoi. Small cymbals, used by the ancient Greeks [Gk]

L'Elisir D'Amore. The Elixir of Love (Donizetti) [It]

Le Métro. Paris subway [F]

lemniscus. Fillet worn by the Greeks [Gk]

lempira. Monetary unit of Honduras [Sp]

lengua. Language; tongue [Sp]

lento. Slow; a slow tempo, between *adagio* and *andante* [It]

Lenz. Spring [G]

Leo. Lion [L]

lepus. Hare [L]

Le Rêve. The Dream (*Manon*, Act II; Massenet) [F]

Le Rire. Laughter; the comical (title of a work by Bergson) [F]

Le roi est mort; vive le roi! The king is dead; long live the king! [F]

Le roi s'avisera. The king will take the matter under advisement [F]

Le Roman Expérimental. The Experimental Novel (essays by Zola; 1880) [F]

les. The (*pl.*) (in phrases, see also below succeeding word) [F]

lesche. Ancient building having covered courts with porticoes [Gk]

lèse-majesté. Treason [F]

Le Sette Giornate del Mondo. The Seven Days of the World (Tasso; 1607) [It]

Le Soldat Inconnu. The Unknown Soldier [F]

lesovodstvo. Forestry [R]

Le style, c'est l'homme. Style is the man (often misquoted for *Le style est l'homme même*) [F]

Le style est l'homme même. Style is the man himself (Buffon) [F]

L'état, c'est moi! I am the state! (Louis XIV) [F]

leto. Summer [R]

l'étoile du nord. The North Star (motto of Minnesota) [F]

letopisi. Annals [R]

letrado. Advocate [Sp]

letto. Bed [It]

lettre de cachet. Letter issued by the kings of France authorizing imprisonment of a person without legal process [F]

lettre de créance. Letter of credit [F]

lettre de récréance. Recredential; letter of appreciation and credential for departure, issued to a diplomat [F]

leukos. White [Gk]

levaya. Funeral [Heb]

levée. Early reception held by a person of high rank [F]

levée en masse. Spontaneous armed rising by civilians to resist an invader [F]

levis. Light; slight; trifling [L]

Levizje Nacional Clirimtare. Albanian resistance movement in World War II

lex. Law (*pl.* leges) [L]

Lex est dictatem rationis. Law is the dictate of reason [L]

lex loci. Law of the place [L]

Lex, Lux. Law, Light (motto of Emory University) [L]

lex non scripta. Unwritten law [L]

lex sacramentalis. Purgation by oath [L]

lex salica. The Salic law; legal code of the Salian Franks (5th century) [L]

lex talionis. Law of retaliation; an eye for an eye [L]

ley. Law [Sp]

lezginka. Oriental dance of the Caucasus [R]

L'Heure Exquise. The Enchanted Hour (Verlaine-Hahn) [F]

l'homme. Man [F]

li. Reason; law; the rational principle; code of manners; profit; benefit [C]

liaison. Linking; affair; go-between; connection; facilities and personnel for inter-communication and co-ordination [F]

lib. See *liber*

libellus. Small book; publication; journal; pamphlet; libel [L]

libellus divortii. Bill of divorcement [L]

libellus famosus. Defamatory publication [L]

libellus rerum. Inventory [L]

libellus supplex. Petition [L]

liber. Book; chapter; free [L]

libera arbitria. Free decisions [L]

liber evangeliorum. Gospel book [L]

libertad. Liberty; freedom [Sp]

libertas. Liberty; freedom; franchise; privilege [L]

libertas arbitrii. Freedom of choice [L]

Liberté, Egalité, Fraternité. Liberty, Equality, Fraternity; slogan of the French Revolution [F]

liber judiciarum. Book of judgment; doom-book [L]

liberum arbitrium. Free choice [L]

liberum arbitrium indifferentiae. Freedom of indifference; ability of the will to choose, independently of antecedent determination [L]

liberum voluntatis arbitrium. Free choice of the will [L]

Libiam Nei Lieti Calici. A Bumper We'll Drain (*La Traviata*, Act I; Verdi) [It]

libido. Lust; sexual drive or impulse, suppression of which leads to psychoneurosis [L]

libra. Pound; English unit of currency; balance [L]

libraio. Bookseller [It]

librairie. Book shop; book trade [F]

libre. Free [F]

librejo. Pamphlet [Sp]

libretto. Book; words of an opera (*pl.* libretti) [It]

libro. Book [It] [Sp]

Libro cerrado no saca letrado. A closed book does not produce a learned man [Sp]

licenciado. Licentiate (in jurisprudence); attorney [Sp]

licentia. License; permission [L]

licentia vatum. Poetic license [L]

licenza. Licence; freedom of style or interpretation [It]

licet. It is allowed; although; notwithstanding [L]

lictor. Binder; officer who

walked before a Roman magistrate [L]

Lidice. Czech town exterminated by the Nazis in World War II as a retaliatory measure; any ruthless extermination of an entire community

Liebe. Love [G]

Liebchen. Dearest; sweetheart [G]

Liebesfreud'. Joy of Love [G]

Liebesleid. Sorrow of Love [G]

Liebeslied. Love Song [G]

Liebeslieder Walzer. Love-Song Waltzes (Brahms) [G]

Liebestod. Love Death (*Tristan und Isolde*, Act III; Wagner) [G]

Liebestraum. Dream of Love (Liszt) [G]

Liebesverbot. Forbidden Love (title of an opera by Wagner) [G]

Lied. Song; a type of song having a close union of the music with the words, and an attempt to express in tones the subjective mood or feeling of the poem [G]

Liederkranz. Singing circle; a type of *Limburger* cheese [G]

liefern. To deliver [G]

Lieferung. Delivery; fascicle; number; part [G]

lienzo. Linen [Sp]

lieu. Place [F]

lieu d'aisance. Lavatory; toilet [F]

ligare. To bind [L]

ligna et lapides. Sticks and stones [L]

lignum. Wood; firewood [L]

lignum vitae. Wood of life; a hard, tropical wood [L]

Lilium candidum. Madonna Lily; Annunciation or Lent Lily [L]

Lilium longiflorum. Easter Lily [L]

Lilium pardalinum. Leopard or Panther Lily [L]

Lilium tigrinum. Tiger Lily [L]

Lille. City in France; bobbin lace made there [F]

Limburger. Cheese having a strong odor, disagreeable to some people [G]

Limoges. City in France; fine enamel work or pottery made in that city [F]

limosna. Alms [Sp]

linea. Line; line of descent [L]

linea recta. Straight, direct, or vertical line [L]

Lindenbaum. Linden Tree (Schubert) [G]

linge. Linen [F]

lingerie. Silken underthings [F]

lingua franca. International or auxiliary language; mixed language spoken in parts of Tunisia and Tripolitania; any common language spoken by people of different nationalities [L]

lingua romanica. European Latin of the 7th century [L]

Linke. Left hand [G]

links. Left; to or on the left [G]

Linosyris. Goldilocks; a perennial flower [L]

linum. Flax [L]

liquet. It is clear or apparent [L]

liqueur. Thick, sweetened alcoholic drink [F]

lira. Italian unit of currency (*pl. lire*) [It]

lire. To read [F]. *Pl.* of *lira* [It]

liriodendron. Species of poplar [L]

lis. Controversy; dispute; lawsuit [L]

lit. Bed [F]

litera. Letter (*pl.* literae) [L]

literae. Letters; literature [L]

literae humaniores. Humane letters; studies including Greek, Latin, philology, logic, ethics, metaphysics, *etc.* [L]

literae scriptae manent. Written words last [L]

literati. The learned; literary men [L]

literatum. Literally [L]

Literaturwissenschaft. Science of literature; methodical investigation of literature [G]

Litfass-säule. Advertizing pillar (Litfass was the inventor) [G]

lithocolla. Cement or adhesive used by gem cutters [Gk]

lithoglyph. An engraved gem [Gk]

lithos. Stone [Gk]

lithostrotum. Mosaic pavement of colored marble [Gk]

litotes. Expression of an affirmative by denial of its contrary; *e.g.* "he's not a bad sort" [Gk]

litre. Unit of capacity, equal to the volume of 1 kilogram of pure water at a temperature of 4° C. =10 pints=0.22 gallon [F]

Litt.D. See *Litterarum Doctor*

litterae humaniores. See *Literae humaniores*

Litterae sine moribus vanae. Literature without character is vain (motto of the University of Pennsylvania) [L]

Litterarum Doctor. Doctor of Literature [L]

littérateur. Man of letters [F]

littérature comparée. Comparative literature [F]

Litteris dedicta et omnibus artibus. Dedicated to literature and all the arts (motto of the University of Nebraska) [L]

litus. Bank; shore; coast [L]

lituus. Twisted wand used by augurs among the ancients [L]

Livorno. Leghorn [It]

livraison. Delivery; fascicle; number; part [F]

livre. Book; pound [F]

livre à clef. Book in which actual persons figure under fictitious names [F]

livro. Book [Port]

llanos. Flat plains of the Orinoco River [Sp]

LL.B. See *Legum Baccalaureus*

LL.D. See *Legum Doctor*

L.N.C. See *Levizje, etc.*

lo. The (in phrases, see also below succeeding word) [It]

loa. Praise; prologue [Sp]

locandiera. Hostess; innkeeper; landlady [It]

locataire. Tenant; renter; lessee [F]

loc. cit. See *loco citato*

loco. Place [It]

loco citato. In the place or passage cited [L]

locomotor ataxia. Trembling or unsteadiness of limbs [Gk]

loco parentis. See *in loco parentis*

Locos y niños dicen la verdad. Children and fools speak the truth [Sp]

locum tenens. Holding a place (for someone else); a deputy [L]

locus. Place (*pl.* loci) [L]

locus classicus. Classical source [L]

locus delicti. Place where an offense was committed [L]

locus standi. Attitude in a matter that justifies participation [L]

lodevole. Excellent [It]

loge. Box in a theatre [F]

loggia. Gallery or portico projecting from a building; paintings used to decorate a loggia [It]

logodaedalus. One who is artful or tricky in the use of words [Gk]

logomachy. Dispute over words [Gk]

logos. Word; discourse; account; theory; science; law; reason [Gk]

loi. Law [F]

loin. Far; distant [F]

Loin des yeux, loin du coeur. Out of sight, out of mind [F]

L'Oiseau de Feu. Fire Bird (Composition by Stravinsky) [F]

Lollards. English followers of Wycliffe, 14th to 15th centuries

Lombards. Italian merchants of the 12th and 13th centuries

Lo mejor de los dados es no jugarlos. The best cast at dice is not to play [Sp]

Londres. London [F]

longeron. Longitudinal fuselage member [F]

longue haleine. Long-winded; exhaustive [F]

longueur. Length [F]

lontano. Far [It]

loofah. Plant used as a brush in a Turkish bath [Arab]

Lo pasado pasado. Let bygones be bygones [Sp]

loquela. Colloquy; talk [L]

loquitur. Term used to introduce a speaker in a play or novel [L]

Lorelei. Legendary siren who lured mariners to their destruction; any seductive female [G]

lorgnette. Eye-glasses with a long handle; opera glasses [F]

los. The (*pl.*) [Sp] (in phrases, see also below succeeding word)

Los niños y los locos dicen las verdades. Children and fools speak the truth [Sp]

los panaderos. Traditional dance in costume [Sp]

lotería. Lottery [Sp]

Louis-d'or. Former French gold coin [F]

loup. Wolf [F]

louve. She-wolf [F]

louvre. Ventilator in the eaves of a building or in the hood of an engine or machine [F]. See also *Louvre*

Louvre. Famous art museum in Paris [F]

lubricum linguae. Slip of the tongue [L]

luch. Ray [R]

Lucifer. Light-bearer; name of Venus as the morning star; Satan [L]

lucri causa. For the sake of gain [L]

133

luctus. Mourning [L]

Lucus a non lucendo. A grove is so called because it excludes the light; a ridiculous derivation; any *non sequitur* [L]

ludere. To play [L]

ludiones. Religious dramadances [L]

ludus. Drama; celebration; game (*pl.* ludi) [L]

Lufthansa. Germany's civil air service prior to 1939 [G]

Luftschiffahrt. Aeronautics [G]

Luftwaffe. Air arm; the German air force as a subdivision of the *Wehrmacht* [G]

lugar. Place [Sp]

Luger. Name of a German automatic pistol [G]

luglio. July [It]

Lügner. Liar [G]

luli kebab. Baby lamb broiled on a skewer [R]

lumbago. Pain in the loins [L]

lumen. Light; window (*pl.* lumina) [L]

lumen fidei. Light of faith; divine revelation [L]

lumen gratiae. Light of grace [L]

lumen naturalis rationis. Natural light of reason [L]

lumière. Light [F]

lumina. See *lumen*

lune. Moon [F]

lunedì. Monday [It]

lunes. Monday [Sp]

lunette. Small vault constructed in a larger one; small window above a large one; paintings on a lunette [F]

lunga. Long [It]

lunkah. Type of cigar [Hindu]

luogo. Place [It]

lupanar. Wolf's nest; house of prostitution [L]

lupus. Wolf [L]

Lusitania. Portugal [L]

Lust. Desire [G]

lustig. Merry, gay; funny [G]

lustrum. Period of five years [L]

Lustspiel. Comedy [G]

lusus naturae. Freak of nature [L]

lutefisk. Lye-cured fish.

lutin. Goblin [F]

lux. Light [L]

Lux aeterna. Eternal Light; part of the Requiem mass [L]

Lux Benigna. Kindly Light (musical version by Dykes for Newman's "Lead Kindly Light") [L]

Lux est Umbra Dei. Light is the Shadow of God (Symonds) [L]

Lux et Lex. Light and Law (motto of the University of North Dakota) [L]

Lux et Veritas. Light and Truth (motto of Yale and University of Indiana) [L]

Lux, Libertas. Light, Liberty (motto of the University of North Carolina) [L]

Lux mundi. Light of the world [L]

lycée. High school [F]

M

M. Thousand [L]. See also *meridie*

ma. But [It]

macabre. Gruesome; referring to death [F]

macaronic. Mixture of two or more languages in a poem, especially Latin and a modern tongue, usually for humorous purposes [ ]

macédoine. Referring to a mixture of vegetables or fruit, with or without meat, generally in jelled sauce [F]

maceta. Flower pot [Sp]

mache. Battle [Gk]

ma chère. My dear (*fem.*) [F]

machete. Large knife used for hacking [Sp]

Machiavelli. Italian writer and diplomat (1469-1537); any person employing unscrupulous means to achieve success in negotiations

Macht. Power; might; force [G]

Machtpolitik. Power politics [G]

Machtstaat. Power state; state using military and economic powers to attain its ends [G]

Machu Picchu. An ancient Inca fortress

macro-. See *makros*

macrologia. Long-winded language; unnecessary repetition in lengthy phrases and clauses [Gk]

macte virtute. Continue in virtue [L]

maculatum. Spotted; term used in flower and plant classification [L]

Mädchen. Girl [G]

Madeleine. Church in Paris in the form of a Greek temple; originally built by Napoleon to glorify his army

Madelon. French soldier's song (in World War I)

mademoiselle. Miss; young lady; governess [F]

madera. Wood [Sp]

Madonna. My Lady; reference to or representation of the Virgin Mary [It]

madre. Mother [It] [Sp]

madrepore. Type of coral [It]

madriguera. Burrow; den; hole [Sp]

madroñero. Picturesque Spanish dress often worn by dancers [Sp]

madrugada. Morning [Sp]

Maenades. Same as *Bacchantes*

maestoso. Majestic; stately [It]

maestranza. Guild [It]

maestro. Master [It]

maffia. Sicilian secret organization engaging in extra-legal acts such as blackmail, murder, *etc.*

mafia. See *maffia*

ma foi. Upon my faith [F]

magadis. Type of ancient harp [Gk]

magasin. Store; shop [F]

maggio. May [It]

maggiore. Major [It]

Maggiore fretta, minore atto. The more haste, the less speed [It]

Magi. See *magus*

Maginot. French minister of war responsible for the system of fortifications known as the Maginot Line; symbol of unsuccessful reliance on fixed fortifications in an era of air and mobile warfare

magis. More; more fully; rather [L]

magister. Master; ruler; learned person [L]

Magister rerum usus. Use is the master of things [L]

Magistra rerum experientia. Experience is the mistress of things [L]

magma. Molten lava; soft igneous mass [Gk]

Magna Charta. The Great Charter; constitutional charter granted by King John of England (1215) [L]

Magna Christi Americana. Great Works of Christ in America (Cotton Mather) [L]

magna culpa. Great fault; gross negligence [L]

magna cum laude. With great praise, honor, or distinction [L]

Magna Est Veritas. Great is Truth (Patmore) [L]

Magna est veritas et praevalebit. Truth is great and will prevail [L]

Magna est veritas et praevalet. The truth is mighty and it prevails (Vulgate; III, *Esdras*, 4-41) [L]

magnas inter opes inops. Poor in the midst of wealth [L]

Magnificat. (My soul) doth magnify [L]

Magnificat (anima mea Dominum). My soul doth magnify the Lord (Luke, 1-46; hymn used in the vesper service of the Catholic Church) [L]

magnifico. Type character of the rich merchant in the *commedia dell' arte* [It]

magnifico. Magnificent; excellent; a nobleman; a lordly personage; one who affects the grand style [Sp]

magnum bonum. A great good [L]

magnum opus. Great work [L]

magot. Grotesque figure; *genre* picture of mediocre style [F]

magrepha. Name of the organ in the Temple of Jerusalem in Biblical days; a "fire shovel" [Heb]

maguey. The American aloe [Sp]

magus. Member of a priestly caste of ancient Persia; one of the wise men who visited the infant Jesus (*pl.* magi) [Pers-Lat]

Magyar. Hungarian

Mahabharata. The Great (War of the) Bharatas, an Indian epic [Skr]

Maharajah. Great rajah; highest title of a prince of a native state of India [Hindu]

Maharaj Shiromani. Chief Maharajah (title of president of councils of Rajputana Princes)

Maharanee. Wife of a *Maharajah* [Hindu]

Mahatma. The great soul; term of respect as applied to Gandhi; in philosophy, the transcendental self or the Absolute [Skr]

Mahdi. Mohammedan messiah; title assumed by several Moslem leaders [Arab]

mahout. Elephant driver [Hindu]

Mahratta. Member of a warlike Indian people [Hindu]

maia. Midwife [Gk]

mai a. Steamed banana [Hawaian]

maiale. Pork [It]

maidan. Parade ground [Persian]

mailloche. Double-knobbed stick used to beat the bass drum [F]

maillot. Bathing suit [F]

Maillot. See *Porte Maillot*

main. Hand [F]

Maire. Mayor; head of a *Commune*, elected by the municipal council [F]

mairie. Government building of each commune; municipal building [F]

maison. House; firm [F]

Mais où sont les neiges d'antan? But where are the snows of yesteryear? (François Villon) [F]

maître. Master; teacher [F]

maître d'hôtel. Steward; butler; *major domo* [F]

Majlis. Iranian Parliament [ ]

Majolica. Fine Italian pottery of the Renaissance; modern pottery of this style [It]

major. Greater [L]

major domo. Steward [L]

makhorka. Tobacco substitute [R]

makros. Long; large [Gk]

makuta. Headdress [Skr]

mal. Bad; ill; evil [F]

maladie. Ailment; sickness; disease [F]

maladie du pays. Homesickness [F]

maladroit. Awkward; bungling; tactless [F]

mala fide(s). Bad faith; in bad faith [L]

Málaga. Spanish seaport east of Gibraltar; species of pale-green grapes [Sp]

malagueña. Spanish dance somewhat like the *fandango* [Sp]

mala in se. Wrongs in themselves; acts morally wrong [L]

malaise. Uneasiness; illness [F]

malaka. Milk [R]

malapropos. Inopportunely [F]

mal de mer. Seasickness [F]

Maler. Painter; artist [G]

Malerei. Painting [G]

malgré lui. In spite of himself [F]

malgré moi. In spite of myself; against my will [F]

malgré tout. In spite of all [F]

malheur. Misfortune [F]

mali exempli. Of bad example [L]

malik. Chieftain [Arab]

malitia praecogitata. Malice aforethought [L]

mallard. Wild duck [F]

malo animo. With an evil mind or intent; with malice [L]

malo grato. In spite; unwillingly [L]

malo modo. In a bad manner [L]

Malo mori quam foedari. Death before dishonor [L]

malum in se. Evil in itself; crime against nature [L]

malus pudor. False shame; false modesty [L]

Malva. Genus name of Mallow flowers [L]

Ma Mère L'Oye. Mother Goose [F]

mañana. Morning; tomorrow [Sp]

manas. Mind [Skr]

manche. Sleeve; channel (La Manche=the English Channel) [F]

manchette. Cuff; wristband; ruffle [F]

manco. Cripple [Sp]

mandamus. We command; a legal writ commanding performance of a particular act [L]

mandato. Order [It]

mandat-poste. Postal money order [F]

manduchus. Grotesque mask worn by Roman actors or pastoral players [L]

manège. Riding technique; art of horsemanship; riding school [F]

manes. Shades; ghost [L]

mangiare. To eat [It]

mania. Madness [L]

mania a potu. Mania as a result of drinking; *delirium tremens* [L]

manica. Sleeve; arm-guard; wrist-guard used by archers [L]

manicotti. Baked noodles and cheese with tomato sauce [It]

Manifesta probatione non in-digent. Things manifest do not require proof [L]

Manilovism. Smug complacency; inactivity; futile daydreaming: from Manilov, a character in Gogol's "Dead Souls" [R]

manioc. Plant from which *farinha* is made; a staple food of Brazil [Port]

Mannigfaltigkeit. "Manifold-ness"; aggregate nature or quality [G]

männlich. Masculine [G]

mano. Hand [It]

manqué. Missed; frustrated; failed [F]

mansard. Window on the slope of a roof; name of a French architect in the 17th century [F]

mantecado. Ice cream [Sp]

mantilla. Lace scarf worn over the head [Sp]

manto. Chilean shawl [Sp]

mantón. Shawl [Sp]

mantra. Pious thought; the poetic portion of the *Veda* [Skr]

manu forti. With a strong hand [L]

manus. Hand [L]

manzanilla. White sherry wine [Sp]

manzo. Beef [It]

Mapai. Socialist party in Palestine [Heb]

Mapam. Leftist party in Palestine [Heb]

M'Appari. Like a dream (*Martha*, Act III; Flotow) [It]

Mappe. Portfolio; briefcase [G]

maquereau. Pimp; pander; procurer; brothel-house keeper [F]

maquillage. Make-up [F]

maquis. Scrub; bush; French underground organization in World War II [F]

mar. Sea [Sp]

marabout. Mohammedan hermit [Arab]

maraca. Cuban musical instrument; a gourd containing dried seeds or pellets, used as a rattle [Sp]

marais. Marsh; bog; swamp; morass [F]

maraschino. Type of cherry (liqueur) [It]

marcato. Marked; accented [It]

marché. Market [F]

marché aux fleurs. Florists' market [F]

marché aux puces. Flea market (second-hand antiques fair in Paris) [F]

Märchen. Tale; fairy tale, legend [G]

marché noir. Black market [F]

mardi gras. Shrove Tuesday; festival [F]

Mar Dulce. Fresh-water Sea; name given to the Plata River [Sp]

mare. Sea [L]

mare clausum. Sea under jurisdiction of a country; sea closed to free commerce [L]

mare liberum. Sea open to all (*i.e.* not controlled by one country) [L]

Mare Liberum. The Sea Free (treatise by Grotius on the freedom of the seas) [L]

marengo. See *à la marengo*

mare nostrum. Our sea; *i.e.* the Mediterranean [L]

Marguerite. Common name given to a number of daisy-like plants [L]

mari. Husband [F]

mariachi. Mexican instrumental ensemble

mariage de conscience. Marriage of conscience (*i.e.* to legalize an illicit relationship) [F]

mariage de convenance. Marriage for practical reasons [F]

mariana. A *Flamenco* dance [Sp]

Marianne. Feminine figure symbolic of France

Mari Magno. On the Great Sea; "Tales on Board" (Clough) [L]

marimba. Type of xylophone made of wooden bars and gourds [Sp]

marinade. Liquor in which meat or fish is steeped [F]

marine. Navy [F]

mariné(e). Pickled in brine [F]

marinierter Hering. Pickled herring [G]

Mark. March; buffer state; border region [G]

Markgraf. Margrave; old German title of nobility [G]

Markgräfin. *Fem.* of *Markgraf*

markofki. Carrots [R]

marli. Inside border of a plate or dish [F]

marmelo. Quince [Port]

marmite. Pot; saucepan; boiler; potful [F]. See also *petite marmite*

marmot. Little monkey; little chap; grotesque figure [F]

maroquin. Moroccan [F]

marqueterie. Inlaid or mosaic work or decoration; marquetry [F]

marquis. Marquess; title of nobility [F]

marquise. Roof projecting from the *façade* of a building; markee; title of nobility; *fem.* of *marquis*; marchioness [F]

marron. Chestnut [F]

marrons glacés. Candied chestnuts [F]

Marsala. Sherry-like wine from Sicily [It]

Marseillaise. French national anthem, composed by Rouget de Lisle, 1792 [F]

mart. March [R]

marteau. Hammer [F]

martedì. Tuesday [It]

martel. Hammer [F]

martellato. Strongly marked or accented [It]

martello. Hammer; knocker [It]

martes. Tuesday [Sp]

Marzipan. Almond-paste candy [G]

marzo. March [It]

maschere. Mask [It]

Maschinenbaukunst. Mechanical engineering [G]

masla. Butter [R]

masorah. Tradition [Heb]

massé. Billiard shot made with upright cue [F]

massektot. Tractates [Heb]

masseur. Male professional massage expert [F]

masseuse. Female professional massage expert [F]

massif. Compact chain of mountains [F]

mässig. Moderate(ly) [G]

masurek. Mazurka; a Polish dance; a musical composition suggested by or in the style of the mazurka [Polish]

Más vale maña que fuerza. Skill is better than strength [Sp]

Más vale saber que haber. Wisdom is better than wealth [Sp]

Más vale tarde que nunca. Better late than never [Sp]

Más ven cuatro ojos que dos. Four eyes see better than two; two heads are better than one [Sp]

matachines. Buffoons; merry dances [Sp]

matador. Killer; bull-fighter who despatches the bull with a sword [Sp]

mate. Paraguay tea [Sp]. See also *hierba mate*

matelassé. Stuffed; padded; provided with a mattress or upholstery; a silk or rayon fabric woven on a *Jacquard* loom, and having a puckered surface [F]

matelot. Sailor [F]

matelote. Fish stew with wine [F]

mater. Mother [L]

Mater artium necessitas. Necessity is the mother of invention [L]

Mater Dolorosa. Sorrowing Mother (the Virgin Mary; painting by Titian) [L]

materfamilias. Mother of a family [L]

materia. Materials; matter; substance; subject-matter [L]

materia medica. Substances of healing; medicines; drugs; pharmacology [L]

matin. Morning [F]

matita. Pencil [It]

matrix ecclesia. Mother church [L]

matte. Impure metallic residue; dull finish [F]

matzos. Unleavened bread (eaten during Passover) [Y]

maudit. Cursed [F]

maugré. In spite of; against the will of [F]

mauvaise honte. False shame [F]

mauvais goût. Bad taste [F]

mauvais quart d'heure. A short but trying experience [F]

mauvais sujet. Rascal; black sheep [F]

mauve. Seagull [F]

maxima cum laude. With greatest distinction [L]

maximus in minimis. The greatest in the least [L]

maxixe. Popular dance in Brazil [Port]

Maya. Veil (covering reality) power of obscuring; a state producing error and illusion [Skr]

mazapán. Almond paste [Sp]

mazarines. Entrees of forcemeat and fillets of poultry, fish, *etc.* [F]

mazuma. Money [Y]

mazzel-tov. Happy day; good luck; congratulations [Y]

M.D. See *Medicinae Doctor*

mea cùlpa. The guilt is mine [L]

Mea maxima culpa. Through my very great fault; I am very guilty [L]

Mecca. City in Saudi Arabia; birthplace of Mohammed; shrine; place of pilgrimage

Meconopsis integrifolia. Yellow Chinese Poppy [L]

meden agan. Shun excess [Gk]

médecin. Doctor [F]

Media in vitae in morte sumus. In the midst of life we are in death [L]

Medicinae Doctor. Doctor of Medicine [L]

medii aevi. Of the Middle Ages [L]

medius. Middle [L]

Médoc. Vineyards on the left bank of the Gironde; district of fine wines [F]

Medusa. Hideous creature with hair of snakes, decapitated by *Perseus*; Gorgon [Gk]

Meer. Sea; ocean [G]

Meereskunde. Oceanography [G]

Meerschaum. Sea-foam; a white mineral found in Asia Minor; a pipe made of this mineral [G]

megas. Large [Gk]

meglio tardi che mai. Better late than never [It]

Mehr Licht! More light! (Goethe's last words) [G]

meilleur. Better [F]

Mein Kampf. My Battle (autobiography by Adolf Hitler) [G]

Meissen. City in Germany noted for its porcelain ware; sometimes used synonymously with *Dresden* china [G]

Meistergesang. Middle - class continuation of *Minnesang*; fostered by German city artisans at the close of the Middle Ages [G]

Meistersinger. Master singer(s) poet from among the city artisans of Germany at the close of the Middle Ages; Wagner's opera, *Die Meistersinger von Nürnberg* [G]

meizon horos. Major term; the predicate of the third term of a syllogism [Gk]

me judice. I (being) judge; in my judgment [L]

melaço. Molasses [Port]

melancholia. Extreme mental depression [Gk]

mélange. Mixture; confusion[F]

mélange de genres. Mixture or confusion of styles or categories [F]

melanzana. Egg-plant [It]

melas. Black [Gk]

Melba. Referring to thin crisp toast [ ]

mele. Apples [It]

mêlée. Fight; brawl; mix-up; free-for-all [F]

melior. Better [L]

Melissa. Genus of Balm flowers [L]

Melius est omnia mala pati quam malo consentire. It is better to suffer every ill than to consent to ill [L]

melopoeia. The musical element in Greek tragedy [Gk]

melos. Song or *Lied*; a sort of melodic recitative used by Wagner [Gk]

membra disjecta. Scattered parts [L]

membrum virile. Penis [L]

même. Same; -self; even [F]

memento mori. Reminder of death; a type of poetry in the Middle Ages [L]

mémoire. Petition; document; note [F]

memorabilia. Things worth remembering [L]

Memorabilia. Things worthy of being remembered; recollections (title of a work by Browning) [L]

memorandum. To be remembered [L]

memoria technica. Artificial memory; aids to memory [L]

memoriter. By memory [L]

ménage. Household [F]

mendigo. Beggar [Sp]

Mene, Mene Tekel Upharsin. (Weighed and) found lighter and lighter; weighed and found wanting (Daniel, v; the words on the wall at *Belshazzar's* Feast, forecasting his downfall) [Aramaic]

Menge. Quantity; amount; volume; a lot, a great number; a crowd [G]

menhir. Celtic monument consisting of an enormous stone standing vertically [Celtic]

meninas. Court maidens; title of a Velasquez painting [Sp]

meno. Less [It]

Menorah. Candelabrum; name of various Jewish organizations [Heb]

mens. Mind; intention; meaning; understanding; will [L]

mensa. Table; goods [L]

mensa et thoro. From bed and board [L]

Mens agitat molem. Mind moves the mass (motto of the University of Oregon) [L]

Mensch. Human being; man; person [G]

Menschheit. Humanity; humankind; mankind [G]

mens conscia recti. A good conscience [L]

Mensheviki. Minority party; Lenin's opponents [R]

menshinstvo. Minority [R]

mensis. Month [L]

mens legis. The spirit of the law [L]

mens rea. Guilty mind; criminal intent [L]

Mens sana in corpore sano. A sound mind in a sound body (Juvenal; *Satires*; 10-356) [L]

menstruus. Monthly [L]

mensuel. Monthly [F]

menteur. Liar [F]

menton. Chin [F]

menuet. Courtly dance consisting of variations of bows and curtsies [F]

meo voto. By my wish [L]

mer. Sea [F]

mercato. Market [It]

mercatum. Market [L]

merci. Thanks; mercy [F]

mercoledì. Wednesday [It]

Mercury. Roman counterpart of *Hermes*; quicksilver [L]

merde. Excrement [F]

mère. Mother [F]

meridie. At midday; at noon[L]

meringue. Whipped whites of eggs with sugar [F]

merismus. Elaboration; detailing [Gk]

Merker. Judge presiding at the singing contests of the *Meistersinger* [G]

merlon. Raised part of a parapet in interval between loopholes [F]

Mertensia virginica. Bluebell or Virginia cowslip [L]

merveilleux. Miraculous; supernatural; marvellous [F]

mesa. Table; tableland; plateau [Sp]

mésalliance. Marriage of unequals; marriage to one of lower social status [F]

mesarchia. Likeness of sound at beginning and middle of a line [Gk]

Mesa Verde. Green Tableland; National Park in Colorado[Sp]

meshuggah. Crazy [Y]

meshummad. Apostate; converted Jew [Y]

mesiats. Month [R]

meso-. Middle; between [Gk]

mesodiplosis. Repetition of a word in the middle of successive lines or sentences [Gk]

mesos horos. Middle term (of a syllogism) [Gk]

mesoteleuton. Likeness of sound at middle and end of a line [Gk]

mesothesis. Reconcilement idea suggested to link two apparently contradictory thoughts or principles [Gk]

messa di voce. Gradual swelling and subsiding on a single tone in singing [It]

Messe. Mass; fair [G]

Messidor. Tenth month of the calendar used during the French Revolution [F]

mestizo. Person of mixed blood, part Spanish, part Indian [Sp]

mestoso. Sadly [It]

meta. After; with [Gk]; Goal; boundary; landmark; turning-point [L]

metabasis. Transition [Gk]

metalepsis. Far-fetched; substitution of a distantly related idea [Gk]

metanoia. Penitent; making a remark, then at once retracting or softening it [Gk]

metastasis. Figure of remove; passing over a matter with scant attention as if it were unimportant [Gk]

meta ta physika. After the physics (the metaphysics, which came after the physics in Aristotle's works) [Gk]

metathesis. Change in order of words or sounds [Gk]

methomania. Irresistible craving for liquor [Gk]

methu. Wine [Gk]

métier. Craft; trade; specialty; profession [F]

metonymia. Misnamer; figure of speech in which one name is used with the intention that another be understood [Gk]

mètre. Meter=0.914 yard= 0.304 foot [F]

Métro. See *Le Métro*

metron. Measure [Gk]

metrum. Meter (in poetry) [L]

metus. Fear; terror [L]

meubles. Furniture; movables [F]

meum et tuum. Mine and thine; rights of property [L]

meunier. Miller (*fem.* meunière) [F]

meunière. See *meunier*

mezhdunarodnyi. International [R]

mezquita. Mosque [Sp]

mezza. Half [It]

mezzanotte. Midnight [It]

mezzo. Semi- [It]

mezzo-forte. Moderately loud [It]

mezzogiorno. Noon [It]

mezzo-piano. Moderately soft [It]

mezzo-relievo. Half relief; said of sculptured work of which half projects from its ground [It]

mezzozeugma. Middle marcher; setting a word between two expressions to which it equally refers [Gk]

miao. Mystery; subtlety [C]

Mi Chiamano Mimi. My name is Mimi (*La Bohème*, Act I; Puccini) [It]

micro-. See *mikros*

Micromeria chamissonis. See *Yerba buena*

midi. Noon; south [F]

midinette. Working girl who goes out to lunch at 12 noon [F]

miedo. Fear [Sp]

miel. Honey [F]

Mientras en mi casa estoy,

rey soy. A man's home is his castle [Sp]

miércoles. Wednesday [Sp]

miesto. Office [R]

mignon. Small and delicate [F]

migraine. Headache [F]

Mihi cura futuri. My care is for the future [L]

mikros. Small [Gk]

mil. Thousand [Sp]

miles. Soldier (*pl.* milites) [L]

miles gloriosus. Boasting soldier; braggart or swaggerer, usually a coward at heart [L]

milieu. Center; environment [F]

Milla. A type of lily [L]

millefiori. A kind of mosaic Venetian glass [It]

millier. 1,000 kilograms=2,200 lbs. [F]

milligramme. Milligram = 0.001 gram [F]

millimètre. Millimeter=0.001 meter [F]

milreis. Unit of Portuguese currency

mimesis. Imitation [Gk]

Mimosa pudica. Sensitive Plant or Humble Plant [L]

minacciando. Menacingly; threateningly [It]

Minatur innocentibus qui parcit nocentibus. He threatens the innocent who spares the guilty [L]

Minenwerfer. Mine thrower; heavy grenade launcher [G]

minestra. Soup [It]

minestrone. Vegetable soup [It]

ming. Name; designation; fate; destiny; the decree of Heaven [C]

ministerium. Ministry [L]

minium. Red lead; peroxide of lead [L]

Minne. Love [G]

Minnesang. German love poetry of the 12th and 13th centuries, the Middle High German period [G]

Minnesänger. Love-poet(s) of the 12th and 13th centuries, the Middle High German period[G]

Minnesinger. Same as *Minnesänger*

minor. Less; lower; inferior; minor [L]

Minseito. One of Japan's major political parties before World War II

minus. Less; less than [L]

minutiae. The slightest details; trifles [L]

Mi Par D'Udir Ancora. I Hear as in a Dream (*Pearl Fishers*, Act I; Bizet) [It]

mirabile dictu. Wonderful to tell [L]

mirabile visu. Wonderful to behold [L]

Mirabilis jalapa. Four o'clock; a species of flower [L]

miroton. Thin slices of meat in a *ragout*, served in circular form [F]

mise en scène. Staging; players and setting taken as a whole [F]

Miserere (mei, Domine). Have mercy (on me, O Lord) (Psalms 51; hymn sung for the Good Friday service); musical setting to this in Verdi's *Il Trovatore*; a small seat in Gothic churches [L]

Miserere mei, Deus. Have mercy on me, Lord [L]

Miserere nostri. Have compassion on us [L]

miséricorde. Mercy; pardon; quarter; grace; a small dagger for delivering the *coup de grâce*; small bench in a church [F]

misericordia. Pity; mercy; a fine [L]

Misericordia Domini. God's mercy [L]

Misericordias Domini. God Have Mercy on Us [L]

Mishnah. Repetition; title of the older part of the *Talmud* [Heb]

mismo. Self [Sp]

miso. I hate [Heb]

missa. The mass [L]

mi-souverain. Semi-sovereign; said of a state lacking full powers of sovereignty [F]

misra. Metrical unit in poetry [Arab]

misterioso. Mysteriously [It]

mit. With [G]

Mitarbeiter. Collaborator [G]

mitior sensus. In a better sense; the more favorable acceptation [L]

Mitius imperanti melius paretur. The more mildly one commands, the better he is obeyed [L]

Mitleid. Pity; compassion [G]

mitrailleuse. Machine-gun [F]

Mitsubishi. Great Japanese financial house; name of a wealthy family

Mitsui. Largest Japanese financial house, dissolved in 1946; name of a wealthy family

Mittelalter. Middle Age(s); medieval times [G]

Mitteleuropa. Central Europe; concept of an integrated central Europe with Germany in the dominant role [G]

mittimus. We send; order to imprison [L]

Mitteilung. Communication[G]

mloda polska. Young Poland [Polish]

mneme. Memory [Gk]

mnemonikos. Pertaining to memory [Gk]

mobile perpetuum. Something in perpetual motion [L]

mobilia. Movables [L]

Moderamen inculpatae tutelae. The regulation of justifiable defense [L]

moderato. Moderate tempo [It]

modicum. Proper measure; moderate; small measure [L]

modiste. Milliner; dressmaker [F]

modo et forma. In manner and form [L]

modulus. Measure (of relative size or quantity); factor; model [L]

modus. Manner; means; way; mode; measure; standard [L]

modus operandi. Mode of operating; way of working; method of doing something [L]

modus tenendi. Manner of holding (tenure) [L]

modus vivendi. Way or mode of living (together); practical method of getting along despite difficulties [L]

moed. Feast [Heb]

Moerae. The Fates. [Gk] See *Moira*

moeurs. Manners; customs; *mores* [F]

Mogen Dovid. Star of David [Heb]

Möglichkeit. Possibility [G]

moha. Distraction; perplexity; delusion [Skr]

mohur. Gold coin equal to 15 *rupees* [Pers]

moidore. A Portuguese gold coin

Moira. Goddess of fate; fate [Gk]

moiré. Watered (silk); a watered effect woven in silk, rayon, or cotton [F]

moksa. Liberation; salvation [Skr]

molina. Mill [L]

Moll. Minor (music) [G]

molossus. Metrical foot of 3 long syllables [ ]

molotov. Hammer [R]

molto. Much; extremely; a great deal [It]

momzer. Bastard [Y]

Mona Lisa. Lady with a cryptic smile; name of the famous painting by Leonardo da Vinci [It] See also *La Gioconda*

monas. Unit [Gk]

Monat. Month [G]

Monatsbericht. Monthly report [G]

mon cher. My dear [F]

Mon Coeur S'Ouvre à ta Voix. My Heart at thy Sweet Voice (*Samson and Delilah*, Act II; Saint-Saëns) [F]

Mond. Moon [G]

mondain(e). Worldly; secular [F]

monde. World [F]

Mon dieu! Good Heavens! [F]

mones. Single [Gk]

moneta. Money [L]

mono. Monkey [Sp]

monologue intérieur. Interior monologue; stream of consciousness [F]

monos. One; alone [Gk]

monos sabios. Wise monkeys; attendants who sprinkle fresh sand in the bull ring [Sp]

mon petit chou. My little cabbage (a phrase of endearment) [F]

monseigneur. Title of princes and bishops; monsignor [F]

monsieur. Mister; sir; gentleman [F]

monsignore. Title of princes and bishops; monsignor [It]

monstrum. Box in which relics are kept; muster of soldiers [L]

monstruo de naturaleza. Prodigy of nature; Cervantes' appellation of Lope de Vega [Sp]

mons veneris. Mount of Venus; pubic delta [L]

montage. Moving-picture technique which superimposes two or more scenes on the same frame [F]

Montani semper liberi. Mountaineers are always freemen (motto of West Virginia) [L]

Montagne. Group of the more violent members of the French revolutionary convention, among whom were Robespierre and Danton [F]

montera. Knitted cap with drooping peak and earlaps [Sp]

monumentum aere perennius.
A monument more enduring
than bronze [L]

moolah. See *mullah*

mora. Unit of quantitative
measure; duration of a short
syllable in classical verse (*pl.*
morae); delay; default; neglect
[L]

moraine. *Débris* deposited by a
glacier [F]

morbidezza. Delicate; subtle;
vivid (rendering of flesh tones
in painting) [It]

mordant. Biting; fixing agent in
colors [F]

morendo. Dying away [It]

More Nebukim. Guide for the
Perplexed (title of a philosophic
treatise by Maimonides) [Heb]

mores. Usage(s); customs; folk-
ways; conventions; traditions;
manners [L]

morgen. Tomorrow [G]

Morgen. Morning; measure of
land of about 2 acres [G]

Morgengruss. Morning Greeting [G]

**Morgenstund' hat Gold im
Mund.** The early bird catches
the worm [G]

morgue anglaise. Haughty reserve as a British trait [F]

Morir! Sì Pura E Bella! To
Die, So Pure and Lovely!
(*Aïda*, Act IV; Verdi) [It]

morisco. Baptized Moor [Sp]

Morituri Salutamus. We about
to die salute (Longfellow) [L]
See also *Ave Caesar, etc.*

Moro. Moor [Sp]

morphe. Form [Gk]

morra. Game of guessing the
number of fingers suddenly displayed by the opponent [It]

mors. Death [L]

Mors Benefica. Kindly Death
(Steadman) [L]

mors et vita. Death and life [L]

Mors janua vitae. Death is the
gate of life [L]

morskoi. Naval [R]

Mors omnia solvit. Death dis-
solves all things [L]

morte. Death [It]

mortis causa. By reason of
death; in contemplation of
death [L]

mortuus. Death [L]

mortuus sine prole. Dead
without issue [L]

morus papifera sativa. Japanese tree, the bark of which is
used for making fine paper [L]

mosca. Fly [Sp]

Moscato. An Italian grape or
wine [It]

mosque. Moslem place of worship

mosso. Movement; motion;
speed [It]

mostra. Sample [It]

mot. Word; saying [F]

mot de guet. Watchword [F]

mot d'ordre. Watchword [F]

motif. Motive; cause; design;
theme [F]

mot juste. Precise word; the one
inevitable word for the unique
and particular occasion [F]

moto. Motion; movement [It]

Moto Perpetuo. Perpetual
Motion (Paganini) [It]

mot propre. Exact term; calling
a spade a spade [F]

mouche. Fly; speck; spot; patch;
beauty spot; spy; parasite [F]

moue. Pout; grimace [F]

mouiller. To moisten; to add
water in cooking [F]

moujik. Peasant [R]

moulin. Mill [F]

Moulin Rouge. Red Mill (French
cabaret) [F]

mourire. To die [F]

mousse. Moss; having a mossy
or smooth texture or consistency; applied to frozen whipped cream, *etc.* [F]

mousseline de soie. A sheer,
light, plain-woven silk fabric,
slightly stiff [F]

mouton. Sheep [F]

**Mouvement Républican Popu-
laire.** Popular Republican
Party; World War II resistance
party led by de Gaulle, continued as a political party after
the war [F]

Moyen Âge. Middle Age(s) [F]

mozárabe. A Christian under
Moorish domination [Sp]

mozo. Youth; lad; servant [Sp]

m.p. See *mezzo piano*

M.R.P. See *Mouvement, etc.*

mu. 12th letter of the Greek
alphabet (Mμ)

muchacha. Girl [Sp]

muchacho. Boy (*la muchacha*=
girl) [Sp]

mudéjar. Mohammedan residing in Spain [Sp]

muerte. Death [Sp]

muerto. Died; dead; dead man
[Sp]

muestra. Sample [Sp]

muet. Mute; silent [F]

muezzin. Crier who proclaims
the time of prayer [Arab]

mufti. Teacher of the law;
Moslem religious leader of Jeru-
salem; title of Haj Amin el
Husseini, assumed in 1930
[Arab]

mujer. Woman [Sp]

mukti. Liberation [Skr]

mula. Mule [Sp]

muladí. Apostate [Sp]

mule. Slipper [F]

mulier. Woman; virgin; wife;
legitimate child [L]

mullah. Mohammedan theolo-
gian [Arab]

Müllerin. Miller's wife or
daughter [G]

Multa fidem promissa levant.
Many promises lessen confidence [L]

**Multi multa, nemo omnia
novit.** Many have known
much; no one has known
everything [L]

multum in parvo. Much in
little [L]

Münchener. From or pertaining
to Munich, city in South Germany; Münchener beer

mundus intelligibilis. The
world of intelligible realities [L]

mundus sensibilis. The world
of things perceived by the
human senses [L]

Mundus vult decipi. The world
wants to be deceived [L]

Munera Pulveris. Gifts of the
Dust (Horace; *Odes*; 1-28)
(essays on political economy by
Ruskin) [L]

muni. Philosopher; sage; one
who has taken a vow of silence
[Skr]

Münster. Name of a German
city; a cathedral [G]

munus. Gift; office; benefice;
show or spectacle [L]

Münzkunde. Numismatics [G]

mürber Teig. Kind of dough
for piecrust [G]

musca. Fly [L]

Muscipula. The Mousetrap
(painting by Joshua Reynolds)
[L]

Museo del Prado. The Prado
Museum; art gallery in Madrid
famous for its Velasquez paintings [Sp]

musette. A kind of bagpipe; a
side-slung pouch or bag [F]

musica di camera. Chamber
music [It]

muslim. True believer; Moslem
[Arab]

mussaca. Oriental dish of spring
lamb, egg plant and tomatoes
[R]

Mussolini ha sempre ragione.
Mussolini is always right [It]

mustizo. Offspring of an Indian
and a negro [Sp]

Mut. Courage [G]

mutaquarib. Metrical form in
poetry [Arab]

mutatio nominis. Change of name [L]

mutatis mutandis. Things being changed that ought to be changed; the necessary changes being made [L]

mutato nomine. Change of name [L]

Mutum est pictura poema. A picture is a poem without words (Horace) [L]

mutus. Dumb; mute [L]

mutuus consensus. Mutual consent [L]

muy. Very [Sp]

muzhik. Peasant [R]

myasa. Meat [R]

myosotis. Forget-me-not [Gk]

myriamètre. 1,000 kilometers = 6.21 miles [F]

mythos. Myth; legend; tale [Gk]

N

na. Well [Gk]; At; by; for; to; with [R]; Here [Y]

nabliudatelnyi. Board [R]

Nach Canossa gehen wir nicht. We are not going to Canossa; *i.e.* we are not going to submit (Bismarck; 1872; reference to the humiliation of Henry IV before Gregory VII at Canossa, Italy, in 1077) [G]

Nachdruck. Reprint; emphasis [G]

Nachfühlen. "After-experiencing"; mimpathy; sympathy or pity [G]

Nachlass. Estate; legacy; remaining effects and belongings of the deceased [G]

Nachtigall. Nightingale [G]

Nachtmusik. Nocturne [G]

Nachrichten. News [G]

Nachrichtenbüro. News office or agency [G]

Nachtrag. Appendix; supplement [G]

Nachwort. Epilogue [G]

nacimiento. Manger scene depicting the Nativity [Sp]

nada. Nothing; anything [Sp]

nadie. Nobody; anybody [Sp]

naga. Dragon; name given to a kind of jar among the Dyaks of Borneo [ ]

naga-uta. Long poem [J]

naïf. Innocent lad [F]

naissance. Birth [F]

naïveté. Innocence [F]

naiv und sentimentalisch. Realistic and idealistic; classical and romantic; antithesis developed by Schiller in his essay, *Über naive und sentimentalische Dichtung*; 1795 [G]

nakaz. Mandate [R]

nakladnaia. Invoice [R]

nalisniki. Pancakes stuffed with meat [R]

nam. For; because [L]; South [C]

nama-rupa. Name and form; word and beauty [Skr]

Namu Amidabutsu. Holy Name [J]

naos. Center of a Greek temple [Gk]

Napoléon. Cake baked in thin strips put together with jam and cream [F]

naranja. Orange [Sp]

Narcissus. Person in Greek mythology; name used for the common Narcissus as well as for Daffodils and Jonquils

narghile. Water pipe for smoking [Pers]

nariz. Nose [Sp]

narod. People [R]

Narodniki. Populists; a pre-Marxist revolutionary party in Czarist Russia [R]

narodnyi. National [R]

Narr. Fool [G]

Narrenschiff. Ship of Fools (title of a work by Brant; 1494) [G]

nascetur ridiculus mus. See *parturiunt montes, etc.*

nasci. To be born [L]

Nascimur poetae, fimus oratores. We are born poets, we are made orators [L]

nasciturus. About to be born; future offspring [L]

nashim. Women [Heb]

nasilshchik. Porter [R]

nasledstvennost. Heredity [R]

nastika. Unorthodox, *i.e.* not acknowledging the authority of the *Veda* [Skr]

nasturtium. Nose-twister; a flower with a pungent odor [L]

Natale di Roma. Founding of Rome; national holiday on April 21st [It]

natale solum. Native soil [L]

Nationalsozialistische Deutsche Arbeiterpartei. National Socialist German Workers Party; the Nazi party (1920-45) [G]

Natura appetit perfectum. Nature covets perfection [L]

Natura il fece, e poi ruppe la stampa. Nature made him, then broke the mold [It]

natura naturans. Nature "naturing", a term for God in Scholastic philosophy [L]

natura naturata. Nature "natured", *i.e.* created things [L]

Naturrecht. Natural right or law [G]

Naturwissenschaft. Natural science [G]

natus. Born [L]

natya. Dance-drama [Skr]

naufrage. Shipwreck [F]

naufrago. Shipwreck [It]

nauka. Science [R]

naumachia. Sea fight; aquatic spectacle; amphitheatre in which sham sea-fights were staged [Gk]

naushnyi. Scientific [R]

nausia. Seasickness [Gk]

nauta. Sailor; seaman; navigator; ship-owner [L]

nautikos. Naval [Gk]

navarin. Brown stew of mutton [F]

Navidad. Nativity; Christmas [Sp]

navire. Ship [F]

navis. Ship [L]

nawab. Native ruler or nobleman in India [Arab]

Nazi. See *Nationalsozialistische, etc.* [G]

N.B. See *nota bene*

néant. Nothingness [F]

nebel. A plucked-string instrument somewhat like a psaltery [Heb]

Nebel. Fog; smoke or gas (military) [G]

Ne cede malis. Do not yield to misfortune [L]

necessitas. Necessity [L]

Necessitas non habet legem. Necessity has no law [L]

Nec more nec requies. Neither delay nor rest [L]

Nec pluribus impar. Not unequal to many; a match for the whole world (motto of Louis XIV) [L]

necro-. See also *nekro-*

necrophilia. Love for corpses [Gk]

nedelia. Week [R]

née. Born; having had as a maiden name [F]

ne exeat. Let him not depart [L]

Nefasti dies. Unlucky days; days on which courts do not sit [L]

Ne fronti crede. Do not trust the face [L]

nefyr. A type of trumpet [Arab]

negligé(e). Neglected; unstudied; careless; a loose robe or gown worn indoors by women [F]

negro. Black [Sp]

Negus. Ruler of Abyssinia

neige. Snow [F]

neiges d'antan. Snows of yester-year [F]. See also *Où sont les neiges, etc.*

nein. No [G]

nekrologium. Death-register [Gk]

nekropolis. City of the dead; burial place [Gk]

nekros. Corpse [Gk]

nelumbium. Lotus [L]

nemetskii. German [R]

nemine. No one [L]

nemine contradicente. No one contradicting; unanimously [L]

nemo. No one; no man [L]

Nemo cogitationis poenam patitur. No one suffers punishment on account of his thoughts [L]

Nemo me impune lacesset. No one will attack me with impunity (motto of Scotland) [L]

Ne moveas Camarinam. Don't disturb Camarina (a lake in Sicily); *i.e.* Let well enough alone [L]

nenia. Song of praise for the departed [L]

ne nimium. Not too much [L]

neo-. New [Gk]

neoterici. Moderns [L]

nepeta cataria. Catnip [L]

nepos. Grandson [L]

ne plus ultra. No more beyond; furthest point; acme [L]

neptis. Granddaughter [L]

Neptune. God of the sea; Poseidon (in Greek mythology) [L]

Ne quid nimis. Be wisely moderate [L]

nereides. Sea-nymphs; daughters of *Nereus* [Gk]

Nereis. See *Nereus*

Nereus. A god of the sea [Gk]

nero. Black [It]

nervos belli. The sinews of war [L]

nervus probandi. Nerve of proof; crux of the argument [L]

nesciens. Ignorant [L]

n'est-ce pas ? Isn't it so? [F]

Ne sutor supra crepidam. Let not the cobbler (judge) above his last [L]

Ne sutor ultra crepidam. Let the shoemaker stick to his last [L]

neti, neti. Not this, not that [Skr]

netsuke. Carved button on the fastener of a medicine box [J]

nettoyage à sec. Dry-cleaning [F]

Neudruck. Reprint [G]

Neufchâtel. A type of soft, sour cream cheese [F]

neumes. Musical notation marks of the Middle Ages [Gk]

nevada. Snow-covered; snowy [Sp]

névé. Glacial snow not yet compressed to ice [F]

neveu. Nephew [F]

nexus. Bond; tie [L]

nezikin. Damages [Heb]

Nibelungenlied. Song of the Nibelungs; old German epic fusing motifs of Germanic mythology [G]

Nicht-Ich. Non-ego; not-self; anything which is not the subjective self; the external world [G]

nicht wahr ? Isn't it true? [G]

nicotiana. Genus name of various tobacco plants [L]

nidra. Sleep [Skr]

niellatori. Artists who practised *niello* engraving [It]

niello. A process of decorating metal used by Italian goldsmiths of the 15th century; a metal plate thus decorated [It]

nieve. Snow [Sp]

niger. Black [L]

nihil. Nothing [L]

nihil ex nihilo. Nothing out of nothing; *i.e.* nothing comes from nothing [L]

Nihil humani a me alienum puto. I consider nothing human to be strange to me [L]

nihil interit. Nothing dies [L]

Nike. Goddess of victory [Gk]

nil. See *nihil*

nil admirari. To wonder at nothing; a jaded or *blasé* attitude [L]

Nil desperandum. Nothing must be despaired of; never despair (Horace; *Odes*; 1-7-27) [L]

nil dicit. He says nothing [L]

nil ligatum. Nothing bound; without obligation [L]

Nil nisi cruce. Nothing save by the cross [L]

Nil sine Deo. Nothing without God [L]

Nil sine numine. Nothing without the divine will (motto of Colorado) [L]

nimbus. Rain cloud; luminous circle around the head of a saint in religious art; any aura or halo [L]

n'importe. Never mind; no matter [F]

ninguno. None; any [Sp]

niño. Child; little boy (la nina = little girl) [Sp]

Niobe. Figure in Greek mythology whose children were slain; symbol of grief [Gk]

nirguna. Devoid of qualities [Skr]

nirvana. Blown out; complete extinction of individuality without loss of consciousness; a Buddhist concept denoting a state in which pain and mental anguish have ceased; oblivion [Skr]

Nisei. Second generation (of children born to Japanese parents outside Japan); a general term for American citizens of Japanese descent [J]

nisi. Unless [L]

Nisi Dominus, frustra. Unless the Lord is with us, our efforts are in vain (motto of Edinburgh) [L]

Nisi prius. Unless before; a legal writ to convene a jury [L]

Nivôse. Fourth month of the calendar used during the French Revolution [F]

Nizam. Ruler of Hyderabad; Turkish army or soldier [Arab]

N.K.V.D. People's Commissariat for Internal Affairs; Soviet secret police; successor to the *O.G.P.U.* [R]

no. See *numero*

nô. See *noh*

noblesse. Nobility [F]

noblesse oblige. Privilege involves responsibility; lofty rank, lofty sentiments [F]

nocentia. Guilt; transgression [L]

noche. Night [Sp]

Nochebuena. Christmas Eve [Sp]

nocturne. A musical composition in emotional style representing poetic feelings aroused by evening or night [F]

Noël. Christmas; a Christmas song [F]

noema. Figure of close conceit; statement that seems to say its opposite [Gk]

No es oro todo que reluce. All that glitters is not gold [Sp]

No faltaba más! That was the last straw! [Sp]

noh. Lyric drama [J]

No hay atajo sin trabajo. No gains without pains [Sp]

No hay mal que por bien no venga. It's an ill wind that blows no good [Sp]

noiabr. November [R]

noir. Black [F]

noisette. Bits of cooked meat, generally lamb [F]

noix de muscade. Nutmeg [F]

Nolens volens. Whether he will or not; willy-nilly [L]

Noli Me Tangere. Touch Me Not (words of Jesus to Mary Magdalene; John, xx. 17) [L]

nolle prosequi. (I) will no further prosecute; plaintiff's declaration that he will not proceed any further in a criminal action [L]

nolle prosse. See *nolle prosequi*

nolo. I am unwilling [L]

nolo contendere. I will not contest it; plea similar to a plea of guilty in a criminal action [L]

nolo episcopari. Unwillingness to accept office [L]

nol. pros. See *nolle prosequi*

nolumuks. Politics [R]

nom de guerre. Pseudonym [F]

nom de plume. Pen name; assumed name; pseudonym [F]

nomen. Name; designation; noun (*pl.* nomina) [L]

Nome Vostro Ditemi. Tell Me Your Name (*Rigoletto*, Act II; Verdi) [It]

nomina. See *nomen*

nominalis. Belonging to a name [L]

nominatim. By name; expressed one by one [L]

nomine. By name; in the name of; under the name of [L]

nomotheta. Lawgiver [Gk]

non. Not [L]

Non Angli, sed angeli. Not Angles, but angels (said by Pope Gregory at the sight of British slaves) [L]

Non capisco. I don't understand [It]

non causa pro causa. No cause for cause; a logical fallacy known as false cause, incident to the method of proof by *reductio ad absurdum* [L]

non compos mentis. Not sound of mind; insane [L]

non constat. It does not appear; it is not clear or evident [L]

nondum editus. Not yet published [L]

non ens. Nonentity [L]

nones. Fifth or seventh day of the month in the Roman calendar, (nine) days from the *ides* [L]

non est. It is not; it is nonexistent [L]

non (est) inventus. He has not been found; he is missing; wanted [L]

Non è ver. It is not true [It]

non libet. It does not please me [L]

non liquet. It is not clear; verdict deferring decision [L]

non placet. It is not pleasing; negative vote [L]

non plus ultra. See *ne plus ultra*

Non Mi Dir, Bell' Idol Mio. Do Not Say, Beloved Mine (*Don Giovanni*, Act II; Mozart) [It]

Non ministrari sed ministrare. Not to be ministered unto but to minister (Matthew, xx. 28; Mark, x. 45) [L]

nonnette. Gingerbread made in Reims [F]

Non nobis. Not unto us; rendering praise to God, not to oneself; a song of rejoicing (Psalms, 115) [L]

nono. Ninth [It]

non obstante. Notwithstanding [L]

non olet. It does not stink (said of money from questionable sources) [L]

Non omnis moriar. I shall not altogether die (Horace; *Odes*, 3-30-6) [L]

Non Più Andrai. No Longer Will You Flutter (*Marriage of Figaro*, Act I; Mozart) [It]

non possumus. We cannot; plea of inability [L]

non quis, sed quid. Not who, but what [L]

non seq. See *non sequitur*

non sequitur. It does not follow; a fallacy in which there is no connection between premises and conclusion; an unwarranted conclusion [L]

Non sibi, sed omnibus. Not for oneself, but for all [L]

non so che. I do not know what; an indefinable something [It]

non sui juris. Not his own master [L]

nonus. Ninth [L]

noques. Dumplings boiled in soup [F]

noria. Primitive water-wheel [Sp]

norma. Rule [L]

norma agendi. Rule of conduct [L]

Nosce teipsum. Know thyself [L]

No se ganó Zamora en una hora. Rome wasn't built in a day [Sp]

nosos. Disease [Gk]

nosotros. We [Sp]

nota. Note [L]

nota bene. Mark well; note this; observe [L]

Nota notae est nota rei ipsius. A known component of a thing is known by the thing itself [L]

Not bricht Eisen. Necessity is the mother of invention [G]

noticias. News [Sp]

notiones communes. Common notions; *i.e.* good, evil, existence of God, *etc.* [L]

Notre Dame. Our Lady; cathedral in Paris [F]

notwendig. Necessary [G]

nougat. Almond and honey candy [F]

nouilles. Strips of paste made of eggs and flour [F]

noumenon. Object of the mind; object of a non-sensuous intuition [Gk]

nous. Mind; reason; the faculty of intellectual apprehension and of intuitive thought [Gk]; we; us [F]

nous pathetikos. Passive reason [Gk]

nous poietikos. Creative mind; the active reason [Gk]

nouvelle. New; short novel or novelette [F]

nouvelles. News [F]

novanta. Ninety [It]

nova rimada. Rhymed narrative of courtly love [Provençal]

Novaya Zhizn. New Life (an early Bolshevik newspaper) [R]

nove. Nine [It]

novela picaresca. Picaresque novel [Sp]

novella. Short prose narrative [It]

Novelle. Prose narrative shorter than a novel [G]

novellozza. A short musical composition in a somewhat humorous style [It]

noventa. Ninety [Sp]

Noverint universi per praesentes. Know all men by these presents [L]

Novial. An auxiliary language devised by Jespersen

novio. Suitor [Sp]

novus homo. A new man; founder of a new generation; one who has been pardoned of a crime [L]

noxa. Damage; injury [L]

noyau. A liqueur [F]

Nozze Di Figaro. Marriage of Figaro (Mozart) [It]

N.S.D.A.P. See *Nationalsozialistische, etc.*

nu. 13th letter of the Greek alphabet (Nν); Well? so what? [Y]

nuage. Cloud [F]

nubilis. Marriageable; one who is of marriageable age [L]

nudis verbis. In plain words[L]

Nuestra Señora. Our Lady[Sp]

nueve. Nine [Sp]

nuevos. New [Sp]

nuevos cristianos. Neo-Christians; name given to Jewish converts to Christianity [Sp]

nuit. Night [F]

Nulla dies sine linea. No day (shall pass) without a line (of music or poetry) [L]

nulla fides fronti. No trust in the countenance; *i.e.* do not trust a person's intention on the basis of his appearance [L]

nullah. Ravine; watercourse [Hindu]

nullius filius. Son of nobody; *i.e.* bastard [L]

Nullum quod tetigit non ornavit. He touched nothing which he did not adorn (Dr. Johnson's epitaph on Oliver Goldsmith) [L]

numen. Nod; command; will; divine will; God [L]

numero. In number [L]

numerus. Rhythm [L]

nunca. Never [Sp]

nunc aut nunquam. Now or never [L]

Nunc dimittis. Now lettest thou (thy servant) depart [L]

nuncio. Papal diplomatic representative [It]

nuncius. Envoy [L]

nunc pro tunc. Now for then; any action with a retroactive effect [L]

nunquam. Never [L]

Nunquam dormio. I never sleep [L]

nunquam non paratus. Never unprepared [L]

nuovo. New [It]

Nur Wer Die Sehnsucht Kennt. None But the Lonely Heart (Goethe-Tchaikovsky) [G]

Nussbaum. Nut Tree (Schumann) [G]

nux. Nut [L]

nux vomica. Seed yielding strychnine [L]

nye ponimayu. I don't understand [R]

nyet. No [R]

nymphaea. Genus name of the water lily [Gk]

nymphomania. Morbid and excessive craving for sexual intercourse [Gk]

nyssa. Genus of gum trees [L]

O

O. For Greek words, see also under *ho-*

ob. If [G]; for; on account of [L]. See also *obiit*

obbligato. Solo passage; an obligatory passage that should not be omitted [It]

Obers. Cream [Austrian]

Oberst. Colonel [G]

obertass. A dance resembling the polka [Polish]

obiit. He (she) died (used in old epitaphs) [L]

obit. (He) died; funeral; anniversary of death [L]

obiter. By the way; incidentally; in passing [L]

obiter dictum. Incidental or collateral remark or opinion by a judge; incidental statement by way of illustration, analogy, or argument (*pl.* obiter dicta) [L]

oblatio. Gift or offering [L]

oblatorium. An apse in a Christian *basilica*, where the bread and wine were blessed [Gk]

obmen. Exchange [R]

obozrenie. Review [R]

obra. Work; book [Sp]

obscurum per obscurius. The obscure by the obscure; defining something obscure in terms still more obscure [L]

obshchestvennyi. Social [R]

obsta principiis. Resist the first (encroachments) [L]

obtrectatores. Detractors [L]

ocarina. Small wind instrument [It]

Occhi Turchini. Blue Eyes [It]

occultatio. Concealment [L]

ochenta. Eighty [Sp]

ochlos. Mob [Gk]

ocho. Eight [Sp]

O Cieli Azzurri. Oh, Azure Sky (*Aïda*, Act III; Verdi) [It]

octa-. Eight [L] [Gk]

octavo. See *in octavo*

octavus. Eighth [L]

octohedron. Solid body having eight sides [Gk]

octroi. Duty; customs; toll; tax; grant; privilege; concession [F]

oculus. Eye [L]

odalik. Female slave in a harem [Turk]

odin. One [R]

odinnadtsat. Eleven [R]

odium. Hatred [L]

odium medicum. Hatred among doctors [L]

odium theologicum. Theological hatred; doctrinal hatred [L]

odontoglossum. Genus of tropical American orchids [Gk]

O Du Mein Holder Abendstern. O Thou Sublime Evening Star (*Tannhäuser*, Act III; Wagner) [G]

Odyssey. Adventurous travels [Gk]

oeconomus. Manager [L]

Oedipus Rex. King Oedipus (title of a drama by Sophocles)

oenothera biennis. European evening primrose [L]

œuf. Egg [F]

œufs à la coque. Boiled eggs [F]

œufs brouillés. Scrambled eggs [F]

œufs sur le plat. Fried eggs sunny side up [F]

œuvre. Work [F]

œuvres complètes. Complete works [F]

Offenbarung. Revelation [G]

offertoire. Church music [F]

offertorium. Offerings; place where these are made or kept; service at Communion [L]

officia. Functions [L]

officier. Officer; 2nd grade of the *Légion d'Honneur* [F]

Officier d'Académie. Officer of the Academy; 1st grade of the *Palmes Académiques* [F]

Officier de l'Instruction Publique. Officer of Public Instruction; 2nd grade of the *Palmes Académiques* [F]

Offizierslager. Officer P.W. camp [G]

Oflag. See *Offizierslager*

oggi. Today [It]

ogive. Gothic style; Gothic arch [F]

oglavlenie. Table of contents [R]

ogni giorno. Every day [It]

O.G.P.U. United State Political Department; a Soviet agency known as the *Cheka* (1919-22); secret police organization replaced by the N.K.V.D. in 1934 [R]

ohne. Without [G]

oikei mania. Domestic insanity; unreasonable but intense hatred of wife or child [Gk]

oiseau. Bird (*pl.* oiseaux) [F]

Oiseau de Feu. Firebird (Stravinsky) [F]

Ojos que no ven corazón que no siente. Out of sight, out of mind [Sp]

Okhrana. Czarist secret police [R]

okimono. Decorative ornaments or objects [J]

okroshka. A cold soup [R]

okto-. Eight [Gk]

oleum. Oil [L]

Olim meminisse juvabit. It is pleasant to recall things afterwards [L]

olio. Mixed dish; stew; medley [Sp]

olla. A baked-clay, household jar [L]

olla podrida. Stew; miscellaneous mixture; hodgepodge [Sp]

ologeta. All together [PE]

olympiad. Grecian epoch; space of four years [Gk]

ombre. Shadow [F]

Ombre Légère. Fleeting Shadow (*Dinorah*; Meyerbeer) [F]

omega. 24th letter of the Greek alphabet (Ωω)

omen faustum. Favorable omen [L]

omicron. 15th letter of the Greek alphabet (Oo)

Omne vivum ex vivo. Every living (thing) from a living (thing) (Harvey's law) [L]

Omnia ad Dei gloriam. All is for the glory of God [L]

Omnia bona bonis. All things are good to the good [L]

Omnia mors aequat. Death levels all [L]

Omnia mutantur, nihil interit. All things change, nothing dies (Ovid; *Metamorphoses*; 15-165) [L]

Omnia mutantur, nos et mutamur in illis. All things change and we also change with them [L]

Omnia vanitas. All is vanity [L]

Omnia vincit amor; nos et cedamus amori. Love conquers all; let us yield to its power (Virgil) [L]

Omnia vincit labor. Labor conquers all [L]

Omnia vincit veritas. Truth conquers all [L]

Omnibus ad quos praesentes literae pervenerint, salutem. To all to whom the present letters shall come, greeting [L]

omnis. Every [L]

omnium. Whole; aggregate [L]

Omnium gatherum. Miscellaneous collection (*gatherum* is mock Latin) [L]

omphalodes. Navelseed or navelwort flower [Gk]

on. Being [Gk]

once. Eleven [Sp]

oncidium. Variety of tropical orchid [L]

onde. Wave [F]

on dit. It is said [F]

oneratio. Load; cargo [L]

onna-kata. Female impersonators in a play [J]

On ne badine pas avec l'amour. There's no trifling with love; you can't play with fire [F]

onomatopoeia. Formation of words in imitation of natural sounds [Gk]

onta. Existing things [Gk]

onuma. Name [Gk]

onus. Burden; load; cargo; weight; charge; incumbrance [L]

onus probandi. Burden of proving; responsibility for proof [L]

oom. Uncle [Du]

op. See *opus*

O Patria Mia. My Native Land (*Aïda*, Act III; Verdi) [It]

opera. Works [L]

opéra-bouffe. [F] See *opera buffa*

opera buffa. Comic opera; light opera [It]

opera omnia. Complete works [L]

opera seria. Tragic opera [It]

Opfer. Sacrifice [G]

opisthodomus. Part of a temple where treasure was kept [Gk]

optimus. The best [L]

opus. Work; labor (*pl.* opera) [L]

opus alexandrinum. Type of geometrical mosaic pavement [L]

opusculum. Little work; small book [L]

opus incertum. Unsquared or rubble masonry [L]

opus isodomum. Masonry in courses of equal height; Greek masonry [L]

opus magnificum. Manual labor [L]

opus reticulatum. Reticulated masonry; checkerboard masonry [L]

opus spicatum. Herring-bone masonry [L]

ora e sempre. Now and always [It]

Ora et labora. Pray and work [L]

oraison funèbre. Funeral oration [F]

ora kali. Happy hour; goodby [Gk]

Ora pro nobis. Pray for us [L]

Orare est laborare. To pray is to work [L]

orario generale. Complete railroad timetable [It]

Orator fit, poeta nascitur. The orator is made, the poet is born [L]

oratorio. A musical drama on a sacred theme [It]

Orbis Factor. Maker of the world [L]

Orbis pictus. The World in Pictures (Textbook by Comenius, 1592-1670) [L]

orbis terrarum. Terrestrial globe [L]

orden. Order [Sp]

ordinandi lex. Law of procedure [L]

ordinatum est. It is ordered [L]

ordines majores. Superior orders; *i.e.* priest, deacon, and subdeacon [L]

ordines minores. Inferior orders; *i.e.* chanters, psalmists, *etc.* [L]

ordo albus. White order; *i.e.* Augustine friars [L]

ordo griseus. Gray order; *i.e.* Cistercian order [L]

ordo niger. Black order; *i.e.* Benedictine order [L]

oreille. Ear [F]

oreja. Ear [Sp]

ore tenus. Orally; by word of mouth [L]

orexis. Striving; desire [Gk]

orfèvre. Goldsmith [F]

organo. Organ [It]

organon. Instrument; instrument of philosophical inquiry; title of Aristotle's logical treatises [Gk]

Orgbureau. Organization bureau of the central committee of the Russian Communist party [R]

Orgel. Organ [G]

orgue. Organ [F]

orgullo. Pride [Sp]

oriflamme. Standard of the ancient kings of France; banner; pennant [F]

origine contrôlée. Bonded as to name and grade; government license to wine growers [F]

origo. Origin [L]

origo mali. The origin of evil [L]

ornithia. Fowl; birds [Gk]

orpiment. A red pigment [F]

orthos logos. Right reason; law or order in the world to which human action should correspond, according to Stoic philosophy [Gk]

ortolan. Redbird; bobolink; any bird considered as a table delicacy [F]

osen. Autumn [R]

O si sic omnia! Oh, if all were thus! [L]

O Soave Fanciulla. Oh, Lovely Maiden (*La Bohème*, Act I; Puccini) [It]

ossia. Or [It]

osso buco. Marrow-bone [It]

ostensoir. Monstrance; transparent vase in which the host is placed [F]

osteon. Bone [Gk]

ostinato. Obstinate; sustained; persistent [It]

Ostmark. Nazi name for Austria; East Mark [G]

ostranenie. Estrangement [R]

Otchi Chornaya. Dark Eyes [R]

O tempora! O mores! Oh the times! Oh the manners! (Cicero) [L]

O Terra Addio. Farewell, Oh Earth (*Aïda*, Act IV; Verdi) [It]

otium cum dignitate. Leisure with dignity; dignified ease [L]

otium sine dignitate. Ease without dignity [L]

otoño. Autumn [Sp]

otrabotki. Labor-rent; rent for farms, paid off in labor on an owner's estate [R]

otrezki. "Cuts"; portions of land cut off from farms of emancipated serfs in Czarist Russia [R]

otrub. Tract of land [R]

ottanto. Eighty [It]

ottava rima. Rhymed octave; Italian verse-form with 8-line stanzas, rhymed ababcc [It]

ottavina. Piccolo [It]

ottavo. Eighth [It]

otto. Eight [It]

Otzovisti. Recallists; faction within the early Communist Party in Russia demanding recall of Social-Democrat deputies from the *Duma* [R]

otzyv. Recall [R]

ou. Or [F]

où. Where [F]

oublié. Forgotten [F]

ousia. Essence [Gk]

Où sont les neiges d'antan? Where are the snows of yester-year? (Villon) [F]

outopia. No place [Gk]

outopos. Land of nowhere [Gk]

outré. Extreme; eccentric; exaggerated; excessive; strained; incensed [F]

outre-mer. Ultramarine [F]

outre-tombe. Beyond the tomb [F]

ouvert(e). Open [F]

ouvrage. Work [F]

oveja. Sheep [Sp]

ovum. Egg; embryo [L]

oxubaphoi. Small cymbals, used by the ancient Greeks [Gk]

oxus. Sharp [Gk]

oxy-. Sour; acidy [Gk]

oxydendrum arboreum. Sour-wood tree [L]

oxymoron. A statement with two seemingly contradictory ideas [Gk]

oy! Ouch! Woe! [Y]

oyer. Hearing [OF]

oyez. Hear ye [OF]

P

pabulum. Food (for thought, *etc.*) [L]

Pace et bello. In peace and in war [L]

Pace, Pace, Mio Dio. Peace, Peace, Oh My Lord (*Forza del Destino*, Act III; Verdi) [It]

pace tua. By your leave [L]

pacta conventa. Conditions agreed upon; diplomatic compact [L]

pacta sunt servanda. Pacts are to be observed; treaties must be honored [L]

pactum. Pact; agreement; convention (*pl.* pacta) [L]

padre. Father [It]

padrone. Boss; employer [It]

paella. Valencian dish of rice and meat; chicken and rice[Sp]

paeonia. Peony [L]

paesano. Native (fellow) countryman [It]

paese. Town [It]

página. Page [Sp]

paideia. Education [Gk]

paidia. Play [Gk]

pain. Bread [F]

paix. Peace [F]

Pajaloosta. Please [R]

pájaro. Bird [Sp]

Palacio Nacional. Famous palace in Madrid, once known as the *Palacio Real* [Sp]

Palacio Real. Royal Palace in Madrid, later called the *Palacio Nacional* [Sp]

palaestra. Place where athletes were trained among the ancient Greeks [Gk]

palaieo. Ancient; old [Gk]

palais. Palace [F]

Palais de Chaillot. Meeting place of the United Nations in Paris [F]

palaios. Ancient [Gk]

palazzo. Palace [It]

Palazzo Venezia. Palace in Rome in which Mussolini's offices were located [It]

paletot. Cloak [F]

palette. Thin piece of wood with a thumb hole upon which artists hold and mix colors [F]

palimpsest. Re-used parchment with writing over an erased original text [Gk]

palin. Again [Gk]

palindrome. Line reading same backward as forward [Gk]

palio. Race (track) [It]

palla. A long robe worn by women [Gk]; Cloak [L]

Palladium. Protection; support; image of Pallas Athene said to safeguard Troy [L]

Pallas Athene. See *Athene*

pallini. Small bowling ball used as a target in *bocce* [It]

pallium. A large cloak [Gk]

palma. Palm tree [L]

Palmach. Striking force; *élite* corps of Israeli troops [Heb]

Palmam qui meruit ferat. Let him who has won the palm bear it (motto of Lord Nelson and of the Royal Naval School in England) [L]

Palma non sine pulvere. No palm without the dust (Horace) [L]

Palmes Académiques. Honorary French order founded in 1808 for service in education (originally), and in the arts [F]

paloma. Dove; pigeon [Sp]

palu. Lowland vineyard [F]

paludamentum. Cloak worn by Roman officers over their armor [L]

pampas. Grassy plains in the Argentine [Sp]

pan. All [Gk]; Lord; nobleman [Polish]; Bread [Sp]

Pan. God of flocks and herds, said to be the inventor of the shepherd's pipe, Pan's pipe[Gk]

panache. Plume; symbol of gallantry or bravado [F]

panade. French bread soup; soaked bread [F]

Panageia. Holy Virgin [Gk]

Panchatantra. The Five Books (collection of Indian fables) [Skr]

Pan de Azúcar. Sugar-Loaf; summit of the island in the Bay of Rio de Janeiro [Port]

Pandectae. Pandects; digest (of Roman law) [L]

pandereta. Tambourine [Sp]

pane. Bread [It]

panecillo. Roll [Sp]

panem et circenses. Bread and the show of the circus; free doles and spectacular shows (to appease the mob) [L]

paner. To cover fried or baked food with bread crumbs [F]

Pange, lingua. Sing, my tongue (opening words of the Catholic liturgical hymn) [L]

Pangloss. Character in Voltaire's *Candide*; symbol of optimism

Panglossa. Universal Tongue;

auxiliary language devised *ca.* 1942 by Hogben

panimayu. I understand [R]

panini. Rolls [It]

panis. Bread; loaf [L]

panne. Breakdown [F]

panné. Velveted; plushed; a high-luster finish used on satins and velvets [F]

pannier. Basket [F]

Pantalone. Pantaloon; stock figure of stupid old man in the *commedia dell' arte* [It]

Pantheon. Temple consecrated to the worship of all the gods; building serving as a memorial to famous men [Gk]

Panthéon. Pantheon; neogrecian building in Paris serving as a hall of fame [F]

pantoufles. Slippers [F]

pantoum. Oriental verse-form [Malay]

Panzer. Armor; tank [G]

paon. Peacock [F]

papa. Potato [Sp]

Papagei. Parrot [G]

papaver. Genus name of poppy flowers [L]

papaver somniferum. Opium poppy [L]

papel. Paper [Sp]

papier mâché. Paper pulp plastic figures or ornaments made of this pulp [F]

papillon. Butterfly [F]

papillote. See *en papillote*

papirosi. Cigarettes [R]

paprika. Red pepper [Hungarian]

Pâques. Easter [F]

par. Equal [L]; By [F]

para. By; from; of; next to [Gk]; For; to; in order to [Sp]

para-. Side; beside; beyond[Gk]

Pará. Port at the mouth of the Amazon River; rubber exported from this city

paradiastole. A euphemism especially by a synonym that softens the tone [Gk]

paradigma. Model [Gk]

parakataloge. Melodramatic declamation [Gk]

paralipomena. Appended items that have been omitted in the body of a work [Gk]

para mirar y ser mirado. To see and be seen [Sp]

páramo. High plateau (of Ecuador) [Sp]

paranoia. Insanity; chronic psychosis [Gk]

parataxis. Coordination of clauses [Gk]

Parcae. The Fates [L]

par delictum. Equal guilt [L]

parekbasis. Digression [Gk]

Parendo vinces. You will conquer by obedience [L]

parenesis. Urging to action; exhortation [Gk]

parens. Parent [L]

parenthurson. Misplaced enthusiasm [Gk]

pareo. Wrapped garment of printed cotton worn in Tahiti [ ]

pares. Peers; equals [L]

pares curiae. Peers of the court [L]

paresis. Laxness; incomplete paralysis; slight palsy [Gk]

pares regni. Peers of the realm [L]

par excellence. Excellent; to a superlative degree [F]

parfait. Dessert or ice-cream dish with thick hot sirup poured over it [F]

pari causa. With equal right; upon an equal basis [L]

par ici. This way [F]

pari materia. Of the same matter; on the same subject [L]

pari passu. By an equal progress; equably; without preference [L]

pari ratione. For the same reason; by the same mode of reasoning [L]

parisia. Begging pardon in advance [Gk]

Pari Siamo! Yon Assassin's My Equal (*Rigoletto*, Act II; Verdi) [It]

parisosis. Even balance in the parts of a sentence [ ]

Paris vaut bien une messe. Paris is well worth a mass (attributed to Henry IV of France) [F]

parlando. Speaking; in a declamatory style [It]

Parmentier. Cream of potato soup, named after the 18th century explorer who introduced this vegetable into France [F]

parmi. Among [F]

parmigiana. Of Parma; Parmesian; as in "Veal cutlet Parmigiana" (breaded and with melted Parmesan cheese) [It]

Parmigiano. Parmesan; an Italian cheese [It]

Parmi Veder Le Lagrime. Art Thou Weeping? (*Rigoletto*, Act III; Verdi) [It]

parodos. Side entrance to orchestra of the ancient theatre; ode sung by chorus entering from side [Gk]

paroemia. Wise saying; proverb [Gk]

parole. Word; prisoner-of-war's pledge to return, if released; pledge not to take up arms against captors, if released [F]

parole d'honneur. Word of honor [F]

paromoion. Alliteration [Gk]

parousia. Presence [Gk]

Par pari refero. I return like for like; tit for tat [L]

parrhesia. Frankness; bluntness [Gk]

pars. Part; party (*pl.* partes) [L]

pars pro toto. Part for the whole [L]

parterre. Flower-bed; orchestra; audience [F]

parti. Match; catch; person considered with a view to marriage [F]

Parteitag. Party day; Nazi Party Congress held annually in September in Nuremberg [G]

particeps criminis. Sharer of the crime; accomplice [L]

partigiano. Partisan [It]

parti pris. Preconceived view; prejudice; bias [F]

partisan. Member of irregular resistance forces [F]

Partitur. A full score (music) [G]

parturiunt montes, nascetur ridiculus mus. The mountains are in labor; there will be born a ridiculous mouse [L]

partus. Child; offspring [L]

parum. Little [L]

parvenu. Upstart; one risen from obscurity [F]

pas. No; not; step; footprint; precedence[F]

pasa. Raisin [Sp]

Pasach. Passover [Heb]

pasa doble. A South American dance [Sp]. See *paso doble*

pas battus. Beating steps; type of ballet embellishment [F]

Pascha Floridum. Palm Sunday [L]

Pascua. Easter [Sp]

Pascua Florida. Feast of Flowers; Easter Sunday [Sp]

pas de Basque. Ballet embellishment; an alternating step with a swinging movement from side to side [F]

pas de bourrée. A ballet step based on the *bourrée* [F]

pas de chat. Ballet step suggesting the steps of a cat [F]

pas de cheval. Ballet step imitating a trot [F]

pas de deux. Dance for two persons [F]

pas des écharpes. Scarf dance [F]

pas du tout. Not at all [F]

paseo. Procession [Sp]

pas glissé. Gliding step [F]

pasha. Officer of high rank [Turk]

paso. Passage; procession; short play or interlude; float in a parade [Sp]

paso de Vasco [Sp]. See *pas de Basque*

paso doble. Two-step; a gay march played at bull-fights after the bull has been killed; a rapid modern ballroom dance [Sp]

pas perdus. See *Salle des Pas perdus*

pasquinade. Satirical poem or diatribe against an enemy; a troubadour verse-form [F]

passacaglia. A slow dance in triple rhythm, thought to be derived from "passo gallo", rooster step [It]

passant. Passer-by; pedestrian [F]

passé. Past; out of date; past one's prime [F]

passementerie. Trimming of braid, beads, *etc.* [F]

passe-partout. Pass everywhere; master key; blanket passport; mount permitting insertion of different pictures; *factotum* [F]

passepied. Rapid dance in triple time [F]

pas seul. Exhibition solo dance [F]

passiflora. Passion flower [L]

passim. Everywhere; scattered far and wide; here and there (in the same work or author) [L]

passus. Step; chapter; canto [L]

pasta. Paste; dough; pulp; piece of pastry; minced sausage-meat [It]

pasta asciutta. Pastry made with cheese, butter, *etc.* [It]

pastel. Colored-crayon drawing; crayon used for this purpose; referring to tones or shades resembling such drawings or colors [F]

pasticcio. A work patched together from various sources; imitation of another's work; an operatic medley [It]. See also *pastiche*

pastiche. Imitation of a work of art [F]

pastor. Shepherd [Sp]

pastorelle. Pastoral poem; an idyll; a shepherds' dialogue [F]

patchouli. An East-Indian perfume [Hindu]

pâté. Paste; patty [F]

pateat universis per praesentes. Know all men by these presents [L]

pâté de foie gras. Goose-liver paste [F]

pater. Father [L]

patera. Shallow dish; circular ornament [L]

paterfamilias. Father of a family; head of a family [L]

Pater Filio. Father to Son (title of a poem by Robert Bridges) [L]

Pater noster. Our Father (first words of) the Lord's prayer; the rosary (by which the prayer is said); a kind of fishing line with spaced hooks like a rosary [L]

pater patriae. Father of (his) country [L]

patetico. Pathetic [It]

pathein. To suffer [Gk]

pathopoeia. Figure, passage, or scene that appeals to the feelings [Gk]

pathos. Suffering; passion [Gk]

patina. Pan; dish; layer of corrosion on bronze; tone acquired by a painting or statue as a result of year-long exposure to

light or atmospheric conditions [L]

patineur. Skater [F]

patio. Courtyard [Sp]

pâtisserie. Pastry; confectioner's shop [F]

patois. Dialect; *argot*; slang [F]

patria. Country [L]

patria chica. Dear homeland; affectionate reference to Spain [Sp]

Patria est ubiconque est bene. Our country is wherever we find happiness [L]

patrie. Fatherland; native land [F]

patron. Master; head of a firm [F]

patronne. Mistress; head of a firm; madame (of a house of ill-repute) [F]

patte. Paw; hand; skill [F]

paucis verbis. In few words; in brief [L]

Pauke. Kettledrum [G]

paulo post futurum. A little past the future; future perfect tense [L]

paupiettes. Slices of rolled meat [F]

pavana. [Sp]. See *pavane*

pavane. Courtly dance consisting of poses, curtsies, retreats and advances [F]

pax. Peace; an ornamental metal plaque used in early Christian church services [L]

pax ecclesiae. Peace of the church; sanctuary [L]

Pax Romana. Roman peace; peace enforced on States subject to Rome [L]

pax tecum. Peace (be) with you [L]

pax vobis. Peace (be) to you [L]

pax vobiscum. Peace (be) with you [L]

payada. Song composed by a *Gaucho* minstrel [Sp]

payador. Gaucho minstrel [Sp]

payrtsu. Pepper [R]

pays. Country [F]
paysan. Peasant [F]
paz. Peace [Sp]
pazhalusta. Please; you're welcome [R]
peau. Skin; fur; pelt [F]
peau d'agneau. Sheepskin [F]
peau de soie. Silk skin; a finely
woven silk taffeta [F]
pecado. Sin [Sp]
peccato. It is a pity [It]
Peccavi. I have sinned [L]
pêche. Peach [F]
pechatnik. Printer [R]
pêcheur. Fisherman [F]
Pêcheurs de Perles. Pearl
Fishers (opera by Bizet) [F]
pecora. Cattle; livestock [L]
pectiné. Comb-shaped; toothed
[F]
pecunia. Cattle; property or
wealth consisting of cattle; property in general; money [L]
Pecuniae obediunt omnia. All
things yield to money; money
rules the world [L]
pecus. Cattle; beast [L]
pedes muscarum. "Fly-track"
notation; *i.e.* a medieval system
of musical notation [L]
pedido. Order; request [Sp]
pedum. Shepherd's crook [L]
peignoir. Woman's dressing
gown [F]
peineta. Tall comb [Sp]
peinture. Painting [F]
pek. North [C]
pelagos. Sea [Gk]
pelargonium. Genus name of
the garden geranium [Gk]
pelar la pava. Courting at the
window-grating; custom of
serenading a *señorita* on her
balcony [Sp]
pèlerin. Pilgrim [F]
pélerinage. Pilgrimage [F]
pèlerine. Pilgrim (*fem.*); ulster;
wrap; broad collar [F]
pellis. Skin [L]
pelmeni. Dumplings stuffed with
chopped lamb [R]

pelo. Hair [Sp]
pelota. Type of handball game
played with special rackets on
a three-walled court; *jai-alai*
[Sp]
penates. Guardians of the inner
house [L] See *lares et penates.*
penchant. Leaning; inclination
[F]
pendente lite. Pending the suit;
pending litigation [L]
penitente. Penitent friar [Sp]
pensée. Thought; maxim [F]
penseur. Thinker [F]
pensieri. Thoughts [It]
pensio. Payment; rent [L]
pensum. Task; duty; homework
[L]
penta-. Five [Gk]
pentaptych. Ornamented panel
consisting of five folded leaves
[Gk]
pentathlon. Contest of five
events; running, jumping,
wrestling, discus and spear
throwing [Gk]
penumbra. Part of a shadow
having a light area due to
divergent rays [L]
peón. Peasant; laborer; serf [Sp]
peplum. Long robe worn by
Greek women [Gk]
pepsis. Digestion [Gk]
pequeño. Small [Sp]
per. By; for; through [It]; by;
in; through, with [L]
per accidens. Through accident; *i.e.* imposed from without;
externally caused [L]
perakim. Chapters [Heb]
Per angusta ad augusta.
Through difficulties to glory;
through straits to honors [L]
per annum. Per year [L]
Per Ardua Ad Astra. Through
difficulties to the stars (motto
of Royal Air Force) [L]
percale. A plain-woven cotton
fabric; a fine muslin [F]
per capita. Per head; per person
[L]

per caput. Per head; each [L]
per cent. See *per centum*
per cent(um). By the hundred; on each hundred [L]
Perchtentanz. Costume pantomime dance of Salzburg in honor of Perchta or *Freya* [G]
per conto. On account [It]
per contra. On the contrary; on the opposite (side of the account) [L]
per curiam. By the court [L]
perdendosi. Dying away; decreasing in power [It]
per diem. By the day; wage or allowance for each day [L]
Perdone. Excuse me [Sp]
perdreaux. Partridges [F]
perdu(e). Lost; hidden; out of sight [F]
père. Father [F]
perepeteia. Turn of action; turning-point in a drama [Gk]
per eundem. By the same [L]
perevod. Translation [R]
per extensum. At length; exhaustively [L]
per fas et nefas. Through right and wrong [L]
per favore. Please [It]
pergola. Garden walk arched with climbing plants [It]
peri. Beautiful woman; fairy [Pers]
peri-. About; around [Gk]
periaktoi. Triangular revolving prisms used as scenery in the ancient Greek theatre [Gk]
pericolo. Danger [It]
periculum. Peril; danger; hazard; risk [L]
periculum in mora. Danger in delay [L]
peridrome. Covered gallery running around a building [Gk]
periergia. Overlabor; building up a minor point by repetition and elaboration [Gk]
peripeteia. Sudden reversal (of condition or fortune), considered by Aristotle as an essen-

tial element in the plot of a tragedy [Gk]
periphrasis. Circumlocution [Gk]
peristyle. Colonnade around the interior of a courtyard or of an ancient temple [Gk]
per mensem. Per month [L]
perpetuum mobile. Something in perpetual motion [L]
Per piacere. Please [It]
per procurationem. By the agency of; by proxy [L]
per quod. Whereby [L]
per recte et retro. Forward and backward [L]
perron. An outside staircase or step; step(s) before a house [F]
per saltum. At a bound; suddenly; all at once [L]
per se. By himself or itself; in itself; inherently; in isolation; as such [L]
per se esse. To be by itself [L]
Persephone. Daughter of Zeus, carried off to the lower world by Hades [Gk]
per se subsistere. To subsist by itself [L]
Perseus. Slayer of Medusa the Gorgon [Gk]
persienne. Window-shutter with inclined lattices [F]
persiennes. Slat window blinds [F]
persifiage. Raillery; irony [F]
persona. Mask [L]
persona grata. Person acceptable as a diplomat to a receiving country [L]
persona ingrata. See *persona non grata*
persona non grata. Person not acceptable as a diplomat to a receiving country [L]
Personenzug. Local train [G]
personne. Person; no one [F]
Persönlichkeit. Personality [G]
perruque. Wig [F]

per veritatem vis. Through truth power (motto of Washington University) [L]

per viam. By way of [L]

per vivam vocem. By the living voice [L]

pervyi. First [R]

pes. Foot [L]

Pesach. Passover [Heb]

pescado. Fish [Sp]

Pescatori di Perle. Pearl Fishers (opera by Bizet) [It]

pesce. Fish [It]

peseta. Small silver coin [Sp]

peso. Unit of currency in Argentina, Colombia, Mexico, Uruguay, and other South American countries [Sp]

pessimus. The worst [L]

pet. Five [R]

pétard. Firecracker; bombshell; said of a word or an action which is loud and vulgar [F]

petere. To seek [L]

petimtse. A kind of felspar used with *kaolin* as an ingredient of Chinese porcelain [C]

petit. Little; small; petty [F]

petit bourgeois. Lower middle class; petty bourgeois [F]

petite marmite. Sandwich or *hors d'oeuvres* spread with bouillon paste or butter; sponger; parasite [F]

petite nature. Smaller than life-size [F]

petitio principii. Begging the question; a logical fallacy involving assumption of one or more propositions identical with the conclusion to be proved [L]

petit maître. Fop [F]

petit point. Fine lace; fine needlework [F]

petits battements. See *battement*

petits-chevaux. A gambling game [F]

petits fours. Mixed cookies in a variety of styles and shapes [F]

petits pois. Green peas [F]

petits soins. Small attentions [F]

petit sujet. Minor dancer in a *corps de ballet* [F]

petit verre. Small glass of liqueur [F]

petra. Rock [Gk]

peu à peu. Little by little [F]

peu de bien, peu de soin. Little gain, little pain [F]

peu de chose. A small matter [F]

peur. Fear [F]

pezzo. Piece; coin [It]

Pflicht. Duty [G]

phainein. To show; to appear [Gk]

phala. Result; effect; fruit [Skr]

phalanstère. Co-operative association, proposed by *Fourier* [F]

phantasia. Appearance [Gk]

phantasma. Appearance [Gk]

phaos. Light [Gk]

Pharos. Name of an island near Alexandria; lighthouse [Gk]

Ph.B. See *Philosophiae Baccalaureus*

Ph.D. See *Philosophiae Doctor*

phero. Carry; bear [Gk]

phi. 21st letter of the Greek alphabet (Φφ)

philein. To love [Gk]

phileo. Love [Gk]

philophronesis. Friendly feeling [Gk]

philos. Dear [Gk]

philosophe. Philosopher; sceptical materialist; one of the writers of Diderot's *Encyclopédie* [F]

Philosophiae Baccalaureus. Bachelor of Philosophy [L]

Philosophiae Doctor. Doctor of Philosophy [L]

philosophia mundi. Philosophy of the world [L]

phobia. Fear; dread [Gk]

phoinix. An ancient string instrument [Gk]

phone. Sound [Gk]

phorminx. An ancient string-instrument [Gk]

phos. Light [Gk]

photon. A *quantum* of light [Gk]

phronesis. Practical wisdom; knowledge of the proper ends of conduct [Gk]

physalis. Chinese lantern plant [Gk]

physike episteme. Natural science [Gk]

physis. Nature [Gk]

pi. 16th letter of the Greek alphabet (Ππ)

pièce. Piece; room; play [F]

piacere. Pleasure [It]

piacevoli. In a pleasing style [It]

Pia Desideria. Things Religiously Desired (title of a work by Spener); the manifesto of the pietistic movement [L]

pia fraus. Pious fraud; justifiable lie or injustice [L]

pia mater. Tender mother; inner membrane enveloping brain and spinal cord; one's brain or wits [L]

piangendo. Weepingly; plaintively [It]

piangere. To weep [It]

pianissimo. Very soft(ly) [It]

pianoforte. Piano; a type of old piano [F] [It]

piastre. Small Turkish coin [Gk]

piat. Five [R]

piatdesiat. Fifty [R]

piatnadtsat. Fifteen [R]

piatnitsa. Friday [R]

piatto. Plate [It]

piatti. Cymbals [It]

pica. Lance [Sp]

picador. Lancer; bull-fighter on a blindfolded horse, carrying a *pica*, or lance [Sp]

picaro. Rogue; rascal [Sp]

piccolo. Short for *flauto piccolo*, little flute [It]

picea. Spruce tree [L]

Pickelhäring. Fool; clown; stock character in 17th century German plays [G]

picot. Splinter; pick; purl (of lace) [F]

pièce bien faite. Well-made play; artificial play with neatly arranged plot [F]

pièce de résistance. Main dish in a meal; the roast; main event or feature [F]

pied-à-terre. Footrest; place of abode or shelter [F]

Piedigrotta. Song festival in Naples [It]

Piedra movediza no coge musgo. A rolling stone gathers no moss [Sp]

pien. Argumentation; dialectics [C]

pie quebrado. Broken foot; short line of verse [Sp]

pierna. Leg [Sp]

pietà. Picture of the Virgin and the dead Christ [It]

Pietà, Signore! Have Mercy, O Lord! [It]

pietra. Stone [It]

piffara. Shepherd's pipe [It]

pikinini. Child(ren) [PE]

pilaff. Oriental dish of rice and meat [Pers]

pilau. See *pilaff*

pimiento. Red pepper [Sp]

pimientos morrones. Sweet red peppers [Sp]

Pinacotheca. Hall in Athens where pictures were displayed; picture gallery. See *Pinakothek* [Gk]

Pinakothek. Art museum in Munich [Gk]

pineau. A type of grape vine [F]

pintoresca. Picturesque [Sp]

pinus. Pine tree [L]

pinus ponderosa. Western yellow pine [L]

pinus resinosa. Norway pine [L]

pinus rigida. Pitch pine [L]

pinus strobus. White pine [L]

pinx. See *pinxit*

pinxerunt. They painted [L]

pinxit. He painted [L]

pi ping. Picking flaws; criticism [C]

piquante. Sharp; biting [F]

piqué. Piqued; stitched; a ribbed cotton or rayon fabric [F]

piquer. To lard with strips of fat, bacon, *etc.* [F]

piquet. A card game [F]

piqué tour. Ballet figure in which the dancer approaches her partner in a stage-covering circle picking her steps with daintiness [F]

pire. Worse [F]

pirogen. Chicken and mushrooms covered with French dough and served with white sauce [R]

pirojok. Puff-cake stuffed with meat or cabbage [R]

pirouette. A turn or spin on one foot only, or in the air [F]

pis aller. Course adopted for want of a better; last resort; extremity [F]

pisces. See *piscis*

Pisces. Fish; sign of the zodiac so-called [L]

piscis. Fish (*pl.* pisces) [L]

piscina. Swimming-pool; basin in a church [L]

Pisco. Name of a city in Peru; Peruvian liquor made from grape juice; Chilean brandy [Sp]

pisé. Rammed earth and gravel [F]

piselli. Peas [It]

pistis. Faith [Gk]

pitanie. Nutrition [R]

pito. Finger-snapping (in Spanish dancing) [Sp]

più. More [It]

più lento. Slower [It]

pizza. Egg-shaped cheese bun; flat, melted-cheese pancake [It]

pizzeria. Italian restaurant [It]

pizzicato. Plucking of the violin strings [It]

placebo. I shall be pleasing; medicine of no efficacy, given to pacify a patient; pacifier [L]

Placebo Domino in regione vivorum. I shall be acceptable to the Lord in the land of the living (Psalms; 116; opening anthem in the vespers for the dead) [L]

placet. It pleases; official order or decree; affirmative vote [L]

plagiarius. Kidnapper [L]

plagiaulos. An ancient woodwind instrument; a side flute [Gk]

plagio. Kidnap [L]

Plaît-il? What did you say? Will you, please? *etc.* [F]

planche. Plank; plate [F]

planh. Verse-form of the French troubadour poets, usually a dirge or poem of mourning [OF]

plat. Flat; plate; dish; item on a menu [F]

platanus occidentalis. Sycamore [L]

plateresco. Filigreed; elaborately ornamented [Sp]

platero. Silversmith [Sp]

plaza de toros. Bull-ring; bullfight stadium [Sp]

plebs. Common people; commoners; common citizens of ancient Rome, exclusive of the patricians and senators; plebeians [L]

Pléiade. Pleiades; constellation of 7 stars; group of 16th century French poets [F]

plein air. Open air; a school of modern French painters who paint in the open air; products of this school [F]

plene. Completely; fully; sufficiently [L]

pleno jure. With full authority [L]

plenum. Full-membership meeting [L]

plenum dominium. Full ownership [L]

pleroma. Filling up; the world of light; the spiritual world [Gk]

pleura. Rib [Gk]

plier. To bend [F]

plinth. Square block at the base of a column; base of a statue [Gk]

plissé. Plaited; folded; puckered; a finish on cotton cloth to produce a puckered effect [F]

pluie. Rain [F]

plumbum. Lead [L]

Plus ça change, plus c'est la même chose. The more it changes, the more it is the same thing [F]

Plus vident oculi quam oculus. Eyes see more than eye; *i.e.* two heads are better than one [L]

pluviers. Plovers [F]

Pluviôse. Fifth month of the calendar used during the French Revolution [F]

P.M. See *Post Meridiem*

pneuma. Breath; spirit; soul [Gk]

Pneuma Hagion. The Holy Ghost [Gk]

pnigos. Strangler; long verse recited without pause for breath [Gk]

pnxt. See *pinxit*

pobedo. Victory; name of a Soviet automobile [R]

Poblacht na h-Eireann. The Irish Republic [Gaelic]

pobre. Poor [Sp]

pobreza. Poverty [Sp]

pochade. Rough sketch [F]

poché. Poached [F]

poco. Little; a little [It] [Sp]

poco a poco. Little by little [It]

pococurante. Caring little; unconcerned; indifferent; lacking enthusiasm [It]

poco fa. A while ago [It]

podium. A low projecting wall; a platform [L]

poêle. Frying-pan [F]

poelée. Soup stock for boiling fowl [F]

poena. Punishment; penalty (*pl.* poenae) [L]

poena corporalis. Corporal punishment [L]

poesía gauchesca. Gaucho poetry or minstrelsy [Sp]

Poeta nascitur, non fit. The poet is born, not made [L]

pogrom. Devastation; organized massacre of helpless people [R]

poi. Then; after that; next [It]

poids. Weight [F]

poiesis. Making; creating; artistic production [Gk]

poignard. Dagger; poniard [F]

point. Point; period; stitch; lace [F]

point d'Angleterre. English lace; lace with hexagonal mesh or ground [F]

point d'appui. Support; fulcrum [F]

point d'esprit. A fine dotted net [F]

point de France. French lace; specifically, all French hand-made laces up to 1665 [F]

pointe. Point; witty or subtle thrust [F]

pointe sèche. Dry-point (engraving) [F]

pointillage. Dotting; stippling; dotted line [F]

poire. Pear [F]

pois. Pea(s) [F]

poisson. Fish [F]

polemonium caeruleum. Jacob's Ladder; variety of flower [L]

polemos. War [Gk]

polenta. Thick soup or pudding of chestnuts, corn, *etc.* [It]

polianthes tuberosa. Tuberose [Gk]

police d'assurance. Insurance policy [F]

polis. City [Gk]

politikon zoon. Political animal (Aristotle's characterization of man) [Gk]

politique de pire. Policy of (making things) worse [F]

pollice presso. Thumb pressed (in the palm); concurrence in a plea or suggestion [L]

pollice verso. With thumb turned down (thus spectators indicated death for a gladiator's adversary); rejection of a plea or suggestion [L]

pollita. Chick [Sp]

pollo. Chicken [It]

polo gitano. A gypsy dance in 3-8 rhythm [Sp]

polonaise. Stately Polish dance; a musical composition on such a theme [F]

polotno. Linen [R]

polus. Many [Gk]

poly-. Many; several [Gk]

polygala. Genus of the milkwort flower [Gk]

polyphthongos. An ancient string-instrument [Gk]

pomidor. Tomatoes [R]

pomme. Apple [F]

pomme de terre. Potato [F]

pommes frites. Fried potatoes [F]

pomodoro. Tomato [It]

poncho. Blanket with an opening for the head, worn as a cape [Sp]

poncif. Hackneyed idea or expression presented with a show of originality [F]

ponedelnik. Monday [R]

ponere. To place [L]

pons asinorum. Asses' bridge; any device for beginners or simpletons; an aid to logic or reasoning for students; the fifth proposition in Euclid [L]

ponte. Bridge [It]

Ponte dei Sospiri. Bridge of Sighs (in Venice) [It]

Ponte Vecchio. Old Bridge (in Florence) [It]

ponticello. Bridge of a violin or other stringed instrument [It]

Pont Neuf. Famous old bridge in Paris [F]

populus. The people; genus name of aspen and cottonwood trees [L]

poputchiki. Fellow-travelers [R]

por el amor de Dios. For the love of God [Sp]

pordiosero. Beggar [Sp]

Por donde fueres, haz como vieres. While in Rome, do as the Romans [Sp]

Porgi Amor. Grant, O Love (*Marriage of Figaro*, Act II; Mozart) [It]

portamento. The carry-over of one note into the next; management of the voice in singing or of the hands in playing [It]

porte-cochère. Covered driveway; gateway for coaches [F]

Porte Maillot. One of the gates of Paris; name of a famous restaurant and its dishes [F]

portero. Doorman [Sp]

portico. Covered gallery or colonnade open on one side [It]

portière. Curtain at the sides of a door; small door in a train [F]

portmanteau. Traveling-bag; suitcase; composite word made up of initial letters of a phrase [F]

portulaca. Purslane; a type of flower [L]

posada. Lodging-house [Sp]

Posaune. Trombone; large trumpet [G]

Poseidon. God of the sea; Neptune (in Roman mythology) [Gk]

poseur. Person who poses [F]

poshchechina obshchestvennomu vkusu. Slap in the face of public taste (slogan of the Russian Cubo-futurists of 1912) [R]

posse. Possibility [L]

posse comitatus. Power or force of the county; those whom a sheriff may summon to his assistance [L]

Possunt quia posse videntur. They are able because they

seem to be able; they can because they think they can (Vergil; *Aeneid*, 5-231) [L]

post diem. After the day [L]

poste restante. General delivery [F]

posteriores. Descendants [L]

post facto. After the fact [L]

Post hoc, ergo propter hoc. After this, therefore in consequence of this; logical fallacy of considering a subsequent event a result of a preceding one merely because of sequence [L]

postillion. Coachman [F]

post meridiem. After midday; afternoon [L]

post mortem. After death; autopsy or examination of a dead body; examination of the reasons for a failure or calamity [L]

post natus. Born after [L]

post obitum. After death [L]

post res. After things [L]

post scriptum. Written afterward [L]

postulatum. Demand; assumption (*pl.* postulata) [L]

potage. Thin soup [F]

potage du jour. Soup of the day [F]

pot-au-feu. Beef (broth) [F]

potentia. Power; possibility [L]

potentilla. Genus name of *cinquefoil* [L]

potio. Drink [L]

potior. More powerful; stronger [L]

Potior est qui prior est. He is preferred who is earlier; first come, first served [L]

potpourri. Mixture; medley; medley of musical fragments[F]

poularde. Fat pullet [F]

poulet. Chicken [F]

poult-de-soie. Fine silk [F]

poupée. Doll [F]

Poupée Valsante. Dancing Doll (Poldini-Kreisler) [F]

Pour. For [F]

pourboire. Tip; gratuity [F]

Pour le Mérite. Order of Merit; highest German military decoration, under the Hohenzollerns [F]

pourparler. Preliminary conversation before official meeting of diplomats [F]

Pourquoi Me Réveiller? Why Awaken Me? (*Werther*, Act III; Massenet) [F]

pou sto. Where I may stand; fulcrum; place from which force may be exerted [Gk]

praam. Flat-bottomed boat[Du]

practica. Business [L]

Prado. See *Museo del Prado*

praeceptor. Master; chief clerk [L]

praecipe. Writ; command [L]

praeco. Herald; crier [L]

praecognita. Things to be previously known [L]

praedia. Pl. of *praedium*

praedia bellica. War booty [L]

praedicabilia. Predicates; those things which may be affirmed or denied of a subject in a logical proposition [L]

praedicamentum. (Category of) things predicated; a term in Kantian philosophy [L]

praedictus. Aforesaid [L]

praedium. Lands; estates; properties (*pl.* praedia) [L]

praedo. Robber [L]

praefatus. Aforesaid [L]

praefecturae. Prefectures; conquered towns governed by a *praefectus* [L]

praefectus. Prefect; governor of a town and surrounding area [L]

praemissas sententias. Aforesaid statements; premises [L]

praemium. Reward; compensation [L]

praemunire. Statutes of 1353 and 1392 for punishment of advocates of papal jurisdiction in England [L]

praemunitio. Warning [L]

praenomen. Forename; first name [L]

praeses. President; governor [L]

praestat cautela quam medela Prevention is better than cure [L]

praesul. Prelate; head priest in ancient Rome [L]

praesumitur pro negante. It is presumed for the negative (rule of the House of Lords when numbers are equal on a motion) [L]

praetor. Municipal officer of the ancient city of Rome; chief judicial magistrate [L]

pragma. Things done [Gk]

Praha. Prague

Prairial. Ninth month of the calendar used during the French Revolution [F]

Prajapati. Lord of Creatures [Skr]

prajna. Realization; insight [Skr]

prakrti. Prinary matter or substance; nature [Skr]

praline. Burnt almond [F]

pramana. Measure; standard of action or reasoning; a criterion or mode of proof [Skr]

prana. Breath; vital air; life [Skr]

pranayama. Breath exercise [Skr]

pranzo. Dinner [It]

prasada. Inclining towards; favor; grace [Skr]

Prater. Famous street in Vienna

pratique. Practice [F]

Pravda. Truth; official Communist newspaper [R]

pravo. Law [R]

praxis. Action; practice; conduct; activity that has its goal within itself [Gk]; Use; custom; practice [L]

pré. Meadow; duelling-ground [F]

preces. Prayers; petitions [L]

précieuse. Fem. of *précieux*

Précieuses ridicules. Farce satirizing the extravagances of *préciosité*, by Molière, 1659 [F]

précieux. Precious; valuable; affected in language; over-refined in speech; given to *préciosité*; member of a literary group about Mme de Rambouillet (1588-1665) [F]

precio. Price [Sp]

préciosité. Excessive refinement of manners and language, cultivated by the group about Mme de Rambouillet (1588-1665) [F]

précis. Abstract; summary [F]

Predigt. Sermon [G]

Préfet. Prefect; head of a *département* [F]

préfecture. Office of a *préfet*

preghiera. Prayer [It]

Prego. Don't mention it [It]

pregunta. Question [Sp]

prehendere. To seize [L]

Preislied. Prize Song (*Meistersinger*, Act III; Wagner) [G]

premier coup. First blow or stroke; executed without retouching or revision [F]

première. First (occasion or performance) [F]

première danseuse. Leading dancer of a *corps de ballet* [F]

premio gordo. First prize [Sp]

prensa. Press [Sp]

presbyter. Elder; priest [Gk][L]

presbyterium. Part of church where the priest performs divine offices; choir; chancel [L]

presepio. Manger; stable [It]

Presidium. Executive committee of the Supreme Soviet of the *U.S.S.R.* [R]

prestissimo. Extremely fast; at the fastest tempo possible [It]

presto. Very rapidly [It]

prêt. Loan; ready; prepared [F]

prêt(e). Ready [F]

preterition. Summary mention of a thing while seeming to pass it by [Gk]

pretium. Price; cost; value [L]
premirovannyi. Awarded a prize [R]
prie-dieu. Prayer stool [F]
prigione. Prisoner [It]
prima colazione. Breakfast [It]
prima donna. First lady; opera star [It]
prima facie. On the face of it; at first sight; presumably [L]
primaria ecclesia. The mother church [L]
primavera. Spring [It] [Sp]
prima volta. The first time [It]
primera espada. Chief matador [Sp]
primo. First (*fem.* prima) [It]; Cousin (*fem.* prima) [Sp]
primo nomo. Best performer [It]
primogenitus. First-born or eldest son [L]
primula. Primrose [L]
primula veris. Cowslip [L]
primum cognitum. That which is first known; the most primitive intellectual cognition of the mind [L]
primum mobile. Prime mover; primary motive; moving power [L]
primus. First [L]
Primus in orbe deos fecit timor. Fear was the first creator of gods in the world (Statius) [L]
primus inter pares. First among peers; spokesman of a group of equals [L]
princeps. Prince; emperor [L]
principia. See *principium*
principia, non homines. Principles, not men [L]
principiorum non est ratio. There is no reasoning of principles; no argument is needed to prove fundamental rules [L]
principium. Principle; beginning (*pl.* principia) [L]
principium individuationis. Principle of individuation; the

intrinsic factor in an existing thing which causes its individuality [L]
printanière. Dressing or garnishing of early spring vegetables [F]
printemps. Spring [F]
prior. Former; earlier; elder; preceding; superior in rank, right, or time; head of a monastery [L]
priori petenti. To the person first applying [L]
privatum commodum publico cedit. Private good yields to public; the interest of an individual should give place to the public good [L]
privilegium. Privilege; right; favor; special obligation (*pl.* privilegia) [L]
privilegium clericale. Benefit of clergy [L]
prix. Price; prize [F]
prix-courant. Price list [F]
prix fort. List price [F]
pro. For; in respect of; on account of; in behalf of [L]
proairesis. Reflective choice; deliberate desire [Gk]
probatio. Proof; direct evidence [L]
probatum est. It is tried or proved [L]
problema. That which is thrown forward; question proposed for solution; problem [Gk]
pro bono et malo. For good and ill [L]
pro bono publico. For the public good [L]
procatalepsis. Anticipation; forestalling an argument [Gk]
proceres. Nobles; lords [L]
procès-verbal. Minutes; written report or statement of facts of what has been said verbally; official minutes or proceeding of a conference [F]
prochain. Next; near [F]

procinctus. Girding for battle [L]

procurator. Proctor; agent; proxy; churchwarden; church collector; attorney (*pl.* procuratores) [L]

procureur. Attorney; prosecutor [F]

Pro Deo et Patria. For God and Country (motto of the American University) [L]

proemium. Introduction [L]

pro et con(tra). For and against [L]

profanum vulgus. The common people [L]

pro forma. As a matter of form [L]

progymnasma. Preliminary exercise; title of a textbook of rhetoric [Gk]

pro hac vice. For this occasion only [L]

proizvedenie. Works [R]

projet. Project; plan; draft of proposed treaty or agreement [F]

projet de loi. Project of law; projected bill sponsored by the French cabinet [F]

pro juventute. For youth [L]

prolegomenon. Preface; introduction (*pl.* prolegomena) [Gk]

prolepsis. Assuming a future act as already bearing consequences; notion; preconception; any notion that arises spontaneously in the mind, as distinguished from concepts resulting from conscious reflection [Gk]

proles. Offspring; progeny; issue [L]

proletarius. Person of poor or mean condition; person in ancient Rome who was so poor he could not serve the state with money but only with his children (*proles*) (*pl.* proletarii) [L]

promyshlennost. Industry [R]

promythium. Opening moral of a fable [Gk]

pronoia. Providence [Gk]

pronominatio. Substitution of an epithet for a proper name [L]

pro nunc. For now [L]

prooemium. Introduction; prelude [L]

Propaganda. See *Congregatio,etc.*

Pro Patria. For (one's) Native Land (title of a poem by Thomas Moore) [L]

propios. Municipal lands [Sp]

propos. Chat; essay [F]

proposition de loi. Bill sponsored by a member of the French legislature [F]

proprietas. Property; propriety [L]

proprietates verborum. Proprieties of words; proper meanings of words [L]

proprio motu. Of one's one accord [L]

proprio vigore. By its own force; by its intrinsic meaning [L]

proprium. Property; attribute [L]

propter. For; on account of [L]

Propylaea. Building at the entrance of the Acropolis at Athens; vestibule of a temple [Gk]

pro rata. Proportionately; according to a certain rate, percentage, or proportion [L]

pro rata (**parte**). According to a calculated part; in proportion [L]

pro re nata. According to what comes up; for the matter at hand; adapted to meet a particular occasion [L]

prosapodosis. Direct reply to an argument [Gk]

proscenium. Portion of a stage from the curtain to the footlights [L]

Proschaii! Goodby! [R]

pro scientia et religione. For science and religion (motto of Denver University) [L]

prosciutto. Ham [It]

prosequitur. He follows up or pursues; he prosecutes [L]

prosit. May it do good; to your health (*or* success) [L]

Prosit Neujahr! Happy New Year! [G]

prosodiacus. Processional [Gk]

prosodium. A song in religious processionals; entrance and exit of the tragic chorus [Gk]

prosonomasia. Nicknamer; use of a jesting name resembling the original; repeated sound in a pithy saying [Gk]

prosopopée. Apostrophe addressed to inanimate things or persons [F]

prosopopeia. Personification [Gk] See *prosopopoeia*

prosopopoeia. Counterfeit impersonation; giving human action to non-human and absent things [Gk]

pro tanto. For so much; for as much as may be; as far as it goes; to that extent [L]

protasis. Placed first; a proposition; premise in a syllogism [Gk]

protectio trahit subjectionem. Protection draws (with it) subjection; protection by government depends on submission to its laws [L]

protégé. Person having a protector or patron [F]

pro tem. See *pro tempore*

pro tempore. For the time being; temporarily; provisionally [L]

prothalamion. Song heralding Hymen, god of marriage; title of a poem by Spenser, 1597 [Gk]

protista. Primary living cell [Gk]

protos. First [Gk]

protreptikos. Hortatory or persuasive discourse [Gk]

proviso quod. It being provided that [L]

Provençal. Region in southern France; dialect spoken in southern France [F]

Provolone. An Italian cheese [It]

prox. See *proximo*

P.S. See *post scriptum*

proxime accessit. He came very near; a runner-up in a contest; second place [L]

proximo (mense). Of next (month) [L]

proximum genus. Nearest kind [L]

prunus. Genus of the cherry tree [L]

prurio. Itch [L]

psuedos. False; deception [Gk]

pseudotsuga taxifolia. Douglas fir [L]

psi. 23rd letter of the Greek alphabet (Ψψ)

psitt-. Parrot [Gk]

psychagogia. Mental abstraction [Gk]

Psyche. The beloved of *Eros*; soul; spirit; mind; World-Soul [Gk]

psychosis. Giving of life or soul; any mental process; a pathological condition of mind [Gk]

ptera. Wings [Gk]

pteron. Wing [Gk]

pterux. Wing [Gk]

pubes. Genitals; pubic hair [L]

publici juris. Of public right [L]

puce. Flea [F]

pucelle. Virgin [F]

Pucelle d'Orléans. Maid of Orleans; name for Jeanne d'Arc [F]

puchero. Earthenware pot; mixed stew [Sp]

pucka. Regular; good; reliable [Hindu]

pudenda. Genitals [L]

pudor. Shame [L]

pueblo. People; population; town; municipality; village [Sp]

puer. Child (boy or girl); boy [L]

puerto. Port [Sp]

puggaree. Turban; scarf [Hindu]

puisard. Cesspool [F]

pukkah. See *pucka*

puis. Then; since; afterwards [F]

puisné. Later born; junior [F]

puissance. Power [F]

Pulcinella. Clown of the *commedia dell' arte*; original of the English Punch [It]

pulmonaria. Lungwort, a perennial creeping plant [L]

pulpitum. Stage [L]

pulque. Fermented juice of the *maguey*; an alcoholic liquor drunk in Mexico [Sp]

pulvis. Powder [L]

punctum contra punctum. Note against note; counterpoint [L]

punctum temporis. Point of time; instant [L]

pundit. Scholar; authority on a subject; interpreter of Hindu law; learned Brahmin [Hindu]

punkah. Swinging fan actuated by a rope [Hindu]

punto tirato. Drawn stitch; drawn-work lace [It]

pupillus. Ward; infant; person under the authority of a *tutor* [L]

pur. Old French of *pour*

purana. Ancient; title of a series of ethical and philosophical treatises [Skr]

purée. Thick soup; vegetables, meat, or fish converted to a smooth pulp; any sieved and thick paste [F]

purdah. Curtain; system of seclusion of females [Hindu]

Purim. Feast of Lots; a festival commemorating the defeat of Haman's plot to destroy the Jews [Heb]

pur sang. Full-blooded; genuine [F]

purusa. Pursuits; wealth [Skr]

purus idiota. Congenital idiot [L]

purusartha. Object of (man's) pursuits; statement of aims which Indian philosophers preface to their works [Skr]

pusma. Protesting question [Gk]

put. Path [R]

putain. Street-walker; prostitute [F]

putj. The way [R]

Putsch. Unsuccessful revolutionary outbreak; abortive uprising; attempted *coup d'état* [G]

pu tung hsin. Maintaining a firm will; state of unperturbed mind [C]

pxt. See *pinxit*

pyat. Five [R]

pylon. Corner tower; bridge tower [Gk]

pyr. Fire [Gk]

pyrethrum. Variety of chrysanthemum; insecticide made from its dried flowers [Gk]

Pyrrhus. King of Epirus, who defeated the Romans in 279 B.C., but at the same time lost a large part of his army

Q

Q.E.D. See *quod erat demonstrandum*

Q.E.F. See *quod erat faciendum*

Q.E.I. See *quod erat inveniendum*

q.s. See *quantum sufficit*

qua. Considered as; in the character or capacity of; as far as; how [L]

quacunque via data. Whichever way you take it [L]

Qua Cursum Ventus. Where the Wind Their Course (guides) (Clough) [L]

quadragesima. Fortieth; first Sunday in Lent (40th day before Easter) [L]

quadrans. Fourth part; quarter [L]

Quadrat. Square; the sign for a natural (music) [G]

quadriennium. Period or term of four years [L]

quadrivium. Four ways; the second and more advanced group of liberal arts studies in the Middle Ages; arithmetic, geometry, astronomy and music [L] See *trivium*

Quaecumque sunt vera. Whatsoever things are true (motto of North-western University) [L]

quae est eadem. Which is the same [L]

Quae nocent docent. Things that hurt us teach [L]

Quae pars orationis ? What part of speech? [L]

quaere. I should like to know; it is a question [L]

quaeritur. It is asked; the question arises [L]

quaestio. Question; problem[L]

quai. Wharf; dock [F]

Quai d'Orsay. Embankment along the Seine River in Paris; location of the French foreign ministry; the French foreign ministry [F]

qualis. Of what kind [L]

Qualis artifex pereo. What an artist dies in me (Nero, before his death) [L]

Qualis vita, finis ita. The way you live determines the way you die [L]

quand. When [F]

quand même. Nevertheless; all the same; despite consequences [F]

quando. When [L]

Quandoque bonus dormitat Homerus. Sometimes even good Homer nods; even the best authors are sometimes dull [L]

Quante teste, tanti cervelli. Many men, many minds [It]

quantum. How great; an indivisible unit of any physical quantity; name of a theory of physical mechanics [L]

quantum libet. As much as you please [L]

quantum sufficit. As much as suffices; enough [L]

quaranta. Forty [It]

Quartier Latin. Artist's quarter in Paris; the Latin Quarter [F]

quarto. Fourth [It]. See also *in quarto*

quarto die post. On the fourth day after [L]

quartus. Fourth [L]

quasi. As if; seemingly; not really; half; almost [L]

quaternio terminorum. (Fallacy) of four terms; failure to provide a common middle term between major and minor premisses of a syllogism [L]

quatre. Four [F]

quattordici. Fourteen [It]

quattro. Four [It]

quattrocentisti. Artists or painters of the *quattrocento* period [It]

quattrocento. 1400; referring to the style or school of 15th century Italian painters; the Pre-Raphaelites [It]

quatuor. Four [L]

quebracho. Hardwood tree, symbol of Paraguay; bark used in tanning [Sp]

Quechua. Dialect of the Quechua Indians of Peru

Queda el rabo por desollar. The worst is yet to come [Sp]

Que faire ? What shall I do? [F]

Qué hora es ? What time is it? [Sp]

quelque. Some [F]

quelque chose. Something [F]

Quem di diligunt adolescens moritur. Whom the gods love dies young [L]

Quem quaeritis ? Whom do ye seek? Opening words of dialogue between women at the tomb of Christ, in medieval drama [L]

quena. Peruvian flute [Sp]

quenelles. Shapes produced by forcing mashed ingredients through a pastry bag into boiling soup [F]

quercus. Oak [L]

quercus alba. White oak [L]

quercus rubra. Red oak [L]

quercus velutina. Yellow oak [L]

querido. Dear (*fem.* querida) [Sp]

queso. Cheese [Sp]

Questa O Quella. The One is as Fair as the Other (*Rigoletto*, Act I; Verdi) [It]

Quest' Assisi Ch' Io Vesto. These Clothes that I Wear (*Aida*, Act II; Verdi) [It]

Qu'est-ce que c'est que cela ? What's that? [F]

Qu'est-ce qu'il y a ? What's the matter? [F]

questura. Police station [It]

quetzal. Monetary unit of Guatemala [Sp]

quia. Because; whereas; inasmuch as [L]

Qui a bu, boira. Ever drunk, ever dry; one drink leads to another [F]

Qui bene distinguit bene docet. He who makes good distinctions teaches well [L]

Qui bene interrogat bene docet. He who questions well teaches well [L]

quicquid. Whatever [L]

quicunque vult. Whosoever will; the Athanasian creed [L]

quidam. Somebody; person unknown [L]

quidditas. "Whatness"; essence; that which is described in a definition [L]

Quid est veritas ? What is truth? (Pilate; John 18-38) [L]

Quid faciendum ? What is to be done ? [L]

Quid hoc sibi vult ? What does this mean? [L]

Quid nunc ? What now? [L]

quidnunc. What now; gossip; newsmonger [L]

quid pro quo. Something for something; substitution of one thing for another; compensation in kind [L]

quién ? Who? [Sp]

Quien mal anda, mal acaba. He who lives ill, dies ill [Sp]

Quien mal dice, peor oye. He who speaks evil, hears worse [Sp]

Quien no se atreve no pasa la mar. Nothing ventured, nothing gained; faint heart ne'er won fair lady [Sp]

Quien no se ventura, no ha ventura. Nothing ventured, nothing gained [Sp]

Quién sabe ? Who knows? [Sp]

Qui invidet minor est. He who envies is inferior [L]

Qui Laborat Orat. He Who Labors (also) Prays (Clough) [L]. See also *Laborare est orare*

Qui male agit odit lucem. He who acts badly hates the light [L]

quina. Quinine [Sp]

quince. Fifteen [Sp]

Quinctili Vare, legiones redde. Quintilius Varus, give me back my legions [L]

quincunx. Checkerboard pattern; form of the five spots on dice [L]

quindici. Fifteen [It]

Qui non negat fatetur. He who does not deny, admits [L]

quinquennium. Period of five years [L]

quinta essentia. Fifth essence; a fifth element which, according to Aristotle, is found in celestial bodies, as distinguished from the four earthly bodies; the purest and most concentrated form of anything; quintessence [L]

quintal. 100 kilograms = 220 lbs. [F]

quinto. Fifth [It]

quintus. Fifth [L]

Qui parcit nocentibus innocentes punit. He who spares the guilty punishes the innocent [L]

quipus. Knotted, colored strings (supposed to have been used by the Incas for keeping records) [Sp]

Quirinal. One of the 7 hills of Rome; location of Italian king's palace; former term for the Italian government

quisling. Traitor; derived from Vidkun Quisling, leader of the Norwegian Nazis, who betrayed his country to the Germans

quisquis. Whoever; everyone [L]

Qui tacet, consentire videtur. He who is silent is supposed to consent [L]

quite. Parry; dodge [Sp]

Qui transtulit, sustinet. He who transplanted, sustains (motto of Connecticut) [L]

qui vive. Long live who? (sentry's challenge); alert; watchful [F]

Qui va là ? Who goes there? [F]

quo ad. As regards [L]

quoad hoc. To this extent; so far; as to this; so far as this is concerned [L]

Quo animo ? With what intention? [L]

quocunque modo. In whatever way [L]

quod. What(ever); that (which) [L]

quod erat demonstrandum. Which was to be shown or proved [L]

quod erat faciendum. Which was to be done [L]

quod erat inveniendum. Which was to be found [L]

quodlibet. Anything whatever [L]

Quod necessitas cogit, defendit. That which necessity compels, it justifies [L]

quod nota. Which note; which mark [L]

quod semper, quod ubique. That which always, that which everywhere (has found acceptance); principle used as a test for great literature [L]

quod vide. Which see [L]

quo fata vocant. Whither the fates call [L]

quo hoc. In this respect [L]

quo jure? By what law? By what right? [L]

Quomodo? In what manner? [L]

quondam. Formerly; one time [L]

qoran. See *Koran*

Quot homines, tot sententiae. How many people, so many opinions (Terence) [L]

quodlibet. How many soever; indeed [L]

quod quid est. That by which it is; that which makes a thing what it is; a thing's essence or substance [L]

quotidien(ne). Daily [F]

quoties. Whenever [L]

quousque. How long; how far; until [L]

Quousque tandem (abutere patientia nostra)? How long (will you abuse our patience)? (Cicero) [L]

Quo Vadis? Whither Goest Thou? (title of a novel by Sienkiewicz) [L]

quovis modo. In whatever manner [L]

quum. When [L]

q.v. See *quod vide*

R

Raagnis. Musical modes in ancient Indian or Hindu music [Skr]

rabbi. Master [Heb]

rabochaya mysl. Workers' thought [R]

rabocheye delo. Workers' cause [R]

rabochii zhurnal. Workers' journal [R]

rabota. Works [R]

Rache. Revenge [G]

rachem. Mercy [Heb]

radix. Root (*pl.* radices) [L]

ragion. Right; reason [It]

ragout. Thick, highly-seasoned stew [F]

rahatlakoum. Turkish candy

Rahmenerzählung. Story within a story; cyclical framed tale [G]

raion. County [R]

rais de coeur. Heart-shaped design [F]

raison. Reason; right [F]

raison d'état. Reason of state [F]

raison d'être. Reason for being [F]

raisonneur. Commentator; character in a play who represents the author's ideas and points the moral or message [F]

rajah. Prince or ruler of one of the states of India [Hindu]

Rajpoot. One of a military caste [Hindu]

Rajpramukh. Chief Prince (governor of a combined unit of merged states in India)

rajput. East Indian warriors [Hindu]

rakia. Expanse; space; the firmament [Heb]

rallentando. A gradually decreasing tempo [It]

Rama. Hero of the *Ramayana*

Ramadan. Ninth month of the Mohammedan year; period of fasting [Arab]

ramal. Metrical form in Arabic poetry [Arab]

Ramayana. Title of an East Indian philosophical epic, celebrating the doings of Rama and his wife Sita [Skr]

rameaux. Palms [F]

ramequin. Tidbit of baked cheese [F]

rampant. Rearing; poised (to strike) [F]

rampion. Bellflower; roots and leaves of this flower used in salads [F]

rancho. Ranch; collection of men or dwellings; hamlet [Sp]

ranseur. Spear having a long blade with two smaller projecting blades [F]

ranunculus. Buttercup [L]

ranz-des-vaches. Swiss herdsmen's melody played on an Alpine horn [F]

rape. Turnips [It]

rapport. Relation; kinship; association [F]

rapporteur. Reporter or secretary of a committee (either in the French parliament or at a conference of the United Nations) [F]

rapprochement. Relationship, kinship; approach; meeting of views, ideas, policies, *etc.*; re-establishment of friendly relations [F]

rara avis. Rare bird; a wonderful thing [L]

Rara avis in terris, nigroque simillima cygno. A rare bird on earth and very like a black swan (Juvenal; *Satires*; 6-165) [L]

rasas. Flavors; impressions to be induced by a work of art [Skr]

rasprodannoe. Out of print [R]

Rassemblement Démocratique Révolutionnaire. Democratic Revolutionary Assembly; a moderate left-wing political movement in France [F]

Rat. Council [G]

rataplan. Imitation of a drumbeat; rub-a-dub-dub [F]

ratatiné. Shriveled; rough-surfaced fabric [F]

raté. Missed fire; failed [F]

Rathaus. Town hall [G]

ratiné. See *ratatine*

ratio. Rate; proportion; degree; reason; understanding; case; judgment [L]

Ratio est radius divini luminis. Reason is a ray of the divine light [L]

rationale. Statement of reasons; exposition of principles [L]

ratione materiae. By reason of the subject-matter involved [L]

Rätsel. Riddle; puzzle [G]

Ratskeller. Restaurant and bar in the basement of a *Rathaus* [G]

Räuber. Robber(s) (title of a play by Schiller, 1781) [G]

Raum. Space; room [G]

raviolo. A kind of meat patty [It]

rayah. Flock; non-Mohammedan Turkish subject [Arab]

rayère. Light-slit in a wall [F]

razón. Reason; cause; right [Sp]

razzia. Raid; plundering or slave - collecting expedition [Arab]

R.D.R. See *Rassemblement Démocratique, etc.*

re. In the matter of; in the case of [L]

real. Spanish monetary unit; old Spanish coin

realia. Real things; the real or physical aspects of a culture or civilization, *i.e.* geography, industry, communications, *etc.*; materials for teaching foreign culture; visual aids [L]

Realpolitik. Politics or policy based on real or material factors; power politics [G]

Réaumur. Thermometer scale from freezing water=0, to boiling water=80; name of a French physicist

rebab. A type of stringed musical instrument [Arab]

rebeck. Ancient three-string violin [Arab]

rebus. A word or name represented by a picture [L]

rebus sic stantibus. Things remaining as they were; basic assumption for continuing validity of a contract or treaty [L]

recensio. Recension; (critical) review [L]

réchauffé. Reheated; warmed over [F]

recherché. Esoteric [F]

recherches. Investigations; research; inquiries [F]

Recht. Right; justice; equity; law [G]

rechts. Right; on the right [G]

Rechtswissenschaft. Jurisprudence [G]

recipe. Take (used on prescriptions) [L]

recitativo. A sustained passage in a vocal selection having a limited range; a passage in the style of a recitation [It]

recitativo secco. A *recitativo* with little accompaniment except for occasional chords [It]

recitativo stromentato. A *recitativo* with full and varied accompaniment [It]

réclame. Notoriety; publicity; reputation or vogue established by advertizing [F]

Recondita Armonia. Strange Harmony (*La Tosca*, Act I; Puccini) [It]

reconquista. Reconquest (of Spain from the Moors) [Sp]

recta ratio. Right reason [L] See *orthos logos*

recto. On the right; right-handed page [L]

rectus. Right [L]

rectus in curia. Upright in court; one who has an honest case [L]

recua. Pack-train (of llamas) [Sp]

recueil. Collection (of writings) [F]

redacteur. Editor [F]

reddendo singula singulis. By referring each to each [L]

redif. Soldier of the reserve; military reserves [Turk]

redingote. Frock coat; style of women's dress fashioned after the English riding coat [F]

redivivus. Living again; restored [L]

redondilla. Quatrain of octosyllabic verses [Sp]

reductio ad absurdum. Reduction to the absurd; a method of indirect proof by deducing a contradiction from the negation of a proposition taken together with other propositions previously proved or granted [L]

reductio ad impossibile. Reduction to the impossible; a method of establishing a proposition by showing that its contradictory involves impossible consequences; disproving a proposition by showing that its consequences are absurd, *i.e. reductio ad absurdum* [L]

referendarius. Officer who presented cases and petitions to the Roman emperor [L]

reditus. Rent; income; profit[L]

refrán. Popular proverb in verse [Sp]

refresco. Soft drink [Sp]

regalia. Things pertaining to a king; trappings suggestive of royalty [L]. See also *jura regalia*

regia via. Royal way; the king's highway [L]

régie. Direction; regulation; state tobacco monopoly [F]

régime. System of rules or regulations; government [F]

regina. Queen [L]

régisseur. (Stage) director [F]

Regisseur. Director [G]

Regius Professor. Royal professor; title of professorship, originally founded by Henry VIII, in English universities [L]

règle. Rule [F]

reglement. Regulation; rule; manual of rules and regulations [F]

Regnant populi. The people rule (motto of Arkansas) [L]

regnum. Kingdom; reign [L]

regula. Rule [L]

regula fidei. Rule of faith [L]

Reich. Empire; realm; Germany [G]

Reichsbahn. German Railroad(s) [G]

Reichsbank. National bank of Germany [G]

Reichskanzler. Imperial Chancellor [G]

Reichsrat. Upper house of the *Reichstag*, representing states [G]

Reichstag. German legislative body with representation based on population [G]

Reichswehr. German regular army [G]

Reigen. Round-dance; hands around [G]

rein. Pure; clean; sometimes used as a short form for *herein!*, "come in!" [G]

reine. Queen [F]

Reine-Marguerite. Queen Marguerite; China Aster [F]

re infecta. Thing undone; without accomplishing one's object [L]

rei publicae. In matters of the state [L]

reja. Iron window - grating [Sp]

rejet. The run-over part of a line of verse [F]

relevé. Raised; type of ballet step involving sharp rise to the toe [F]

relevé de potage. Dish of boiled food immediately following the soup [F]

Religio Laici. Religion of a Layman (Dryden) [L]

Religio Medici. Religion of a Physician (Sir Thomas Brown) [L]

reliquiae. Remains [L]

remoulade. Salad dressing; spicy sauce [F]

Rem tene, verba sequentur. Grasp the matter, the words will follow; choose a subject, and the words will follow (Cato) [L]

Renaissance. Re-birth (of Latin and Greek studies); revival of learning in Italy and then in Europe, 15th and 16th centuries [F]

rendezvous. Meeting place; appointment [F]

rendición. Surrender [Sp]

renegado. Apostate; renegade; originally a Spaniard who embraced Mohammedanism [Sp]

renga. Poem sequence [J]

renseignements. Information [F]

rente. Annual return on invested capital; interest; annuity; income from investments; dividend [F]

rente foncière. Perpetual or long-term annuity based on land rental [F]

Rentenmark. German mark introduced in 1923 after the inflation [G]

rentier. Investor in French Government funds; person having an income from investments or property [F]

renversé. Reversed; ballet step involving backward sweep of the arms and body in a complete turn [F]

répétiteur. Rehearsal director; coach [F]

répétition générale. Dress rehearsal [F]

Répondez s'il vous plaît. Please answer [F]

repos. Repose; rest [F]

repoussé. Rebuffed; repulsed; hammered into relief from the reverse side [F]

reprise. Resumption [F]

repudium. Breaking of marriage contract [L]

Requiem aeternam. A part of the Requiem mass [L]

Requiem aeternam dona eis, Domine. Grant them eternal rest, O Lord (antiphon in the mass for the dead) [L]

Requies. Rest [L]

Requiescant in pace. May they rest in peace [L]

Requiescat in pace. May he (she) rest in peace [L]

reredos. An altar screen; an open fireplace [ ]

rerum primordia. First elements of things [L]

res. Thing; object; matter; action; proceeding [L]

Res accendent lumina rebus. One thing throws light upon others [L]

res adjudicata. Thing adjudicated; decision of a court [L]

res angusta domi. The poverty of one's home [L]

res cogitans. Thinking substance; the mind; the substance which pervades all individual minds (Descartes) [L]

res controversa. Matter in controversy; thing in question [L]

res derelicta. Abandoned property [L]

reseau. Network [F]

reseda. Mignonette [L]

Res est ingeniosa dare. It is a noble thing to give; it is better to give than to receive (Ovid) [L]

res extensa. Extended substance (Descartes) [L]

res extra mentem. Thing outside of the mind; objective datum [L]

res gestae. Things done; transactions; essential circumstances and facts surrounding a subject [L]

residuum. That which remains; residue; balance [L]

res ipsa loquitur. The thing speaks for itself [L]

res judicata. Matter upon which judgment has been passed [L]

Res non posse creari de nilo. Matter cannot be created from nothing (Lucretius) [L]

res nullius. Thing belonging to nobody; previously unoccupied territory [L]

Respice finem. Look to the end; look before you leap [L]

respondeat superior. Let the master answer [L]

res publicae. Things belonging to the public; public property [L]

ressault. Projection of moulding beyond the surface of a building [F]

ressenti. Forcible expression of form in a drawing or painting [It]

résumé. Summary [F]

Resurgam. I shall rise again [L]

retas. Semen [Skr]

retro. Back(ward); behind [L]

rétroussé. Turned up [F]

Reue. Repentance [G]

reus. Defendant; person accused; party to a suit; litigant [L]

revanche. Revenge; retaliation [F]

rêve. Dream [F]

revers. Reverse; rear side; turned-over lapel [F]

revista. Review [Sp]

revocatur. It is recalled; set aside; annulled [L]

rex. King [L]

Rex Iudaecorum (or **Judaeorum**) King of the Jews (part of the inscription on the cross of Christ) [L]

Rex non potest peccare. The king can do no wrong [L]

Reyes Católicos. Spanish Sovereigns; specifically, Ferdinand and Isabella [Sp]

Reyes Magos. The Magi; (three) Kings of the Orient[Sp]

rez-de-chaussée. Ground-floor [F]

rhamnus. Buckthorn tree [L]

rhapsode. Stitcher of song; minstrel; bard [Gk]

rhetor. Teacher of rhetoric; public speaker; orator [Gk] [L]

rho. 17th letter of the Greek alphabet (Pρ)

rhus. Species of sumac [L]

rhyparographus. A painter of still life and *genre* subjects among the ancient Romans [Gk]

rhyton. An ancient drinking cup in the shape of a horn [Gk]

riabinovka. An alcoholic drink [R]

ribi. Fish [R]

ricercari. Research; a type of esoteric, intricate music [It]

ricinus communis. Castor bean [L]

ricochet. Bounce [F]

ricorsi. Refluxes [It]

Ricotte. A hard, Italian cheese made from albumen whey [It]

ridere. To laugh [It]

ridotto. Club; gambling salon [It]

rien. Nothing [F]

Riesensteg. Giant's causeway [G]

Riesling. Type of grape grown in Alsace; wine of this grape [G]

rifacimento. Re-making; re-hash; copy or imitation [It]

rigaudon. A rapid dance; riga-doon [F]

rigor mortis. Stiffness of death; rigidity of a corpse; stiffening of muscular tissue and joints setting in a few hours after death [L]

rigor juris. Strictness of law [L]

rigsdag. Parliament [Dan-Swed]

riksdag. See *rigsdag*

rillettes. Pork hash [F]

rime riche. Rich rhyme; perfect rhyme; identical rhyming of sounds although in words of different meanings [F]

rinascimento. Rebirth [It]

rinceau. A scroll ornament consisting of sprigs of foliage [F]

Rinderpest. Cattle plague [G]

rinforzando. Reinforced; accented [It]

rinnce fadha. An ancient Irish dance [Gaelic]

rio. River [Sp]

R.I.P. See *Requiescat in Pace*

ripa. Banks of a river [L]

riqueza. Wealth [Sp]

rire. Laugh; laughter; humor [F]

ris de veau. Sweetbreads [F]

riso. Rice [It]

risoluto. Resolute; determined; bold [It]

Risorgimento. Resurgence; revival; emergence of Italy as a unified, independent state in the middle of the 19th century, under the leadership of Mazzini and Garibaldi [It]

risotto. A savory rice dish [It]

risqué. Daring; beyond the bounds of propriety [F]

rissolé. Sun-tinted; golden-brown; browned; minced fish or meat rolled in thin pastry and fried [F]

ritardando. Retarding; a gradual delay of tempo [It]

ritenuto. Retained; held back; more slowly [It]

Ritorna Vincitor. Return Victorious (*Aïda*, Act I; Verdi) [It]

Ritter. Knight [G]

robe. Dress; gown [F]

robe de style. Full-skirted gown [F]

robinia. Species of locust tree [L]

rocaille. Having scrolls and foliage; a term applied to the art in vogue at the time of Louis XV [F]

Rocinante. Steed ridden by Don Quixote; a scrawny nag [Sp]

rococo. Decorative style with a profusion of meaningless ornament; Louis XIV style; tawdry [F]

rodeo. Round-up [Sp]

rogo. I ask; I request [L]

roi. King [F]

Roi de Thulé. King of Thule (*Faust*, Act III; Gounod) [F]

Roi d'Yvetot. Minor king of Normandy made famous by a song by Béranger; jovial type [F]

roinek. Red-neck; nickname for British soldier [S. Afr. Du]

roi soleil. The Sun King (*i.e.* Louis XIV) [F]

rojo. Red [Sp]

roman. Novel; epic narrative [F]

roman à clef. Key novel; novel in which fictitious names are used for actual persons in real life [F]

roman bourgeois. Middle-class novel [F]

romancier. Novelist [F]

roma peditae. Pilgrims who traveled to Rome on foot [L]

Romería. Religious pilgrimage [Sp]

rondar. To linger; hang around [Sp]

rond de jambe. Ballet step consisting of a circle described by the foot [F]

rondeau. Metrical form of 3 stanzas of 15 lines each [F]

ronde-bosse. Rounded sculpture as distinguished from reliefs [F]

rondo. Musical movement of several parts, each ending with a repetition of the preceding part [It]

rond-point. Semi-circular termination of a building or avenue [F]

Rossiia. Russia [R]

ropa. Clothes [Sp]

Roquefort. Cheese made from goat's milk, having a strong odor and taste [F]

rosa chinensis fragrans. Tea rose [L]

rosa gallica. French rose [L]

rosa moschata. Musk rose [L]

rosa multiflora. Rambler rose [L]

Rosh Hashanah. The Hebrew New Year [Heb]

rosserie. Sordidness [F]

rossignol. Nightingale [F]

rosso antico. Antique red; red marble with white veins [It]

rostra. Raised platform; tribune; pulpit in the ancient Roman *forum* [L]

rostrum. Ornamented prow of a ship; a tribune or speaker's platform in the Roman *forum* [L]

rota. Succession; rotation; ancient court at Rome [L]

rôti. Roast [F]

rôtisserie. Restaurant specializing in grilled or broiled meats [F]

rôtissoire. Dutch oven [F]

rotunda. Circular building or part of a building, usually surmounted by a cupola [L]

roturier. Plebeian [F]

rouble. See *ruble*

roucou. A red paste used in gilding [F]

roué. Debauchee; rake; dissipated person [F]

rouet. Spinning wheel [F]

rouge. Red [F]

rouge et noir. Red and black; a card game [F]

roulade. Roll; quick succession of notes; florid vocal phrase [F]

roulette. Roller; an engraving tool used to trace a series of points; a gambling wheel [F]

route. Way; direction; road [F]

roux. Mixture of butter and flour for thickening soup or sauce [F]

roy. Old French for *roi*

R.S.V.P. See *Répondez, etc.*

ruba'i. Ancient Arabic verseform; song [Arab]

rubai. Quatrain (*pl.* rubaiyat) [Arab]

Rubaiyat. Pl. of *rubai*; poems by Omar Khayyam (d. 1123), translated by Edward Fitzgerald (1859–1868) [Arab]

rubato. The extension of one note at the expense of another in order to gain expression [It]

ruber. Red [L]

rubia tinctorum. Madder root, used for pigments [L]

ruble. Russian monetary unit

rubric. Illuminated initial letter in red on medieval manuscripts; a title or caption [L]

ruche. Lace frill [F]
Rückblick. Retrospect [G]
Rückkehr. Return [G]
Rucksack. Knapsack; pack [G]
Rücksicht. Consideration [G]
rudbeckia hirta. Black-eyed susan [L]
ruelle. Lane; alley; narrow space between bed and wall; bedroom used as a reception room by the *précieuses* at the time of Louis XIV [F]
ruggera. A pantomime dance [It]
Ruhm. Fame [G]

rukovodstvo. Manual [R]
Rundfunk. Radio broadcast(ing) [G]
Rundschau. Review [G]
rupee. Unit of currency in India [Skr]
rusé. Sly; given to ruses [F]
ruse de guerre. Trick in war; stratagem [F]
rus in urbe. Country in town; place or house combining the conveniences of both [L]
rutilant. Shining; brilliant [F]
ryot. Indian peasant [Hindu]

S

S. See *Seite*

S.A. See *Sturmabteilung*

sábado. Saturday [Sp]

sabato. Saturday [It]

sabda. Sound; word; testimony [Skr]

sablière. Horizontal supporting beam [F]

sabot. Wooden shoe [F]

sabotage. Interference with production; intentional damage or disruption to delay or stop something [F]

saboteur. One who attempts or carries out an act of *sabotage* [F]

sacellum. Small roofless temple or shrine [L]

sacerdotalis. Pertaining to a priest [L]

Sache. Thing; matter; cause [G]

sacheru. Sugar [R]

sachet. Small bag of perfume[F]

sachlich. Factual [G]

sächlich. Neuter [G]

Sachverhalt. State of affairs; existing facts; the situation as it stands; the facts of the matter [G]

Sackpfeife. Bagpipe [G]

Sacrae (or **Sanctae**) **Theologiae Doctor.** Doctor of Sacred Theology [L]

sacramentum. Oath [L]

sacra rappresentazione. Sacred representations; early religious plays [It]

sacrarium. Repository of sacred things [L]

Sacré Du Printemps. Rite of Spring (Stravinsky) [F]

sacrilegium. Theft of sacred things [L]

sacrosanctae theologiae professor. Professor of Sacred Theology [L]

saeculum. Age; era [L]

saepe. Often [L]

sagittarius. Archer [L]

saguna. Possessed of qualities [Skr]

sahib. Friend; native title for Europeans in India [Arab]

sainete. Farce [Sp]

saison. Season [F]

sakti. Strength; might; the female generative power in the universe [Skr]

salaam. Peace [Arab]

salame. Spiced sausage [It]

sal atticum. Attic salt; intellectual acuity; stinging wit [L]

sale. Dirty [F]

salida. Exit [Sp]

salix. Genus name of willow trees [L]

salle. Room; hall [F]

salle à manger. Dining room [F]

salle d'attente. Waiting room [F]

salle des pas perdus. Long hall or gallery in front of a courtroom or audience chamber [F]

salmagundi. Seasoned dish of chopped meat, anchovies, eggs, *etc.* [F]

salmi. Game-bird ragout [F]

salmis. Hash made of game [F]

salon. Reception room; exhibition hall [F]

Salon Carée. Square room; exhibition hall in the *Louvre* [F]

salpiglossis. Painted Tongue; variety of garden flower [Gk]

salpinx. An ancient bronze trumpet [Gk]

saltarello. An Italian dance somewhat similar to the *tarantella* [It]

saltation. Dance [F]

salud. Health [Sp]

salus. Health; prosperity; safety; welfare [L]

salus populi. Welfare of the people (motto of the University of Missouri) [L]

Salus populi suprema lex. The welfare of the people is the supreme law [L]

Salus populi suprema lex esto. The welfare of the people shall be the supreme law (motto of Missouri) [L]

Salus reipublicae suprema lex. The welfare of the state is the supreme law [L]

Salut, Demeure. Hail, thou Dwelling (*Faust*, Act III; Gounod) [F]

Salvam fac reginam, O Domine. God save the Queen[L]

Salvator Mundi. Savior of the World [L]

Salve! Hail! Welcome! (motto of Idaho) [L]

Salve Regina Misericordiae. Hail, Queen of Mercy; an old Catholic hymn to the Virgin[L]

salvia. Genus name of sage flowers [L]

salvo. Simultaneous firing of guns; round of applause [It]

sal volatile. Solution of ammonium carbonate, used as smelling salts [L]

salvo pudore. Without offense to modesty [L]

samadhi. Final stage in the practice of Yoga, in which individuality is given up while merging with the object of meditation [Skr]

samanya. Similar; generic; generality; universality [Skr]

samba. A South American dance [Sp]

sambuca. An ancient string-instrument [Gk]

sambucus. Elder tree [L]

Sammlung. Collection [G]

sämmtlich. Complete; collected [G]

samnyasin. Wise man, philosopher [Skr]

samovar. Tea cooker [R]

samsara. Going about; passage of the soul through the different stages of transmigration [Skr]

samskara. Mental impression; memory [Skr]

samurai. Feudal class composed of warriors and nobility [J]

sanae mentis. Of sound mind [L]

sanbenito. Penitential shirt [Sp]

san chiao. The three systems or religions, *i.e.* Confucianism, Buddhism, and Taoism [C]

Sancho Panza. Don Quixote's squire; uneducated but shrewd and realistic person [Sp]

sancta simplicitas. Blessed simplicity [L]

Sancte Pater. Holy Father [L]

sanctum. Holy place; private room [L]

sanctum sanctorum. Holy of holies; private place; esoteric doctrine [L]

sanctus. Holy; beginning of the hymn "Holy, holy, holy" in the Communion [L]

sandhi. Linkage [Skr]

sanft. Gentle; soft; mild [G]

sang. Blood [F]

sanga. Sticking to; attachment to material things [Skr]

sangar. Stone breastwork [Hindu]

Sängerfest. Song Festival [G]

sangfroid. Cool-blood; coolness in the face of difficulty or danger [F]

sangre. Blood [Sp]

sanguinaria. Bloodroot flower [L]

sanguis. Blood; consanguinity [L]

sanjak. Administrative district; subdivision of a *vilayet* [Turk]

sankhya. Name of a system of Indian philosophy [Skr]

San Nicola. Santa Claus [It]

sans. Without [F]

sans culottes. "Breechless"; nickname given to patriotic Frenchmen during the Revolution for discarding the aristocratic knee-breeches and hose, and adopting long trousers [F]

sans doute. Undoubtedly [F]

sans façon. Unceremoniously; abruptly; outspoken [F]

sans gêne. Without constraint or embarrassment; nerve; "cheek" [F]

sans peur et sans reproche. Without fear and without blame; of chivalrous character [F]

sans phrases. Without beating around the bush; direct; outspoken [F]

sans recours. Without recourse [F]

sans souci. Without care; unconcerned; without a worry in the world [F]

Santa Fé. Holy Faith [Sp]

Santiago de Compostela. St. James of Compostela; shrine in Galicia, Spain, famous since 800 A.D. [Sp]

Santo Oficio. Holy Inquisition [Sp]

sapiens. Wise (man) [L]

sapientia. Wisdom [L]

saponaria. Soapwort flower [L]

saraband. A solo dance of Spanish origin, executed with raised arms and slow gliding footwork [F]

sarcophagus. Flesh-decayer; tomb [Gk]

sardana. Country dance in north-eastern Spain [Sp]

sari. East Indian robe [Hindu]

sarracenia. Pitcher plant [L]

sarto. Tailor [It]

Sartor Resartus. The Tailor Retailored (Carlyle) [L]

sastra. A Sanskrit textbook[Skr]

sat. Being [Skr]

satem. 100; name given to a classification of languages based on resemblance of sound in their words for 100; distinguished from the *centum* languages [Avestan]

satis. Enough [L]

satis superque. Enough and too much; more than enough [L]

Satsuma. A royal family of Japan; fine stoneware produced in factories owned by this family [J]

Saturnalia. Riotous festivals in honor of Saturn(us), held in December in ancient Rome [L]

satyam. Truth [Skr]

satyriasis. Morbid and excessive craving for sexual intercourse [Gk]

Satz. Sentence; proposition; set [G]

Satzlehre. Syntax [G]

sauce blanche. White sauce [F]

sauce piquante. Sharp sauce, with lemon or vinegar [F]

saucisson. Sausage [F]

Sauerbraten. Roast in sweet-and-sour sauce [G]

Sauerkraut. Pickled cabbage [G]

sauté. Cooked in a small quantity of fat [F]

sauter. To jump; to cook in a small quantity of fat [F]

Sauternes. A French township famous for its wines; special wines made from over-ripe grapes [F]

sauve qui peut. Let him find safety who can; let every man look out for himself [F]

Sauwetter. Awful weather [G]

savannah. Plain [Sp]

savant. Learned man; scholar; scientist [F]

savate. Boxing in which feet as well as fists are used [F]

savoir faire. Ability to do the right thing; self-assurance; tact [F]

savoir vivre. Knowing how to behave; good breeding; knowledge of manners [F]

savon. Soap [F]

saxifraga. Sassafras [L]

sbirro. Policeman [It]

sc. See *scilicet*

scabellum. Footstool; square pedestal topped by a bust [L]

scaenae frons. Ornamental façade or stage background [L]

scagliola. Imitation stone masonry of plaster; artificial marble made of gypsum and glue [It]

Scaramouche. Boastful coward; stock figure in the *commedia dell' arte* [It]

scaramuccia. Skirmish [It]

scarpe. Shoes [It]

scarpellino. Workman employed by a sculptor to do either rough or finishing work in marble [It]

scélérat. Scoundrel; villainous [F]

scena. A vocal composition having a variety of styles, either independent or part of an opera; dramatic recitative, as in an opera [It]

scène à faire. Obligatory scene in every *pièce bien faite* [F]

Scènes de la Vie de Bohème. Scenes of Bohemian Life (title of a novel by Henri Murger, 1848, depicting the life of artists of the *Quartier Latin* in Paris) [F]

sch-. See also *sh-*

Schadenfreude. Malice; malicious joy [G]

Schall. Sound [G]

Schatz. Treasure; sweetheart [G]

Schauspiel. Play; drama [G]

Schauspielhaus. Theatre [G]

schaygetz. Gentile boy [Y]

Schein. Appearance; illusion; certificate; banknote; bill [G]

schema. Figure; external form; plan; construction; figure [Gk]

schematismos. Stylistic pattern of a speech [Gk]

Scherz. Joke; prank [G]

scherzando. Jestingly [It]

scherzo. A jest; a composition of lively tempo and jesting style [It]

schicker. Drunk(ard) [Y]

Schicksal. Fate; destiny [G]

Schicksalstragödie. Fate-drama [G]

Schiedam. Holland gin [place]

schiksa. Gentile girl [Y]

Schimpflexikon. Dictionary of invective [G]

Schinken. Ham [G]

schipperke. Lapdog [Du]

Schlacht. Battle [G]

Schlagobers. Whipped cream [Austrian]

Schlagwort. Slogan [G]

Schlamperei. Slovenliness; sloppiness [G]

schlemihl. Helpless individual; unlucky fool [Y]

schleppend. Dragging; drawling [G]

Schlimmverbesserung. An improvement in reverse; an improvement that makes matters worse [G]

Schmalz. Fat; suet; sentimentality [G] [Y]

Schmerz. Pain [G]
Schmetterling. Butterfly [G]
schmus. Gossip; chew the fat[Y]
Schmutz. Dirt; smut; filth [G]
Schnaderhüpferl. Folk dance [G]
Schnapps. Brandy; whiskey [G]
Schnecken. Snail; type of cake [G]
schnell. Fast; quick; rapid [G]
Schnellzug. Express train [G]
Schnitzel. Shaving(s); cutlet[G]
Schnitzelbank. Sawbuck; song chart [G]
Schnörkel. Spiral; scroll; volute; flourish; curleycue; periscope-like device for providing air to a submarine [G]
schnorrer. Beggar [Y]
Schnur. String [G]
schochet. Ritual slaughterer [Heb]
scholium. Annotation; gloss (*pl.* scholia) [L]
schön. Beautiful; fine; nice; all right; good [G]
schöne Seele. Beautiful soul; *bel esprit* [G]
Schottische. Dance in Scottish style [G]
Schrecklichkeit. Frightfulness; policy of terror [G]
Schrift. Script; writing; written publication [G]
Schuhplatteltanz. Bavarian clog-dance involving rapid slapping of shoes and leather breeches [G]
Schuhplattler. See *Schuhplatteltanz*
schul. See *shool*.
Schuld. Guilt; blame [G]
Schupo. Cop; policeman (*abbr.* of Schutzpolizist) [G]
Schuster, bleib' bei deinem Leisten. Every cobbler should stick to his last [G]
Schutz. Defense; guard; protection [G]
Schütze. Marksman; rifleman; bowman; huntsman [G]

Schutzstaffel. Elite bodyguard of the Nazi party [G]
Schwächling. Weakling [G]
Schwanengesang. Swan song [G]
Schwank. Medieval comic folktale in prose [G]
Schwärmerei. Raving; enthusiasm [G]
schwarz. Black; sombre; pessimistic [G]
Schwarzes Korps. Black corps; name given to members of the black-uniformed *Schutzstaffel*[G]
Schweinskopf. Pig's head; an uncomplimentary epithet; a name given to the medieval musical instrument, the psaltery, because of its shape [G]
Schweizerkäse. Swiss cheese[G]
Schwulst. Bombast; grandiloquence [G]
schwungvoll. Animated; lively [G]
scie. Saw; boring observation or platitude [F]
scie d'atelier. Boring observation or refrain; practical joke; witty allusion to current events; traditional annoyances in the French artists' *atelier* [F]
sciendum est. It is to be known; be it known [L]
scienter. Knowingly [L]
scientia. Knowledge; science[L]
scientia intuitiva. Intuitive knowledge [L]
Scientia sol mentis est. Knowledge is the sun of the mind (motto of the University of Delaware) [L]
scilicet. That is to say; to wit [L]
scilla. Squill or Bluebell [L]
scintilla. Spark; least particle [L]
sciolto. With freedom; according to taste; light; free [It]
scire. To know [L]
scire facias. That you cause to know; that you show cause [L]

scire feci. I have caused to know; I have caused notice to be given [L]

scissio auricularum. Cropping of the ears [L]

scolion. Drinking song; collection of 6th century Athenian songs [Gk]

scop. Poet or minstrel [AS]

scribere. To write [L]

scribere est agere. To write is to act [L]

scrinium. Circular case used to hold rolls of parchment [L]

scriptor classicus. Aristocratic writer; writer for the few [L]

scriptor proletarius. Proletarian writer; writer for the masses [L]

scriptum. Something written; a writing or written document[L]

Scoppio del Carro. Annual festival in the city of Florence [It]

scorpio. Scorpion [L]

scrotum. Pouch enclosing the testicles [L]

scrutin de liste. Electoral system for choosing members of the Chamber of Deputies by groups from each electoral district [F]

sculpsit. Engraved [L]

scusa. Excuse me [It]

Scuto bonae voluntatis tuae coronasti nos. With the shield of thy good will hast thou crowned us (motto of Maryland) [L]

scutum. Oblong, curved shield carried by Roman foot-soldiers

se. If [It]

séance. Session [F]

sec. Dry [F]

sécateurs. Pruning-shears [F]

secco. Dry [It]

Secentismo. Literary reaction against classicism in the 17th century [It]

secentisti. Poets of the *secentismo* [It]

séchiste. Dry-point engraver [F]

secundi adjacentis. A proposition in logic consisting of subject and predicate, but without a copula or connection [L]

secundum. According to [L]

secundum aequum et bonum. According to what is just and right [L]

secundum artem. According to the rules of the art; skillfully [L]

secundum bonos mores. According to good usages; according to established custom [L]

secundum naturam. According to nature; naturally, not artificially [L]

secundum quid. Relatively; in some respect; in a qualified sense; a fallacy arising from the use of a general proposition without attention to tacit qualifications which would invalidate the use made of it [L]

secundus. Second [L]

sed. Thirst [Sp]

seda. Silk [Sp]

sedarim. Orders [Heb]

sedente animo. With settled purpose [L]

sederunt. They are sitting; session [L]

sedes. A see; the dignity of a bishop [L]

sedici. Sixteen [It]

sed quaere. But inquire; examine this further [L]

Seele. Soul; psyche; mind [G]

sefer. Book [Heb]

Segel. Sail [G]

Segen. Blessing [G]

segno. Sign [It]

segue. It follows; now follows [It]

seguedilla. A rapid dance in 6-8 rhythm [Sp]

seguidilla. Improvised song of 4 verses [Sp]

seguro. Sure [Sp]

Sehnsucht. Longing; nostalgia [G]

sehr. Very (much) [G]

sei. Six [It]

Seicento. Italian literature of the 17th century [It]

Seigneur. Lord [F]

Seil. Rope; cable [G]

Se Il Mio Nome. If you want to know my name (*Barber of Seville*, Act I; Rossini) [It]

sein. To be; his or its; being or existence (when capitalized) [G]

seis. Six [Sp]

Seises. A religious dance [Sp]

Seite. Page; side [G]

Sejm. National legislature of Poland

Sekundenstil. Style of minute and exact observation of detail; phonographic reproduction of spoken words as a style of naturalistic writing [G]

sel. Salt [F]

Selbsttäuschung. Self-deception [G]

Selbstzweck. Self purpose; said of anything engaged in for its own sake [G]

selene. Moon [Gk]

selig. Blessed; beatific [G]

sella curulis. Official seat; seat of honor [L]

selon. According to [F]

Seltzer(wasser). Mineral or carbonated water; seltzer [G]

selva. Forest [Sp]

selyanka. A Russian soup [R]

sem. Seven [R]

sema. Sign; symbol [Gk]

semaine. Week [F]

semana. Week [Sp]

Semana Santa. Holy Week; week before Easter [Sp]

semasia. Signification of a term [Gk]

semble. Seems; would appear [F]

seminarium. Tree-nursery [L]

semitae sapientiae. Paths of wisdom [L]

Semmel. Bread roll [G] [Y]

semnadtsat. Seventeen [R]

semolino. A coarse flour [It]

semper. Always [L]

semper eadem. Always the same (motto of Queen Elizabeth) [L]

Semper ego auditor tantum ? Am I always to be a listener only? (opening words of Juvenal's *Satires*) [L]

semper felix. Always fortunate [L]

semper fidelis. Always faithful [L]

semper idem. Always the same [L]

semper paratus. Always prepared (motto of the Boy Scouts) [L]

Semper specialia generalibus insunt. Particulars are always included in generals [L]

semplice. Simple; unaffected [It]

sempre. Always; constantly; continuously [It]

sempre diritto. Straight ahead [It]

sen. Coin worth one-hundredth of a *yen* [J]

senatus. Senate [L]

senatus populusque romanus. The Roman senate and people [L]

senectus. Old age [L]

senex. Old (man) [L]

senex bis puer. An old man (is) twice a child [L]

seniores priores. Elders first [L]

señor. Mister; sir; gentleman [Sp]

señora. Madam; lady; matron [Sp]

señorita. Miss; young lady [Sp]

sensibilia communia. "Common sensibles"; the qualities of a sense object that may be apprehended by several senses [L]

sensiblerie. Sentimentality [F]

sensus. Sense; meaning [L]

sententia. Sense; import; sentence; maxim; opinion [L]

sentiabr. September [R]

sentido. Path [Sp]

sententiae. Propositions; collection of logical or philosophical propositions and explanations of them; sentences [L]

Sententia facit jus. Judgment creates right [L]

sentire. To feel [L]

senza. Without [It]

senz' anno. No date [It]

senza tempo. With freedom from strict time [It]

separatim. Severally [L]

Sepharad. Spain [Heb]

Sephardim. Spanish-Portuguese Jews, as distinguished from Polish-German Jews, or *Ashkenazim* [Heb]

sepo. Rot [Gk]

sept-. Seven [L]

septimus. Seventh [L]

septuagesima. Seventieth (day before Easter) [L]

septuaginta. Seventy [L]

Septuagint(a). Seventy; reference to the Greek translation of the Hebrew scriptures (*ca.* 275 B.C.), supposed to have been made by 70 persons [L]

septum. Inclosure [L]

sepultura. Offering to the priest for burial of a dead person [L]

seq. (*pl.* seqq.) See *et sequens*

sequela. Consequence; result (*pl.* sequelae) [L]

sequentiae. (Musical) sequences (of the Mass) [L]

sera. Evening [L]

seraglio. Harem [It]

serang. Petty officer of Lascar seamen [Pers]

serenata. Serenade [Sp]

sereno. Watchman; clear [Sp]

seriatim. Severally; separately; one by one [L]

serment. Oath; vow [F]

Sermo index animo. Speech is an index of the mind [L]

Servabo fidem. I will keep faith [L]

serventese. Form of satirical lyric [It]

servette. Maid-servant [It]

serviette. Napkin [F]

servitium. Service; obedience [L]

servitor. Servant; serving man [L]

servitus. Slavery; bondage; servitude [L]

servus. Slave; bondman [L]; At your service! [G]

sesenta. Sixty [Sp]

sessanta. Sixty [It]

sesterce. Ancient Roman coin [L]

sestet. Last six lines of an Italian sonnet [L]

sestina. Poetic form of 6 stanzas each of 6 lines, with an *envoi* of 3 lines [F]

sesto. Sixth [It]

seta. Silk [It]

setenta. Seventy [Sp]

settanta. Seventy [It]

sette. Seven [It]

settimo. Seventh [It]

Sèvres. French town noted for its fine pottery [F]

sexagesima. Sixtieth (day before Easter); second Sunday before Lent [L]

sextus. Sixth [L]

s.f. See *sub finem*

sforzando. Forced; accented [It]

sfregazzi. Method of shading color in painting by using the finger instead of the brush [It]

sfumato. Vague in outline; soft focus [It]

sgraffito. A kind of *fresco* painting using white color on black stucco [It]

sh-. See also *sch-*

shaar ha-shamayyim. The gate to Heaven [Heb]

shabbos. (Day of) rest; sabbath [Heb]

shadchen. Marriage broker; matchmaker [Y]

Shah. King of Persia [Pers]

sha'ir. Poet; knower [Arab]

shako. High, stiff military hat or headdress, formerly of fur [Hungarian]

Shalom Aleichem. Peace be with you; pseudonym of a writer of humorous short stories in Yiddish [Heb]

shaman. Priest(ess) [Tungusic]

shan. Goodness; the practice of virtue [C]

Shariah. See *Sheria*

Shavuoth. Feast of Weeks [Heb]

shayst. Six [R]

shchav. Soup made of sour greens [R]

shean treuse. A rollicking pantomime dance [Scottish]

shechinah. Visible glory of God [Heb]

sheikh. Chief [Arab]

shekari. See *shikaree*

shekel. Ancient weight and coin (*pl.* shekels=money, riches) [Heb]

shen. Spirits; spiritual power; spirited style [C]

sheng. Sage; ruler; male lead in a play [C]

shen jen. The spiritual man [C]

Sheria. Sacred Moslem law, including the *Koran* and the sayings of Mohammed [Arab]

shest. Six [R]

shestdesiat. Sixty [R]

shestnadtsat. Sixteen [R]

shetar. Covenant [Heb]

Shiah. Mohammedan sect; person adhering to Shiah doctrine [Arab]

shih. Actuality; substance; authority; force; movement; verse; poetic quality [C]

shih chi. Historical records [C]

shih fei. Right and wrong [C]

Shiite. See *Shiah*

shikaree. Hunter; native attendant [Pers]

Shinto. Way of the gods; former Japanese state religion emphasizing the divinity of the emperor [C] [J]

Shir Hashirim. Song of Songs [Heb]

shish kebab. Broiled filets of lamb [Arab]

shite. Hero; leading man in a play [J]

Shiva. The kind one; name of the God Rudra in the religion of Shivaism [Skr]

shogun. Leader of the army; title of feudal rulers of Japan from the 12th to the 19th century [J]

sholom. Peace [Heb]

Sholom aleicham. Peace be with you [Heb]

shool. Synagogue [Y]

shto ? What? [R]

shto-takoi ? What's that? [R]

shu shu. Divination and magic [C]

si. West [C]; If; yes indeed! [F]

sì. Yes [It]

siao. A wind instrument [C]

Sibylla Palmifera. The Sibyl Carrying a Palm (Rossetti) [L]

sic. So; thus (used parenthetically to call attention to an error or an unreasonable statement) [L]

Sicherheit. Safety; security [G]

sic eunt fata hominum. Thus go the fates of men [L]

si contingat. If it happen [L]

sic passim. Thus everywhere [L]

Sic semper tyrannis. Thus always to tyrants (motto of Virginia; words of Edwin Booth after shooting Lincoln) [L]

Sic transit gloria mundi. Thus passes away the glory of the world [L]

sicut ante. As before [L]

sicut me deus adjuvet. So help me God [L]

siddhi. Attainment (of supernatural powers); a *Yoga* ideal [Skr]

Si Dieu n'existait pas, il faudrait l'inventer. If God did not exist, it would be necessary to invent him (Voltaire) [F]

sidi. Chieftain [Arab]

si diis placet. If it please the gods [L]

siècle. Century [F]

siècle d'or. Golden age [F]

Sieg. Victory [G]

Siegheil! Hail to victory! [G]

siempre. Always [Sp]

sierra. Mountain range [Sp]

siesta. Nap [Sp]

siete. Seven [Sp]

sigillum. Seal [L]

siglo. Century [It]

Siglo de Oro. Golden Age (of Spanish literature; 16th and 17th centuries) [Sp]

sigma. 18th letter of the Greek alphabet (Σσ)

signor. Mr.; gentleman [It]

signora. Mrs.; married lady; madam [It]

signorina. Miss; unmarried lady [It]

si ita est. If it be so [L]

Sikh. Member of a military sect in the Punjab; disciple [Hindu]

sikinnis. Satirical dance [Gk]

Si latet ars, prodest. If the art is hidden, it succeeds [L]

silent leges inter arma. The power of law is suspended during war [L]

Silenus. Drunken old man; rollicking old drunkard; foster-father of Bacchus [Gk]

silex. Flint [L]

silpa. The arts [Skr]

silva. Wood; forest [L]

s'il vous plaît. Please [F]

Simchath. Rejoicing; happy event(s) [Heb]

Simchath Torah. Rejoicing in the Law, a Hebrew holiday [Heb]

Simikion. A type of ancient harp [Gk]

Similia similibus curantur. Like (ailments) are cured by like (remedies) [L]

Similia similibus percipiuntur. Like things are apprehended through like things [L]

similiter. Likewise; the like; similarly [L]

Si monumentum requiris, circumspice. If you seek a monument, look around (epitaph of Sir Christopher Wren in St. Paul's Cathedral in London) [L]

simpático. Congenial; nice, pleasant; winsome; sympathetic [Sp]

Simplex Munditiis. Simple in Neatness (Horace; *Odes*; 1-5; Ben Jonson) [L]

simpliciter. Absolutely [L]

simulacrum. Likeness; image; copy of an original [L]

simul et semel. Together and at one time [L]

Simultanbühne. Multiple set; stage set having several locales at once [G]

sindicato. Trade union [Sp]

sine. Without [L]

sine cura. Without charge; without care [L]

sine die. Without (assigning a) day [L]

sine dubio. Without doubt [L]

sine mora. Without delay [L]

sinensis. Chinese; term used in plant classification [L]

sine odio. Without hatred [L]

sine qua non. Without which not; indispensable requisite or condition [L]

sineva. Blue [R]

singaut-sorri. "Sing-out sorry" public lamentation; plea for aid [PE]

Singspiel. A play with songs, a precursor of the modern opera [G]

sinistrati. Lost or forgotten ones [It]

Sinn. Sense; thought(s) [G]

Sinnbild. Symbol [G]

Sinn Fein. "We ourselves"; the Irish nationalist movement which led to the establishment of the Irish Free State in 1922 [Gaelic]

Sinngedicht. Didactic poem [G]

Sinnlichkeit. Sensibility [G]

sin(o). To; toward; as far as [It]

sinus. Curve; fold; bay or gulf; a (winding) cavity [L]

si paret. If it appears [L]

Si Pùo! If You Please (*Pagliacci*, Prologue; Leoncavallo) [It]

Si quaeris peninsulam amoenam, circumspice. If you seek a delightful peninsula, look about you (motto of Michigan) [L]

Sirdar. General; British commander-in-chief of the Egyptian army [Pers]

sirniki. Cottage cheese cakes fried in butter and served with sour cream and sugar [R]

sirocco. Hot, oppressive wind reaching Italy from Africa [It]

siru. Cheese [R]

sirvente. A war song or metrical diatribe against an enemy; a verse-form in troubadour poetry [F]

sirventes. See *serventese*

Siste viator. Stop, traveler [L]

Si te vi, ya no me acuerdo. Out of sight, out of mind [Sp]

Sitten. Morals; customs; manners; ethics [G]

Sittenlehre. Ethics; theory of morals [G]

sittlich. Moral; ethical [G]

Sittlichkeit. Morality [G]

Sit tibi terra levis. May the earth rest lightly on thee [L]

Sit venia verbis. Let the words be pardoned [L]

Sitzkrieg. Sit-down war; phony war; slang term used to describe the initial period of relative inactivity in World War II after the fall of Poland [G]

Siva. See *Shiva*

Si vis me flere dolendum est primum ipsi tibi. If you wish me to weep, you must first weep yourself [L]

Si vis pacem, para bellum. If you want peace, be prepared for war [L]

sivodnya. Today [R]

sixtine. A troubadour verse-form having 6 stanzas of 6 lines each [F]

sjambok. Hide whip [Pers]

skald. Scandinavian minstrel of the Viking period

skazka. Verse folk-tale [R]

skene. Scene; acting area of the stage [Gk]

skiamachia. Fight with the shadow; a dance pantomime of combat [Gk]

skleros. Hard [Gk]

Skolka? How much? [R]

skopeo. Look at [Gk]

skralat. A Swedish folk-dance [Swed]

Skupshtina. Parliament of Yugoslavia [Serbian]

sloka. Verse form [Skr]

slovar. Dictionary [R]

sloyd. Education by manual training [Swed]

smetane. Sour cream [R]

smorgasbord. Swedish *hors d'oeuvres* [Swed]

smorzando. Dying away [It]

sobranie. Convention; meeting; society [R]

Sobranje. Parliament [Bulgarian]

sobre. On; about [Sp]

sobre. Above; over; upon [Sp]

Sobre gustos no hay disputas.
There is no disputing about
tastes [Sp]

soccus. Soft shoe worn by actors
in comedy [L]

sociedad. Society; partnership
[Sp]

sociedad anonima. Business
corporation [Sp]

sociétaire. Stock-holder [F]

société anonyme. Limited liability corporation [F]

socius. Companion; associate;
partner [L]

socle. Pedestal; base [F]

sodeistvuiushchii. Co-operative [R]

soeben erschienen. Just published [G]

Soedinennye Shtaty. United
States [R]

soeur. Sister [F]

sog(enannt). So-called [G]

sogno. Dream [It]

soi-disant. Self-styled; pre-
tended [F]

soie. Silk [F]

soir. Evening [F]

soirée. Evening (gathering or
entertainment) [F]

soit. Let it be; be it so [F]

soixante-quinze. Seventy-five
(mm. gun) [F]

sol. Sun; monetary unit of Peru
[Sp]

solarium. Terrace over a porch
or on the roof of a house; open
space exposed to the sun's rays
[L]

solatium. Solace; compensation
[L]

sola topi. Pith helmet [Hindu]

soldanella dulcamara. Bitter-
sweet [L]

soleil d'or. Golden sun; species
of rose of the pernetiana variety
[F]

Solenne In Quest' Ora. Swear
In This Hour (*Forza del Destino*,
Act III; Verdi) [It]

solfeggio. Singing by note
names; *e.g.* do, re, mi, *etc.* [It]

soli. Salt [R]

solidago. Goldenrod [L]

solidum. Whole; undivided
thing [L]

solitaire. Alone; lonely; a single
diamond in a setting; card
game for a single player [F]

**Solitudinem faciunt, pacem
appellant.** They make a soli-
tude and call it peace (Tacitus)
[L]

solus. Alone [L]

Solvitur Acris Hiems. Severe
Winter is Melting Away (Horace; *Odes*; 1-4; Clough) [L]

soma. Body [Gk]

sombra. Shade [Sp]

sombrero. Hat [Sp]

somnus. Sleep [L]

son. Sound; his; her [F]

Sonderdruck. Special print; reprint [G]

songe. Dream; nostalgic thought
[F]

son mariachi. Round song or
dance [Sp]

Sonnenaufgang. Sunrise [G]

Sonnenuntergang. Sunset [G]

soobshchenie. Communications
[R]

sopherim. Scribes [Heb]

sophia. Wisdom; theoretical as
distinguished from practical
wisdom [Gk]

sophistikoi elenchoi. Refuta-
tions of sophistries; title of the
last of Aristotle's logical treatises, dealing with fallacies in
argumentation [Gk]

sophos. Wise [Gk]

sophrosyne. The virtue of tem-
perance [Gk]

sopra. Above; over; before [It]

sopra bianco. Italian glazed
pottery with a white design on
a white background [It]

sor. Forty [R]

sorbet. Sherbet; frozen punch;
ices with fruit [F]

Sorbonne. School for advanced study in sciences and letters, in Paris; founded 1257 by Robert de Sorbon; Palace of the Sorbonne [F]

sordini. Mutes [It]

sordino. Mute [It]

Sorge. Concern; worry [G]

soror. Sister [L]

sortie. Exit [F]

sostenuto. Sustained; holding notes to their full length [It]

sot. Comedian; clown; fool; drunkard [F]

sotnia. Hundred [R]

sotrudnik. Collaborator [R]

sottie. Comic vaudeville of the 15th and 16th centuries [F]

sottise. Stupidity [F]

sotto. Under; below [It]

sotto voce. In an undertone [It]

sou. Popular French term for a five-*centime* piece; trifle [F]

soubriquet. Nickname [F]

souchong. Fine tea [C]

soufflé. Blown or puffed up; baked custard of fruit, eggs, cheese, flaked fish, minced meat *etc.* [F]

souffleur. Whistler; prompter [F]

soupçon. Suspicion; dash; trace; tinge [F]

soupir. Sigh [F]

source. Spring; well [F]

sourd. Deaf [F]

sourire. Smile [F]

souris. Bat [F]

sous. Under [F]

Sous-Préfet. Sub-Prefect; head of an *arrondissement* [F]

souteneur. Panderer; man living on a prostitute's earnings [F]

Soviet. Council; revolutionary organization of soldiers and workers in 1917; pertaining to the Russian government or communist Russia [R]

soyez ferme. Be firm [F]

Soyez le bienvenu. Welcome [F]

Sozialwissenschaft. Social science; sociology [G]

spa. Name of a town in Belgium; a mineral spring, or any locality frequented for its mineral springs [Place]

Spasibo. Thank you [R]

Spass. Joke; fun [G]

spät. Late [G]

spatje. Sleep [R]

spatula. Trowel-shaped or blade-shaped instrument used for mixing, spreading or smoothing out colors or cement [L]

species. Particular thing as distinguished from *genus*; form; shape; figure; fashion [L]

spectemur agendo. Let us be judged by our deeds [L]

speculum. Mirror; looking-glass; title of many ancient books and compilations [L]

speculum vitae. Mirror of life [L]

spes. Hope [L]

spes sibi quisque. Each man must rely upon himself [L]

sphyrelata. Hammered metalwork [Gk]

spianato. Smooth; even [It]

spiccato. Separated; detached; a style of violin playing having a semi-staccato quality [It]

spichik. Matches [R]

Spiel. Play; long harangue [G]

Spielmann. Minstrel [G]

Spieltrieb. Play instinct [G]

spina. Thorn; spine; low wall down the center of the ancient Roman circus [L]

Spinnrad. Spinning wheel [G]

spirito. Spirit; fire; energy [It]

spirituelle. Witty; refined; sensitive; intelligent [F]

spiritus rector. Ruling spirit [L]

Spokoinoi notchi! Good night! [R]

spondee. Metrical foot of 2 long syllables [Gk]

sponte sua. Of one's own accord [L]

sporran. Pouch hung in front of a kilt [Gaelic]

Sportsverein. Sport club [G]

sposo. Bridegroom (*fem.* sposa; *pl.* sposi=married couple) [It]

Sprache. Speech; language [G]

Sprachgesellschaft. Speech society; society to promote the vernacular and eliminate foreignisms [G]

Sprachwissenshaft. Linguistics [G]

Sprichwort. Proverb [G]

springbok. Gazelle [Du]

sprogvidenskab. Linguistics [Danish]

spumone. Ice-pudding with whipped cream [It]

sputum. Saliva [L]

st. See *stet*

Staatenbund. Confederation of states [G]

Stabat Mater. The Mother was standing; beginning of an old Latin hymn, set to music by Haydn, Rossini, and others [L]

staccato. Detached; separate; notes made as short as possible [It]

stadion. Ancient Greek unit of linear measurement; a course laid out for foot-racing; stadium [Gk]

squadristi. Members of Italian squads or armed bands [It]

S.S. See *Schutzstaffel*

stadtholder. Viceroy; lieutenant governor [Du]

Stahl. Steel [G]

Stahlhelm. Steel helmet; German veterans organization after World War I [G]

stakan chayu. Glass of tea [R]

Stakhanov. A Russian coalminer who set a record for time-unit work (Donetz Basin, 1935)

Stalag. Base camp for P.W.'s (*abbr.* of Stammlager) [G]

stalin. Steel [R]

stamen. Warp; thread; threadlike part of a flower (*pl.* stamina) [L]

Stamm. Tribe; ethnic unit [G]

stamnos. A vase with an ovoidal body, two handles, and a lid [Gk]

Ständchen. Serenade (Schubert) [G]

Stati Uniti. United States [It]

stantsiia. Station [R]

stare decisis. Doctrine that preceding court decisions are law [L]

starina. Narrative folk-song [R]

stasimon. Ode sung and danced by the chorus [Gk]

stasis. Standing [Gk]

status. State; condition [L]

status quo. Existing state of things [L]

status quo ante. Situation existing before (an event) [L]

status quo ante bellum. Situation existing before the war [L]

Stavo ben, ma per star meglio, sto qui. I was well, but trying to be better, I am now here [It]

Sta' zitto! Be quiet! [It]

St. Cyr. Location of the French military school; the "French West Point"

S.T.D. See *Sacrae Theologiae Doctor*

Stechleinwand. Buckram [G]

stele. Ancient monument in the form of a vertical monolith [Gk]

stellaria. Easter bell; a species of flower [L]

St. Emilion. Famous winegrowing region in southern France [F]

stemma codicum. Family tree of manuscripts (for studying the text history of a literary work) [L]

stenanthium lutea. Variety of lily; "lily of the field" [L]

steppe. Heath [R]

stère. One cubic meter of cordwood = 1.31 cubic yards = 35.32 cubic feet [F]

stereos. Solid [Gk]

Sternkunde. Astronomy [G]

Sternwarte. Observatory [G]

stesso. The same [It]

stet. Let it stand [L]

Steuermann. Helmsman [G]

sthenos. Strength [Gk]

sticciato. *Bas relief* which hardly projects from the surface upon which it has been carved or moulded [It]

stichomythia. Disputatious dialogue [Gk]

stichos. Line [Gk]

Stille Nacht, Heilige Nacht. Silent Night, Holy Night (Gruber) [G]

stilus. Instrument for writing on wax tablets [L]

Stimme. Voice; vote [G]

Stimmung. Mood; atmosphere [G]

stipendium. Soldier's pay; wages; stipend [L]

stirps. Root; stock of descent or title [L]

sto. Hundred [R]

stoa poikile. Painted porch; place frequented by Zeno, founder of the Stoic school of philosophy [Gk]

Sto bene. I am well [It]

Stofftrieb. Impulse toward material things; sensuous instinct [G]

stola. Long gown worn by Roman matrons [L]

Stollen. A loaf-shaped cake [G]

Stolz. Pride [G]

stoma. Mouth [Gk]

Storch. Stork; light reconnaissance plane [G]

storia. History [It]

storiagrafia. Historography; writing of history [It]

stornello. Short popular lyric [It]

Storthing. The Norwegian Parliament

Storting. See *Storthing*

S.T.P. See *sacrosanctae, etc.*

strada. Road [It]

strambotti. Epigrams on love [It]

strapassé. Said of figures which are twisted or distorted [F]

strata. See *stratum*

strategos. General [Gk]

stratum. Layer (*pl.* strata) [L]

Streiche. Pranks; tricks; practical jokes [G]

Streit. Quarrel; altercation; conflict [G]

Streitgedicht. Contest in verse; metrical disputation [G]

strepito. Noise [It]

stretto. A round-song or melody extending through other voices; part of a fugue [It]

strepitoso. Noisily [It]

striae. Narrow fillets between the flutings of a column [L]

strigil. Skin-scraper [L]

stringendo. Hurrying; accelerating [It]

stromenti. Instruments [It]

Strudel. Twist cake or bread [G]

stucco. Mixture of slaked lime and pulverized marble or stone, used as a coating for walls [It]

Stück. Piece; fragment; selection; musical composition [G]

studiis et rebus honestis. For studies and noble achievements (motto of the University of Vermont) [L]

Stuka. Dive bomber (*abbr.* of Sturzkampfbomber) [G]

Sturmabteilung. Storm troops; *Nazi* party strong-arm squads using force to down opposition and bring their party to power [G]

Sturm und Drang. Storm and stress; revolt against the rationalism of the 18th century Enlightenment in Germany [G]

style empire. Empire style; a variant of classical Greek style in vogue during the reign of Napoleon I [F]

stylobate. Moulding running around the base of a building; projecting sub-basement [Gk]

stylus. See *stilus*

sua cuique sunt vitia. Everyone has his own vices [L]

sua sponte. Of his own will [L]

suaviter in modo, fortiter in re. Gentle in manner, firm in matter(s); gently but firmly; with iron hand in velvet glove [L]

sub. Under; upon [L]

subahdar. Native officer in a company of Indian troops [Hindu]

subbota. See *subota*

sub conditione. Upon condition [L]

sub finem. Towards the end [L]

subito. Suddenly; immediately [It]

sub judice. Under the judge; still in question; not yet decided [L]

sublata causa, tollitur effectus. The cause being removed, the effect is taken away [L]

sub modo. Under a qualification; subject to a restriction or condition [L]

subota. Saturday [R]

sub poena. Under penalty; writ requiring a person's appearance in court [L]

subpoena ad testificandum. Subpoena to testify [L]

subpoena duces tecum. Subpoena compelling witness to appear in court and bring evidence with him [L]

sub quandam aeternitatis specie. Under a certain form of eternity; said of knowledge or reason as distinguished from opinion or imagination, in Spinoza's *Ethica* [L]

sub rosa. Under cover; in confidence; in secret [L]

subsella. Semicircular bench in the Christian *basilica* [L]

sub silentio. In secret; tacitly; in silence [L]

sub specie aeternitatis. See *sub quandam etc.*

substratum. Foundation; support [L]

sub verbo. Under the word [L]

sub voce. Under the word; under the (main) entry [L]

succès de scandale. Success due to notoriety or scandal [F]

succès d'estime. Success as measured by critics and connoisseurs rather than by popular acclaim [F]

succès fou. Great hit [F]

Succoth. Feast of Tabernacles [Heb]

succursale. Branch (of a firm) [F]

suche. Peruvian species of fish [Sp]

sucre. Sugar [Fr]; monetary unit of Ecuador [Sp]

suède. Swedish; undressed kid (leather) [F]

sueño. Dream [Sp]

suerte. Luck [Sp]

sufi. Pantheist [Arab]

suggestio falsi. Misrepresentation short of a direct lie [L]

suif. Tallow; grease [F]

sui generis. Of its own kind; of a class to itself; unique [L]

sui juris. Of one's own right; in one's own power; of full age and capacity; independent [L]

suite. Series; sequence; set; collection having a certain order of subjects, ideas, or events; applied to rooms, paintings, musical compositions, *etc.* [F]

sukhoveyi. Hot, dry winds from the Caspian Sea and deserts of central Asia [R]

sul. Upon; near [It]

sul ponticello. A style of violin playing; bowing close to the bridge of the violin [It]

summa. Greatest; highest; sum; compendium; name given to comprehensive treatises [L]

summa cum laude. With highest distinction [L]

summa potestas. Supreme power; ruling part of a state[L]

summa summarum. Sum total [L]

summum bonum. The supreme or highest good [L]

summum genus. The largest (and most inclusive) type or classification [L]

summum jus. Strict right; rigor of the law [L]

summum jus summa injuria. Greatest right, greatest wrong; extreme enforcement of law may lead to injustice [L]

Sunni. An orthodox Moslem [Arab]

suo nomine. In his own name [L]

sup. See *supra*

super-. Above; over; on top of; up; high; great; in addition [L]

super. Upon; above; over [L]

Super Flumina Babylonia. By the Rivers of Babylon (Psalms; 137-1; Swinburne) [L]

supplicatio. Petition for pardon or reversal of judgment [L]

supplicium. Punishment [L]

suppressio veri. Suppression of truth; tacit misrepresentation [L]

suppressio veri, suggestio falsi. Suppression of the true (is a) suggestion of the false [L]

supra. Above; over; on the upper side; beyond; more; formerly; close upon [L]

suprême. Said of any special or complex way of preparing certain dishes [F]

sur. On; upon [F]

sur canapé. On toast [F]

surd. Deaf; irrational (number); voiceless (sound) [L]

surdus. Deaf (person) [L]

sûreté. Safety; security [F]

sur les pointes. On the tip of the toes; referring to toe-dancing [F]

sursum. Upwards (motto of Arizona University) [L]

Sursum Corda. Upward Hearts; *i.e.* Lift up Your Hearts (title of a poem by Mrs. Browning) [L]

sursum reddere. Render up; surrender [L]

surtout. Above all; especially; a close-fitting, long-skirted overcoat [F]

sus. per coll. See *suspendatur, etc.*

suspendatur per collum. Let him be hanged by the neck [L]

sutra. Treatise of the late Vedic period; poetic treatise; mnemonic rule; string; aphorism [Skr]

suttee. Custom of widow's casting herself on her husband's funeral pyre [Skr]

suum cuique. To each one his own [L]

suum cuique tribuere. To render to every man his due [L]

suus cuique mos. Everyone has his own way [L]

s.v. See *sub voce; sub verbo*

svaraj. Self-rule; self-determination; a designation for the home-rule movement in India [Skr]

svelte. Slender; lissom [F]

svinini. Pork [R]

Swahili. Inter-tribal African language [ ]

swaraj. See *svaraj*

sylva. See *silva*

symposium. Banquet; feast; collection of opinions of learned men [L]

syn. With [Gk]

synchoresis. Concession (as a rhetorical device) [Gk]

syncope. Contraction; omission of one or more letters in a word; shifting of accent in a line [Gk]

synecdoche. Understood together; figure of speech including part for the whole, genus for the species, material for the thing made of it, *etc.* [Gk]

synesis, Logical rather than grammatical or verbal agreement [Gk]

synezeugmenon. Linking of two or more words in a construction to another one in the same construction [Gk]

syrinx. An ancient wind- instrument consisting of a set of tubes [Gk]

syzygy. Yoke; joined pair of terms; pair of metrical feet considered as one unit [Gk]

sznyceleki. Meat cutlet [Polish]

szolo. A dance in which the woman is swung through the air by her male partner [Hungarian]

T

Taanith Esther. Fast of Esther [Heb]

tabarro. Cloak [It]

tabatière. Snuff-box [F]

tabella. Tablet; ballot [L]

tableau vivant. Living tableau; representation of an incident or scene by a silent and motionless person or group [F]

table des matières. Table of contents [F]

table d'hôte. Regular menu [F]

tablinum. Archive room in the ancient Roman house [L]

tabor. Tambourine [Arab]

tabula. Tablet; table (*pl.* tabulae) [L]

tabula rasa. A scraped tablet; a clean slate [L]

Tabulatur. The set of rules for the compositions of the *Meistersinger* [G]

tâche. Task; duty; job; spot; stain; blemish; touch (in painting) [F]

tachiste. Impressionist painter using strong touches of color [F]

tacita. Things unexpressed [L]

tacite. Silently; by way of implication; tacitly [L]

tackjern gjutjern. Cast iron; pig iron [Swed]

taedium vitae. Weariness of life [L]

Tag. Day [G]

Tagebuch. Day-book; diary; journal [G]

Tagetes. Genus name of Marigold [L]

täglich. Daily [G]

Tagmuleh Ha-Nefesh. Reward of the soul (title of a philosophical work by Hillel) [Heb]

tagua. Ivory nut [Sp]

t'ai. The great unit [C]

t'ai chi. The great ultimate; the moral law [C]

T'ai Chi. Being [C]

taille. Tax or assessment on real estate; waist; size [F]

taille d'épargne. Spare cut; an engraving process [F]

taille douce. Soft cut; an engraving process [F]

talaria. Ancient sandal with thongs between toes, and wings on the ankle-strap [L]

tales. Such; such men [L]

talio. Like for like; punishment in kind; an eye for an eye [L]

tallia. Tax; tribute; share of income or property [L]

Talmud. Learning; an encyclopedic work representing the oral tradition of Judaism in the form of commentary on the Old Testament; it consists of the *Mishnah* and the *Gemara* [Heb]

talus. Slope of ground, wall, or fortification [L]

Talweg. Valley road; middle or main channel of a river, serving as a boundary if between two countries [G]

tamale. Mexican dish made of crushed corn seasoned with meat and red pepper [Sp]

tamasha. Show; function; occasion [Arab]

tambour. Drum [F]

tamis. Sieve; strainer [F]

tan. Female lead in a play [C]

Tanagra. City in ancient Baeotia; *terra cotta* figures made there [Gk]

tango. Argentinian dance in 4-4 rhythm [Sp]

tanka. Short poem of 31 syllables [J]

tannaim. Repeaters [Heb]

tante. Aunt [F]

tant mieux. So much the better [F]

tanto. So much; as much; too much [It]

tant pis. So much the worse [F]

tan tzu. Fiction written in rhymed doggerel [C]

Tao. The Way; principle; cosmic order; nature; the moral law [C]

tapage. Racket; uproar [F]

tapis. Carpet; rug [F]

tarantella. Costume dance based on the theme of the *morra* game; a swift Neapolitan dance in 6-8 rhythm [It]

tarantismos. A kind of hysteria [It]

tarantula. Spider [It]

taraxacum. Genus of Dandelion; drug made from dandelion [L]

tarboosh. Tasseled skull-cap [Arab]

tarde. Afternoon; late [Sp]

Tarnhelm. Helmet of invisibility [G]

Tarnung. Camouflage; concealment [G]

tarsia. Ornamental wooden inlay-work [It]

tartana. Gaily decorated cart [Sp]

TASS. See *Telegrafnoe Agenstvo*, *etc.*

tassets. Hip-armor hanging in strips from the waist [F]

Tartarin. Character in a novel by Daudet; symbol of a boastful southerner [F]

Tartufe. Character in a play by Molière; a hypocrite [F]

Tatsache. Fact [G]

tau. 19th letter of the Greek alphabet (Tτ)

Taube. Dove [G]

taupe. Mole; moleskin [F]

taurus. Bull [L]

Täuschung. Illusion [G]

tautologia. Repetition; excessive alliteration [Gk]

tautotes. Frequent repetition of the same word [Gk]

taxus brevifolia. Western yew [L]

Te Adoramus. We Adore Thee [L]

Teatro Colón. Famous theater in Buenos Aires [Sp]

techne. Art [Gk]

Technik des Dramas. Technique of the Drama (title of a treatise by Gustav Freytag; 1863) [G]

tedesco. German; in German style [It]

tedesco furor. German fury [It]

Te Deum. See *Te Deum laudamus*

Te Deum laudamus. We praise thee (Oh) God [L]

tedium. Weariness [L]

Teig. Dough [G]

teja. Roof tile [Sp]

telamones. Male figures used as columns in ancient architecture [Gk]

tele. At a distance [Gk]

Telegrafnoe Agenstvo Soyusa Sovetskih. News agency of the Soviet Socialist Republics; Tass [R]

Tel-el-Amarna. Egyptian city where the *Amarna* tablets were unearthed.

Tellermine. Flat-shaped anti-personnel contact mine [G]

telos. End; purpose [Gk]

Tel père, tel fils. Like father, like son [F]

tema. Theme [Sp]

tema con variazioni. Theme with variations; humorous verse or parody [It]

tempera. Method of painting in which dry colors are diluted in glue [It]

tempo. Time; rate or speed; pace at which a composition is to be played or sung [It]

Tempora Acta. Times Past (Lytton) [L]

Tempora mutantur, et nos in illis (mutamur). All things change and we also change with them [L]

tempore. In the time of [L]

temps. Time; weather; dance movement [F]

tempus. Time; season [L]

tempus, edax rerum. Time, consumer of things [L]

Tempus fugit. Time flies [L]

Tempus omnia revelat. Time reveals all [L]

tençon. Form of poetic debate [F]

tendere. To stretch [L]

ten do ji. Heavenly children [J]

ténèbre. Shade [F]

tenebrosi. School of Venetian painters whose effects were produced by strong lights and shadows [It]

tenendum. Holding; to be holden; to hold [L]

tenere. To hold [L]

tenerezza. Tenderness [It]

tenore di grazia. Delicate tenor; lyric tenor [It]

tenore robusto. Strong tenor; dramatic tenor; heroic tenor [It]

tenson. Dialogue in verse; an old troubadour verse-form [F]

tenuto. Sustained (note) [It]

tenzone [It]. See *tençon*

terebinth. A resinous substance; liquid made from it, used as brush cleaner and paint remover [Gk]

teremas. House of Russian style [R]

termini technici. Technical terms or terminology [L]

terminus. Boundary; limit; end (*pl.* termini) [L]

terra. Earth; soil; arable land [L]

terra cotta. (A type of) baked clay (used for making artistic objects and figures); earthenware [It]

terra culta. Cultivated land [L]

terra di Sienna. A kind of mineral earth used as a pigment; burnt sienna [It]

terra firma. Solid earth; solid ground [L]

terra incognita. An unknown land [L]

terra nova. New land; newly reclaimed land [L]

terras irradient. Let them illumine the lands (motto of Amherst) [L]

terra verde. Mineral earth used as a green pigment [It]

terre. Ground; earth; territory; land [F]

tertium non datur. The third (term) not being given; the law of excluded middle in formal logic [L]

tertium quid. A third something; *e.g.* a third factor that reconciles or explains the first two; a compromise [L]

tertius. Third [L]

tertius gaudens. Third party who profits by the disagreement of two others [L]

tertulia. Party; social gathering [Sp]

terza rima. Verse form of hendecasyllabic tercets rhyming aba, bcb, cdc, . . . mnm, n;

invented by Dante for the *Divina Commedia* [It]

terzo. Third [It]

Teshu Lama. Chief Lama of Thibet [Thibetan]

tessitura. The location of a majority of tones in a musical composition [It]

testatum. It is testified [L]

testis. Witness (*pl.* testes) [L]

tête à tête. Intimate conversation [F]

tetra-. Four [Gk]

teuchos. Book [Gk]

Teufel. Devil [G]

Teufelsdröckh. Devil's offal; pedant in *Sartor Resartus* [G]

thanatos. Death [Gk]

thaumazein. Primitive awe [Gk]

Théâtre du Vieux Colombier. Paris theater founded by Copeau [F]

Théâtre Libre. Free Theatre; founded by Antoine in Paris, 1887 [F]

thé dansant. Afternoon tea and dance at a hotel or restaurant [F]

thelema. Will [Gk]

theologoumena. Writings concerning God or the Divine [Gk]

theos. God [Gk]

therm-. Hot; heat [Gk]

thermae. Hot springs; hot baths; Roman bath house [L]

Thermidor. 11th month of the calendar used during the French Revolution; style of sea food cooked in wine or brandy [F]

thesaurus. Treasure; store; collection; dictionary arranged according to ideas [L]

thesaurus inventus. Treasure-trove [L]

thèse. Theme; thesis [F]

Thespis. Dramatic poet of the 6th century B.C.; an actor [Gk]

theta. 8th letter of the Greek alphabet (Θθ)

thuja. Species of cedar [L]

thuja plicata. Red cedar [L]

thymelikoi. Pantomimists; choristers [Gk]

thyrsus. Staff carried by Bacchus; staff covered with branches and flowers carried in religious processions [L]

tiara. Headdress; crown [Gk]

tibia. Shin bone; wind instrument made of the shin-bone of an animal; an ancient Roman flute [L]

tidskrift. Periodical [Swed]

Tiefland. Lowland (title of an opera by D'Albert) [G]

tiempo. Time [Sp]

Tiempo ni hora no se ata con soga. Time and tide wait for no man [Sp]

Tiens! Well! [F]

t'ien ti. Heaven and earth [C]

Tiergarten. Zoo [G]

tierra. Earth; land; (native) country [Sp]

tiers état. Third estate; the common people [F]

tifosi. Teen agers [It]

tige. Top; summit; crown (of a tree) [F]

tilia. Basswood [L]

tilyatini. Veal [R]

timbale. Unsweetened custard baked in a mold, usually seasoned with fish, meat, or vegetables; *kettledrum* [F]

timbre. (Postage) stamp; quality of a tone [F]

Timeo Danaos et dona ferentes. I fear the Greeks even when bringing gifts (Vergil; *Aeneid*; 2-49) [L]

timpani. Kettledrums [It]

tirage. Edition [F]

tirailleur. Sharpshooter; skirmisher [F]

tiro. Recruit; novice [L]

tirocinium. Recruit; novice; apprenticeship [L]

Tishabov. See *Tish'ah B'Ab*

Tish'ah B'Ab. Fast of the ninth of Ab, a Jewish period involving abstention from bathing in the ocean in July and August [Heb]

Tnuat Haherut. Freedom Party [Heb]

toccata. A touch-piece; musical composition designed to exhibit the player's touch [It]

Todtentanz. Dance of Death (Liszt) [G]

Tod und das Mädchen. Death and the Maiden (Claudius-Schubert) [G]

Tod und Verklärung. Death and Transfiguration (Richard Strauss) [G]

toga. Robe worn by Roman citizens [L]

toga virilus. Robe of manhood [L]

toharot. Purifications [Heb]

toile. Linen-cloth; sail-cloth; canvas; embroidery backing; foundation of a lace pattern [F]

toit. Roof [F]

to kalon. The beautiful [Gk]

tomar. To take [Sp]

tombola. A kind of lottery [It]

Tonart. Scale; mode; key [G]

Tondichtung. Tone poem [G]

Tonfarbe. Tone-color [G]

tonka. Bean used as a substitute for the vanilla bean [Sp]

ton meta ta physika. That which came after the physics; (the metaphysics came after the physics in Aristotle's works) [Gk]

tonneau. Cask; rounded-rear type of auto [F]

Töpfchen. Pot; chamber pot [G]

to prepon. The proper; the fit; the becoming [Gk]

toque. Small, turban-like hat [F]

Tor. Gate; fool [G]

torchère. Vase or figure holding a torch, lamp, or candle(s); an electric fixture or candelabrum of this description [F]

tordion. A lively folk-dance [F]

toreador. Bullfighter [Sp]

torero. Bullfighter; pertaining to bullfighting [Sp]

toreuma. Bas reliefs executed in metal [Gk]

toreutic. Referring to fashioning or ornamenting ivory, stone, or silver [Gk]

toro. Bull [Sp]

Torte. Tart; layer cake; round cake [G]

torsade. Design of twisted rope or cable [F]

tostadas. Toast [Sp]

totem. A feature of primitive social organization whereby the members of a tribe possess group solidarity by virtue of their association with a class of animals, plants, or inanimate objects [Ojibway]

Toteninsel. Isle of the Dead (painting by Boecklin; symphonic poem by Rachmaninoff) [G]

totidem verbis. In so many words [L]

toties quoties. As often as occasion shall arise [L]

totis viribus. With all one's might [L]

toto caelo. By the whole sky; indicative of a wide difference of opinion; diametrically opposed [L]

totum. The whole [L]

totum divisum. Divided whole; a unit capable of being divided [L]

touché. Hit (in fencing); remark that strikes home; apt retort [F]

toucher. To cash [F]

touffu. Tufted; bushy; leafy [F]

toujours. Always; constantly [F]

toupet. False hair (covering part of the head) [F]

tour. Tower; trip; turn; trick, lathe [F]

tourbillon. Whirlwind [F]

tour de force. Feat of strength;

accomplishment by sheer skill or clever technique [F]

Tour Eiffel. Eiffel Tower [F]

tourelle. Small tower; turret [F]

tourmaline. A hard stone of various colors [F]

tournure. Roundness; gracefulness of lines; characteristic aspect of a figure or drawing [F]

tourte. Tart; pie [F]

tourteau. Round tart or cake[F]

tout à coup. Suddenly [F]

tout à fait. Entirely [F]

tout à l'heure. A little while ago; in a little while; just now [F]

tout au contraire. Quite the contrary [F]

Tout comprendre, c'est tout pardonner. To understand all is to forgive all [F]

tout court. Quite simply [F]

tout de suite. Immediately [F]

tout ensemble. Taken as a whole [F]

Tout est dit. All has been said [F]

tout le monde. Everybody [F]

tovarishch. Comrade [R]

toxiphobia. Morbid fear of being poisoned [Gk]

trabajo. Work [Sp]

tracasserie. Chicanery; treachery [F]

tractent fabrilia fabri. Let smiths perform the work of smiths [L]

tradición. Tradition; long anecdote from history or legend[Sp]

traditio. Delivery; transfer of possession [L]

traduction. Translation [F]

traduttore, traditore. Translator traitor; *i.e.* the translator is a betrayor of the author's style [It]

trafe. Unclean; not *kosher* [Yid]

trag oidia. Goat song; literal meaning of the word "tragedy" [Gk]

trahere. To draw; to pull [L]

trahison. Betrayal; treason [F]

Trahison des clercs. Betrayal of the intellectuals (title of philosophical essays by Julien Benda; 1928) [F]

traité. Treatise; tract; treaty [F]

traje. Suit [Sp]

tranche de vie. Slice of life; term descriptive of naturalistic writing [F]

Träne. Tear [G]

tranquillo. Tranquil; calm; peaceful [It]

transit in rem judicatam. It passes into a matter adjudged [L]

trapezium. Quadrilateral figure with two parallel sides and all the sides unequal [Gk]

Tras los años viene el juicio (*or* **seso**). Wisdom comes with years [Sp]

tratado. Treatise [Sp]

Trauerspiel. Tragedy [G]

Traum. Dream [G]

trauma. Wound; injury [Gk]

Traumdeutung. Interpretation of dreams (title of a work by Freud) [G]

Träumerei. Reverie (Schumann) [G]

Trau, schau, wem. Mark well the man whom you trust; look before you leap [G]

Trauung. Betrothal; wedding; marriage [G]

travail. Labor; work [F]

travaux. Works [F]

travertino. Name of a species of limestone used in ancient Roman buildings [It]

tre. Three [It]

trece. Thirteen [Sp]

tredicesimo. Thirteenth [It]

tredici. Thirteen [It]

trèfle. Trefoil; clover; shamrock; clubs (cards) [F]

Treibhaus. Hothouse [G]

treinta. Thirty [Sp]

tremolo. Trembling; quavering [It]

trenta. Thirty [It]

trente et quarente. A card game; thirty and forty [F]

trepak. A lively dance [R]

tres. Three [Sp]

trescona. A pantomime dance [It]

trêve de Dieu. The Lord's Armistice; religious law of 1041 forbidding combat from Thursday nights to Monday mornings [F]

tri. Three [R]

Tribunal de las Aguas. Peasant court of Valencia, Spain (having jurisdiction over irrigation matters) [Sp]

trich-. Hair; capillary [Gk]

triclinium. Dining-room of the ancient Roman house, having three seats, upon each of which three persons could recline [L]

tricolore. Flag of the French Republic, having three vertical stripes of red, white, and blue [F]

tricorne. Three-cornered hat [F]

tricot. Knitted cloth; Jersey cloth; flat-knit rayon goods [F]

tridtsat. Thirty [R]

triduum. Three days of prayer preceding the Feast of the Immaculate Conception [L]

triforium. Gallery above the nave of a church [L]

trigo. Wheat [Sp]

trigon. An ancient harp [Gk]

trimurti. Having three shapes; the Hindu trinity, *Brahma, Vishnu,* and *Shiva* [Skr]

trinadtsat. Thirteen [R]

triplice. The triple (alliance) [It]

tripotage. Mess; jumble [F]

triptych. A picture painted on a panel with two side-leaves mounted on hinges [Gk]

triste. Sad [F]

tristesse. Sadness [F]

tristezza. Sadness; pensiveness [It]

trivia. (Junction of) three roads; commonplace (things, ideas, etc.) [L]

trivium. Three ways; the first three disciplines in the medieval educational system of the seven liberal arts; grammar, rhetoric, and dialectic. See *quadrivium* [L]

Trocadéro. Palace serving as an exposition and concert hall in Paris; name of a Spanish citadel captured by the French in 1823 [F]

trois-temps. Waltz time [F]

tromba. Trumpet [It]

Trommel. Drum [G]

trompe-l'oeil. Deceptive to the eye; illusion of reality [F]

trop. Too (much) [F]

tropos. Manner [Gk]

troppo. Too much [It]

trotzdem. In spite of that; nevertheless [G]

trouvaille. Lucky find; windfall [F]

trouvère. Troubadour; minstrel; French court poet of the Middle Ages [F]

trovatore. Troubadour [It]

truc. Knack; technical mastery [F]

trucage. Manufacturing of artistic forgeries [F]

trudodni. Pay units; workday units used as the basis for computing pay of collective-farm workers [R]

Trudoviki. Petty-bourgeois group formed in 1906 from among peasant members of the first Czarist *Duma* [R]

trudy. Transactions; works [R]

truffes. Truffles [F]

truites. Trout [F]

trulli. Conic-shaped stone houses [It]

truqueur. Fraud in art; manufacturer of artistic fakes [F]

tsar. See *czar*

tsuga. Hemlock [ ]

tuber. Bump; knob (on a root of a plant) [L]

tuches. Backside [Y]

Tugend. Virtue [G]

Tuileries. Palace surrounded by famous gardens, in Paris; residence of various French kings [F]

tulipe noire. Black tulip [F]

tulle. Fine silk net [F]

tumbo. Peruvian fruit; a sweet punch made of it; its creepers and vines [Sp]

tumulus. Cairn; stones in the form of a cone or mound [L]

tung. Activity; motion; being moved or awakened; east [C]

tu quoque. Thou also; accusation of an accuser; identical retort [L]

turba. Multitude; mob [L]

turca. Turkish; in Turkish style [It]

turitulum. Censer; incense-burner; thurible [L]

Turnfest. Gymnastic festival [G]

Turnhalle. Gymnasium [G]

Turnverein. Athletic club [G]

turrón. Spanish nougat [Sp]

tussore. Kind of East-Indian silk [Hindu]

tutela. Tutelage; guardianship [L]

tutius erratur ex parte mitiore. It is safer to err on the gentler side [L]

tutor. Guardian [L]

tutta forza. With all force [It]

Tutte Le Feste. On Every Festal Morning (*Rigoletto*, Act III; Verdi) [It]

tutti. All together [It]

tutti-frutti. Mixed fruits [It]

tutti i giorni. Every day [It]

tutti quanti. Every one [It]

tutto. All; the whole [It]

Tyche. Fortune; chance; name of the goddess of fortune or chance [Gk]

tympanum. Triangular arch or structural unit; bracket-shaped support of a column and beam; membrane; the middle ear [L]

typos. Form [Gk]

tyro. See *tiro*

tysiacha. Thousand [R]

Tzigane. Hungarian gypsy [Magyar]

Tzom Gedaliah. Fast of Gedaliah [Heb]

tz'u. (Parental) love; kindness; affection [C]

tzu. Musical verse written to a prevailing tune [C]

U

u. For Greek words, see also under *hu-*

u.a. See *unter anderm*

uaimm. Alliteration [Gaelic]

Überbrettl. Cabaret; floor show; night club [G]

Überfall. Attack [G]

Überläufer. Deserter [G]

Übermensch. Superman [G]

Überwindung. Supersedence; surmountal; overcoming [G]

ubi. Where [L]

Ubi bene, ibi patria. Where it is well with me, there is my country [L]

Ubi libertas, ibi patria. Where liberty is, there is my country [L]

Ubi mel, ibi apes. Where the honey is, there are the bees [L]

ubique. Everywhere [L]

ubi sunt? Where are . . .? Frequent opening words of medieval Latin songs and poems [L]

ubi supra. Where (mentioned) above [L]

uborshitsa. Maid [R]

ubriaco. Drunk [It]

Übung macht den Meister. Practice makes perfect [G]

Uccidiamo il chiaro di luna. We will do away with the moonlight (slogan of Italian futurists) [It]

udarnik. Shock-worker [R]

ukase. Law or ordinance of the czar of Russia [R]

Ulema. Scholars of the sacred law of the Moslems [Arab]

ulmus. Elm tree [L]

ult. See *ultimo* (*mense*)

ultima ratio. Final reason or argument (*i.e.* force) [L]

ultima Thule. Farthest Thule; any far-off, mystical place; some unattainable goal [L]

ultimo (mense). Preceding (month) [L]

ultimum supplicium. Extreme punishment or penalty, *i.e.* death [L]

ultimus Romanorum. Last of the Romans [L]

ultra. Beyond; outside of [L]

ultra licitum. Beyond what is permitted [L]

ultra mare. Beyond the sea [L]

ultra posse. Beyond possibility [L]

ultra vires. Beyond one's power or authority; unauthorized; unwarranted [L]

umbellularia californica. California laurel tree [L]

umbra. Shade [L]

umore. Humor; playfulness [It]

unanimisme. Unanimism; philosophy that emphasizes the group aspect of individual existence; formulated by Jules Romains in "La Vie unanime", 1908 [F]

Una scopa nuova spazza bene. A new broom sweeps clean [It]

una voce. With one voice;

unanimous(ly); without dissent [L]

Una Voce Poco Fa. A little voice I hear (*Barber of Seville*, Act II; Rossini) [It]

Una Furtiva Lagrima. A Furtive Tear (*Elisir d'amore*, Act II; Donizetti) [It]

Un Ballo in Maschera. The Masked Ball (Verdi) [It]

unberufen. Unbidden; without invoking bad luck; interjection used to ward off bad luck after speaking well of someone [G]

uncial. Referring to capital letters [L]

Undank ist der Welt Lohn. Ingratitude is the world's reward [G]

undicesimo. Eleventh [It]

undici. Eleven [It]

Ungeduld. Impatience [G]

Unkraut. Weed(s) [G]

Un Nido Di Memorie. A Song of Tender Memories (*Pagliacci*, Act I, Prologue, Leoncavallo) [It]

uno animo. With one mind [L]

Unsinn. Nonsense [G]

und so weiter. And so forth; *etcetera* [G]

unendlich. Infinite [G]

unguentarium. Jar or vase containing oil [L]

unio. Union; uniting [L]

unio mystica. Mystical union; the merging of the individual consciousness with a superior or supreme consciousness [L]

unitas. Unity [L]

universitas. Whole; aggregate; corporation; university [L]

uno actu. In a single act [L]

uno flatu. At one breath [L]

unter anderm. Among other (things); and others; *etcetera* [G]

Untergang. Decline; fall; destruction [G]

Untergang des Abendlandes. Decline of the West (title of a philosophical work on history by Oswald Spengler, 1918-22) [G]

Unterhaltung. Conversation; diversion; entertainment [G]

Unterricht. Instruction [G]

Untersuchung. Investigation; examination; search [G]

unus nullus. One (is) none; legal principle that testimony of a single witness is not valid [L]

unwesentlich. Inessential; irrelevant; accidental; contingent [G]

uomo. Man [It]

uova. Eggs [It]

Upanishad. (Pupils) sitting opposite (the teacher); one of a large number of philosophic Indian treatises antedating Greek philosophy [Skr]

upas. Poison; Javanese tree yielding arrow poison [Malay]

upravlenie. Administration [R]

upsilon. 20th letter of the Greek alphabet (Υυ)

Urbild. Primitive image; original image; prototype [G]

urbs. City; town [L]

Ursa Major. The Great Bear [L]

Ursa Minor. The Little Bear [L]

Ursprung. Origin [G]

Urteil. Judgment [G]

Urteilskraft. (Power of) judgment [G]

uscita. Exit [It]

uso. Use; usage [Sp]

usque. Up to; until [L]

usque ad nauseam. To the point of disgust [L]

usquebaugh. Water of life; whisky [Gaelic]

Ustaschi. Pro-German Croatian terrorist organization led by Pavelich in 1941 after the invasion of Yugoslavia by the Nazis

usted. You [Sp]

usus bellici. Warlike use; contraband [L]

usus loquendi. Usage of speech (Cicero; *Orator*; 48-160) [L]

u.s.w. See *und so weiter*

ut. As [L]; first note of the scale, or C [F]

utile dulci. The useful with the agreeable [L]

Utimur pro necessitate. We use (things) because of necessity [L]

ut infra. As (shown) below [L]

uti possidetis. As you hold; principle of international law whereby belligerents hold possession of conquered land [L]

Ut pictura poesis. As is painting, so is poetry; maxim by Horace in his *Ars Poetica* [L]

Ut potior sit qui prior est. That he may be preferred who is first (Terence) [L]

ut prosim. That I may be of service; that I may do good [L]

ut saepe. As often [L]

ut supra. As (shown) above [L]

uva. Grapes [It]; grape [Sp]

uxor. Wife [L]

uyezd. District [R]

V

v. See *vide*

vac. Voice [Skr]

vache. Cow [F]

vada. Theory; doctrine [Skr]

Vade in pace. Go in peace [L]

vade mecum. Go with me; one's constant companion; a guide; a book or other article constantly carried with one [L]

vadi. Water [R]

Vae victis. Woe to the vanquished! (Livy; 5, 48, 9) [L]

vafvax vadna. Pantomime dance based on the theme of weaving [Swed]

vale. Farewell [L]

Valenciennes. City in northern France; flat lace with diamond-shaped mesh ground [F]

valentia. Value; price [L]

Valet anchora virtus. Virtue is an effective anchor [L]

Valete ac plaudite. Farewell and applaud [L]

valeur. Value [F]

Valle Padana. Po Valley [It]

vallum. Wall [L]

valor. Value [L]

valuta. Foreign currency; exchange [R]

vámonos. Let's go! All aboard! [Sp]

vamoose! Beat it! [Sp]

Vanitas vanitatum. Omnia vanitas. Vanity of vanities. All is vanity [L]

vaquero. Cowboy; herdsman [Sp]

vara. Measure of length equal to about 33 inches [Sp]

varia lectio. A different reading (in texts of historical or literary works) (*pl.* variae lectiones) [L]

variété. Variety; miscellany [F]

variazoni. Variations (on a musical theme) [It]

varilla. Bar [Sp]

variorum. Of different (men); referring to an edition of a work with notes or versions by various editors [L]

Varium et mutabile semper femina. Woman is always a fickle and changeable thing (Vergil; *Aeneid*; 4-569) [L]

var. lect. See *varia lectio*

vasco. Basque [Sp]

vascuence. Basque (language) [Sp]

vates. Seer [L]

vates sacer. Sacred seer or poet; inspired poet [L]

vaurien. Good-for-nothing [F]

vawsim. Eight [R]

v'chira. Train [R]

veau. Calf [F]

Veau d'Or. Calf of Gold (*Faust*, Act III; Gounod) [F]

Vecheka. Extraordinary Commission (set up after the Russian Revolution to combat counter-revolution and sabotage) [R]

vecino. Neighbor [Sp]

Veda. Knowledge; collectively, the ancient sacred literature of India [Skr]

Vedanta. The end of the *Veda*; the final goal or meaning [Skr]

vedette. Mounted outpost or sentinel [F]

Vedi Napoli e poi mori. See Naples and then die [It]

veinte. Twenty [Sp]

veintiuno. Twenty-one [Sp]

vekhi. Landmarks [R]

veldt. Wild grass-land [Du]

velillo. Veil [Sp]

vellum. Calfskin; parchment [L]

veloce. Swiftly; speedily [It]

velours. Velvet [F]

velours de coton. Velveteen [F]

velours de soie. Silk velvet [F]

velours du nord. Northern velvet; a heavy, coating velvet [F]

velouté. Velvety; smooth (to the palate); a rich sauce [F]

velum. The dangling end of the roof of the mouth; the soft palate; a curtain used as a sunshade for skylights [L]

Vendémiaire. First month of the calendar used during the French Revolution [F]

vendimia. Grape harvest; vintage [Sp]

venerdì. Friday [It]

Venezuela. Little Venice; republic in South America [Sp]

Venia necessitati datur. Indulgence is granted to necessity [L]

Veni, Creator Spiritus. Come, Holy Ghost, our souls inspire [L]

venire facias. Cause to come; a writ of summons [L]

Veni, sancte Spiritus. Come, Holy Spirit [L]

Venite. O come [L]

Venite quì! Come here! [It]

Veni, Vidi, Vici. I came, I saw, I conquered (Caesar, following his victory at Zela, 47 B.C.) [L]

vent. Wind [F]

venta. Roadside inn [Sp]

ventana. Window [Sp]

vente. Sale [F]

ventesimo. Twentieth [It]

venti. Twenty [It]

Ventôse. Sixth month of the calendar used during the French Revolution [F]

ventre. Belly; womb [F]

ventre à terre. At full speed; belly (close) to the earth [F]

ventuno. Twenty-one [It]

Venus. Goddess of love; the Roman counterpart of *Aphrodite* [L]

Venusberg. Mount of Venus [G]

Venus Verticordia. Venus, Turner of Hearts (Rossetti) [L]

verano. Summer [Sp]

verba. See *verbum*

Verba sunt indices animi. Words are indices of the mind [L]

verbena. Foliage; branches [L]

verbi gratia. For the sake of example [L]

Verbot. Prohibition; denial [G]

verboten. Prohibited [G]

verbum. Word; verb (*pl.* verba) [L]

verbum mentis. Mental word; intra-mental concept [L]

Verbum sapienti sat est. A word to the wise is sufficient [L]

Verbum sat sapienti. A word to the wise is sufficient [L]

verdad. True; truth [Sp]

verde antico. Antique green; natural or artificial bronze *patina* [It]

verdigris. Green of corroded copper [F]

verdura. Green vegetables [It]

verecundia. Modesty; bashfulness; coyness; respect; reverence [L]

veredictum. Declaration of truth; verdict [L]

Verein. Union; club [G]

vereinigt. United [G]

Vereinigte Staaten. United States [G]

Verfasser. Author [G]

vergebens. In vain [G]

Vergeltungswaffe. Weapon of retaliation [G]

Vergissmeinnicht. Forget-Me-Not [G]

Vergleich. Comparison; simile [G]

vergleiche. Compare; *confer* [G]

vergogna. Shame [It]

verhandling. Treatise; proceeding [Du]

verismo. Realism; a realistic school of opera founded by Mascagni; naturalism [It]

veritas. Truth [L]

Veritas. Christo et Ecclesiae. Truth. For Christ and the Church (motto of Harvard) [L]

Veritas et Virtus. Truth and Virtue (motto of Pittsburgh University) [L]

Veritas liberabit vos. Truth shall make you free (motto of Southern Methodist University) [L]

Veritas odium parit. Truth engenders hatred [L]

Veritas praevalebit. Truth will prevail [L]

Veritas vincit. Truth conquers [L]

Veritas vos liberabit. Truth shall make you free (motto of Johns Hopkins University) [L]

Veritatem cognoscetis et veritas vos liberabit. Ye shall know the truth and the truth shall make you free (John; 8-32; motto of the University of Tennessee) [L]

Veritatem dilexi. I have loved the truth (motto of Bryn Mawr) [L]

Veritatis simplex oratio est. The language of truth is simple [L]

vérité. Truth [F]

vérité de fait. Truth of fact, as distinguished from truth derived by reasoning [F]

vérité de raison. Truth of reason, as distinguished from *vérité de fait*, truth of fact; truth derived by reasoning [F]

verkehrt. Perverse; wrong [G]

verklärt. Transfigured [G]

Verklärte Nacht. Transfigured Night (Schönberg) [G]

Verklärung. Transfiguration [G]

Verlag. Publishing house [G]

verlassen. Deserted; left [G]

vermicelli. Thin rolls of dough made with flour, cheese, egg-yolks and saffron [It]

vermoulu. Worm-eaten [F]

vernacular. Domestic [L]

Vernier. French mathematician of the 17th century; scale or slide-rule invented by him for measuring small dimensions [F]

Vernunft. Reason [G]

vernünftig. Reasonable [G]

Verrat. Betrayal [G]

verrückt. Crazy [G]

vers. Verse; poetry; towards [F]

Versailles. Palace near Paris, built by Louis XIV and designed by Lenôtre; seat of the French government at the beginning of the 3rd Republic; scene of historic events

Versammlung. Meeting; convention [G]

Verschweigung. Reticence; secrecy [G]

vers de société. Light verse; occasional verse; satire on the superficialities of polite society [F]

Versicherung. Assurance; insurance [G]

versi martelliani. Alexandrines [It]

vers libre. Free verse [F]

verso. Left-hand page [L]

verso sciolto. Blank verse [It]

verst. Linear distance of about two-thirds of a mile [R]

Verstand. Understanding [G]

verstehen. To understand [G]

Versuch. Essay; experiment; attempt [G]

versus. Towards; opposite; against [L]

vert(e). Green [F]

vertere. To turn [L]

vertex. Turning point; top (point about which a thing turns) (*pl.* vertices) [L]

vertices. See *vertex*

vertigo. Turning; whirling; dizziness [L]

Vertrau' auf Gott. Trust in God [G]

vervain. Verbene; a perennial flowering plant [L]

Verwaltung. Administration[G]

Verweile doch! Du bist so schön. Stay! Thou art so fair (*Faust*; Goethe) [G]

Verwendung. Application; use [G]

verworren. Confused [G]

Verzeichnis. Table; index [G]

vesica piscis. Fish bladder; elliptical design or aureole [L]

vesper. Evening (star); evening service or prayer [L]

Vesta. Goddess of domesticity; symbol of purity and chastity [L]

vestido. Dress; costume [Sp]

vestigia. Footsteps; traces; vestiges [L]

Vesti La Giubba. On With the Motley (*Pagliacci*, Act I; Leoncavallo) [It]

veto. I forbid [L]

vettura. Carriage; hack [It]

vetturino. Hackman [It]

v.g. See *verbi gratia*

vgl. See *vergleiche*

via. Way; road [L]

Via Crucis. Way of the Cross (title of a novel about the second Crusade; F. Marion Crawford) [L]

via dolorosa. Way of sorrow; the way traversed by Jesus to the place of crucifixion [L]

via media. Middle way; middle course between extremes [L]

Viaticum. Provision for the journey; the Eucharist, administered to the sick [L]

viator. Traveler [L]

vibrato. Vibrated; recurrent swells and subsidences in a tone [It]

vice. In the place or stead [L]

vice versa. The succession being turned; the terms or situation being interchanged or reversed [L]

vichy. Mineral water [place]

Vichy. Resort in South France; seat of the French government under Nazi domination from 1940 to 1944

vicino. Near [It]

vicuña. South American animal of the camel family; wool of this animal [Sp]

vide. See [L]; empty; vacant [F]

vide ante. See the preceding [L]

Vide et crede. See and believe [L]

vide infra. See the following [L]

videlicet. That is to say; to wit; namely [L]

vide post. See the following [L]

vide supra. See above [L]

Vide ut supra. See what is stated above [L]

vidya. Knowledge [Skr]

vie. Life [F]

Vie de Bohème. Bohemian life; title of an opera by Puccini, based on a novel by Murger[F]

viejo. Old (man) [Sp]

vieillard. Old man [F]

vieille. Old [F]

vierge. Virgin [F]

viernes. Friday [Sp]

Viernes Santo. Good Friday [Sp]

Vierteljahrschrift. Quarterly [G]

vi et armis. By force and arms; by armed force [L]

Viet Nam. Name of the Indo-China Republic, formerly *Annam*

vieux. Old [F]

vieux jeu. Old game; old stuff; outworn style [F]

vignette. Small vine; floral decoration; illuminated letter(s) with design of vine tendrils; cut or engraving in book illustration; short literary essay or character study [F]

viis et modis. Ways and means [L]

vijnana. Consciousness [Skr]

vilayet. Turkish province; district [Arab]

villanelle. Verse-form of 5 tercets rhymed aba plus a final quatrain, all on two rhymes [F]

ville. City [F]

villegiatura. Country sojourn [It]

Vim vi repellere licet. To repel force by force is lawful [L]

vin. Wine [F]

vinaigrette. Meat seasoned with vinegar; vinegar sauce; type of chair [F]

vinca. Periwinkle flower [L]

Vincam aut moriar. I will conquer or die [L]

vincere aut mori. To conquer or to die [L]

Vincit veritas. Truth conquers [L]

vinculum. Bond; fetter; tie; a mathematical sign tying together certain quantities [L]

vingakersdans. Pantomime dance in which two women compete for the same man [Swed]

vingt et un. Twenty-one; a card game [F]

vin léger. Light wine [F]

vin mousseux. Smooth wine (as distinguished from sparkling wine) [F]

vino. Wine [It]

vin ordinaire. Common wine; cheap wine served free with meals in restaurants [F]

vint. Screw; card game [R]

viola da gamba. A large, cello-like viol [It]

viola odorata. Sweet violet [L]

viola tricolor. Pansy [L]

viol da gamba. A six-stringed musical instrument of the violin family; name of a reedy-toned organ stop [It]

viol d'amore. A musical instrument somewhat like the viola; an organ stop having a thin and delicate note [It]

viol d'amour. See *viol d'amore*

vir. Man; husband [L]

viracocha. Peruvian-Indian name for a white man; name of an Aztec god [Sp]

virago. A manlike woman; a fierce or abusive woman [L]

vires. Pl. of *vis*

Vires acquirit eundo. It gains strength as it goes (Vergil; *Aeneid*; 4-175) [L]

Virginibus Puerisque. For Girls and Boys (Stevenson); something innocent [L]

Virginibus puerisque canto. I sing for girls and boys (Horace; *Odes*; 3-1) [L]

virgo intacta. Pure virgin; untouched virgin [L]

virtu. Virtue; prudence [It]

virtuoso. Virtuous; strong; competent in art or science; person having these qualities; connoisseur; master of an art; master performer [It]

virtus. Virtue; virility; strength of character [L]

virtute cujus. By virtue whereof [L]

virtute securus. Secure through virtue [L]

virtutis amore. By the love of virtue [L]

Virtutis laus omnis in actione consistit. All the merit of virtue consists in action [L]

virus. Slime; poisonous liquid; infectious agent [L]

vis. Force; power; energy; violence; faculty (*pl.* vires) [L]

vis aestimativa. The animal faculty; *i.e.* the sensory, vegetative, and locomotive faculties [L]

vis armata. Armed force [L]

vis a tergo. Force from behind [L]

vis-à-vis. Opposite; face to face [F]

vis cogitativa. The rational faculty, *i.e.* intellect, rational will, *etc.* [L]

vis comica. Comic talent [L]

vis divina. Divine force; act of God [L]

visé. Examined; indorsement on passport [F]

Vishnu. Deity of the Hindu trinity, *trimurti*; Supreme Being and Creator of the world; in philosophy, the principle of conservation and stability [Skr]

vis inertiae. Force of inertia [L]

Vision Fugitive. Fleeting Vision (*Hérodiade*, Act II; Massenet) [F]

vis major. Superior or irresistible force; act of God; *force majeure* [L]

vis poetica. Poetic force or genius [L]

Vis unita fortior. Union is strength [L]

vis vitae. Vigor of life [L]

vita. Life [L]

vita brevis. Life is short [L]

Vita brevis, ars longa. Life is short and art is long [L]

Vita Nuova. New Life (Dante; 1292) [It]

vitello. Veal [It]

Vitia erunt, donec homines. As long as men live, there will be vices (Tacitus) [L]

vitium. Error; fault [L]

vitium clerici. Clerical error [L]

vitium scriptoris. Copyist's error; clerical error [L]

vitrine. Show-window; showcase; shop window; glass case in a museum [F]

Viva! Long live——! [It]

viva agua. Running water [L]

vivace. Lively; animated; a brisk, lively tempo [It]

Vivamus atque amemus. Let us live and love [L]

vivandier. Seller of provisions to troops: sutler [F]

vivandière. *Fem.* of *vivandier*

Viva Il Vino. Hail the Red Wine (*Cavalleria Rusticana*, Mascagni) [It]

Vivat! Long live——! [L]

Vivat respublica! Long live the republic! [L]

Vivat rex! Long live the king! [L]

viva voce. By living voice; by word of mouth; oral(ly) [L]

Vive le roi! Long live the king! [F]

Vive memor leti. Live mindful of death [L]

Vive ut vivas. Live that you may live [L]

Vivit post funera virtus. Virtue survives the grave [L]

vivre. To live [F]

Vixere fortes ante Agamemnona. Brave men lived before Agamemnon [L]

viz. See *videlicet*

vizir. Mohammedan minister of State [Arab]

v.l. See *varia lectio*

vocabula artis. Words of art; technical terms [L]

vocalise. Music for exercising the voice [F]

voce. Voice [It]

voce di petto. Chest voice; natural voice [It]

voce di testa. Head voice; falsetto [It]

vodka. Grain whisky [R]

voennyi. Military [R]

Vogel. Bird [G]

Vogel Als Prophet. Bird As Prophet (Schumann) [G]

Vogt. Governor [G]

Voi Che Sapete. What is this Feeling? (*Marriage of Figaro*; Act II; Mozart) [It]

Voilà! There! [F]

Voilà l'affaire. That's the very thing [F]

Voilà le malheur. That's the trouble [F]

voile. Veil; mask; sail; fine silk fabric [F]

Voi Lo Sapete. Now You Shall Know (*Cavalleria Rusticana*; Mascagni) [It]

voisin. Neighbor(ing) [F]

voiture. Carriage; coach [F]

voiturette. Light car [F]

voix. Voice [F]

voix blanche. A female voice of pure, clear quality [F]

volaille. Fowl [F]

Volapük. World speech; an auxiliary language devised 1880 by Schleyer

vol au vent. A large, light patty [F]

volens. Willing [L]

volens et potens. Willing and able [L]

voleur. Thief [F]

volgarizzare. Make popular; translate into the vernacular [It]

Volk der Dichter und Denker. Nation of poets and thinkers (*i.e.* the Germans) [G]

Völkerkunde. Ethnology [G]

Volkskunde. Folklore [G]

Volkslied. Folk-song [G]

Volksmärchen. Folk-tale [G]

Volkssturm. People's army; home guard recruited for last-ditch defense of Germany near the end of World War II [G]

volkstümlich. Popular [G]

Volkswagen. People's car; cheap German auto [G]

Volkswirtschaft. Economics [G]

vollbracht. Fulfilled [G]

volo. I fly [L]

volost. Rural district [R]

volte. A dance in which the man whirls his partner by her raised hand [It]

volte-face. About face [F]

volti. Turn over [It]

voluntas. Volition; will; intention [L]

Voluntas reputatur pro facto. The intention is to be taken for the deed [L]

vomitoria. Exits of large public buildings [L]

voortrekker. Pioneer; trailbreaker [Du]

Vorläufer. Predecessor(s) [G]

Vorlesung. Lecture [G]

Vorrede. Foreword; preface [G]

Vorsicht ist die Mutter der Weisheit. Discretion is the better part of valor [G]

Vorspiel. Prelude [G]

Vorstellung. Introduction [G]

vortex. See *vertex*

vosotros. You [Sp]

Vota vita mea. My life is devoted [L]

votum. Vow; promise [L]

Vouloir, c'est pouvoir. Where there's a will, there's a way [F]

voussure. Curve of an arch [F]

vox. Voice [L]

Vox audita perit, litera scripta manet. The heard voice perishes, but the written letter remains [L]

Vox clamantis in deserto. The voice of one crying in the wilderness (Matthew; 3-3; motto of Dartmouth University) [L]

vox humana. Human voice; an organ stop [L]

vox populi. Voice of the people; public opinion; popular belief [L]

Vox populi, vox Dei. The voice

of the people (is) the voice of God [L]

Vperyod. Forward; an early Bolshevik newspaper [R]

vrai. True; truth [F]

vraisemblance. Verisimilitude [F]

vrille. Spiral ornament or design; corkscrew design [F]

vs. See *versus*

vtornik. Tuesday [R]

vuelta. Turn; *pirouette* [Sp]

vulgaris. Common; term used in many Latin classifications of plants and flowers [L]

vulgaris purgatio. Common purgation; trial by ordeal [L]

vulgo. Commonly [L]

vulgo concepti. Spurious children; bastards [L]

vulgus. The people [L]

Vulneratus, non victus. Wounded, not conquered [L]

vulpes. Fox [L]

W

Wachtlied. "Watch-song", a type of poem in the Middle High German period [G]

Wafd. Delegation; Nationalist Party of Egypt [Arab]

Waffe. Arm; firearm; weapon [G]

Waffenschmied. Armorer; gunsmith or swordsmith; ordnance technician or repairman [G]

wagon-lit. Sleeper [F]

Wahn. Illusion [G]

Wahrheit. Truth [G]

Wahrscheinlichkeit. Probability [G]

Wahrscheinlichkeitsrechnung Calculation of probabilities [G]

Währung. Currency; money [G]

Wald. Forest [G]

Waldesrauschen. Forest Murmurs (Liszt) [G]

Waldhorn. Forest horn [G]

Walküre. Valkyrie; one of the nine daughters of Wotan, whose function was to convey slain heroes to Walhalla; an opera by Wagner [G]

Wallfahrt. Pilgrimage [G]

Wanderjahre. Journeyman years; years of travel (as a part of one's education) [G]

Wanderlust. Desire for travel [G]

Wanderschaft. Wandering; journeying; journeyman period [G]

Wandervogel. Migratory bird; member of a hiking-club youth movement before World War II (*pl.* Wandervögel) [G]

Wange. Cheek [G]

Ware. Ware(s); goods [G]

warum. Why [G]

Wasserfahrt. Water Voyage (Heine-Mendelssohn) [G]

wayang wong. Javanese dance-drama

Weber. Weaver(s) [G]

weezen. Essence; nature; being; character [Du]

Wegweiser. Guidepost [G]

Wehrwirtschaft. Military economy [G]

Wehrmacht. Defense force; collective term for all the German armed forces, including army, navy, and air force [G]

weiblich. Feminine [G]

Weiche, Wotan, Weiche! Relent, Wotan, Relent! (*Das Rheingold*, Wagner) [G]

Weihnachten. Christmas [G]

Weimar. Goethe's residence; scene of drafting of the German Republic's constitution, 1919; symbol of the German Republic and of the humanistic spirit of the German classicists

weinen. Weep [G]

Weinstube. Tavern [G]

Wein, Weib, und Gesang. Wine, woman, and song [G]

Weltanschauung. World-view; philosophy; perspective of life; conception of things [G]

Weltbegriff. Concept of the world [G]

Welträtsel. Riddle of the Universe (title of a philosophical work by Ernst Haeckel; 1899) [G]

Weltschmerz. World woe; romantic melancholy and sentimental pessimism [G]

wen. Culture; appearance; superficiality; letters; literature [C]

Wendepunkt. Turning point[G]

wenig. Little; few; a little [G]

wen li. Classical Chinese [C]

weregild. Price of homicide; money paid to the kin of a slain man [AS]

Wer nie sein Brot mit Tränen ass. Who ne'er his bread in sorrow ate (from Goethe's *Wilhelm Meister*) [G]

Wert. Value; worth [G]

wertfrei. Value-free; neutral with regard to values [G]

Werther. See *Leiden des jungen Werthers*

Werttheorie. Theory of value [G]

Wesen. Being; essence; nature or character; class or institution (in compound words) [G]

Wesensschau. Intuition of essence; immediate grasp of essences [G]

Wesenswissen. Knowledge of essences [G]

wesentlich. Essential(ly) [G]

Widerspruch. Contradiction [G]

Widmung. Dedication (Rückert-Schumann) [G]

Wiederbelebung. Revival [G]

Wiegendrucke. Incunabula [G]

Wiegenlied. Cradle Song; Lullaby (Brahms) [G]

Wiener Schnitzel. Breaded veal chop or steak [G]

wijk. District [Du]

Wilhelmstrasse. Street in Berlin; location of government offices; the German foreign office; the German government [G]

willkürlich. Arbitrary [G]

Winterreise. Winter Journey (Song Cycle; Schubert) [G]

Wipfel. Treetop [G]

Wirklichkeit. Reality [G]

Wirtshaus. Tavern [G]

Wissenschaft. Science; knowledge [G]

Wissenschaftslehre. Theory of science [G]

witenagemote. Assembly of wise men; council of the ancient Saxons in England [AS]

Wochenschau. News film [G]

Wochenschrift. Weekly [G]

Woher ? Whence? [G]

Wohin ? Whither? [G]

Wolfram. Tungsten [G]

Wollt ihr immer leben ? Do you want to live forever? (Frederick the Great) [G]

Wortspiel. Pun [G]

Wotan. Ruler of the gods

wu. Non-being; the non-self; creatures; things; matters; affairs [C]

wu ch'ang. The five virtues (of Confucianism); family virtues [C]

wu chi. Non-being [C]

wu chiao. See *wu ch'ang*

wu hsing. The five agents or elements, water, fire, wood, metal, and earth [C]

Wurst. Sausage [G]

Wurstmaxl. Hot-dog vendor[G]

Wurst wider Wurst. Tit for tat [G]

Wut. Rage; frenzy [G]

wu wei. Following nature; inactivity or passivity [C]

X

xenophobia. Dislike of foreign things and persons [Gk]

Xeres. Town in Spain famous for sherry wine

xi. Fourteenth letter of the Greek alphabet (Ξξ)

xoanon. Primitive wooden image [Gk]

xuda. God [Pers]

xylo-. Wood(en) [Gk]

xyst. Exercise room [Gk]

Y

y. There [F]; and [Sp]. For Greek words, see also under *hy-*, or *hu-*

Yahveh. Jehovah; the personal name of God in Hebrew theological and philosophical writings [Heb]

yajna. Sacrifice [Skr]

yama. Moral restraint; a *Yoga* concept [Skr]

yang. Male principle; active force [C]

Ya ni znayu. I don't know [R]

yarna. Color [Skr]

yashmak. Moslem woman's veil [Arab]

yataghan. Type of sword without a guard; dagger with a curved blade [Turk]

yayits. Eggs [R]

yedinstvo. Unity [R]

yen. Strong desire [C]; unit of Japanese currency [J]

yentzer. Cheater [Y]

Yerba buena, Perennial creeping plant; *Micromeria chamissonis* [Sp]

yerba mate. Paraguay tea [Sp]. See also *hierba mate*

Yizkor. Memorial service for the departed [Heb]

yesod mora. Foundation of the knowledge of God [Heb]

Yiddish. Middle High German dialect used by Jews [Y]

Yildiz Kiosk. Sultan's palace [Turk]

yin yang. Passive and active (principles); female and male (cosmic forces) [C]

yo. I [Sp]

yo fu. Musical verse [C]

Yoga. Yoking; restraining (of the mind); an Indian philosophy emphasizing self-discipline for the purpose of gaining peace of mind and insight into the nature of reality [Skr]

Yogasutras. Yoga aphorisms or verses; title of a work by Patanjali, on which the Indian philosophy of *Yoga* is based [Skr]

Yogin. Yogi; one who practices *Yoga* [Skr]

Yom Kippur. Day of Atonement [Heb]

yoni. Womb; source; origin; matrix; first cause [Skr]

Yquem. Famous French sauterne [F]

yu. Being; existence; space; desire [C]

yuan. Beginning; originating power; government council; building in which it meets [C]

Yuan. Chinese government agency; unit of Chinese currency [C]

yumi. You and I [PE]

yung. (Moral) courage; harmony [C]

Z

Z. See *Zeile*

zabaione. Custard mixed with wine [It]

zaftra. Tomorrow [R]

Zahlentheorie. Theory of numbers [G]

zakon. Law [R]

zamar. Oboe [Arab]

zantedeschia. Calla lily [L]

zapateado. Spanish tap-dance [Sp]

zapatero. Shoemaker [Sp]

zapatilla. Slipper, pump [Sp]

zapato. Shoe [Sp]

zapoviednik. Prohibited area [R]

zarabanda. Saraband; a solo dance of Spanish origin [Sp]

zariba. Protective hedge or palisade [Arab]

zart. Tender(ly); gently [G]

zärtlich. Tender; delicate [G]

zarzuela. Play performed to music; forerunner of the opera [Sp]

Zauber. Magic [G]

Zauberberg. Magic Mountain (title of a novel by Thomas Mann) [G]

Zauberflöte. Magic Flute (opera; Mozart) [G]

Zauberlehrling. Sorcerer's Apprentice (title of a poem by Goethe, set to music by Dukas in the form of a *scherzo* entitled "L'Apprenti Sorcier") [G]

za-um. Beyond reason [R]

zaumnyi. Transrational (language); ungrammatical style of the Russian Cubo-futurists of 1912 [R]

zayim. Chief; leader [Arab]

z.B. See *zum Beispiel*

Zdrav'stvuitye! Hello! [R]

Zeile. Line [G]

Zeit. Time [G]

Zeitalter. Age; era; epoch [G]

Zeitgeist. Spirit of the time; prevailing intellectual atmosphere [G]

Zeitschrift. Periodical; magazine [G]

Zeitung. Newspaper [G]

zemindar. Bengali land owner [Pers]

zemledelie. Agriculture [R]

zemsky nachalnik. Administrative official in Czarist Russia; rural prefects in Czarist Russia [R]

zemsky sobor. Assembly of representatives of the estates convened in Russia in the 17th and 18th centuries [R]

zemstvo. Elective district council [R]

zenana. Secluded women's chamber in India [Pers]

Zendavesta. Commentary and text; title of sacred scriptures of the Parsis, an Indo-Iranian religious sect [Mid. Persian]

Zentrumspartei. (Catholic) Center Party; one of the largest

German parties before Hitler's assumption of power [G]

zeraim. Seeds [Heb]

zeta. 6th letter of the Greek alphabet (Zζ)

Zeug. Gear; tool; stuff and nonsense [G]

zeugma. See *synezeugmenon*

Zeus. King of the gods in Greek mythology [Gk]

zia. Aunt [It]

ziemlich. Somewhat; rather; fair(ly) [G]

zierlich. Graceful; neat; ornamented [G]

Zigeuner. Gypsy [G]

Zigeunerlied. Gypsy song [G]

Zigeunerweisen. Gypsy Airs (Sarasate) [G]

zingani. Gypsies [It]

zingara. Referring to potted beef preserved in wine [R]

zinzolin. See *cinzolino*

Zis. Name of a Soviet auto

Zitti, Zitti. Silently, Silently (*Barber of Seville*, Act: III Rossini) [It]

zloty. Small Polish coin [Polish]

zoe. Life [Gk]

Zoe mou, sas agapo. My life, I love thee [Gk]

zögernd. Hesitating; retarding [G]

Zollverein. Customs union [G]

zona. Girdle [L]

zonam solvere. To untie the girdle; to marry a woman [L]

zoophorus. Decorative design of foliage and animals [Gk]

zotheca. Sleeping niche or cubicle in ancient Roman bedrooms [L]

zouave. Member of French-Algerian army; referring to military uniform worn by a zouave; short jacket [F]

zoubrovka. An alcoholic drink [R]

z.T. See *zum Teil*

zucca. Squash [It]

zucchero. Sugar [It]

zucchini. Squash [It]

zueco. Wooden shoe [Sp]

Zufriedenheit. Satisfaction; contentment [G]

Zug. Draft; procession; train; trait; feature; traction; platoon [G]

Zugvogel. Bird of passage [G]

Zukunft. Future [G]

zum Beispiel. For example; *exempla gratia* [G]

zumpogna. An ancient type of bagpipe [It]

zum Teil. In part [G]

zur Ansicht. For examination; on approval [G]

Zveno. Name of a pro-Russian party in Bulgaria, organized 1943 [ ]

zvezda. Star [R]

Zwei Seelen und ein Gedanke. Two souls with but a single thought [G]

Zwei Seelen wohnen, ach, in meiner Brust. Two souls, alas, dwell within my breast (Goethe) [G]

Zwerg. Dwarf [G]

Zwieback. Toasted bread sticks [G]

Zwiebel. Onion(s) [G]

Greek supplement

by *Konrad Gries,* Ph.D.

Department of Classical Languages,
Queens College, Flushing,
New York

ἀγάπα τὸν πλησίον. Love thy neighbor (Thales)

ἀγεωμέτρητος μηδεὶς εἰσίτω. Let no one who does not know geometry enter (inscription said to have been placed over Plato's door)

ἀγνώστῳ θεῷ. To the Unknown God (Acts xvii. 23)

ἀετὸς ἐν νεφέλαισι. An eagle in the clouds; *fig.*, an unattainable object

αἰδὼς ὄλωλεν. Modesty has perished (Theognis)

αἰδὼς οὐκ ἀγαθή. False shame (Hesiod)

αἰὲν ἀριστεύειν. Always to excel (Homer)

αἰτεῖτε, καὶ δοθήσεται ὑμῖν· ζητεῖτε, καὶ εὑρήσετε· κρούετε, καὶ ἀνοιγήσεται ὑμῖν. Ask, and it shall be given you; seek, and ye shall find, knock, and it shall be opened unto you (Matthew vii. 7)

Ἄλφα καὶ Ὦ μέγα. Alpha and Omega (the first and last letters of the Greek alphabet); the beginning and the end

ἀνάγκη. Necessity; force; constraint

ἀνδρῶν ἐπιφανῶν πᾶσα γῆ τάφος. For famous men the whole earth is a sepulchre (Thucydides)

ἀνεμώλια βάζειν. To speak vain words

ἀνέχου καὶ ἀπέχου. Bear and forbear (Epictetus)

ἀνήριθμον γέλασμα. The numberless laughter (of the sea) (Aeschylus; *Prometheus Bound*)

ἄνθρωπός ἐστι πνεῦμα καὶ σκιὰ μόνον. Man is but a breath and a shadow (Euripides)

ἄνθρωπος φύσει ζῷον πολιτικόν. Man is by nature a social (*lit.* civic) animal (Aristotle)

ἄξιος γὰρ ὁ ἐργάτης τοῦ μισθοῦ αὐτοῦ. For the laborer is worthy of his hire (Luke x. 7)

ἅπαξ λεγόμενον. (A word or phrase) said or recorded only once. See *Hapax legomenon*

ἀπόδοτε οὖν πᾶσι τὰς ὀφειλάς. Render therefore to all their dues (Romans xiii. 7)

ἀπόδοτε οὖν τὰ Καίσαρος Καίσαρι καὶ τὰ τοῦ θεοῦ τῷ θεῷ. Render therefore unto Caesar the things which are Caesar's; and unto God the things that are God's (Matthew xxii. 21)

ἄριστον μὲν ὕδωρ. The best (of the four elements) is water (Pindar)

ἄριστον μέτρον. The best is the middle course (Cleobulus)

ἀρκετὸν τῇ ἡμέρᾳ ἡ κακία αὐτῆς. Sufficient unto the day is the evil thereof (Matthew vi. 34)

ἀρχὴ ἄνδρα δείξει. Power (*or* authority) will reveal the man (Bias)

ἀρχὴ δέ τοι ἥμισυ παντός. But the beginning is really the half of the whole; well begun is half done (ascribed to Hesiod or Pythagoras)

ἄσβεστος γέλως. Inextinguishable laughter (Homer)

αὐτὸς ἔφα. He himself said so (said by his disciples of Pythagoras). Cf. *Ipse dixit*

βοὴν ἀγαθός. Good at the battle cry (Homer)

βοῦς ἐπὶ γλώσσῃ. An ox on the tongue; *fig.*, a weighty reason for silence (Aeschylus)

βοῶπις πότνια "Ηρη. The ox-eyed Lady Hera (Homer)

γαμεῖν ὁ μέλλων εἰς μετάνοιαν ἔρχεται. He who is about to marry is on the way to a change of mind

γάμος γὰρ ἀνθρώποισιν εὐκταῖον κακόν. For marriage is an evil that men pray for (Menander)

γέλως ἄκαιρος ἐν βροτοῖς δεινὸν κακόν. Ill-timed laughter among mortals is a grievous evil (Menander)

γῆν ὁρῶ. I see land; *fig.*, I see the end of my work (Diogenes)

γηράσκω δ' ἀεὶ πολλὰ διδασκόμενος. But I grow old always learning many things (Solon)

γλαῦκ' εἰς 'Αθήνας. An owl to Athens; coals to Newcastle (Aristophanes)

γνῶθι σεαυτόν. Know thyself (inscription over the entrance of the temple of Apollo at Delphi)

γυναικὶ μή πίστευε, μηδ' ἂν ἀποθάνῃ. Don't trust a woman, not even if she's dead

δάκρυ' ἀδάκρυα. Tearless tears (Euripides)

δεῖ τοῖσι πολλοῖς τὸν τύραννον ἀνδάνειν. The prince must please the many (Euripides)

δέχεται κακὸν ἐκ κακοῦ αἰεί. Evil ever follows upon evil (Homer)

διὰ δυσφημίας καὶ εὐφημίας. By evil report and good report (II Corinthians vi. 8)

δὶς κράμβη θάνατος. Cabbage twice (*i.e.* warmed over, served a second time) is death. Cf. *Crambe repetita*

δόξα ἐν ὑψίστοις θεῷ καὶ ἐπὶ γῆς εἰρήνη ἐν ἀνθρώποις εὐδοκίας. Glory to God in the highest and on earth peace, good will toward men (*or* peace among men who meet with his approval *or* men of good will) (Luke ii. 14)

δόσις δ' ὀλίγη τε φίλη τε. A gift at the same time small yet welcome (Homer)

δός μοι ποῦ στῶ καὶ κινῶ τὴν γῆν. Give me (a place) where I may stand and I (can) move the earth (Archimedes)

ἑαυτὸν τιμωρούμενος. The self-tormentor (Menander; title of a comedy by Terence)

εἶδος; pl. εἴδη. Form; species, kind; *philos.*, "idea"

εἷς ἀνὴρ οὐδεὶς ἀνήρ. One man no man; *i.e.* two heads are better than one

εἰς αὔριον τὰ σπουδαῖα. (Save) serious matters for tomorrow; *i.e.* don't bother me with business today (Archias, Spartan general noted for his procrastination)

εἷς Κύριος, μία πίστις, ἐν βάπτισμα. One Lord, one faith, one baptism (Ephesians iv. 5)

εἰς ὄνυχα. To a finger nail; *fig.*, to perfection (from the sculptor's practise of applying the finishing touches to the model with his nail). Cf. *Ad unguem*

εἰς τὸ πῦρ ἐκ τοῦ κάπνου. Out of the smoke into the fire; out of the frying pan into the fire (Lucian)

ἐκ γὰρ τοῦ περισσεύματος τῆς καρδίας τὸ στόμα λαλεῖ. For out of the abundance of the heart the mouth speaketh (Matthew xii. 34)

ἐκεῖνος ἦν ὁ λύχνος ὁ καιόμενος καὶ φαίνων. He was a burning and a shining light (John v. 35)

ἐκ Ναζαρὲτ δύναταί τι ἀγαθὸν εἶναι; Can there any good thing come out of Nazareth? (John i. 46)

ἐκ τοῦ στόματός σου κρίνω σε. Out of thine own mouth will I judge thee (Luke xix. 22) ἐλεύθερός ἐστιν ὁ ζῶν ὡς βούλεται. Free is he who lives as he chooses (Epictetus)

ἕλιξ ἕλικα τέρπει. Like pleases like

ἐμοῦ θανόντος, γαῖα μιχθήτω πυρί. When I am dead, let the earth be mingled with fire (anonymous Greek writer quoted by Suetonius). Cf. *Après nous le deluge*

ἐμποδίζει τὸν λόγον ὁ φόβος. Fear hinders speech (Demades)

ἐν οἴνῳ ἀλήθεια. In wine there is truth. Cf. *In vino veritas*

ἐν πιθήκοις ὄντα δεῖ εἶναι πίθηκον. When among monkeys one must be a monkey (Apollodorus)

ἔξω τοῦ πράγματος. Beside the question

ἔπεα πτερόεντα. Winged words (Homer)

ἐπὶ γήραος οὐδῷ. On the threshold of old age (Homer)

ἐπὶ ξυροῦ ἀκμῆς. On the razor's edge; *fig.*, at the critical moment (Homer)

ἔρως. Love

ἔσσεται ἦμαρ ὅταν ποτ' ὀλώλῃ Ἴλιος ἱρή. There will be a day when sacred Ilium will perish (Homer)

εὖγε. Fine!; Bravo!

εὐθανασία. A pleasant death

εὕρηκα. I've found it (Archimedes, on discovering the solution to a difficult scientific problem)

εὐτυχία πολύφιλος. Prosperity has many friends

εὐτυχῶν μὲν μέτριος ἴσθι, ἀτυχῶν δὲ φρόνιμος. In prosperity be moderate, in adversity sage (Periander)

εὐτυχῶν μὴ ἴσθι ὑπερήφανος, ἀπορήσας μὴ ταπεινοῦ. In prosperity don't be arrogant, in adversity don't be abject (Cleobulus)

εὐφήμει; pl. εὐφημεῖτε. Silence! (*lit.*, speak words of good omen)

ἕως κόρακες λευκοὶ γένωνται. Till the crows turn white; *i.e.*, never

ζεῖ χύτρα, ζῇ φιλία. (While) the pot boils, friendship flourishes

ζωὴ καὶ ψυχή. My life and soul (used as a term of affection)

ζώη μοῦ. Life of mine; my darling

ζώη μοῦ, σάς ἀγαπῶ. Life of mine, I love thee (refrain, in modern Greek, to Byron's "Maid of Athens")

ζῶμεν ἀλογίστως, προσδοκῶντες μὴ θανεῖν. We live thoughtlessly, expecting not to die (Menander)

ζῶμεν οὐχ ὡς θέλομεν, ἀλλ' ὡς δυνάμεθα. We live not as we wish, but as we can

ἡ ἀλήθεια ἐλευθερώσει ὑμᾶς. The truth shall make you free (John viii. 32)

ἡ ἀξίνη πρὸς τὴν ῥίζαν τῶν δένδρων κεῖται. The axe is laid unto the root of the trees (Luke iii. 9)

ἥβη. Youth

ἡγεμονία. Hegemony; leadership; sovereignty

ἡ γλῶσσ' ὁμώμοχ', ἡ δὲ φρὴν ἀνώμοτος. The tongue has sworn, but the mind is unsworn (Euripides)

ἥδιστον ἄκουσμα ἔπαινος. The sweetest sound is praise (Xenophon)

ἡδὺ δούλευμα. Sweet bondage (said of love)

ἢ θήριον ἢ θεός. (Man is) either a brute or a god (Aristotle)

ἢ πῖθι ἢ ἄπιθι. Either drink or depart

ἡ πίστις σου σέσωκέν σε. Thy faith hath saved thee (Luke vii. 50)

ἢ τὰν ἢ ἐπὶ τάν. Either (with) it or upon it (a Spartan mother telling her son how he should return from battle, in reference to his shield)

θάλαττα! θάλαττα! The sea! The sea!; *fig.*, safe at last! (the Greek soldiers in Xenophon's *Anabasis* upon finally fighting their way through the Persian

Empire to the Greek-colonized shores of the Black Sea)

θάρσει, ἔγειρε, φωνεῖ σε. Be of good comfort, rise; he calleth thee (Mark x. 49)

θαρσεῖτε, ἐγώ εἰμι· μὴ φοβεῖσθε. Be of good cheer, it is I; be not afraid (Matthew xiv. 27)

θεὸς ἐκ μηχανῆς. A god from the machine; *fig.*, a providential intervention. Cf. *Deus ex machina*

θεῶν ἐν γούνασι κεῖται. It lies on the knees of the gods; it rests in the lap of the gods (Homer)

ἰατρέ, θεράπευσον σεαυτόν. Physician, heal thyself (Luke iv. 23). Cf. *Medice, cura te ipsum*

ἰδοὺ ὁ ἄνθρωπος. Behold the man (John xix. 5)

'Ιλιὰς κακῶν. An Iliad of woes; *fig.*, an endless series of calamities

Καδμεία νίκη. A Cadmean victory; *i.e.*, a victory that ruins the victor, a Pyrrhic victory

κάθαρσις. Cleansing; purification

καὶ ἐδικαιώθη ἡ σοφία ἀπὸ τῶν ἔργων αὐτῆς. But wisdom is justified of her children (*lit.*, by her works) (Matthew xi. 19)

καὶ ἐδικαιώθη ἡ σοφία ἀπὸ τῶν τέκνων αὐτῆς πάντων. But wisdom is justified of all her children (Luke vii. 35)

καὶ κεραμεὺς κεραμεῖ κοτέει καὶ τέκτονι τέκτων. And potter bears grudge against potter and carpenter against carpenter (Hesiod)

καιρὸν γνῶθι. Know your opportunity (Pittacus)

καὶ σύ, τέκνον. Thou too, child (according to Plutarch, Caesar's dying words, addressed to Brutus). Cf. *Et tu, Brute*

καὶ τὰ λοιπά. And the rest; and so forth; et cetera. *Abbr.* κ. τ. λ.

κακὸν ἀναγκαῖον. A necessary evil

κακοῦ κόρακος κακὸν ᾠόν. From a bad crow a bad egg; *fig.*, like father, like son

καλόν ἐστιν ἡμᾶς ὧδε εἶναι. It is good for us to be here (Matthew xvii. 4)

καλὸς κἀγαθός. A gentleman (*lit.*, handsome and good)

καλῶς. Well said! Bravo! Good! Cf. εὖγε. *Also used to mean* No, thank you

καρπὸς μέγιστος ἀταραξία. The greatest blessing is serenity (*lit.*, absence of agitation) (the philosophical principle of Epicurus)

κατ' ἐξοχήν. Preeminently; *par excellence*

κατ' ἔπος. Word by word, *i.e.* in detail

κάτθανε καὶ Πάτροκλος, ὅπερ σέο πολλὸν ἀμείνων. Even Patroclus died, and he was much better than you (Homer)

κατόπιν ἑορτῆς ἥκειν. To arrive after the party; *fig.*, to be too late (proverb quoted by Plato)

κινεῖν πάντα λίθον or πᾶν χρῆμα. To move every stone or thing; to leave no stone unturned

κοινὰ τὰ τῶν φίλων. The belongings of friends are common (attributed to Pythagoras and also to Socrates)

κολοιὸς ποτὶ κολοιόν. Jackdaw with jackdaw; birds of a feather flock together

κόσμος. Order; harmony; the universe

κούφη γῆ τοῦτον καλύπτοι. May the earth lie light upon him (*lit.*, may the earth cover him lightly) (a commonly used epitaph). Cf. *Sit tibi terra levis*

κρείσσων χρημάτων. Superior to money; *i.e.* inaccessible to bribery

κτῆμα εἰς ἀεί. A possession for all time (Thucydides)

κῦδος. Glory; fame

κύριε ἐλέησον. Lord, have mercy

λαγὼς καθεύδων. A sleeping hare; *fig.*, a person feigning sleep

λάθε βιώσας. Live in such a way that you will not be noticed (Epicurus)

λεγιὼν ὄνομά μοι. My name is Legion (Mark v. 9)

λήθη. Lethe; oblivion; forgetfulness

λόγιον; *pl.* λόγια. A traditional saying or maxim of a religious teacher; esp., a saying of Jesus unrecorded in the Gospels

λύχνου ἀρθέντος, γυνὴ πᾶσα ἡ αὐτή. When the lamp is removed, all women are the same; in the dark all cats are gray

μακάριόν ἐστιν μᾶλλον διδόναι ἢ λαμβάνειν. It is more blessed to give than to receive (Acts xx. 35)

μάντις κακῶν. A prophet of evils

μέγα βιβλίον μέγα κακόν. A big book is a big evil (Callimachus, adapted)

μεγάλη πόλις μεγάλη ἐρημία. A great city is a great desert

μείζονα ταύτης ἀγάπην οὐδεὶς ἔχει ἵνα τὴν ψυχὴν αὐτοῦ θῇ ὑπὲρ τῶν φίλων αὐτοῦ. Greater love hath no man than this, that a man lay down his life for his friends (John xv. 13)

μελετὴ τὸ πᾶν. Practise is everything (Periander)

μέμνησο ἀπιστεῖν. Remember to be suspicious

μεταβολὴ πάντων γλυκύ. Change of all things is sweet; a change is always pleasant (Euripides)

μέτρον ἄριστον. Moderation is best (Cleobulus)

μὴ αἰσχροκερδεῖς. Not greedy of filthy lucre (I Timothy iii. 8)

μὴ γένοιτο. God forbid! (*lit.*, may it not happen) (Romans iii. 31)

μηδὲν ἄγαν. Nothing too much; nothing in excess. Cf. *Ne quid nimis*

μηδὲν θαυμάζειν. To wonder at

nothing (attributed to Pythagoras). Cf. *Nil admirari*

μὴ κρίνετε, ἵνα μὴ κριθῆτε. Judge not, that ye be not judged (Matthew vii. 1)

μὴ ταρασσέσθω ὑμῶν ἡ καρδία. Let not your heart be troubled (John xiv. 1)

μήτηρ τῆς ἐνδείας ἡ ἀεργία. Idleness is the mother of want

μὴ τὸ θέλημά μου ἀλλὰ τὸ σὸν γενέσθω. Not my will but thine be done (Luke xxii. 42)

μικρὸν ἀπὸ τοῦ ἡλίου μετάστηθι. Stand aside a bit from (in front of) the sun (Diogenes to Alexander the Great, when the latter asked what he could do for him)

μικρὸν κακὸν μέγα ἀγαθόν. A small evil is a great good

μονομαχία. A single combat; a duel

μόνος ὁ σοφὸς ἐλεύθερος, καὶ πᾶς ἄφρων δοῦλος. Only the wise man is free, and every fool is a slave (Stoic maxim)

Μουσῶν ὄρνιθες. The birds of the Muses; *i.e.* the poets

νεκρὸς οὐ δάκνει. A dead man doesn't bite; dead men tell no tales

νέμεσις. Nemesis; retribution

Νεφελοκοκκυγία. Cloudcuckoo land (Aristophanes)

νέφος μαρτύρων. A cloud of witnesses (Hebrews xii. 1)

νίκη δ' ἐπαμείβεται ἄνδρας. Victory comes to men by turns (Homer)

ὁ βίος βραχύς, ἡ δὲ τέχνη μακρή. Life is short, but art is long. Cf. *Ars longa, vita brevis*

ὁ ἐλέφας τὴν μυῖαν οὐκ ἀλεγίζει. An elephant doesn't trouble himself about a fly

οἱ ἀρούρης καρπὸν ἔδουσιν. They who eat the fruit of the soil (Homer)

οἱ γὰρ πολλοὶ μᾶλλον ὀρέγονται τοῦ κέρδους ἢ τῆς τιμῆς. For the people strive for gain rather than for honor (Aristotle)

οἴκοι λέοντες, ἐν μάχῃ δ' ἀλωπέκες. Lions at home, but foxes in the battle (Aristophanes)

οἶνος 'Αφροδίτης γάλα. Wine is the milk of love (Aristophanes)

οἷος ὁ βίος τοῖος ὁ λόγος. As a man's life is, so is his speech

οἱ πολλοί. The many; the majority; the masses; the mob; thè people

ὁ κόσμος οὗτος μία πόλις ἐστί. This world is one city (Epictetus)

ὁ μὲν θερισμὸς πολύς, οἱ δὲ ἐργάται ὀλίγοι. The harvest truly is plenteous but the laborers are few (Matthew ix. 37)

ὁ μὴ ὢν μετ' ἐμοῦ κατ' ἐμοῦ ἐστιν. He that is not with me is against me (Luke xi. 23)

ὄναρ καὶ ὕπαρ. Asleep and awake; at all times

ὃν γὰρ ἀγαπᾷ Κύριος παιδεύει. For whom the Lord loveth he chasteneth (Hebrews xii. 6)

ὃν οἱ θεοὶ φιλοῦσιν ἀποθνῄσκει νέος. He whom the gods love dies young (Menander)

ὄνου πόκαι. Ass's wool; fig., something that does not exist

ὃ οὖν ὁ θεὸς συνέζευξεν, ἄνθρωπος μὴ χωριζέτω. What therefore God hath joined together, let not man put asunder (Matthew xix. 6 and Mark x. 9)

ὅπου γάρ ἐστιν ὁ θησαυρός σου, ἐκεῖ ἔσται καὶ ἡ καρδία σου. For where your treasure is, there will your heart be also (Matthew vi. 21)

ὅπου ἐὰν ᾖ τὸ πτῶμα, ἐκεῖ συναχθήσονται οἱ ἀετοί. For wheresoever the carcase is, there will the eagles be gathered together (Matthew xxiv. 28)

ὅρα τέλος μακροῦ βίου. Look to the end of a long life; i.e. don't pass judgment on a man until he has died (Solon to Croesus). Cf. Respice finem

ὀργὴ φιλούντων ὀλίγον ἰσχύει χρόνον.

Lovers' wrath lasts little time (Menander)

ὀρνίθων γάλα. Birds' milk; "pigeons' milk"; any marvelous good fortune

οὐ γὰρ δοκεῖν ἄριστος ἀλλ' εἶναι θέλει. For he does not wish to seem but to be the best (Aeschylus)

οὐ γνῶσις, ἀλλὰ πρᾶξις. Not knowledge, but practise

οὐδ' εἴ μοι δέκα μὲν γλῶσσαι, δέκα δὲ στόματ' εἶεν. Not even if I had ten tongues and ten mouths (Homer)

οὐδεὶς γὰρ ὃν φοβεῖται φιλεῖ. For no one loves him whom he fears (Aristotle)

οὐδὲν μάτην ἡ φύσις ποιεῖ. Nature does nothing in vain (Aristotle)

οὐδὲν οὕτω δεινὸν ὡς γυνὴ κακόν. There is no evil so terrible as a woman (Euripides)

οὐδὲν οὕτω πιαίνει τὸν ἵππον ὡς βασιλέως ὀφθαλμός. Nothing so fattens a horse as the king's eye; fig., a man's affairs prosper best when he sees to them himself (Plutarch)

οὐδὲν πρᾶγμα. It is no matter; it's of no consequence

οὐδὲν πρὸς ἔπος. Nothing to the purpose (lit., the word); not to the point; off the subject

οὐ δύνασθε θεῷ δουλεύειν καὶ μαμωνᾷ. Ye cannot serve God and Mammon (Matthew vi. 24)

οὐκ αἰσχρὸν οὐδὲν τῶν ἀναγκαίων βροτοῖς. Nothing that is necessary (for life) is shameful foɪ men (Euripides)

οὐκ εἰσὶν οἱ παμπλούσιοι ἀγαθοί. The very rich are not good (Plato)

οὐκ ἐπ' ἄρτῳ μόνῳ ζήσεται ὁ ἄνθρωπος. Man shall not live by bread alone (Matthew iv. 4)

οὐκ ἔστ' ἐραστὴς ὅστις οὐκ ἀεὶ φιλεῖ. He is not a lover who does not love for ever (Euripides) οὐρανός. The sky; heaven, seat of the gods.—οὐρανὸς ἀστερόεις. The starry firmament

ὁ φίλος ἕτερος ἐγώ. A friend is a second self (Aristotle)

παθήματα μαθήματα. Sufferings are lessons (Herodotus)

πάντα γὰρ δυνατὰ παρὰ τῷ θεῷ. For with God all things are possible (Mark x. 27)

πάντα δυνατὰ τῷ πιστεύοντι. All things are possible to him that believeth (Mark ix. 23)

πάντα καθαρὰ τοῖς καθαροῖς. Unto the pure all things are pure (Titus i. 15)

πάντα κάλων ἐξιᾶσι. They are letting out every reef; fig., they are doing all they can (Euripides)

πάντα ῥεῖ. All things flow (the philosophical principle of Heraclitus)

πάντων χρημάτων ἄνθρωπος μέτρον. Of all things man is the measure (Protagoras, as quoted by Plato)

παράγει γὰρ τὸ σχῆμα τοῦ κόσμου τούτου. For the fashion of this world passeth away (I Corinthians vii. 31)

πάταξον μέν, ἄκουσον δέ. Strike, but listen (Themistocles, according to Plutarch)

πῖνε καὶ εὐφραίνου. Drink and be merry (Palladas)

πλέον ἥμισυ παντός. Half is more than the whole (Hesiod)

πλήρωμα νόμου ἡ ἀγάπη. Love is the fulfilling of the law (Romans xiii. 10)

ποιμανεῖ αὐτοὺς ἐν ῥάβδῳ σιδηρᾷ. He shall rule them with a rod of iron (Revelations ii. 27)

πολλὰ μεταξὺ πέλει κύλικος καὶ χείλιος ἄκρου. There's many a slip 'twixt the cup and the lip (Aristotle)

πολλοὶ γάρ εἰσιν κλητοί, ὀλίγοι ἐκλεκτοί. For many are called, but few are chosen (Matthew xxii. 14)

πολλῶν δ' ἀνθρώπων ἴδεν ἄστεα καὶ νόον ἔγνω. And of many men he saw the towns and learned the ways (Homer; Odyssey)

πολλῶν ὁ λιμὸς γίγνεται διδάσκαλος. Of many things does hunger become the teacher

πολύτιμον μαργαρίτην. A pearl of great price (Matthew xiii. 46)

πολυφλοίσβοιο θαλάσσης. Of the loud-resounding sea (Homer)

πομφόλυξ ὁ ἄνθρωπος. Man is a bubble

ποσὶ καὶ χερσίν. With feet and hands; fig., with might and main

ποῦ στῶ. Where I may stand; i.e., a standing place, leverage ground, basis for operation. See δός μοι ποῦ στῶ καὶ κινῶ τὴν γῆν

προλεγόμενα. Preliminary remarks

πῦρ μαχαίρᾳ μὴ σκαλεύειν. Don't poke a fire with a sword; fig., don't provoke an angry man (Pythagorean proverb)

ῥοδοδάκτυλος ἠώς. Rosy-fingered dawn (Homer)

σκιαμαχία. Shadow-fighting; a mock fight

σκιᾶς ὄναρ. The dream of a shadow; fig., anything fleeting or unreal.—σκιᾶς ὄναρ ἄνθρωποι. Men are the dream of a shadow (Pindar)

σκληρόν σοι πρὸς κέντρα λακτίζειν. It is hard for thee to kick against the pricks (Acts xxvi. 14)

σοφός. Skilled; clever; wise.—σοφὸς λέγειν. Clever at speaking

σπεῦδε βραδέως. Make haste slowly (favorite saying of the Emperor Augustus). Cf. Festina lente

στέργει γὰρ οὐδεὶς ἄγγελον κακῶν ἐπῶν. For no one loves a bearer of bad news (Sophocles)

στοργή. Parental or filial affection

συκίνη μάχαιρα. A fig-wood sword; fig., a weak and ineffective argument

243

σύκινοι ἄνδρες. Fig-wood men; *fig.*, weak, good-for-nothing fellows (Theocritus)

συναγάγετε τὰ περισσεύσαντα κλάσματα. Gather up the fragments that remain (John vi. 12)

τὰ σῦκα σῦκα, τὴν σκάφην σκάφην λέγειν. To call figs figs, a tub a tub; to call a spade a spade

τίκτει τοι κόρος ὕβριν. Surfeit truly breeds insolence (Theognis)

τίς οὖν ἄρξει τοῦ ἄρχοντος; Who then will rule the ruler? (Plutarch). Cf. *Quis custodiet ipsos custodes?*

τὸ ἀργύριόν ἐστιν αἷμα καὶ ψυχὴ βροτοῖς. Money is blood and life to mortals (Antiphanes)

τὸ δ' εὖ νικάτω. And may the right prevail (Aeschylus)

τὸ ἦθος ἔθος ἐστὶ πολυχρόνιον. Character is habit of long duration (Plutarch)

τοῖς πᾶσιν γέγονα πάντα. I am made all things to all men (I Corinthians ix. 22)

τὸ καλὸν καὶ τὸ αἰσχρόν. The beautiful and the base; virtue and vice. Cf. *Honestum et turpe*

τὸν θεὸν φοβεῖσθε, τὸν βασιλέα τιμᾶτε. Fear God, honor the king (I Peter ii. 17)

τὸ ὅλον. The whole; the universe (Plato)

τὸ πρέπον. That which is seemly; propriety; decorum

τὸ σάββατον διὰ τὸν ἄνθρωπον ἐγένετο, καὶ οὐχ ὁ ἄνθρωπος διὰ τὸ σάββατον. The sabbath was made for man, and not man for the sabbath (Mark ii. 27)

τοῦ ἀριστεύειν ἕνεκα. In order to excel (punning motto of Lord Henniker)

τοὺς πτωχοὺς γὰρ πάντοτε ἔχετε μεθ' ἑαυτῶν. For the poor always ye have with you (John xii. 8)

τρισκαιδεκάπαχυς. A fellow thirteen cubits tall; a big lunkhead (Theocritus)

τυφλὸς δὲ τυφλὸν ἐὰν ὁδηγῇ, ἀμφότεροι εἰς βόθυνον πεσοῦνται. And if the blind lead the blind, both shall fall into the ditch (Matthew xv. 14)

τῷ θεῷ δόξα. Glory to God.

τῷ τεκόντι πᾶν φίλον. To its parent everything is dear (Sophocles)

ὕβρις. Insolence

ὑγίεια. Health

ὕδραν τέμνεις. You're wounding a Hydra (a many-headed water snake who grew two heads in the place of every head that was cut off); *fig.*, you're laboring in vain; you're making a bad matter worse

ὑμεῖς ἐστε τὸ ἅλας τῆς γῆς. Ye are the salt of the earth (Matthew v. 13)

ὑμεῖς ἐστε τὸ φῶς τοῦ κόσμου. Ye are the light of the world (Matthew v. 14)

ὑμῶν δὲ καὶ αἱ τρίχες τῆς κεφαλῆς πᾶσαι ἠριθμημέναι εἰσίν. But the very hairs of your head are all numbered (Matthew x. 30)

ὕπαγε ὀπίσω μου, σατανᾶ. Get thee behind me, Satan (Matthew xvi. 23 *and* Mark viii. 33)

ὕστερον πρότερον. The latter (become) the former; the cart before the horse. Cf. hysteron proteron (Engl.)

φάγωμεν καὶ πίωμεν· αὔριον γὰρ ἀποθνήσκομεν. Let us eat and drink, for tomorrow we die (I Corinthians xv. 32)

φάρμακον λύπης. A remedy for grief

φάρμακον νηπενθές. A remedy for grief; nepenthe (Homer; *Odyssey*)

φείδεο τῶν κτεάνων. Husband your resources (Lucian)

φιλοσοφία βίου κυβερνήτης. Philosophy the guide of life (motto of Phi Beta Kappa)

φιλοσοφία ὄρεξις τῆς θείας σοφίας. Philosophy is a yearning after heavenly wisdom (Plato) φροντιστήριον. A think shop (Aristophanes)

φύσει σοφὸς μὲν οὐδείς. By nature none is wise (Aristotle)

φωνῇ γὰρ ὁδῶ, τὸ φατιζόμενον. For I see by sound, as the saying goes (Sophocles; the words of the blind Oedipus)

χαῖρε; pl. χαίρετε. Rejoice!; Hello!; Goodbye!

χαλεπὰ τὰ καλά. What's good is difficult

Χάρων. Charon, the ferryman of the dead

χειρῶν νόμος. The law of might

χρήματ' ἀνήρ. Money makes the man (Pindar)

χρήματα ψυχὴ βροτοῖσι. Money means life for mortals (Hesiod)

ψεκάδες ὄμβρον γεννῶνται. The raindrops form the rain

ὡς ἂν μάθῃς, ἀντάκουσον. In order to learn, hear the other side too (Xenophon)